Howard
Hughes
and
TWA

Smithsonian History of Aviation Series

Von Hardesty, Series Editor

The Smithsonian History of Aviation Series is intended to contribute to the overall understanding of the history of aviation—its science and technology as well as the social, cultural, and political environment in which it developed and matured. Some publications help fill the many gaps that still exist in the literature of flight; others add new information and interpretation to current knowledge. While the series appeals to a broad audience of general readers and specialists in the field, its hallmark is strong scholarly content.

The series is international in scope and includes works in three major categories: Smithsonian Studies in Aviation History, works that provide new and original knowledge; Smithsonian Classics of Aviation History, carefully selected out-of-print works that are considered essential scholarship; and Smithsonian Contributions to Aviation History, previously unpublished documents, reports, symposia, and other materials.

Howard Hughes and TWA

Robert W. Rummel

SMITHSONIAN INSTITUTION PRESS *Washington and London*

Editor: Tom Ireland
Production Editor: Duke Johns
Designer: Janice Wheeler

Library of Congress Cataloging-in-Publication Data
Rummel, Robert W.
    Howard Hughes and TWA / by Robert W. Rummel.
      p.   cm.
    Includes bibliographical references and index.
    ISBN 1-56098-017-6 (cloth)
    1. Trans World Airlines—History. 2. Hughes, Howard, 1905–1976.
I. Title.
HE9803.T7R86   1991
387.7′06′573—dc20   90-39534

British Library Cataloging-in-Publication Data is available

Manufactured in the United States of America
98 97 96 95 94 93 92   5 4 3 2

This book is part of the Smithsonian History of Aviation Series. Published in the United States by the Smithsonian Institution Press, this series of books is distributed in the United Kingdom, Europe, the Middle East, and Africa by Airlife Publishing Ltd.

∞The paper used in this publication meets the minimum requirements of the American National Standard for Permanence of Paper for Printed Library Materials Z39.48-1984.

To Marjorie,
with humility and boundless gratitude
to God that she is still by my side

Contents

Acknowledgments

Everyone I turned to for assistance in developing this book was without exception most cooperative and helpful. I could not have been accorded greater consideration or courtesy. Former associates, other direct participants, and industry historians willingly provided information, subjected themselves to interviews, reviewed draft manuscripts, and volunteered constructive suggestions. I owe a very special debt of gratitude to Ralph Bayless, Marshall Cox, Jim Floyd, John Guy, Hall Hibbard, Dixon Speas, Tommy Tomlinson, Dudley Tenney, Ed Wells, and Ed Zak for the extraordinary amount of time they spent being interviewed or reviewing draft manuscripts. The contributions of all who assisted were absolutely outstanding. I extend my sincere gratitude to all of them.

Ralph L. Bayless	Marshall Cox	John C. Franklin
William B. Bergen	Raymond M. Dunn	Harry Gann
Edward G. Betts, Jr.	Jack H. Enders	John E. Guy
Richard F. Brown	Frank Fink	M. Carl Haddon
Cyril Chappelet	J. C. Floyd	Willis M. Hawkins

Hall L. Hibbard
Clarence L. Johnson
Robert E. Johnson
A. E. Jordan
Raymond D. Kelly
Jackson R. McGowen

Norman R. Parmet
J. A. Shaunty
Walter D. Sherwood
Warren H. Spannuth
W. R. Sonnemann
R. Dixon Speas

Paul R. Strohm
Dudley B. Tenney
D. W. Tomlinson IV
Edward C. Wells
Edwin Zak

1.

Hughes— The Man and the Times

This was the golden time, the best years of Howard R. Hughes: aviator, industrialist, and entrepreneur. He became world famous for his aviation exploits; he established major corporations; he became a national hero during war contract Senate hearings, when he turned the tables on the politicians; he produced blockbuster movies; and he built the "Spruce Goose," the world's largest plane. His business interests multiplied and expanded, until finally, he emerged one of the wealthiest men in the world.

It was a period not yet tainted by demonstrations of extreme withdrawal or actions suggestive of a psychopathic condition. Howard was alert, vigorous, analytical, and extremely perceptive. He had enormous retentive capability, was tireless, and exuded vitality. His actions and words revealed an extremely cagey, determined, and organized mind that did not want to stop.

I write with the authority of personal experience. I was closely associated with Howard Hughes during the most challenging and dramatic period in the development of transport aviation. These were the years during which the fledging wings of the Douglas DC-3 workhorse planes gave way

1

to ever-improving piston-powered transports, which, in turn, were replaced by the magnificent jets that propelled the airlines from adolescence to early maturity.

It was a time of intense airline competition, entrepreneurship, and exciting visions of the future, which bred in rapid succession a string of competitive transports produced by leading manufacturers. Each vied for a lion's share of the transport market—a market that was pitifully small considering the enormous sums required to develop, tool, and produce the aircraft. It was a progressive era, paced by technological advances with an insatiable hunger for financial resources.

My direct association with Hughes stemmed from my work at Trans World Airlines (TWA). My primary job was to define, evaluate, and procure TWA's transport fleets. During this period over 200 transport designs—pistons, turboprops, and jets (some original on my part) were investigated. Over $3 billion worth of equipment was purchased by TWA and Hughes, equivalent to at least $24 billion today. This area was Howard's special apple pie, for which he never lost appetite.

Howard's great interest in aviation—probably his first and last real love—and my work generated an extraordinary working relationship between us almost from the first. I joined TWA in 1943, after a successful youthful career in aircraft design. Not long thereafter, Hughes requested through Jack Frye, the president of TWA, that I attend a meeting on aircraft design to be held at the Hughes Aircraft Company in Culver City, California.

About fifteen men were seated around the table when Howard arrived, right on time. By chance, I was seated directly across the table from him. I noticed what seemed to be a pronounced reluctance on the part of the other men to respond to Howard's comments and questions. I thought their reticence a bit odd and out of place. As far as I was concerned, Howard was entitled to the best and most candid professional opinions I could muster. After all, he owned most of the company and certainly would not have called the meeting unless he thought it was important. I decided to respond whenever I thought my comments would be constructive.

The room was not air-conditioned, and the weather was hot and sticky. Every time I spoke, my glasses slipped down my nose almost to the very end. I would push them back and continue, not just once, but several times during each response. A silly situation. As far as I can recall, that never happened before or since. As I continued to try to be helpful by comment-

2

ing and answering questions, and the glasses kept slipping, I noticed a faint smile cross Hughes's face.

The meeting lasted about two hours. When I was leaving, Hughes motioned me to one side for a private chat, during which he thanked me for my candor. I never learned if it were the wisdom of my comments or my slippery nose that attracted his attention. This meeting not only got me off on the right foot with Hughes, but it was also the beginning of a long, unusual working relationship that carried exceptional personal responsibilities far beyond my normal TWA duties.

Howard began to habitually turn to me for advice and action recommendations rather than to my superiors, including TWA presidents, who frequently looked to me for Hughes's position. On occasion, even TWA's chairman would ask me to intercede with Hughes in his behalf. During one period, Howard required that proposed agenda items for TWA's Board of Directors meetings be cleared with me before submission to the board, even though I held no such formal position of authority in TWA.

The exceptional responsibilities thrust upon me through my relationship with Hughes always belied my organizational positions at TWA, which progressed from engineer to vice president. After several years, while remaining on TWA's payroll, I was also placed on the payroll of Howard's wholly owned Hughes Tool Company (then and in this book generally referred to as Toolco) as a special Hughes consultant, a circumstance approved without dissent by TWA's board. All this resulted in a warm but often hectic working relationship with Hughes that lasted nearly 18 years, until Howard lost control of the corporation on December 31, 1960.

The fact that Howard held no position whatever in TWA made no discernible difference to him. He acted as if he were management, dealing directly in any area of corporate activity that gained his fancy, rather than through the board. I always had two bosses, Howard and a TWA superior. To say the very least, this sometimes awkward situation was not always sunshine and roses and might have become intolerable, except that successive senior managements almost always welcomed my relationship as desirable insulation between Hughes and themselves. I discovered early on that I must be physically incapable of developing ulcers.

Howard required full compliance with two strict, unyielding precepts: TWA was not to make any corporate financing arrangements or undertake new aircraft fleet procurement negotiations without his personal, direct approval. Working these areas in customary fashion through senior man-

3

agement to the board for approval was not enough, Howard's control of the board notwithstanding. In every case when management tried to follow an independent course in either forbidden area, Hughes took care of the dissenting presidents by unmercifully replacing them. Jack Frye, whose pioneering efforts were substantially responsible for TWA's emergence as a major carrier, was replaced when he attempted to act on his own in financial matters; LaMotte T. Cohu was replaced when he persisted with aircraft procurement policies incompatible with those of Hughes; Carter L. Burgess was replaced when he attempted to act independently in aircraft procurement affairs. During the management upheavals that inevitably followed, my relationship with Hughes was not affected in the slightest.

I saw nothing wrong in Howard's dominance in aircraft procurement matters, at least during the early years of my association with him. After all, I reasoned with some naivete, because he owned a lion's share of the company, he would do what he considered best for it. If it were good for TWA, it would be good for Hughes, or so I thought. This viewpoint proved to be totally incorrect during the late 1950s, when jets intended for TWA's use were not only denied to it, but sold to its prime competition.

Howard had a marvelous facility for surrounding himself with highly competent people and an equally amazing facility for losing them when they could likely be most productive. Simon Ramo, Dean Wooldridge, and Charles B. ("Tex") Thornton are good examples. All were highly successful in their own right after leaving Hughes. Ramo and Wooldridge cofounded the Ramo-Wooldridge Corporation, which later merged with Thompson Products to become TRW, and Thornton founded Litton Industries.

Howard was a difficult man to work for, but one of the reasons for such departures was his well-known position on granting capital-gains positions to key employees. He would not and did not, no matter what. *Everything* was for Hughes. Nothing substantial rubbed off, anywhere.

Howard's principal and most enduring money fountain was Hughes Tool Company of Houston, Texas, manufacturer of drilling tools for the oil industry. Howard was president and 100-percent owner; however, he took very little interest in the affairs of Toolco per se, relying on his financial watchdog, Noah Dietrich, to monitor its day-to-day operations. Howard's interest was in the money Toolco generated.

It was Howard's Toolco, not TWA, that placed the initial Lockheed Constellation order. Toolco also ordered all of TWA's major new fleets from 1954 on, for as long as Hughes controlled the airline. Yet Toolco and Toolco management played no part whatsoever in the decisions on what to order or in negotiations leading up to placing the orders. It was I who, on Howard's instructions, immediately after we had reached final agreement with the manufacturers, contacted officials at Toolco and arranged for a special Toolco board meeting to be held the next day to formally approve and execute the procurement contracts. Toolco was a strong financial anchor for Howard's dealings.

Howard's management style was peculiar. He personally directed his empire from the West Coast, or wherever he happened to be. The telephone was his lifeline. He dealt with the world primarily through trusted employees. While he personally attended numbers of key meetings, he seldom, if ever, signed key letters, contracts, or other documentation.

Howard had a consummate, unquenchable interest in airplane design. His questions concerning broad design concepts as well as details were crisp, comprehensive, and usually exasperatingly detailed. He wanted to know everything. Working with Howard required exhaustive preparation; but no matter how well prepared I might be, he would frequently probe areas requiring further study. And he had a memory that made the proverbial elephant look like a dunce.

I learned early to pay close attention to every word that Howard spoke, that is, to accept only the literal meaning of his statements rather than be led down the primrose path by jumping to conclusions or being swayed by tone of voice. Howard had the knack of verbally selling his viewpoints and negotiating gains without making any commitment whatsoever, unless he deemed it both timely and absolutely necessary. He was a master of leading one up to the edge of a major decision and then subtly leaving the decision like a fish dangling precariously on the hook, just out of reach. When I was not certain of his intentions and thought it important to know, I would ask. If he thought the time was right, I received a meaningful answer. If he did not, I learned nothing.

He was a master, perhaps one of the greatest of all time, of using procrastination as a weapon. When a decision could be put off, it would be; and frequently, when it should not have been, it was anyway. This often resulted in my negotiating hands being tied at the most contractually awkward times possible. It also led to strained relations with manufacturers who were driven by critical, time-sensitive situations and caused considerable needless extra work. On the other hand, Howard was quite capable of and did make far-reaching decisions, but only when he considered circumstances to be advantageous.

Howard could not be forced into action. He could be reasoned with and persuaded, but never forced. He wanted to know all the facts and potential consequences of any actions he might take before making his mind up. I never knew him to make blind or uninformed decisions, and never when he thought he was being forced. Dealing successfully with Howard required sensitivity to this quirk. If one pushed too far, one incurred the risk of setting in concrete either inaction or the wrong conclusion.

Howard's unconscionable telephone habit is probably one for the record books. At first, his calls to me were infrequent, but they gradually increased, finally averaging about one a day during extended periods when he was active in aviation affairs. Late night calls were standard, when most people, including me, were ready for bed or had retired. It was as if he did not recognize the difference between night and day. Some lasted all night, some only a few hours. The longest I remember was 11 hours, with only one 10-minute break.

The subject matter of Howard's telephone calls was mostly interesting, usually necessary, but not always timely. Three areas were favorite topics: flight safety, airplane design, and current fleet negotiations. For example, with regard to safety, all known aspects of every transport accident were explored at length, including probable causes, human factors, future avoidance, and other pertinent considerations. I welcomed the opportunities to discuss such matters with Howard but grew to intensely dislike the unreasonably late hours and excessive duration of his calls. His words were always thoughtful and considerate, and his manner respectful and kind; but somehow his conversations almost always imposed unwanted obligations on weekends and holidays. He would say in effect that he did not want to impose, but, "If you can just see your way clear to do this, it would be so helpful, and I would be eternally grateful. Bob, I don't want to interrupt your weekend any more than is absolutely necessary, but if you can manage this, I'll be deeply appreciative." His manner made it hard to say no, and he had a special knack for making every project an urgent affair. Some indeed were, usually because of his having failed to act when it was timely. All-out efforts by my staff and me, including a great deal of after-hours work, was the norm rather than the exception. I marvel that my staff put up with it year after year, but I am grateful that they did.

Howard's proclivity for secrecy was legend throughout the industry.

Code words such as "string bean," "Mexico City," and the like were used to identify secret projects and help maintain industrial security for the purpose of gaining competitive equipment advantages for TWA. Initially, such precautions seemed well placed. As time passed, however, Howard insisted that deep secrecy be accorded nearly every activity, including even trivial matters. Secrecy became a way of life with Howard, rather than a carefully exercised option.

If Howard's extreme withdrawal in later life had early manifestations during the years I worked with him, they went by me unnoticed. I thought Howard's carefully managed unavailability reflected deliberate efforts to avoid shysters, salesmen, unwanted promoters, and the like. Similarly, his persistent use of drab-colored Chevrolets and casual dress, in addition to being economical and comfortable, seemed to me only to reflect a desire common to many well-known personalities to avoid public notice. Much has been written about Howard's ill-kept ways, no doubt with some validity, especially in reference to his final years. However, I never saw that side of him. He habitually wore loose-fitting slacks, a white shirt open at the collar, comfortable loafers, and sometimes an open jacket. He always seemed to be physically clean. I always wore a business suit and tie, and, quite frankly, would have preferred to dress like him. On special occasions, he would spruce up and be as presentable as the best of them.

I admired Howard's aviation and business successes, enjoyed the work, especially during the early years, and considered myself fortunate to be associated with him. Our aircraft development programs and planning for TWA's future were especially compelling and exciting activities. We worked on the frontier of aircraft design technology, and I loved it. However, my exuberance diminished as the years passed, yielding to genuine, pressing concerns about the long-term impact his unpredictable aircraft program permutations would have on TWA.

My exuberance also faded because of the impact on my family of his pervasive, burdensome demands on my time. I was on call 24 hours every day and was frequently required to report my whereabouts by telephone when out of direct reach for more than 30 minutes. I was required to be away from home over half of the time. When at home, I was buried in Howard's "urgent" projects and regular TWA work. My work week averaged over 70 hours for 18 years. I knew this was not fair to my wife, Margie, and our family—a perception that wore heavily on my conscience.

I was trapped by the necessity of earning a living and the double-barreled intrigue of my profession and working for Howard.

If I had had even the slightest inkling of what the future held for me, I might have chosen not to continue working for Hughes and TWA. When Howard lost control of TWA in 1960, his stock was put in a voting trust, and TWA's board was reconstituted. The new board hired outside lawyers to determine if cause existed for any legal action on the board's behalf. It did. TWA filed two major suits against Hughes and Toolco, claiming hundreds of millions of dollars in damages. Significantly, both cases involved the very activity I had engaged in with Hughes throughout my long association with him: the procurement of aircraft for TWA.

It seemed to me that the greatest disservice I could do either TWA or Hughes was to withhold information. I answered the lawyers' questions as candidly and completely as memory and research permitted and soon found myself in the unenviable position of having become the chief witness for the plaintiff in both cases. Thus, through circumstances over which I had no control, I was pitted against Hughes and my friends at Toolco. While I had become thoroughly disgusted with Howard's treatment of TWA—it had been obvious for some time that his actions, which made no sense to me whatsoever, were seriously harming the corporation—I was never angry with him and always hoped he understood my compulsion to tell the truth.

My attitude contrasted sharply with that of numbers of TWA officers, who seemed more worried about bringing down the wrath of Hughes on themselves in the event he regained control (which he nearly did in 1964) than about harming TWA by not acting in a forthcoming manner. In one instance, the lawyers handling TWA's case recommended that a corporate officer hire outside counsel to protect himself because he had for days when on the witness stand persisted in forgetting everything concerning Hughes.

It was a wrenching experience. I was on the witness stand surrounded by batteries of opposing lawyers for endless days that added up to more than four months, including two pretrial depositions, a damage hearing, and a trial. That is a very long time, indeed, and every appearance required weeks—often months—of research to prepare myself. To make matters worse, the overall time required to complete legal proceedings associated with the two suits required an astonishing 27 years plus. As the only witness with knowledge of the entire period, I was required up to the end to retain detailed knowledge of Howard's related activities and pertinent events that occurred from 1943 onward—a total of 45 years.

Fortunately, I had required all data pertaining to my work with Hughes to be retained in locked files. My repetitive reviews of that file and other case documentation, and the blessing of a good memory, served TWA well and provided an excellent data base for this book. TWA won one trial and lost one.

Through all the 45 years, Margie was absolutely wonderful. She had a right to be angry, but could not have been more understanding and helpful. The responsibility of raising our five children was more than a full-time job, which she handled beautifully, without complaint. The kids always sparkled, were happy, and along with Margie were the pride of my life. My love and my gratitude defy description.

I can look back today on a life intimately connected with the infancy, adolescence, and early maturity of the aviation industry, in the course of which I worked with and came to know many of the individuals and organizations responsible for the amazing progress that has been realized in transport aviation. For all his faults, there can be no doubt that Howard Hughes belongs in that honorable company. During the years of my association with him, he importantly impacted the course of transport aviation—and for the better. My work and that of my staff contributed to much of that impact. Passing time only clarified the significance of those accomplishments and mollified our disappointments.

2.
My Life
before Hughes

From the age of awakening on, I was interested in aviation. This interest grew until it irresistibly shaped my life, expanding with the passing years and finally embracing the intriguing frontiers of space. Today, nearly 70 years later, the challenging technological horizons are just as vivid and exciting to me as ever. Yet nothing in my early childhood pointed to the course my life was to take.

Dakota, where I was born on August 4, 1915, is located in the fertile farm lands of northern Illinois about 10 miles northeast of Freeport. The countryside was attractive, with rolling hills, lush intermittent woods, brooks, and little fern-covered glens. The town of 300, complete with a railroad station, town center, churches, and recreation halls, was an active, vital community. Altogether, a delightful place.

My mother and dad, my brother Eddie, and I were a happy and caring family. I cannot remember a single cross word between my parents. They were fine, upright, industrious Christians who placed the welfare of the family first.

Dad was a food merchant who worked long, hard hours to become established and make ends meet. His general store was the center of the town's commercial activities. He was busy every waking minute at work, with his family, or with athletic activities. He set a fine example for me by his integrity, honesty, and consideration for others.

So did Mother. She was wonderfully caring, a good teacher, and always helpful and interested in my boyhood activities. Like Dad, she was well liked in the community, very forthright and sincere, well read, and industrious. My parents managed well, and even though we were not wealthy, we never lacked for anything important.

When I was seven years old, Dad sold the business in Dakota and moved to Morrison, Illinois, for a better business opportunity. In time, he acquired a small chain of markets. His formula for success worked well. Each time he bought a market, he would manage it personally until it was well established. Then, as soon as practicable, he would invest management in a trusted employee whom he had personally trained, making it a practice to visit each store weekly. Dad provided a good incentive for his managers to build the business. In addition to a regular salary, they received a percentage of the profits.

After my sophomore year in high school, the family moved to Mount Carroll, Illinois, again for business reasons. My last two years in high school were something else. At 15, I discovered two things: girls, and the fact that I knew very little. While my grades had been above average, I was suddenly faced with the sobering realization that my knowledge in all areas was abysmally low compared to what was available and what I wanted and would probably need to know. This led me to take extra subjects. I took seven major courses each year (four were required for graduation), and I discovered that the more work I took on, the more I seemed to be able to handle. This was a valuable lesson.

The math teacher, Zella Corbett, learned of my interest in math and offered to teach me advanced algebra, trigonometry, and solid geometry, none of which were available at that school. She explained I would be the only student and would not receive credit on the record, but she would be glad to help if I were interested. I jumped at the chance. Later on, at the end of the courses, she explained, "Bob, I can't give you 100-percent grades because I know that somewhere you must have made some error. I don't know what it is, but no one is perfect, so I will give you only 99 percent." She was a wonderfully fine person. I will always be grateful for her kind understanding and good help.

By this time I was talking little else but airplanes. Dad thought flying was unsafe and sent me to the 1933 Boy Scout World Jamboree in Gödöllö, Hungary, with the expressed hope that I would find some other interest. I had never been out of the country and excitedly looked forward to the jamboree and the tour, which included England, Belgium, the Netherlands, France, Germany, Austria, Hungary, Italy, Sicily, and Gibraltar. Seeing different peoples, being with other young men from countries all over the world at the jamboree, and visiting museums and other points of interest was an unforgettable and highly educational experience. Nine of us were fortunate enough to have a private audience with Pope Pius XI after an extensive tour of the Vatican. The pope spoke briefly to each of us in English and blessed the group. He also touched and blessed a dozen rosaries I had, which I gave to Catholic friends on returning home.

Nazi storm troopers seemed to be everywhere in Munich. I left Germany with an uneasy feeling. When giving talks on my return at the local Rotary and Lions clubs, I was brash enough to predict World War II. This was controversial, but I did not change my position.

Of course, Dad's ploy did not work, Years later he said he thought I had made the right career choice; that I never would have been content doing anything else, especially selling bananas in a grocery store.

The Lure of Aviation

I first awakened to the lure of aviation when I was five years old. My brother and I had a child's book filled with drawings of airplanes. The story—I do not recall the title—was about an air race across the United States. I was fascinated. All types of airplanes participated in the race, which required months to complete. With help, I learned to read it and must have read it at least a hundred times. About the same time, while I was playing under the cherry tree in the back yard, a biplane flew over at low level. It was the first real airplane I had ever seen. The speed, the sound of the engine, and the very idea of leaving the ground like a bird thrilled me. I imagined the pilot waved at me. I did not know it then, but these were the first steps toward becoming hooked on aviation.

Later on, the early pioneering flights over the Atlantic and Pacific oceans, including the early zeppelin crossings, were exciting and beckoning to me. All of the pilots were my heroes. Their exploits stirred my imagination and convinced me that aviation would have a truly great future.

If any one event clinched my determination to take up aviation, it was Charles A. Lindbergh's nonstop transatlantic flight of May 20–21, 1927. Unlike NASA's magnificent space exploits of recent years, each of these early flights was mostly the product of only a handful of people. The skill of the pilots and the personal risks they accepted easily justified, in my opinion, every honor accorded them.

I read everything on aviation available in the press and the local library. I purchased monthly the leading aviation magazine of the day, *Aero Digest*. I spent hours sketching aircraft, illustrating design features, and even drawing what I thought were new ideas. This activity evolved into a model-building period. The models were rudimentary. Because prefabricated kits were not available, it was necessary for all my models to be designed and built from scratch with materials at hand.

Of the many models I built, the last was a rocket-propelled car. It was about two feet long, had a wide wheel base, was highly streamlined, and was powered with a single rocket motor made by tamping the propellant into a large glass tube that I wound with wire to keep it from exploding. The propellant was gunpowder I made in my small shop in the basement of our house. Making gunpowder ceased abruptly when Dad found out what was going on, but by then I had enough for one run. It was more successful than I imagined it could be. I found smooth pavement on a little-traveled highway north of Morrison and lit the charge. The model moved at incredible speed. All went well until it crossed a heavy tar strip in the pavement, bounced, took off, landed in a ditch, rolled over, and burned. The toys and construction kits that can be bought today are beautiful. However, I doubt if they are as much fun or as educational as the kinds I and many of my contemporaries made as children.

I had my first airplane ride in 1930 in a Ford trimotor. I visited airports and took in air shows at every opportunity. Lt. J. H. Doolittle, later General Doolittle, performed one Sunday at Sterling, Illinois, in his Travel Air Model R Mystery Ship, a fully cowled, wire-braced monoplane. I had never seen such expert flying. Lieutenant Doolittle demonstrated nearly every possible maneuver with great precision. The show left a lasting impression. The furthest thing from my mind was that our paths would cross numbers of times years later.

14

Curtiss Wright and Early Employment

I could hardly wait to graduate from high school and get on with my life. Nonetheless it was with some trepidation and doubt as to my capabilities that I left home in the fall of 1934. I chose to attend the Curtiss Wright Technical Institute of Aeronautics, in Glendale, California. This school taught aeronautical engineering and aircraft construction and was more like a trade school than a college. I was anxious to become an engineer and correctly thought I could enter industry sooner this way. The school had an excellent reputation. The majority of its students, trained to be productive when first employed, found work on graduation, even during the Great Depression.

The engineering course at Curtiss Wright concentrated on drafting, aerodynamics, structures, design, physics and mathematics, and work techniques used by the airplane manufacturers. It was a fine school, and it gave me a good start. However, it lacked the broad curriculum found in colleges. Later, I often regretted not having taken time to earn a degree. I finished the course about three months early and graduated with honors.

A few days before finishing the course, I was approached by the chief instructor, Carl Stryker, who said that Howard Hughes had a racing plane under development and needed a stress analyst. Was I interested in talking to them? I had heard a great deal about the fabulous Howard Hughes, and I needed a job. After pondering the question all of a tenth of a second, I said, "You bet I am, Carl, thanks." Then, after a pause, I added, "Carl, I'm not really a stress analyst. Do you think I can handle the job if I'm lucky enough to get it?" Carl said he thought they would be glad to help me, and he set up a meeting.

The next day I met with Byron Masterson, the chief of structures for Hughes. He hired me but carefully explained that when the one airplane project was finished, my position would be terminated. Byron was tolerant and understanding of my inexperience, and helpful with difficult problems.

The construction of the Hughes Racer was probably as perfect as that of any plane manufactured up to that time, and possibly since then. Hughes insisted that if a .005-inch-thick feeler gauge could be inserted between the edges of the butt-joined fuselage plates, new, tighter fitting plates had to be installed. The wing was constructed of birch plywood, which presented a completely smooth surface to the airstream. It was a sweet plane, in which

15

Hughes set a transcontinental speed record of 7 hours, 28 minutes, and 35 seconds on January 20, 1937, between Burbank, California, and Newark, New Jersey. The record stood for many years. The plane is presently housed in the National Air and Space Museum in Washington, D.C.

My initial job was to stress analyze (compute the loads and calculate the strength of) the landing gear. The gear was extremely long and spindly. When load was applied, virtually every part of this three-dimensional structure deflected, causing the loads to be redistributed. Calculating the true loads and stress was difficult work for a neophyte. I burned midnight oil over textbooks.

My next job was to calculate maximum stress in the plywood wing skin. The compressive strength of wood is greater when the load is applied in line with the grain rather than perpendicular to it. So, the angles of the grain between the birch plies were varied along the wing span to obtain the greatest strength at the lightest possible weight. By calculating the direction and intensity of the stress, the optimum angles of the grain between the plies could be found.

After that, until the project ended, I was assigned miscellaneous stress analysis jobs. Hughes frequented the plant to inspect construction progress. Because he spent most of his time in the shop rather than the engineering department, it was not my privilege to meet him at that time.

After my work at Hughes was completed, I was hired by Lockheed as a stress analyst to work on the Electra Junior, the Model 12. Stress analysis was interesting, and Lockheed was a fine company to work for, but I hoped to gain broader experience before this type of work somehow limited my career options. While still at Curtiss Wright, I had become convinced that the best career path for me would be to obtain as broad a background as possible rather than become a specialist in only one discipline. I had noticed 50-year-old, pencil-pushing draftsmen at the Douglas factory who apparently had been doing the same work for years. That was probably okay for them, but I was determined not to be pinched into a lifetime of work with limited visibility. I thought that the experience to be gained working for small rather than large companies would be more diverse and intense, and would likely expedite career progress.

While working at Hughes, I became acquainted with W. C. (''Rocky'') Rockefeller and Carlos C. Wood, who were associated with the California Institute of Technology and had worked directly with Hughes on numbers of projects. They took an interest in me and were instrumental in my obtaining two jobs in succession: at the Aero Engineering Corporation, in Long Beach, which produced a small, two-place, all-metal, low-wing prototype monoplane; and at the National Aircraft Company, in Alhambra, which had under development primary and basic trainers for the U.S. Army Air Corps. The considerable detail design and design layout (aircraft configuration) experience gained at both companies was exceptional for a young man, improved my credentials, and helped shape my career. Later on, when I worked directly with Howard, our paths again crossed when Rocky worked for Floyd B. Odlum, who founded the Atlas Corporation, and when Carlos was an engineering executive at the Douglas Aircraft Company.

After National went out of business due to inability to adequately finance the trainer programs, I decided to try the Midwest. I headed by train to St. Louis for a prearranged interview with George Page of Curtiss Wright, who was then responsible for engineering the CW-20 (later, the C-46) twin-engine transport at Lambert Field. On the way I visited the Beech Aircraft Company in Wichita and Rearwin Aircraft in Kansas City.

The fact that I had been part of the West Coast aviation industry, even for a short time, worked like magic. I was offered jobs by all three companies. With that happy situation in hand, I extended my vacation by two weeks and visited my parents in Mount Carroll. While I was there, Rae A. Rearwin, the company's president, telephoned me three times, offering me higher pay each time. I was skeptical about joining Rearwin because it was a family-owned company, and I favored Curtiss Wright. However, I could not afford to turn down the final Rearwin offer. At the end of my short vacation, I moved to Kansas City.

Rearwin

Rae A. Rearwin founded the Rearwin Airplane Company in Salina, Kansas, in 1928 when he was 50 years old. A successful lumber and fuel products dealer, he was attracted to aviation in anticipation that the lightplane industry would boom. His success was especially remarkable considering he was not a pilot and had no prior experience in aviation. The company outgrew several locations and finally settled in the Fairfax Industrial District in Kansas City, Kansas.

By the time I joined Rearwin, October 4, 1937, the Rearwin Ken-Royce biplane (named after his two sons), an excellent performer that had set numerous records, and the Junior, an open-cockpit, two-place tandem (pilot

17

in front of the passenger), strut-braced light monoplane, had been super-seded in production by the Rearwin Sportster, an advanced, more powerful, closed-cabin version of the Junior. Also in arrested development was the Speedster, a high-speed, 150-mph, two-place tandem design started in 1932, which had been unable to pass the required Department of Commerce, Bureau of Air Commerce, spin recovery certification requirements.

Certification of the Speedster was Rearwin's most pressing problem. Several had been sold but could not be prudently manufactured until after federal certification. I was familiar with many of the reports and technical notes published by the National Advisory Committee for Aeronautics (NACA), the forerunner of the National Aeronautics and Space Adminis-tration (NASA), and had acquired a small library of them. The NACA reports on aircraft spins provided solid clues as to the nature of the Speed-ster spin problem and how to correct it. I mentioned this to the chief engineer, who seemed completely unconvinced. Nevertheless, he passed my comments on to Rearwin, who, probably in desperation, quickly gave me carte blanche to solve the problem.

Bill Miller, Rearwin's test pilot and Rearwin Flying School instructor, showed me a foot-high stack of Speedster flight test reports. Each page covered a series of spin tests which, in aggregate, had required several years to complete. I read them all, then asked Bill to demonstrate the problem to me in the prototype. At about 10,000 feet, he put the plane in a spin—the first I had ever experienced. Seventeen turns later, at about 2,000 feet, after putting the controls in various positions on the way down to no avail, Bill had to blast our way out by applying full engine power. We leveled out at about 1,000 feet, which was plenty of altitude. Bill then asked me if I wanted anything else demonstrated. I was a little queasy from the 17 turns and said, "Yes, let's see how this thing lands!"

The first thing I did was to place the airplane in flight attitude in the hangar to check out the flight control system. The heavy friction through-out the control system was almost unbelievable. This was solved by the simple expedient of adding ball and "oilite" (pressed sintered bronze saturated with oil) bearings, along with rudder-centering springs.

Rearwin came past the airplane at least once every hour, urging that the airplane be tested in flight. His frequent, impatient insistence was distract-ing and finally compelled me to remind him of the past years of unpro-ductive flight tests. I assured him I was working as rapidly as possible and that I did not want the airplane flown until I was satisfied it was ready. This startled him, but he acquiesced and did not raise the issue again.

The next step was to redesign the vertical tail surfaces so they remained effective during spins. I also redesigned the "mutilated" slot ahead of the ailerons to smooth the airflow so the wing tips would be less prone to stall at high angles of attack. After about one week of flight tests, the airplane easily passed the federal spin tests, and it was certificated as soon as detailed engineering was completed.

I was surprised to notice Rearwin looking at me with jaundiced eyes shortly after I solved the spin problem, a personal performance that I had thought would favorably impress even the Sphinx. At that time, I was completing detailed engineering and stress analyses required for certification, some of which had been pending for several years. I had no idea why Rearwin was cool until I overheard by accident the chief engineer tell him that I would have the work finished in "two or three days," when, in fact, both he and I knew the work would require nearly a month. I suspected he had been telling Rearwin that for some time, and I did not appreciate being undercut in this manner. I was a fast, accurate, and dedicated worker, but no matter how well my job was being done, Rearwin was being given an entirely incorrect impression.

Later that day while I was mulling this situation over, Rearwin stopped me in the hall and brusquely asked how much longer my work would take. Without mentioning the chief engineer, and with considerable forced composure, I told him exactly what was involved and how long it would take. He listened intently and was, I believe, convinced of my sincerity. He knew I had been working several nights every week and all day Saturdays, not because that was our bargain, but because of my interest in the project. Rearwin confirmed my suspicion and, as we parted, thanked me for my candor. I then went directly to the chief engineer and told him what I said to Rearwin concerning the time required to complete the work. He seemed miffed and would not discuss the subject. A few weeks later Rearwin fired him.

Rearwin then hired a new chief engineer. Unfortunately, Rearwin had not talked to him before he arrived for work. He was likable and probably a good engineer. However, the poor fellow was not given much of a chance to prove it. He stuttered incessantly—not just ordinary stutters, but long, rolling, reverberating-from-the-gut stutters. He was nearly impossible to understand and would sometimes write on a white paper pad he carried rather than speak. This circumstance wore his welcome thin very fast with Rearwin, and his tenure was brief. Rearwin then named me chief engineer. I was 22 years old.

I had a great deal to learn and needed to learn it fast. Troy Keys, the no-nonsense manufacturing foreman who kept the men on their toes, was especially helpful. At first, however, I was not sure a good working relationship could develop. Troy was several years older than me, knew his trade well, had a knack for fabricating components in the most practical manner, and obviously did not need advice from a young engineer. It was fairly common for draftsmen to run to the shop to measure what the shop had already produced to make production drawings, but I had no intention of perpetuating this practice. Engineering had to have the final responsibility for design. This was necessary to avoid unauthorized shop changes and assure that the strength and configuration of the aircraft would always be as represented to the federal authorities and the customers.

Locking horns with Keys on this issue promised to be unproductive and apt to cause long-term resentments. The best solution seemed to be to solicit the ideas and opinions of responsible shop personnel. I had deep respect for their knowledge and experience, and I wanted to benefit from their judgments when it was timely to do so, at the outset of the design process. The initial meetings were followed by joint reviews prior to release of key production drawings. This plan was embraced by Keys and his shop associates, and it worked well. Engineering benefited from constructive suggestions made by shop personnel and made the final design decisions.

Rearwin acquired the LeBlond Aircraft Engine Corporation during the late fall of 1937, moved it from Cincinnati, Ohio, to Kansas City the following spring, and named it the Ken-Royce Aircraft Engine Company. The parent corporation had been founded in Detroit, Michigan, by Capt. E. V. ("Eddie") Rickenbacker and Glen D. Angle, who had designed the engines. Both founders had left LeBlond by the time of Rearwin's purchase. At that time the engines were used by Rearwin, Aeronca, and several other aircraft manufacturers.

The engine company did not run smoothly after its transfer to Kansas City. When production did not improve, Rearwin became suspicious of subtle sabotage; but nothing was proved, then or later. However, when he learned that some of the key people he moved from Cincinnati had arranged financing and planned to buy LeBlond just before he did and that they still coveted the company, he summarily dismissed them, including the shop foreman and chief engineer. Archie Turpin, an experienced foreman and jig builder, was hired as the new shop foreman, and, in a surprisingly short time, the production problems disappeared and the engine shop became a smooth-running, efficient organization.

Rearwin asked me to serve as chief engineer of the engine company while continuing to serve as such for the airplane company. This was flattering, but not altogether welcome, because I was up to my ears in airplane projects, and I did not consider myself an engine man. I pointed this out but on his insistence accepted the added responsibilities.

My first engine projects included modernizing and increasing the power of the two production models. This called for extensive redesign and testing of many components, including the crankshaft, case, cylinders, and heads. These projects were as interesting as they were challenging. This experience broadened my background and helped prepare me for what was to come.

While at Rearwin I designed the Cloudster series of two- and three-place airplanes, powered by Ken-Royce engines, and the smaller, two-place Skyranger series, powered with horizontally opposed engines. I also modernized the Sportster, giving it renewed life in the marketplace. Land plane, float plane, and ski plane versions of all models were engineered and certificated. The planes were certified in Canada, England, and New Zealand, as well as in the United States. They were sold primarily to sport fliers and training schools, although custom-designed trainer versions were manufactured for Pan American World Airways (PAA), TWA, and the government of Iran. Rearwin planes, in aggregate, were being produced at a total average rate of one per day when World War II intervened, a very respectable rate indeed for that era.

The Cloudster was designed, tested, and produced in remarkably short time. Permanent tooling was completed, full certification achieved, and production underway in less than one year from start of design. The Cloudster, like the subsequently produced Skyranger, had excellent flying, stall, and spin-recovery characteristics and quickly earned a worthwhile niche in the marketplace.

I designed a number of safety features into both planes that Rearwin chose not to advertise, perhaps understandably for fear of dissuading prospective customers. For example, the entire structure surrounding the occupants was 20 percent stronger than the rest of the structure to provide additional protection for the occupants during any crash landings that might occur. Also, I required the diagonal steel tubes located ahead of the cabin to be offset so if they failed in compression, they would bend away from the occupants and not become spears during accidents. Additionally, the main landing gear was designed so that in event of failure from excessively hard landings it would separate from the fuselage rather than penetrate it to avoid harming the occupants.

One Cloudster suffered a nearly catastrophic crash on a gravel riverbank not far from the factory after engine failure. The engine was pushed back to the reinforced cabin area, where it stopped; the fuselage was bent nearly double aft of the occupied area; one half of the gear was torn off; the wings were demolished. I was happy to see that the cabin area was virtually undamaged, and the pilot escaped with only a sprained shoulder. It was, and still is, my belief that aircraft structures should be designed efficiently, but in such a manner as to minimize the probability of injury in survivable accidents. Through the years, I have pressed this concept during NACA and NASA Research Advisory Committee meetings, with the Civil Aeronautics Authority (CAA, later the Federal Aviation Administration, or FAA), and with the air transport manufacturers with whom I dealt. Unfortunately, design habits do not always yield easily. Even simple, obvious things like the elimination of potential head knockers and the judicious placement of padding took years to accomplish. As chief engineer for Rearwin, I gained a great deal of engineering and management experience. In addition to designing airplanes and developing engines, I established the Inspection Department, which reported to me; set up the Heat-treat Department; learned to fly; ran flight and structural tests; had full responsibility for the certification programs; and helped with production planning. I averaged over 70 hours per week on the job, not because it was expected, but because of my enthusiasm for and interest in aviation. This experience gave me broad insight into aircraft design, certification, and manufacturing that was extremely valuable later on when dealing with the major airframe and engine manufacturers on behalf of Howard Hughes and TWA.

Margie

I met Marjorie Cox during June 1939, an event that was to forever improve my life. A friend arranged a blind date for me through one of her friends— the first blind date for either of us. It was electric. I liked the way she looked, the way she talked, the way she walked, her mannerisms; in fact,

22

there was nothing I did not like about her—a lot. We had fun, and I asked her for a date the next night, and the next, and every night for the next several months except when I absolutely could not put my work aside. I met her family and finally mustered enough courage to pop the question. We were married at the Cox home in Osawatomie, Kansas, on September 30, 1939.

Before the marriage, as a matter of courtesy I decided to ask her father for her hand. I walked into his shop indicating that I wanted to talk to him. Because several customers were present, he followed me into the back room with a quizzical look on his face. Without preliminaries, I said, "I plan to marry Margie if she will have me, and I'd like your approval."

I did not expect what I heard. He said, "What if I say no?"

I responded, "I hope you don't, but if you do, and Margie will still have me, I'll marry her anyway."

He smiled and said, "I thought you would say that," and then added with a serious tone of voice, "There is something you should know." I could not imagine what was coming next. After a long pause, he said, "She can't keep stockings and breaks heels off her shoes." He laughed, shook my hand warmly, and said he would be glad to welcome me into the family.

We planned to take two weeks to drive to New York City to visit the World's Fair for our honeymoon. I mentioned this to Rearwin, who promptly asked me to postpone the honeymoon "because of the urgency of the work," adding that the honeymoon would keep and that I could take it "anytime."

The only time I had ever taken any time off was a year earlier to visit my parents when both of them were in a hospital in Illinois after suffering an automobile accident while on their way to visit me. During the rest of my tenure at Rearwin, I literally worked night and day, up to the time I met Margie, and I never knew a time when Rearwin did not consider the work urgent. Thinking about this while he was talking, I decided his minimum forbearance should be time off for my honeymoon, especially considering the success of my designs. Besides, I did not want to disappoint Margie, who was eagerly anticipating her first trip to New York.

Rearwin was given to venting his temper on occasion, sometimes turning purple with rage. I had never personally been a target, but I saw dark clouds erupt on his brow when I told him I would see that the work would be handled, but that I planned to go ahead with the honeymoon. For a moment, I thought he might fire me. Instead of exploding, he stared at me coldly for what seemed like a long time and then abruptly turned and walked away without saying a word. Later that day, his son, Kenneth, approached me and said that his father was upset. Ken wondered if I would like to change my mind. I told him I appreciated Mr. Rearwin's viewpoint, that I hoped he appreciated mine, and explained my position to him. I asked Ken to please explain this to his father. The subject never came up again.

A few weeks after the honeymoon, Rearwin invited Margie and me to dinner at the exclusive Kansas City Club rooftop ballroom. Rearwin was most gracious and friendly. It was a great evening, and it put the raw edges behind us.

The honeymoon trip was great. We drove our Oldsmobile coupe to New York, stopping along the way when it pleased us. While there, we did the World's Fair; danced to Guy Lombardo's music at the Roosevelt Hotel, where we stayed; ate at Keene's Chop House; took in a Broadway play; and bought Margie a fur coat. One afternoon on our way to a shop near the Waldorf Astoria Hotel to buy Margie more stockings, she broke the heels completely off both shoes in an iron grate.

Our week in New York seemed to evaporate overnight. On the return drive to Kansas City, I managed to park too close to a steep bank covered with pebbles. With my left arm in the window opening and my right hand on the steering wheel, I stepped out. The pebbles acted like ball bearings. I lost footing and caught myself by my arm in the window and my hand and forearm on the wheel. My weight slammed the door shut on my head and tooted the horn. When my footing was momentarily regained the door would open and the horn would stop, but I could not regain footing. The door kept slamming and the horn tooting. I could not have dreamed up a more ridiculous situation. There I was, beating my head to a pulp with my pretty wife looking on. Margie thought it was funny. Except for this silly incident, the honeymoon was perfect.

A year later, Margie became pregnant. We decided our child would be better off if we had a house in the country. We found a bungalow for rent on two acres of land in the North Kansas City area. We moved in but discovered the country was considerably more than we hoped it would be. We had close neighbors on one side who had chickens and a cow. Every morning around sunrise the cocks would start crowing, and the cow seemed to stick her head in our bedroom window and bellow.

We could have gotten used to that, but neither of us could talk about crops, livestock, or hardly anything else that interested the neighbors. Everyone was friendly, but we had nothing in common. All this, plus the fact that it required over two hours for Margie to get into town because I needed the car for work, caused us to rethink the needs of our unborn child. We found an apartment in Kansas City, Kansas, close to the one we had left several months earlier. Linda Kay, a fine, healthy child, was born on May 23, 1941, and she has shown no ill effects from having been deprived of the country.

Shortly after Linda was born, we decided it would make economic sense to buy our home rather than continue to rent apartments. Although we did not have much money, we decided to look around just in case some unexpected miracle might develop.

The J. C. Nichols Company, a major Kansas City developer, had recently undertaken to develop Prairie Village, a suburb several miles southwest of Kansas City. It consisted of one and a half blocks of foundations and unfinished houses (its population had grown to 24,000 by 1980). Margie fell in love with a small, two-bedroom bungalow at 2816 West 69th Street. I agreed it would be just right for our family. We really wanted it, but we concluded with some anguish that we simply could not afford the down payment.

We met with Miller Nichols, the vice president, to explain our circumstances. Miller was more than helpful. By the time the meeting was over, he agreed to accept a second mortgage for the customary down payment if we would put in $500 and leave for collateral a class ring I was wearing and Margie's engagement ring. We agreed. As we were leaving, Miller said he thought Margie would take good care of her ring and asked if she would like to keep it for him. She almost cried when Miller handed it to her. Miller was a fine gentleman who saw fit to help a young couple on their way. The house was finished right on time. We moved in when Linda was 10 months old.

Prairie Village grew rapidly until World War II sharply curtailed construction. Most of the families were young with lots of children—everyone said the water was responsible—and neighborhood gatherings were commonplace. Our family continued to grow: Sharon Lee was born on February 25, 1943; Marjorie Susan on July 29, 1944; Robert, Jr., on February 19, 1949—a real "buster," who has never stopped even to this day; and Diana Beth on January 26, 1953, our fourth beautiful little girl.

25

Conversion for War

By 1940, it was obvious to most of us that the United States would inevitably be embroiled in fighting World War II despite President Franklin Delano Roosevelt's campaign promises to the contrary. Hardly anyone doubted that Hitler would continue to overrun Europe.

At that time, Rearwin's business outlook was excellent and would likely remain so if the war somehow were not to intervene, and my personal career seemed to be well on track. But the Pearl Harbor outrage on December 7, 1941, decisively erased any harbored thoughts concerning possible avoidance of direct U.S. participation and forever changed what might have been.

With material for the construction of private planes in short supply, the Rearwin factory was converted for war production just as rapidly as acquisition of contracts permitted. Efforts to sell scout versions of the planes to the military did not succeed, but contracts for the manufacture of punches and die for making cartridges, hydraulic actuators for aircraft, test benches, glider tow disconnects, and the like kept the shops occupied. Finally, Rearwin landed a major contract for the construction of CG-3A and CG-4A combat gliders, designed by Waco. The gliders were to be towed by aircraft to move troops to strategic areas, after which they would be released for "power-off" landings. I thought most landings would at best be controlled crashes.

When the glider contract was awarded, Rearwin was a lean and efficient organization. However, like many organizations caught in the exploding war effort, this was about to change drastically. The contracting officer required nearly one-third of the factory to be converted into office space. I considered the conversion exorbitant, wasteful, and counterproductive but was told that management was expected to expand to a stipulated percentage of the number of production workers. This idea ran counter to my grain. I had always believed that personnel in any category should be hired only to satisfy real needs, not to satisfy arbitrary ratios. A great excess of new hands were hired to fill management and production positions, most with little or no experience.

I had been responsible for engineering, inspection, production planning, flight test, and heat-treat operations when the "cost plus" glider contract was awarded. New people were hired to fill all of these positions, except engineering, which became my sole responsibility. Because the gliders had

26

been engineered by Waco, virtually no engineering was required. I now had very little responsibility indeed, compared to the heavy load I had been carrying.

I had trouble accepting this. It was explained that my downgraded position had nothing to do with my past work—it was only the wish of the contracting officer, who, incidentally, personally selected most of the new key people. I seriously considered leaving the company, but because my salary had not been cut (earlier, I had even thought the glider contract would impose greater responsibilities on me with a commensurate salary increase), I decided to stay on.

I tried very hard to get along with the new people, but everywhere I turned, I saw needless inefficiency and waste. My suggestions for making improvements were almost always unwelcome, as if I were trying to move in on someone's turf. My youthful appearance probably did not help my position either.

Commonwealth

Although Mr. Rearwin said nothing to me, I am confident that the extravagance and inefficiencies developed despite his best efforts to the contrary. Waste was contrary to his nature and must have racked him terribly. During the latter part of 1942, he sold Rearwin Aircraft & Engines (the airplane and engine companies had been combined several years earlier) to Empire Ordinance of New York City. He and Ken were out as part of the transaction. (Royce, his other son, had been inactive for some time and was not directly affected). The following January, Empire renamed the Rearwin company Commonwealth Aircraft, Inc.

My first encounters with the new president were disillusioning. One day I discovered a welder cutting up the Cloudster fuselage production jig with an acetylene torch. When I asked him why, he said, "President's orders. Need iron for tools." He quickly added, "I objected, Bob, but was set straight."

Scrap iron, both angle and channel, was still readily available at low prices in almost every junk yard in town! In fact, that is where most of our small tool stock came from. After sandblasting, it was always entirely satisfactory. It did not make any sense whatsoever to destroy a major production tool, especially one that would probably be needed after the war, to retrieve a few lengths of iron.

After my anger subsided and I had collected myself, I walked into the president's office to discuss the matter. I did not want other major tools destroyed. He took my concerns as a challenge to his personal judgment, became very uptight, and did not want to hear anything I said. He dismissed me curtly by saying, "I'm not interested in the Cloudster, and I'm not going to discuss the matter any further. This really isn't your business. I suggest you stop worrying about things that don't concern engineering."

Unfortunately, this meeting proved typical of my frequent concerns and the disposition of them by the president. Such incidents and the waste I observed led me to believe that Commonwealth could not long survive in the competitive postwar world, and I was right.

With the CG-4A contract well underway, the president gave me a specially created job, chief development engineer. I was to propose airplane programs for Commonwealth. This was something I could sink my teeth into and for which I was thoroughly qualified. I developed proposals and supporting technical data for several military versions of the Cloudster and Skyranger, and for a number of brand new airplanes designed to comply with military requirements. Each proposal consumed considerable time and to my dismay received virtually no consideration from Commonwealth's senior management. I was spinning my wheels. It was as if I were being retained for some undisclosed future need.

Moving to TWA

With my situation at Commonwealth becoming more and more unsatisfactory, and after talking it over with Margie, I decided to quietly look around. I did not have to look far.

I had been classified by the local draft board as essential to the war effort. Even though this ruling was justified, I felt some guilt for not being in uniform. With Margie's blessing, I decided to try for a commission in the Air Corps.

I filled out the papers and took my physical examination at Ft. Leavenworth, Kansas. I was flabbergasted with the doctor's findings. In addition to hay fever, which I had had for years, I had a temperature and unacceptably high blood pressure. I could not believe it. Despite my dissatisfaction with Commonwealth, I was working long hours, teaching University of Kansas Extension courses in the evenings, and was otherwise very active. I thought I was in exceptionally good health. In fact, I was.

The fever and high blood pressure were caused by an abscess, which was corrected within the year.

The doctor said he would not send the papers to Washington unless I signed a waiver absolving the government of all liabilities, including insurance. In consideration of Margie, Linda, and Sharon, I could not possibly sign such a waiver. Besides, in any realistic evaluation of what I could do for the war effort, it was obvious that I could be of more value in industry than in the services.

Only a week later, Ken Rearwin, who had joined TWA, called me. He said that John C. ("Jack") Franklin, TWA's vice president of engineering, was looking for an airplane design engineer to help with fleet planning. Ken thought the job would be perfect for me.

I was intrigued with the thought of working for TWA. I knew of TWA's pioneering aircraft development programs; Jack Frye's reputation; the cutting-edge, high-altitude research undertaken by Capt. D. W. ("Tommy") Tomlinson IV, Frye's assistant in technical affairs; and Hughes's ownership. The fact that my first job had been with Hughes was a striking coincidence in light of the unique personal relationship that quickly developed between us, but it did not influence my decision. Principally, I thought that because all my work had been in the manufacturing industry, working for TWA could be an opportunity to gain a broader background for the future—and Margie and I would not have to leave the new home we had built in Prairie Village when Linda Kay was born. I telephoned Jack Franklin for an interview and was hired a few days later. The salary was good by TWA standards, but it was only about half what I had been earning at Commonwealth and by teaching. Even so, leaving the frustrations of Commonwealth was welcome.

While things were not always a bed of roses at Rearwin, I respected the Rearwins and thoroughly enjoyed the work. The concentrated experience gained there could probably not have been duplicated anywhere else. It was with a sense of gratitude to the Rearwins for the opportunities they provided and a keen sense of disappointment concerning the new management that I left Commonwealth.

29

3.
TWA
before
Hughes

Leadership

From the very first, TWA and its corporate progenitors had trailblazed transport skies by producing the best possible services with the most advanced flight equipment. While immediate horizons were always circumscribed by economic and operational practicalities, the founding fathers understood the overriding importance of improving safety and expanding operational frontiers. Over the years, that progress would require major investments in new transport fleets of improved design bred of essential technological advances and hard-won operational experience. Faith in themselves and the future of aviation was absolute.

TWA's founders produced with uncommon entrepreneurial zeal many original contributions to aviation, encompassing virtually every operational phase and including new, precedent-setting aircraft designed specifically to satisfy the company's requirements. The tradition thus established was embraced and fostered by Howard Hughes from the time of his association in mid-1939. Indeed, it is reasonable to believe that TWA's historic aviation leadership was the chief reason for Hughes's initial interest in the company. In my case, it set marvelous precedents for my work and inspired me to future actions.

Jack Frye, Paul E. Richter, and Walter A. Hamilton played vital roles in shaping TWA and in its early success. They formed a lasting friendship during the 1920s while being taught to fly by Burdette Fuller, who ran a small flying school in the Los Angeles area, and they formed the Aero Corporation of California in 1926. Aero provided nearly every type of flying service that could turn a dollar: scenic and charter flights, pilot training, crop dusting, skywriting, towing advertising banners, aerial photography, and so on. It was also a distributor for Fokker transports and other aircraft. Passenger operations were so successful that a subsidiary, Standard Airlines, was soon formed, serving Los Angeles, Tucson, Phoenix, and El Paso.

TWA was formed through acquisitions and mergers involving Standard, Maddux Air Lines, Western Air Express (WAE), and Transcontinental Air Transport (TAT), with the result that Transcontinental and Western Air was formed October 1, 1930. The name was changed to Trans World Airlines on May 17, 1950, to reflect the international character of its expanding operations. Jack Frye was named vice president of operations on TWA's formation and became its president in 1934.

Tommy Tomlinson, whose research flights contributed much to the development of transport aviation, joined the triumvirate in 1930 when TAT-Maddux and WAE merged. He had learned to fly with the Navy, then accepted an offer from Jack Maddux and quickly became vice president of operations, Maddux Air Lines.

While many contributed to TWA's early success, Frye, Richter, Hamilton, and Tomlinson collectively took the bold, decisive steps that firmly established TWA as an innovative pioneer. They instilled a common spirit of camaraderie and excitement throughout the ranks that generated high morale and enthusiastic support for building the corporation.

Jack Frye was a man who led by example. He worked long hours with such great enthusiasm and drive that those about him were caught up in the same spirit of adventure and achievement. He did not need to give orders to get results. We were all eager to do our part and worked with the same kind of infectious zeal. When TWA flight crews complained that the mail schedules Frye had established for Northrop Alphas were too tight, Jack responded by unexpectedly replacing the assigned captain one night at

Newark, rather than issuing memos or verbal orders. He flew the Alpha through heavy weather, landing on time in Kansas City after stops at Pittsburgh, Columbus, Indianapolis, and St. Louis. No more complaints were registered. This incident was a good measure of the man and his management style.

Frye repeatedly demonstrated uncommon business and great technological insight. In addition to pioneering in nearly every operational field, he originated and implemented new transport development programs. The revolutionary Douglas DC-1 and DC-2 transports; the Boeing 307 Stratoliners, the world's first pressurized commercial transports; and the long-range, high-altitude, pace-setting Lockheed Constellations were all sponsored under Jack Frye's tenure. His visionary leadership, later supported by Hughes's interest, ambition, and counsel, contributed greatly to TWA's domestic growth and its expansion into the international arena to become one of the world's greatest airlines. The tragic break between Hughes and Frye, culminating in Frye's forced departure in early 1947, was a major setback, from which the airline did not recover for years.

Paul Richter was Jack Frye's right-hand man. After holding top positions in Operations, he became executive vice president in 1938. A quiet but firm man, he had an instant grasp of aviation matters. He was an excellent listener, but long explanations were unnecessary. Paul's unique attributes as a solid, conservative businessman beautifully complimented Frye's aggressive corporate expansion activities. Paul's leveling judgments were always respected and listened to. Paul and Jack were an excellent synergistic team. Paul took a leave of absence in 1943 to serve the war effort. During late 1945, he resumed duties as TWA's executive vice president. He resigned a few days before Frye left TWA but was prevailed upon to return for several months to assist Howard's new president, La-Motte T. Cohu.

The innate technical skills of the third member of the original triumvirate, Walt Hamilton, were developed and honed at the Duesenberg Auto Company, where he acquired a reputation as an automotive genius. Notwithstanding, airplanes were a challenge he could not refuse. For Hamilton, organizing and handling TWA's maintenance and overhaul functions were as natural as breathing. The TWA Kansas City overhaul facility, which he developed, was quickly emulated by the industry. After serving TWA with great distinction, Walt elected to join the Douglas Aircraft Company on June 1, 1939.

Tommy Tomlinson conducted extensive experimental operations: flights into severe thunderstorm and icing conditions, new instrumentation research, and pioneering high-altitude research flights. His personal exploits proved the practicality of over-weather flying and paved the way for the development of the first pressurized commercial transport.

The Technical Committee

Shortly after TAT's formation on May 16, 1928, the Technical Committee was established, with the primary obligation of developing fleet planning and procurement recommendations for board consideration. It was the policy of the TAT board to make no decisions concerning these matters, or indeed, any technical and operating problems, without the blessing of the Technical Committee—a far-sighted and eminently sound policy.

After the formation of TWA through the TAT-Maddux merger with WAE in 1930, Tomlinson became technical assistant to the president, Richard W. Robbins, and a member of the Technical Committee at New York corporate headquarters. The other members of the committee were Robbins, Frye, and Lindbergh, who served as the first chairman.

A difficult early Technical Committee problem was to deal with the acute flight equipment shortage that followed the March 31, 1931, Knute Rockne accident. A Fokker F-10 operating between Kansas City and Wichita had crashed, killing all on board including Rockne, Captain Bob Frye, and Copilot Jes Mathias. Shortly after that accident, all of TWA's Fokker F-10 trimotors were grounded and later destroyed.

Investigation showed that the right wing of the ill-fated F-10 severed at altitude, probably from encountering rough air, momentary loss of control, or possibly from pulling up from a dive when breaking out under the stormy cloud cover. The exact circumstances that imposed the wing shearing load can only be conjectured. Examination of the wreckage by independent experts confirmed that the wood wing had been weakened from long-term exposure to moisture. The wing was especially vulnerable because it contained blind structure: structure that could not be inspected without tearing the wing apart. This accident doomed the use of wood wings in new transports.

Following the Knute Rockne accident, the Technical Committee was faced with the dilemma of how to make up the capacity of the grounded Fokker F-10's. New transports were either unavailable or believed unsuitable for flight over TWA's mountainous western region. For example, the steel-tube, fabric-covered Curtiss Wright Condor biplane was considered obsolescent, partly because of its hopelessly inadequate ceiling with qne engine inoperative. An improved version with air-cooled Cyclone engines and retractable landing gear was in the works, but it too appeared to lack essential performance.

The all-metal Boeing 247, considerably faster than the new trimotors, was a nicely streamlined, twin-engine, low-wing design in the early stages of development. Boeing, however, had made a marketing mistake that it would long regret and which ruled 247's out of serious TWA consideration: It had sold the first 60 to an affiliate, United Air Lines (UAL), thus closing out any possibility of reasonably early deliveries to any other carrier. Tomlinson also did not like the cramped fuselage or the need for the passengers to climb over the main wing spar to reach the forward seats, but such considerations were moot because of the delivery situation.

Indeed, none of the planes studied by the Technical Committee, available or in the offering, including new Fords, fully met TWA's operational needs. There remained one alternative but time-consuming approach: sponsoring the development of an entirely new design.

The Technical Committee was well aware of the inviting progress made by John K. (''Jack'') Northrop—one of the truly great aviation pioneers—in the development of efficient, all-metal, semimonocoque structures, and by Boeing in the development of its metal-fuselage Monomail and all-metal Model 215 (Y1B-9A) bomber. These aircraft first flew in 1930 and 1931, respectively, and provided a solid basis for development of the 247. Technologically, it was clearly time for the development of better aircraft, but what and how remained active questions.

Jack Frye and TWA's pilots had developed and fostered the idea that any transports TWA bought had to be capable of flying from Winslow, Arizona, over the high country to Albuquerque, New Mexico, or vice versa with one engine inoperative. This appeared attainable with trimotors of brand-new design, but it was questionable with twin-engine aircraft. Nonetheless, Frye decided to require contractual compliance with this capability in any new transport development venture TWA might undertake.

The Technical Committee was split on the question of twins versus trimotors. It engaged in numbers of intense, heated debates. Jack Frye had long been a strong proponent of the trimotor concept and remained adamant. Tomlinson was equally adamant, holding the view that two engines

35

were the right answer; that the center engine had to go because of vibration and fumes. Lindbergh, perhaps deliberately, did not take a strong position either way. And Robbins, who was competent in financial and business affairs, stayed out of it.

When arguments continued to rage, Jack Frye bit the bullet by writing independently of the Technical Committee his historic letter of August 2, 1932, to a number of manufacturers, soliciting interest in the development of a new transport. It read: "Transcontinental and Western Air is interested in purchasing ten or more trimotored transport planes. I am attaching our general performance specifications covering this equipment, and would appreciate your advising whether your company is interested in this manufacturing job. If so, approximately how long would it take to turn out the first plane for service tests?" The letter carried the following postscript: "N.B. [nota bene] Please consider this information confidential and return specifications if you are not interested."

The specifications, consisting of six items loosely filling one page, included "satisfactory takeoffs under good control at any TWA airport on any combination of two engines," that is, with any one engine inoperative. The plane was to carry "at least 12 passengers with comfortable seats and ample room" and have a 1,080-mile range at 150 mph and a one-engine-out service ceiling of 10,000 feet. Although these capabilities are puny by today's standards, compliance represented a major step forward.

Three manufacturers responded favorably: General Aviation (successor to Fokker), Douglas, and Sikorsky. Douglas proposed a twin. The others proposed trimotors much like the Fords and Fokkers. Tomlinson was given the principal task of analyzing the three proposals to judge if the performance, weight, and other claims could be realized.

The Technical Committee impasse on the engine question continued. It was finally resolved by TWA's deciding to proceed with both the Douglas twin, the DC-1; and the General Aviation trimotor, the GA-38. The inviting Sikorsky proposal was outscored. TWA's expressed intent was to complete the development of both prototypes but to order only the best airplane to production.

The General Aviation Program

General Motors had acquired control of Fokker Aircraft Corporation on March 3, 1931, through a newly formed subsidiary, the General Aviation

Corporation. General Aviation had moved from Teterboro, New Jersey, to a new factory in Baltimore by the time Frye's letter was written. The president of General Aviation was a TWA director named Jay Schoomacker, and the chief engineer was Herbert Thaden, who had recently designed and flown an all-metal, high-wing, single-engine plane. Tomlinson flew the plane and considered it ''reasonably successful'' and of good promise re the trimotor proposal. Ernest R. Breech, who much later as chairman of the board was to guide TWA through critical periods following Hughes's loss of control, was at that time assistant treasurer for General Motors and a member of TWA's Board of Directors.

Breech and Lindbergh inspected the General Aviation trimotor in Baltimore during early construction. This trip convinced Breech that the trimotor would be very expensive to manufacture and could not sell close to the price stipulated in the TWA contract. The day following the inspection trip, Breech and Lindbergh met with John Thomas Smith, general counsel for General Motors. Lindbergh convinced Smith that General Aviation should go ahead with the trimotor even though Breech opposed the idea. Breech surmised that Lindbergh wanted competition for Douglas and was fearful that the Douglas plane could not meet TWA's stringent single-engine performance requirements. It might not have, except for the timely development of the Hamilton Standard variable-pitch propeller.

On May 1, 1933, Ernie Breech was elected chairman of the board and of the executive committee and president of North American Aviation, a combine that included General Aviation. A short time later Breech decided that General Aviation should spend no more money on the trimotor even though it had sunk another $800,000 since the Breech-Lindbergh inspection trip. That decision was an example of the soundness of Ernie Breech's often-demonstrated business judgment. The DC-1 flew two months later, July 1, 1933, and soon proved its outstanding capabilities. TWA never would have ordered the General Aviation trimotor to production. It was scrapped before it ever flew.

The Douglas Program

Along with the Boeing 247, the revolutionary Douglas DC-1 was a technological breakthrough that set the pattern of transport design for years. At the time the DC-1 project originated, a wealth of new technology options and design opportunities existed, awaiting only the spark of genius and an imperative need to produce major gains. TWA's need, which generated Jack Frye's famous letter, provided just such an opportunity.[1]

The DC-1 development contract was executed on September 20, 1932, less than two months after Frye's letter. Brief but demanding, it required Douglas to manufacture one prototype and permitted TWA a 30-day shakedown period to check specification compliance. Mockups were "subject to inspection and final approval in writing by the Buyer," and control forces and handling characteristics were subject to TWA's acceptance. It also called for the plane to take off on any regularly used runway at any regular TWA airport and fly to the next regular TWA airport at full gross weight after the failure of one engine at 4/10 the length of the takeoff runway, or not less than 1,000 feet. This contract, written long before federal regulations required one-engine-out airport and en route performance, is evidence of TWA's demanding farsightedness in safety matters.

Tommy Tomlinson was released from his duties in New York and assigned full time at Douglas as the "top TWA representative and test pilot." About the same time, a maintenance department inspector who would later become chief engineer for TWA, Ralph L. Ellinger, was also assigned to Douglas to inspect DC-1 work in progress and provide technical liaison with TWA. An absolutely forthright man blessed with sound intuitive judgment and a good analytical mind, Ralph contributed much to the success of this and other new airplane ventures by insisting on straightforward, practical design features. During the development period, Frye, Richter, Hamilton, and Harlan Hull, TWA's chief pilot, made frequent trips to the Douglas factory in Santa Monica to inspect mockups and monitor the design. The DC-1 was completed and made ready for flight less than one year after Frye's letter of solicitation was written.

Tomlinson understood that he and Edmund T. Allen, the well-known Douglas test pilot, would fly every DC-1 flight, alternating as pilot and copilot. However, for reasons that were never made clear, Douglas had his vice president of sales, Carl Cover, whom Tomlinson considered a good pilot, make the first flight on July 1, 1933, with Eddie Allen as copilot. Tomlinson thought Allen would be in command.

Tomlinson watched Cover take off toward the ocean. To Tomlinson's horror, shortly after leaving the ground the DC-1 lost power in both engines and dropped out of sight where the land fell off rather sharply beyond the runway. Then, with disaster imminent, only seconds before the airplane would have hit the ground, the engines responded and it began to climb. Then the same thing happened, not just once but several times. With the nose up, the engines lost power; with the nose down, the engines came fully alive. Cover, with great skill, fought the airplane around just enough to make an emergency landing on a fairway adjacent to Clover Field. Tommy said later, "Everyone was scared to death thinking the plane would crash."

Ivar Shogran and other Douglas engine experts immediately examined every part of the power systems that could possibly cause the problem, but without results. Surprisingly, the plane was nursed into the air again in this condition, not just once, but three times to discover the problem, but again without success. The flights were extremely touchy and hazardous. Finally, Shogran noticed that the four-barrel carburetor hold-down bolts in the Wright engines were such that the carburetors could be reversed 180 degrees. The carburetors were changed to the "reverse" position, and after that, the engines performed normally. A great lesson was learned once again: Never design anything that can be incorrectly assembled.

One day while Eddie Allen was taxiing the DC-1 at Mines Field (now Los Angeles International Airport), the landing gear collapsed without warning. The airplane was not badly damaged, and, after repairs and the installation of new propellers, it was flown to Santa Monica to resume the flight test program. Unfortunately, the retractable landing gear had been designed without mechanical down locks. Douglas engineers had reasoned that the incompressibility of the hydraulic fluid and off-center strut hinges were all that was needed; mechanical down locks would be an unnecessary complexity.

Tommy encountered similar difficulties, which he described this way: "Sometimes while taxiing I had the horrible sensation that something wasn't quite right. I would look out and see the landing gear struts jumping back and forth, not quite past dead center. We did everything to get Douglas to add a down latch but were refused. Douglas insisted, 'By God, the principle will work, the fluid is incompressible, and there is no damn way the piston can move so the strut can go past dead center.' "

During the 30-day shakedown period, Tomlinson was checking out two experienced TWA pilots, Eddie Bellande and George Rice, when the landing gear struts again went past dead center and collapsed. TWA again heatedly demanded that Douglas install down latches. Douglas again refused. Later on, Tomlinson was flying copilot for Paul Richter on a Wichita demonstration flight. The mayor and other celebrities were on board when the gear again collapsed. Confronted with this embarrassment and emphatic complaints from TWA, Douglas finally agreed to provide mechanical down locks with a signal light in the cockpit.

The crucially important one-engine-inoperative flight demonstration, from Winslow over the Continental Divide to Albuquerque, occurred in early September 1933, shortly before TWA's 30-day shakedown test commenced. The flight was to be made at full gross weight under simulated airline operating conditions. The evening before the test, Tomlinson; Allen; Bailey ("Ozzy") Oswald, chief aerodynamicist for Douglas; and Frank Collbohn, a Douglas flight test engineer, met to review performance calculations and agree on test procedures.

Tomlinson proposed two tests. The first was to be a trial run with the throttle retarded to the idle position rather than with the switch cut, so power could be restored instantly if needed. The second, if all went well during the trial run, was to cut the switch at the 1,000-foot mark on the runway. This sensible procedure, including carrying enough extra fuel on the first flight to avoid refueling for the second, was agreed to by Allen and the others. Oswald confirmed the amount of extra fuel at around 20 gallons.

Tomlinson was aware of the need to reduce aerodynamic drag by retracting the landing gear as soon as possible after takeoff. He knew from experience that a great deal of muscle was required to do this. Retraction required the copilot to place his right hand on the instrument panel coaming to brace himself, lean down, turn a valve, and "pump like hell" with the left hand.

The next morning observers were stationed along the runway at 100-foot intervals starting at 900 feet from start of roll. Large flags clearly marked the 1,000-foot line. The tests did not go as planned. Tommy explained:

I got myself all braced for the takeoff with my head down. I can't be looking out because I want to get that damn gear up just as soon as I can. Jesus! Here we go! All of a sudden I see Eddie reach up for the upper panel where the switches are located. Christ! I see Eddie's hand come up, and goddamn him, he cut the switch instead of doing what we had agreed. I damn near busted a lung pumping that gear up. When we got back, the people on the ground said, "Tommy, your props missed the ground by only about six inches." I was so damn mad I could have cut that bastard's throat. I have been accused of being rash, but have never been a damn fool.

After the harrowing single-engine takeoff at Winslow, the DC-1 climbed to the necessary altitude and flew majestically on one engine to a perfect landing at Albuquerque. It had passed its most critical tests with flying colors. Tomlinson wired the good news to headquarters.

The 30-day service test soon followed. The DC-1 was flown principally by Tomlinson on the night mail run from Kansas City to Glendale, California, with stops at Wichita, Amarillo, Albuquerque, and Winslow, replacing Northrop Alphas. John E. Guy and another top inspector, Frosty Frostrom, were assigned to ride the airplane on alternating weeks.

Tomlinson had been responsible for Guy's joining the airline during early TAT-Maddux days. Tomlinson was as particular about the mechanical condition of his car as he was about airplanes. Nothing short of perfection would do. After trying to have an engine problem corrected by several garages without success, he decided to try the Hollywood Mission Garage. He explained the problem to a young mechanic who worked there. In a remarkably short time the engine was running perfectly. Tomlinson was so impressed that he offered the mechanic, John Guy, a job in the engine shop.

Tomlinson's intuitive perception did well for TWA. Johnny spent a professional lifetime with the airline, became a confidant of Howard Hughes and senior airline executives, and contributed significantly to the high quality and maintainability of many new types of transport aircraft. However, except for a quirky coincidence, his career at TWA might have been entirely different.

During the DC-1 service test period, it was widely rumored that TWA would soon place a substantial order for Douglas transports. If this happened, a TWA inspector's job at the Douglas plant would become available. Guy and Frostrom were qualified, well positioned, and wanted the job. They made their interests known. Guy thought that Frostrom would be chosen because of company seniority and his reputation as a competent inspector. But to John's surprise and delight, he, not Frostrom, landed the job.

A good many years later, Tomlinson told Guy why Frostrom had been passed over. During the service test period, TWA's highly polished and brightly illuminated DC-1 was always parked at the Kansas City terminal well before flight time for publicity reasons. TWA's servicing personnel, dressed in crisp white overalls, performed the servicing functions with practiced, military-like precision. This procedure attracted crowds of the curious, who wanted to see the new ''giant'' aircraft, which was larger and much more imposing than the Fords.

Tomlinson explained that one evening when the service test period was almost over, John A. Collings, TWA's chief of operations, watched the pretakeoff preparations, as was his frequent habit. John was talking to Tommy when Frostrom crossed the ramp on his way to board the DC-1 for the flight to Los Angeles. Frostrom was wearing bedroom slippers! John took one look and exploded. He turned to Tomlinson and with a few well chosen-expletives ordered him to remove Frostrom from the flight, concluding, "He is not to approach that plane again, tonight or any other time." The flight took off without Frostrom, who was immediately assigned a different job. That had been his only transgression.

So John Guy's career, because of bedroom slippers and Collings's sense of propriety, took a permanent turn for the long-term betterment of TWA. Shortly thereafter, TWA ordered 20 DC-2's, the production version of the DC-1, and Guy was transferred to Santa Monica to work for Ralph Ellinger, by then TWA's factory representative at Douglas.

Only one DC-1 was built. The DC-2 was essentially the same design except that the fuselage was lengthened 18 inches ahead of the wing. This stretch, plus shortening the above-floor baggage compartment, permitted installing another row of passenger seats, which increased the capacity from 12 to 14. This added a significant margin of profit with little change in performance or operating cost.

TWA placed DC-2's into commercial operations on its Columbus-Pittsburgh-Newark route on May 18, 1934, and inaugurated DC-2 transcontinental services the following August. Thus, a new era of vastly improved safety, reliability, and comfort was introduced. DC-2's, soon procured by a majority of the airlines, quickly become the preferred standard for air transportation. The steel-tube, fabric-covered transports as well as the corrugated aluminum trimotors yielded and became history.

I well remember watching TWA's DC-2 operations from the Grand Central Air Terminal in Glendale while a student at the Curtiss Wright Technical Institute. Grand Central—now a housing area—was the main Los Angeles air terminal. The sparkling, all-metal DC-2's, patronized by movie stars and other famous personages for whom I and other students were always on the lookout, contrasted sharply with American Airlines' (AAL) fabric-covered Condor biplanes, one of which I saw quickly burn to a skeleton on the parking ramp. I was convinced that DC-2's were the wave of the future.

Saving TWA's Work Force

President Roosevelt canceled all airmail contracts on February 9, 1934, effective 10 days later, and ill-advisedly ordered a poorly equipped U.S. Army to fly the mail. The Airmail Act of 1934, which required the separation of the airlines and manufacturers, followed the cancellation. All this produced chaos in the airline industry: corporate divestitures, reorganizations, and extended economic hard times.

Jack Frye, who was convinced that the Army would do a miserable job, decided to demonstrate the capability of private airlines to carry the mail efficiently and reliably. Frye arranged to fly the DC-1 on the last private mail run from Glendale to Newark, with Capt. Eddie Rickenbacker of Eastern Air Lines (EAL) as copilot. Rickenbacker was equally anxious to make the case in Washington.

Frye wanted as much publicity as possible and called a press conference the day before the flight. The evening before the conference, three Army pilots were killed while flying to assigned airmail stations. When confronted with this news during the conference, Rickenbacker reacted impulsively by loudly exclaiming, ''That's legalized murder!'' His words became headlines in virtually every major newspaper in the country and focused public attention on the flight.

Frye and Rickenbacker took off the evening of February 18 and headed for predicted severe weather conditions in the East. They landed in Kansas City in light snow and at Columbus in blizzard conditions. Taking off almost blind, they made it to Newark ahead of schedule, setting a new transcontinental record of 13 hours and 4 minutes. This flight clearly established the capability of the DC-1 in the public mind but, of course, did nothing to alter Roosevelt's selected course for U.S. aviation.

Loss of the mail contract forced Dick Robbins to furlough all TWA employees on February 18, 1934. Shortly thereafter he resigned, and Jack Frye was elected president on April 17. Frye was convinced it was only a question of time until new airmail contracts would be awarded to the airlines. TWA's immediate problem was to hang on and be ready when this occurred.

When I interviewed John Guy on July 23, 1983, he recalled a pivotal meeting held in Ralph Ellinger's office at the Douglas factory shortly after the furlough:

I was in the office with Jack Frye, Carl Cover, and Ralph Ellinger. Jack told Carl he had complete confidence that the airlines would get the airmail contracts back before very long, that the Army airplanes were not adequately equipped, nor were the pilots sufficiently trained to fly the mail. He predicted pretty disastrous results, including loss of aircraft over the mountains. Jack also told Carl he was convinced TWA would get airmail contracts back and for this reason was willing to let the DC-2 contract stand and would purchase the planes.

Jack continued, saying, "Carl, you don't have enough employees and must hire more people to build the planes. We have hundreds of TWA people all over the system who don't have a job. When you hire people, we want you to hire TWA people. When we get the airmail contract back, we want you to release them so we can rehire them." After conferring with Douglas, Cover agreed to the Frye plan. Jack then did the same thing at Wright Aeronautical, who had contracted to build the engines. Wright also agreed.

Jack Frye then sent a letter to all furloughed employees telling them they could have a job in either Santa Monica or Patterson and that the company would fly them and their families to either point. He also told them that when the airmail contract was renewed they would be offered their jobs back without loss in seniority. This was great news. It was during the depression when jobs simply weren't available. As you can imagine, lots of employees took advantage of this opportunity. This was a wonderful thing that Jack Frye did. It was typical of his consideration for people. I don't think he ever received the credit that is due him.

I was in high school when Roosevelt canceled the airmail contracts and had routinely followed aviation developments as closely as possible from radio reviews and reading *Aero Digest, Popular Mechanics,* and the *Chicago Daily Tribune.* I was absolutely appalled by the loss of the Army pilots, which clearly showed the airlines to be far better equipped and much more adept at flying. I had no sympathy whatsoever for Roosevelt's action and thought he should have known better. Frye and Rickenbacker were my heros, the kind of men I wanted to be associated with, once I became what I was determined to be—an aeronautical engineer.

Records and Research

The Army Air Corps made its last airmail flight on June 1, 1934. Selected airlines including TWA were allowed to resume the carriage of mail shortly thereafter under new federal contracts. By then TWA was in dire financial condition. Jack Frye wanted publicity for TWA and its new Douglas fleet and suggested that Tomlinson try for some records. Tommy gladly agreed and set out to break a number of load and distance records in the DC-1, equipped with extra fuel tanks.

Tommy's description of one of the flights follows:

During May 1935, Joe Bartles and I took off with the fuel tanks loaded to the gills. Every tank was topped off. The plane weighed around 30,000 pounds, which was about twice the design gross weight. . . . When we took off from Floyd Bennett Field, the wing tips must have been up about eight feet; the ripples in the skin were really frightening. I thought Joe would have jumped out if he could. When the fuel load burned down, most of them disappeared. We were in the air 18 hours and could have had dinner in Paris if we had flown in a straight line. We broke two world records and eight American records on that flight.

Tomlinson also flew the DC-1 in thunderstorm research flights because little was known about thunderstorms and how to cope with them. Special Wright Cyclone engines with two-speed blowers and electric variable-pitch propellers were installed, which enabled the DC-1 to fly as high as 27,000 feet.

Tommy explained:

When heavy thunderstorms occurred in the triangle between Kansas City, Chicago, and New York, I'd take off with some pilot if he would hold still, or I might get a meteorologist or someone else to ride with me. It became very clear that in order to fly through thunderstorms, I had to learn to completely ignore rate of climb, airspeed, and altimeter readings. The trick was to fly a constant *attitude,* which the pilot could do by watching the artificial horizon, which we had by that time. Since wind shifts caused the instruments to jump and oscillate violently, there was no way to chase the instruments and maintain safe flight. The thing to do was to just sit there, hang on, and forget the instrument readings, which were unreliable.

I encountered hail and ice on numbers of flights. The hail was always localized. I decided that when you hit hail, the thing to do is to hold course and not turn around, otherwise you are apt to double your exposure. When flying through the anvil heads at around 27,000 feet I encountered white rime ice and really rough air. The part of the thunderstorms I avoided was at the root of the anvil heads, where the clouds were black, purple, and blue and obviously contained a tremendous amount of turbulence.

During the fall of 1935, Goodyear asked Tomlinson to test new wing deicing boots and propeller strips designed to feed glycol along the leading edges. Frye agreed. During that winter Tomlinson made it a point to fly the DC-1 experimentally through extreme blizzard and icing conditions when American, TWA, and United had canceled scheduled flights because of weather. These flights showed that the DC-1 could handle some "pretty miserable stuff," but, even more importantly, they also showed its limitations.

The Experimental Overweather Laboratory

Tomlinson's DC-1 thunderstorm research flights convinced Frye, Richter, and Tomlinson that the only likely way to minimize en route weather exposure was to operate at stratospheric altitudes. To do so, however, required high-altitude research—higher than possible with the DC-1. They decided to devote to this end TWA's Northrop Gamma, which Frye named the "Experimental Overweather Laboratory." Tomlinson, the obvious choice, was assigned to handle this project.

Operating at extreme altitudes required modification of the Gamma. Wright provided a Cyclone engine equipped with a pressurized carburetor. General Electric (GE) made available Dr. Sanford Alexander Moss, the mechanical engineering genius who invented the turbo supercharger. Wright Field provided one of its few GE exhaust-driven turbo superchargers. The plane was extensively modified by TWA in its Kansas City shops and was ready for flight by the spring of 1936.

The first flights were discouraging. Serious engine surging and unacceptable fuel-flow problems were experienced. The latter was solved through a series of fuel system modifications. Engine surging was not solved until the separate throttle and supercharger controls were combined into a single unit. This proved to be extremely difficult. Numbers of designs were tried until one was evolved that worked reasonably well. After that, Tomlinson could fly the Gamma at an altitude of up to 35,000 feet without encountering problems.

Tomlinson's Gamma flights, like the earlier DC-1 flights, illustrate the courageous determination for acquiring knowledge and the zeal for pressing technological frontiers forward that was typical of TWA's early days. One of Tommy's objectives was to determine the wind velocity at altitude.

Discovery of the jet stream followed. He explained: "I repeatedly flew a triangular course between Kansas City, Columbia, and a radio station near Chicago. I could stay on course with drift angles and with the data at hand could figure out the speed of the airplane and the wind. After almost every flight I would come down and tell the meteorologists, 'My God! I had winds of 100 mph to 150 mph!' They just shook their heads. They had no idea what was up there."

During early 1937, Tommy very nearly lost the Gamma and possibly his and Jim Hiestand's lives. In Tommy's words:

During March of 1937, Paul Richter called me at Wright Field and asked me if I would come to Kansas City to fly the Gamma to New York through the strato- sphere. He explained it was a publicity deal, that the Gamma would be featured in a show at the Coliseum. There wasn't anything important scheduled at Wright Field for a few days, so I agreed.

I flew to Kansas City, but the Gamma wasn't ready—something about the liquid oxygen system. I arrived on Friday and wanted to leave on Saturday since the show was on Monday, and a hell of a blizzard was forecast for Kansas City and the East. Jesus! They couldn't get the damn thing ready to go before Sun- day morning. By that time, for Christ's sake, I had about a 200-foot ceiling and snow in Kansas City. United wasn't operating, and TWA wasn't operating east of St. Louis. Blizzard, ice, and the works—everything under the sun was hap- pening.

I figured I had enough experience with the airplane, and on night mail runs, to make it without any sweat. On the night mail runs I used to think if I had 50 feet [ceiling] and ¼ mile [visibility] at Pittsburgh or Newark I could make it. I made a few that close. If it was do or die, you came in, particularly with ice. The trick with ice, of course, was to fly around through the warm air layer above the super-chilled atmosphere and soak the airplane at about 40 degrees, then come in over the cone [radio marker beam] and make the final approach and landing damn fast before the structure cooled enough to accumulate danger- ous ice. So, I wasn't particularly worried about the flight. I was hairy assed in those days, see?

So Jim Hiestand and I took off in the blizzard. I figured it's in the bag: that at 30,000 feet, hell, I'll be sitting on top, fat, dumb, and happy. I got to 32,000 feet by Columbia and was getting on top when I started to pick up a little rime ice. The ice static became horrible because the Gamma wasn't equipped with an ice-static loop. I started to lose the radio. I'd gotten to 33,000 feet by the time I passed St. Louis, but couldn't get any higher. I wanted to get over the goddamn stuff. I got a good fix on the north leg to St. Louis and figured I could fly by dead reckoning to Newark. But, Christ all fishhooks, I'm sitting there with no radio. Once in a while I could get through on the company radio, but the beams were gone, cold.

I dropped down to 15,000 feet thinking I might get between layers. No dice. It was the same all over all the way through. So, I went back up. I didn't know where I was but got through momentarily to Pittsburgh. They told me to turn toward Albany, that Albany had 10,000 feet and broken clouds. I changed course 45 degrees thinking that would take me to Albany where I would break out and get a fix.

I'd been sitting up there about four hours, and it's getting a little tiresome. After about 15 or 20 minutes on the new course, I began to get a few signals and finally picked up Elmira. Jesus! I knew where Elmira was and what the Elmira beam and another one down toward Bellfonte looked like. By then I was at 37,000 feet, and the outside air temperature was 70 degrees below zero. I was getting cold. I picked up what I thought was the southwest leg and figured I'd just go on until I picked up the west leg of Newark. Okay! Great! I think I'm doing pretty damn well and am close to Newark.

Then I came out of a solid wall of clouds that must have reached to 40,000 feet. It was the damndest sight I ever saw. It extended northeast-southwest and was an advancing thing. The minute I came out I got perfect beam reception. Everything came in. Well, by crossing the Albany and Boston legs, I estimated I was about 100 miles off the coast headed for Bermuda and had only about 40 minutes of gas left. The only chance I had was to head north since the coast runs northeast-southwest there. I headed north and waited for the Newark leg. I timed crossing the leg and figured from the width of the beam I was east of Brooklyn somewhere.

My last tank of gas was getting down to empty, and Newark was reporting ¼-mile visibility and from 50-foot to 100-foot ceiling with freezing rain at the airport. I had made it under those conditions with the Alpha and figured I could do it with the Gamma. By now, I'm in the rain between layers at just over 4,000 feet. When I hit the cone, the gas gauge was empty. I knew there might be enough gas for 5 or 10 minutes but, on the other hand, that the engine might quit at any time. If the engine quit while coming down from 4,000 feet, while swinging around or in the approach, the only chance Jim and I would have was to jump out. I had already written him a warning note, but wrote again telling him to get ready to jump. However, since the engine was still running, I headed west because I knew there was a lot of flat country west of Elizabeth and Newark. I wrote Jim another note and told him to tuck himself in, that I was going to ride the Gamma down and crash-land it.

48

I had the engine down to 1,100 rpm and it was going "pt, pt, pt," but it was still turning over. I dropped about one-quarter flap and started coming down through the stuff. I figured I must be over flat country. I had the hatch open and was feeling the windshield for ice. It started to collect at about 500 feet. I'm coming down through this goddamn stuff when all of a sudden, looking over to the side I see a polo field. Polo field! Okay! All I wanted to do was get the wheels on the ground because brother, if you do, the chances are good that you will walk away from it. That is not true of today's airplanes.

I had to make an offset turn, so nosed it down and wrapped it into a flipper turn so I could slideslip into the place. Just as I was well into the bank, the engine quit. It was all through. Well, Christ! I shoved the stick forward and leveled off. I had to take what was ahead. If I changed my approach, I would be in serious trouble. You must make the best of what you have while you are still under control.

I was headed for a low hill. I cleared some wires, went to full flaps, and settled into weeds about three feet high. The weeds hitting against the flaps made the damndest noise I'd ever heard. There was a row of trees on the right, so I instinctively kicked left rudder. It had been raining for days, and the wheel fairing picked up mud, which set the plane on its nose and bent one prop blade. I had been in the air for seven hours and hadn't seen the ground for more than probably a minute.

I was able to radio Newark with the trailing antennae, which was on the ground, and give them my location after a farmer came out to investigate. He confirmed we were about three miles east of Princeton. It turned out that TWA had followed me all the way across. They could hear my transmissions but I couldn't hear them most of the time. Paul Richter was waiting for me in Newark and came out to the plane. We killed a bottle of scotch that night.

TWA was always a can-do airline. That night a truck and crew was sent to the Gamma. They removed the wings and hauled the plane to Newark for cleaning and repair, and then to the Coliseum, where it was reassembled. When the show opened the next morning, it was absolutely clean and polished, as if nothing had happened. With the publicity that was accorded Tommy's flight, it was the hit of the show.

Tomlinson flew many research flights in the Gamma and catalogued scientific information in detail. His exploits contributed valuable meteorological information and demonstrated the important operational advantages that could accrue from high-altitude flight. His work helped shape the future course of transport aviation.

The Douglas DC-3

The Douglas DC-3 was evolved from the DC-2 to satisfy an AAL requirement for modern sleeper planes to replace its old fleet of berth-equipped
Curtiss Condor biplanes. Because the DC-2 was too narrow for berths,
Douglas proposed to widen the fuselage and increase the maximum operating weight to accommodate 21 rather than 14 day passengers.

Douglas kept TWA fully apprised of the DC-3 program and offered good
delivery positions. TWA, skeptical of the plane's performance at numbers
of high-altitude airports, reluctantly concluded that it was underpowered
for TWA's western routes and did not order DC-3's at the outset.

The DC-3 first flew from Clover Field, Santa Monica, on December 17,
1935. Tomlinson flew it on January 6, 1936, and noted that the takeoffs
were sluggish, which seemed to confirm TWA's airport performance estimates. Tomlinson reported his findings, and TWA lost interest. This
proved to be a costly error. A series of engine modifications and improved
propellers corrected the performance deficiency. By the time TWA renewed its interest, valuable delivery positions had been lost to competing
airlines. Jack Frye ordered 10 sleeper DC-3's and 8 day-plane versions,
introducing TWA DC-3 services on June 1, 1937, 10 months after AAL
had done the same.

My first close look at the DC-3 occurred at the old Ambassador Hotel,
Los Angeles, early in 1936, where AAL had its version, the DST, parked
for public display on the lawn off of Wilshire Boulevard. Day plane and
berth sections were shown. As a young engineer, I thought the interior was
extravagantly luxurious and excessively heavy. It was striking, but was it
necessary? I would learn more about airline competition later.

The Boeing Stratoliner Program

Development of the Boeing 307 Stratoliner, the world's first commercial
pressurized transport, was strictly a Boeing-TWA affair. No other airline
was involved until after the design was conceived and agreed to between
the two parties.

The genesis of the four-engine Stratoliner was the Boeing Y1B-17
bomber, developed from the Model 299, which Boeing produced in response to an August 1934 Army bid request. The 299 was rushed to

completion in less than one year and flown to Wright Field for demonstration after only minimal testing. It crashed during a demonstration flight, which technically disqualified it from the competition; however, the Army was so well impressed with its capabilities that it placed an order for 13 Y1B-17 bombers.

Tomlinson, who was well acquainted at Wright Field, was invited to fly a Y1B-17. He did so and was extremely favorably impressed with the performance and potential it offered. He reviewed his evaluation and the B-17 program with Frye and Richter. They agreed that TWA should seriously explore with Boeing the development of a superior high-altitude over-weather commercial variant.

Jack Frye telephoned Boeing, with the almost immediate result that Fred Collins, Boeing's sales manager, and two engineers were dispatched to Kansas City. Boeing had given some prior consideration to a commercial derivative, which would use Y1B-17 wings, engines, horizontal tail, and landing gear. It was obvious that it would be nonsensical to provide oxygen masks for passengers and that the only acceptable alternative would be to pressurize the entire occupied volume. An appropriate purchase agreement and specifications were expeditiously developed following the Kansas City meeting. TWA ordered five Boeing 307 Stratoliners on January 29, 1937.

Ralph Ellinger was transferred to Seattle as the TWA plant representative, and John Guy was promoted to the same position at Douglas, where TWA's DC-3's were being manufactured. Later, after the last DC-3 was delivered in August, Guy joined Ellinger. Tomlinson and others made frequent trips to Boeing to inspect mockups and to critique Boeing's design proposals.

While the 307's were being manufactured, Jack Frye encountered serious problems with a conservative TWA Board of Directors, many of whom lacked foresight and confidence in the future of aviation. The board concluded that Jack had overreached his authority and refused to authorize the expenditure of additional funds due Boeing. During June 1938, John Guy dropped by the TWA office in old Plant No. 1, near the Dwamish River, to confer with Ralph Ellinger. He then proceeded to Plant No. 2 on Marginal Way, where three of the TWA aircraft were in final assembly. He was shocked to see that all TWA markings had been stripped from the planes.

Johnny explained what happened this way:

I immediately contacted the factory supervisor to find out what in the devil was going on, and why the planes had been stripped of TWA markings. He claimed he did not know the reason; the planes had been stripped during the night on orders from Boeing's top management. I called Ralph right away to see if he knew what was going on. At first he didn't believe me, and, I suppose, thought I'd gone off my rocker.

Ralph lost no time in calling Kansas City. He talked to either Jack Frye or Paul Richter—I'm not sure which—who said a Boeing wire had been received that purported to cancel the contract. Ralph was advised that Boeing's position was illegal, that the contract was valid, and that the airplanes were still on order by TWA. He was directed to proceed with inspection and other activities on the basis that the airplanes were still ours. Ralph instructed me to continue to inspect the airplanes, to close out areas, and to write squawks [complaints] as if nothing had happened.

At times this procedure became a bit humorous. I would write up squawks and hand them over to Boeing Quality Control for handling. They would insist the airplanes were not TWA's, and I would insist they were. They fixed some things and some they ignored. They used to say, "Johnny, you're working for us as a Boeing inspector." This farce lasted from June until late December.

The contract required Boeing to deliver the first 307 on December 22, 1938. Because Boeing had stopped work on the TWA planes, it had been obvious for some time that it could not meet the requirement. On December 22, TWA notified Boeing it was canceling the contract for failure to deliver the aircraft. It also filed a $1-million damage suit against Boeing. With that turn of events, Ellinger and Guy gathered up their families and left Seattle.

Note

1. The DC-1 story that follows—I was not a participant—is based on my interview with Tommy Tomlinson, January 22, 1983; remarks by Arthur E. Raymond at the August 13, 1980, San Francisco meeting of the American Society of Mechanical Engineers; and information contained in several publications listed in the bibliography.

4.

Hughes and Frye— A Promising "Partnership"

Howard Hughes Buys In

Jack Frye's position with TWA's board, like TWA's position at Boeing, worsened and became critical. Jack's back was against the wall. It was during this hectic period that Frye approached Howard Hughes to persuade him to invest in TWA. Howard saw this as a rare opportunity to become a major stockholder, revitalize the board to his liking, and attain a position of clout with the management. Howard bought in, and the board was reconstituted. With the board problem behind and new funds available, TWA renewed contract discussions with Boeing during June 1939.

Frye dispatched Ellinger and Guy to Seattle to review the status of "TWA's" 307's. Ralph worked mostly on engineering and contractual items while John inspected the five planes and wrote detailed reports on the production status of each of them. After about 10 days they returned to Kansas City and briefed Frye and Richter.

Boeing had continued with the 307 program after the TWA planes had been set aside because PAA had placed an order for four on March 24,

1937, about two months after the original TWA contract. Boeing had tried desperately to sell the five canceled aircraft without success and found interest at KLM (Royal Dutch Airlines).

TWA and Boeing settled their differences sufficiently to permit TWA to place a new order for the five 307's on September 23, 1939. By that time, the first PAA 307 was in flight test.

The 307 Accident

A short time after the Ellinger-Guy briefing, Harlan Hull, TWA's popular chief pilot, visited Boeing to fly the 307 and report findings to Frye and Tomlinson. Several KLM personnel were at Boeing to fly on a demonstration flight when Hull arrived for the same purpose. The Dutch had the first flight; Hull accepted an invitation to go along as an observer.

The airplane crashed near Mt. Rainier, killing all on board. KLM was flying the plane with two engines inoperative on one side, an unauthorized and dangerous maneuver. Several witnesses on the ground saw a severe yaw, followed by a roll, followed by an uncontrolled descent. The airplane impacted flat, with little forward motion, and was demolished.

Following the accident, Boeing adding a large dorsal fin and made changes to the control system. A similar dorsal was added to the B-17's. Because of this tragedy, PAA received only three of the four 307's it ordered.

About the time of the accident, Hughes was anxious to learn more about the upper atmosphere and flew to Kansas City in his stagger-wing Beech to discuss Tomlinson's high-altitude exploits. Frye had warned Tomlinson of Howard's arrival and asked that he make the data available to him.

Tommy described the meeting this way:

Well, when the man came into my office, I couldn't believe my eyes. He looked like a tramp with long hair and dirty fingernails. He was anything but what I expected to see. He sat down opposite my desk. After some discussion, I was amazed at his knowledge and interest. He knew what he was talking about, and he knew how to ask the right questions. He was pretty damn smart.

When he finally left, I could hardly wait to get to Jack's office. I said, "I just met with this fellow Hughes for several hours. He asked every question under the sun. Do I really have to put up with him?" Jack looked at me and said, "Tommy, he owns the airline."

54

Hughes purchased 1 of the 10 307's Boeing produced. Without the dorsal fin, it was delivered to Burbank with an experimental license. Howard intended to break his earlier round-the-world record with this plane. Extensive modifications were undertaken by a Boeing crew including the installation of fuselage fuel tanks, special navigation aids, and over-water emergency equipment. The modifications, which required over a year to accomplish, were completed with the installation of the dorsal fin.

The impending war forced Howard to cancel plans to try for a new record when it became apparent that suitable landing fields and flight paths had become entirely too limited. Later, Howard sold the plane to Texas oil magnate Glen McCarthy after replacing the fuselage fuel tanks with a plush interior.

Stratoliner Service

The first, much-delayed TWA Stratoliner, Model SA-307B, was delivered on May 6, 1940, nearly two months after PAA had accepted its first 307—this, despite the fact that the PAA planes had been ordered months after TWA's. TWA inaugurated a new era in domestic air transportation with its Stratoliners on July 8, 1940, by providing the first coast-to-coast service with pressurized, over-weather aircraft. PAA began its 307 service on June 3 between New York and Colombia, via Barranquilla and Bogotá.

TWA's 307's were luxurious. No effort was spared to provide the best state-of-the-art meal service and other passenger amenities. The planes accommodated 16 passengers in berths arranged across the commodious fuselage, or 33 day passengers. They could be flown comfortably at 20,000 feet, with the passenger cabin pressurized to 12,000 feet. This permitted the pilot to avoid an appreciable amount of rough air and bad weather; a notable advance over the DC-3's.

Cabin pressurization was a hit with the passengers but produced maintenance headaches. Perhaps this is not too surprising, considering that the GE engine-driven superchargers were the first such attempt. Modifications helped, but they did not cure the problems.

Another serious initial 307 operating problem was carburetor icing. Ralph Ellinger told me years later of early TWA attempts to persuade Boeing to provide improved carburetor air heaters during the development program. In addition to arguments with Boeing, demand letters were written. However, TWA's pleadings fell on deaf ears; Boeing insisted that warm under-cowl air was sufficient, choosing to totally ignore TWA's wealth of airline experience.

Shortly after aircraft acceptance TWA unintentionally proved its point in spades. The CAA required "proving flights" prior to commercial service to demonstrate adequate airline preparations for commercial operations. On one such flight between Kansas City and San Francisco, a TWA 307 under the command of Capt. Otis Bryan suddenly lost all four engines from excessive carburetor ice near Pritchett, Colorado. Otis had no choice but to make an emergency power-off landing, expertly executing a wheels-up landing on soft ground. The impact forced the belly cargo doors open; mud was scooped in, filling the bins. The energy thus absorbed slowed the plane and prevented considerable damage. The crew and other TWA employees on board were uninjured. Raymond M. Dunn, later TWA's senior vice president and system general manager, was the flight engineer during the Pritchett incident.

TWA quickly designed and installed an exhaust-manifold-muff heat system, which Tomlinson found adequate during flight tests. The drawings were given to Boeing so the same modifications could be made in the other 307's, which they of course were without further argument.

After all of TWA's Stratoliners were in service, another near disaster occurred. On January 1, 1941, Capt. Harry Campbell took off from Kansas City on a nonstop flight to New York. It was a bitter cold day. Immediately after takeoff, the nose rose sharply in an uncontrollable manner and put the plane into a dangerous incipient stall condition. Harry applied full power, pushing forward on the control yoke with all of his strength. He did not have sufficient altitude or power to turn and flew straight ahead through downtown Kansas City, narrowly missing the skyscrapers. He somehow wrestled the plane back and landed at Municipal Airport. Passengers, shaken by this experience, said they had looked into the fifth-floor windows of the Kansas City Power and Light Building.

The cause of this near disaster was congealing of hydraulic fluid in the elevator control system boost cylinder due to exceptionally cold weather. It was never clear why this condition was not discovered prior to takeoff because the checklist required flight controls to be exercised to the full extent in all modes. The fix was to drill a small hole in the piston to permit the hydraulic fluid to circulate at all times.

After the usual period of debugging that accompanies any new airplane, the 307's earned a deserved reputation for good, dependable service and rugged reliability, which remained intact throughout their long service history. TWA's Stratoliner services proved to be popular and confirmed what Frye, Richter, and Tomlinson knew all along: Flight above the weather was the correct goal, and as soon as technology permitted, further gains would be inevitable. They resolved to keep TWA in the forefront of these developments.

On December 24, 1941, shortly after Pearl Harbor, TWA turned its Stratoliners over to the Army Air Forces[1] and agreed to operate them in contract services for the Air Transport Command. TWA flew them as C-75's to South America, Africa, and Europe. Over 3,000 wartime transatlantic crossings were made. The experience TWA gained from this operation, along with similar contract operations with a fleet of Douglas C-54 transports and a few C-69 Constellations, helped vault Howard's airline into scheduled transatlantic operations after World War II.

A short time after VE Day, on May 8, 1945, arrangements were made for the return of the five Stratoliners to TWA. One of my first assignments as an employee of TWA was to formulate a plan to restore them for commercial services, which I did, working in collaboration with Boeing. They were now intended for deployment on short- and medium-haul services to dovetail with TWA's anticipated C-54 and long-haul Constellation services. Plans were developed that entailed extensive modifications at Boeing's Seattle facilities and installation of new day-plane interiors (no berths) at TWA's Kansas City overhaul base. Certification flight tests, the first under the CAA's brand-new T-category rules, were to be conducted by TWA. New, more powerful engines to permit compliance with the stringent new performance rules; new wings to eliminate the threat of spar cracks, which had been encountered in early B-17's;[2] and new horizontal tail surfaces to ameliorate the balance problem that had sometimes limited payloads—all of which were available from the B-17 program—were installed along with essential commercial instrumentation and equipment. The cabin pressurization system was eliminated because of excessive maintenance problems encountered before the war. The TWA 307's were the first to receive CAA T-category certification after the modification and flight test programs were completed on schedule.

TWA flew the 307's in short- and medium-haul services until they were sold in 1951 because they had become economically obsolescent. The radiant-wall cabin heating system, the first in any transport, designed by TWA engineers Bob Walker and John Griffin, and the spacious passenger accommodations contributed significantly to the comfort and popularity of TWA's postwar 307's. After leaving TWA, the five planes continued to be flown for many years, testifying to the high quality of Boeing's design and construction practices.

The Birth of the Constellation

After buying a major share of TWA and saving TWA's Stratoliner program, Howard Hughes lost no time in sponsoring the development of much larger, highly advanced transports capable of long-range flights at record-shattering speeds.

Airline competition was severe. TWA was being squeezed by UAL on the north and AAL on the south. Although Lindbergh had done a creditable job pioneering TAT's direct coast-to-coast route with regard to flight aspects, the route lacked the number of major traffic-generating centers enjoyed by TWA's principal competition. For example, TWA had no counterpart cities for Denver, Salt Lake City, Atlanta, or Dallas.

That basic circumstance, which was to limit TWA until deregulation, plus a Board of Directors with myopic aviation vision, had taken its toll by the time Howard bought in. Howard's new investment sorely needed strengthening. He astutely believed that high-speed, super-deluxe planes with over-weather, transcontinental, nonstop capabilities—planes the competition could not come close to matching for years—would do the trick. As a well-established movie entrepreneur, he also believed that if he influenced prestigious Hollywood stars to fly TWA in such planes with attending well-orchestrated publicity, a larger share of the important repeat business market and other traffic would also choose to fly TWA.

Because the best payoff would clearly accrue if TWA had exclusive use for an extended period of the planes he had in mind, and because the likelihood would be minimized that competitive programs might develop, Howard decided the new plane had to be produced in secret. During late 1939, before the first Stratoliner was delivered to TWA, Howard called Jack Frye to discuss such a venture. The call lasted eight hours or more. They discussed the priority need for the new plane to have reliable, high-speed, over-weather capabilities. It was to carry around 50 passengers and 6,000 pounds of cargo in nonstop transcontinental services, and installation of luxurious accommodations, including berths and a private compartment in the rear, would be advisable. By the time Howard's call was over, they had agreed on the plane's conceptual mission and a list of design objectives. Jack Frye would approach several manufacturers in secret to determine the extent of their interest, if any.

Lockheed

The Lockheed Company came on hard times following the 1929 stock market crash, a condition exacerbated by its failure to produce new types of aircraft following Northrop's highly successful, record-setting Vega, Sirius, Altair, and Orion designs. Five years went by without development of a single new type of airplane, a circumstance that could be fatal in an industry that lives on advances in technology. Finally, Lockheed, with only four people remaining on the payroll, found itself in the hands of federal bankruptcy receivers. The company struggled on, but in April 1932, a federal receiver took inventory, valued the assets, and offered them for sale.

Robert E. Gross, Walter T. Varney, and Lloyd Stearman bought Lockheed on June 6, 1932, for $40,000. Gross became chairman and treasurer; Stearman, president; Carl Squier, who early on had distinguished himself selling Lockheeds, became vice president of sales; and Hall L. Hibbard, a graduate of the Massachusetts Institute of Technology and assistant chief engineer for Stearman-Varney Aircraft, became vice president, chief engineer, and a member of the board. About one year later, Clarence L. ("Kelly") Johnson, who was to become one of the preeminent airplane designers of all time, joined Hibbard's staff.

Hibbard's engineering department produced a series of high-speed, twin-engine transport designs that restored Lockheed's leadership position. Included were the piston-powered Model 10 Electra; a smaller executive version, the Model 12 (I was an engineer on this project); the Super Electra, Model 14, one of which Hughes flew around the world with an expert crew in mid-1938 to set a record that stood for years; and the Lodestar, Model 18.

Lockheed had searched several years for a large transport development project suitable for commercial marketing and proposed a four-engine design, the Excalibur, in about 1937. It resembled an oversized Lockheed Electra and was capable of flying 32 passengers 2,000 miles at speeds from 250 to 275 mph. Lockheed entertained discussions with PAA and built a mockup, but the project was soon dropped. Lockheed's attention was focused on the gathering war storm in Europe; however, its keen interest in entering the large transport market at the earliest feasible time did not abate.

Lockheed was technically well positioned to undertake the development of pressurized transports. Approximately one year after Tomlinson's research flights in the high-altitude Gamma and four months after TWA ordered Stratoliners, Lockheed flew its experimental XC-35, a pressurized version of the piston-powered Electra, developed under Army contract. The well-publicized high-altitude flights, flown in shirt-sleeve comfort, only reinforced Tomlinson's and Frye's strong conviction, shared by Hughes, that high-altitude, over-weather flight was the correct goal.

Project Formation

After Howard's call, Jack Frye quietly contacted Bob Gross. (He also contacted Reuben H. Fleet, chief executive officer at Consolidated Aircraft, who had no interest in the proposed venture.) Gross saw this as a tremendous opportunity for the fledgling company he resurrected from bankruptcy only a few years earlier. He jumped at the chance.[3]

The first exploratory meeting was held in Howard's home on Muirfield Road in the elegant old Hancock Park section of Los Angeles near Wilshire Boulevard. The only people present were Howard Hughes, Bob Gross, Hall Hibbard, and Kelly Johnson. All agreed with Johnson that Lockheed should make a fresh start, that no attempt would be made to resurrect and enlarge the Excalibur design. An extended discussion of Hughes's and Frye's design and operational requirements followed. Howard strongly emphasized speed, range, and passenger comfort. Lockheed enthusiastically undertook to study how to best meet the expressed objectives.

The next meeting was held at the Beverly Hills Hotel to review Lockheed's preliminary proposal. Jack Frye and Tommy Tomlinson joined the group. An intense debate erupted concerning whether Wright Aeronautical R-2600 engines, which had demonstrated satisfactory service for the military, or the more powerful Wright 3350's, which were then under development for the Boeing B-29 program, should be used. Frye and Hughes favored R-2600's because they were proven engines. They were leery of 3350's, which were test-stand hardware, unproven in flight. Tomlinson strongly favored the 3350's because they were a much better size for the project. Tomlinson had followed test-stand experience with the 3350's and, knowing the immensity and importance of the B-29 program, was convinced any bugs would be worked out in good time. He believed the 3350's would provide advisable initial performance margins and permit future growth. Johnson agreed. He considered the power of the R-2600 too marginal and thought that it would limit the design to an entirely unsatisfactory degree. Johnson and Tomlinson prevailed. Lockheed returned to the drawing boards to perfect its offering based on use of 3350's.

Hughes insisted on complete secrecy from the outset. Cyril Chappelet, who was responsible for Lockheed contracts, and Charles Barker, Lockheed's treasurer, met with Hughes at his Muirfield home to finalize a preliminary letter of agreement. Hughes, wearing a bathrobe and slippers, greeted them in the library. He wanted numbers of detail changes made in the letter, which the group drafted on slips of paper. Howard tore into small pieces every scrap of paper they used and threw them into the fireplace to erase any possible evidence of the program. Because of his concern, the marked-up draft letter was deposited in Cyril's personal safety-deposit box rather than on Lockheed premises. Howard insisted that every precaution be taken at every turn to ensure secrecy.

The next meeting occurred several weeks later at the Beverly Hills Hotel to review Lockheed's revised design. The TWA group had been expanded to include Jack Franklin, soon to become TWA's vice president of engineering, and Ralph Ellinger. The design proposal Lockheed presented, except for minor variations that occurred during the course of development, became the Constellation. The sleek, curved-down fuselage, triple tail, fully cowled nacelles, and enlarged P-38 wing with Lockheed-Fowler flaps were all there. Lockheed claimed a phenomenal top speed of 340 mph (better that military pursuits) and full mission compliance. A series of meetings followed in one of "Howard's" bungalows at the Beverly Hills Hotel to develop specifications and a contract.

During lax periods between meetings, Tomlinson and Franklin would loll around or play ping-pong by the swimming pool. They, like others who were involved, had been warned of the importance of maintaining absolute secrecy. Tomlinson and Franklin decided that to avoid security slips during idle conversations they would always refer to Hughes as "God" and Frye as "Jesus Christ." Ellinger adopted the further precaution of simply not saying anything even remotely related to the project for fear that some listener might be able to patch together scraps of information and learn of the program. He could not be sure what they might already know and did not want to say anything that might tip them off.

Throughout the negotiation, Hughes's emphasis was on speed, speed, and more speed. Kelly Johnson shared his preoccupation and occasionally took extreme positions. One time, after everyone was getting tired, Franklin said TWA wanted a small, conveniently located metal tab to which servicing personnel could attach a battery clip to ground the airplane. Kelly commented, "Okay, but it will have to be retractable."

Jack Franklin and Ralph Ellinger considered the artistic lines of the fuselage to be beautiful but far from optimum. They argued strongly for a straight-sided, cylindrical fuselage, pointing out that greater passenger and crew utility, ease of design, and economy of manufacturing would result. They opposed the tiny flight deck because crew and instrument space would be severely limited and maintenance access extremely difficult. Bob Gross strongly preferred the beauty of the curved-down form, and Johnson opposed the straight-sided fuselage concept, claiming it would cost 3 mph. Both were adamant, and the now familiar lines were retained.

Franklin and Ellinger also opposed the installation of powered boost control systems and the extremely complicated wing flap system because of weight and probable maintenance costs. Again, Lockheed listened but was unyielding. Unfortunately, operating experience would prove Franklin and Ellinger to be correct. Despite such arguments, however, negotiations progressed surprisingly well, and an acceptable contract and procurement specifications were developed in short order.

One of the practical problems encountered during the negotiation was how to produce the necessary contract papers and maintain total secrecy. Hughes was suspicious of everyone suggested to handle this aspect. Finally, Tomlinson suggested that his wife, Marge, who had been a court reporter and was absolutely trustworthy, would be glad to type the agreements. Frye knew her and thought this would be fine. Hughes and Gross concurred, so she moved in, and Tomlinson got to sleep with the secretary.

Howard read every word of the efficiently prepared contract papers. He wanted numbers of language and a few substantive changes made, which Lockheed agreed to for the larger part. The papers were initialed at the Beverly Hills Hotel and formally executed a few days later at Lockheed.

The contract required Lockheed to produce the first 40 Constellations for the Hughes Tool Company and refrain from even committing to sell additional Constellations to others until 35 had been delivered to Hughes. This arrangement gave TWA about two years exclusivity with the world's fastest, longest-range, and most comfortable transport. The unpressurized Douglas DC-4 and the pressurized DC-6, which was then in the talking stage, could not come close to matching its spectacular performance. Nor could anything else. The Constellation program gave excellent promise for fulfilling Hughes's and Frye's best hopes for TWA.

Hughes elected to have the planes, which cost $425,000 each, purchased by the Hughes Tool Company rather than by TWA. If TWA had purchased them, banks and financial institutions would have become quickly involved and secrecy lost because of disclosure requirements. Besides, TWA's weak financial position, which Howard quite obviously elected not to reinforce, would never have justified such a large order. It was fortunate for the future of TWA that Hughes had the financial muscle and inclination to handle the deal, and to do it secretly.

After the papers were initialed, everyone congratulated everyone, and a few bottle corks were popped. Then the negotiating teams left to attend to regular business.

Project Implementation

John Guy was asked to come to Kansas City the following March to meet with Paul Richter. He had no indication of what Paul wanted. What happened can be best told in Johnny's own words:

Paul asked me if I had any intention of leaving TWA. I was a bit nonplussed but said that I hadn't at that time. He said, "I want you to promise that you will not leave TWA until I release you. What I am going to tell you is something that only five people in TWA know about. It is absolutely secret, and you must swear to keep it that way."

I promised, and Paul continued by explaining the Lockheed project and that he wanted me to act as liaison agent between Lockheed, Hughes, and TWA. He added, "You will continue to work at the Douglas factory, and, as far as anyone will know, that is your only assignment. However, for security reasons I want you to get a house in the Burbank area with a large room in the back that can be used as an office. Make sure that nobody who works for Lockheed lives behind or on either side or across the street from this house.

63

From now on, the word *Lockheed* is stricken from your vocabulary. Don't say it. Don't mention it. If, when you are around Douglas, you hear anything about a plane being built at Lockheed, I want you to let me know at once." I agreed, but thought it would be damn near impossible to locate such a house since almost everyone in Burbank worked for Lockheed. However, I was lucky enough to find one on Cypress Street.

One of the things Mr. Richter instructed me to do when I received letters and data from Lockheed was to go through them and remove all company and personal names. When letters, drawings, or any other Lockheed data came to Cypress Street, I would take a razor blade and cut out all the names and company identification. Drawings were the worst thing. Some of them would take hours and look like Swiss cheese. There was so damn much of it, sometimes it would take me until two or three o'clock in the morning to finish. When I wrote notes, I never used names. They would start "Dear J." for Jack Frye or "Dear H. H." for Hall Hibbard, for example. There was supposed to be absolutely nothing in my home to identify the project with Lockheed, Hughes, or TWA. And there wasn't. Even my wife, Florence, didn't know what was going on.

Face-to-face meetings were sometimes absolutely necessary to thrash things out. To avoid drawing attention to Cypress Street, we would meet at selected places like Griffith Park. Don Palmer, the project engineer; Ed Trapini, the assistant project engineer; and sometimes others would meet me with drawings and data. We would find a secluded park table, spread them out, and go to work. If someone approached, we would hastily cover them or move on. When nighttime meetings were held at the Cypress Street house, I would caution the participants to park away from the house to avoid centering attention there.

Guy regularly forwarded technical data to Hughes for information and to obtain any comments he might want to make. He was careful to always show copies to Jack Frye and make absolutely certain that both men were provided the same material. Hughes would occasionally write comments on the drawings and return them to Guy. More often that not, he would telephone during late evening or early morning hours to discuss his views.

Guy was exceptionally busy, which seemed to be the usual fate for most people who worked closely with Hughes. The days and nights did not have enough hours to accommodate his Lockheed activities, his responsibilities at Douglas and TWA vendors, the night meetings, and Howard's long telephone calls. A good night's sleep became a precious commodity.

The Interior Mockup

As soon as technical progress permitted, Lockheed constructed a full-size mockup of the passenger interior in a shed located in an infrequently used area of the Burbank airport. The mockup was furnished with seats, carefully selected fabrics and upholstery materials, and sample appointments. It was with considerable pride that Lockheed presented it for approval to Hughes and TWA one Sunday morning, selected as the time least likely to attract attention. Even so, the participants arranged to arrive at the mockup building at intervals of about 15 minutes starting at 7:00 A.M. so as to not look like a caravan. Gross, Hibbard, and Johnson were first to arrive, with Frye, Ellinger, and Guy not far behind.

Hughes was last. As he entered the mockup, everyone became silent. Without saying a word, he looked around and deliberately walked very slowly the length of the display. After a pause he turned to Bob Gross and said, "This isn't exactly what I had in mind."

The Lockheed mouths dropped when he spoke. Howard's reaction surprised the TWA contingent as much as it did Lockheed's. After another pause, he added, "Bob, I think you should get Raymond Loewy on this." He then abruptly left, apparently without expecting or receiving an answer from Gross.

Loewy, a world-class industrial designer, had done a creditable job on TWA's DC-3 sleeper interiors. Gross lost no time in getting him on board. During the next several weeks, Loewy developed sample color schemes and sketches, which Guy handed on to Hughes for approval. However, for reasons unknown, Hughes did not respond. Lacking directions to the contrary, Loewy proceeded with his design efforts.

Some time later, when Loewy was visiting Lockheed, Hughes asked Guy to arrange for a meeting with him. Loewy had an important meeting in the East with Studebaker the next day, expressed sincere regrets, and said that while he could not meet with Howard at that particular time, he would be pleased to visit California later at a time convenient for Howard. Guy advised Howard, who absolutely insisted that Loewy change his plans. Loewy reluctantly did so, with considerable effort and personal embarrassment, only to find that Howard was too busy to meet with him. When Loewy prepared to leave, Howard again requested through Guy that Loewy remain. Loewy again acquiesced and shifted plans, and Howard was again too busy. This happened once again, and Loewy's situation became even

65

more critical. It did not help Loewy's frame of mind that he could talk only with Guy, not with Howard.

The three finally met at Howard's house. After waiting several hours, Howard came in dragging a large picture of an airplane interior and said, "Raymond, this is what I have in mind. See what you can do."

Guy was aghast. After persuading Loewy to stand by for days, the meeting ended almost as soon as it started. To make matters worse, Johnny thought the picture looked like an enlarged shot of a standard Douglas interior.

John's Other Work

The visible part of John Guy's job was to work with Douglas and other vendors in the Los Angeles area. He was frequently called upon by TWA's Maintenance Department to locate urgently needed airplane parts, required to return airplanes to scheduled service. Johnny did the best he could. When he could not be reached because of the Lockheed project, he would leave word that he would be at this or that vendor.

Bill Hughes was TWA's superintendent of maintenance in Burbank, then the main terminal for the Los Angeles area. In emergencies, when Guy could not be reached, Bill would call the stipulated vendor only to discover that Guy had not been there and was not expected. With planes to get out, Bill was more than a little perturbed.

After this had gone on a long time, Bill confronted John: "Bill Maxfield had a plane down in Kansas City, and I had to get parts out. I called Airesearch and they said you were at Adel. I called Adel and three other places. You weren't anywhere. You son of a bitch, I don't know what you're doing, but you're not working, and one of these days, I warn you, they're going to catch up with you."

This problem persisted until the Constellation program was made public. On that very day, John Guy made it a point to visit Bill in the airport shops to make peace with him. He said, "Well, Bill, now you know what I was doing all that time."

John Guy worked closely with Howard Hughes throughout the early Constellation development period and on special projects that Hughes requested from time to time. Johnny had this to say about Hughes several years after his death:

66

I always felt at ease with him. I always called him "Howard," and I'm not a brash person. I would never have called Jack Frye, "Jack"; or Mr. Richter, "Paul." They were "Mr. Frye" and "Mr. Richter." With Howard it just seemed to come naturally. He had a lot on the ball. He was terribly demanding, but wasn't hard to work with. He had a good mind and at one time had a memory like an elephant. He never forgot anything. You couldn't cross him up. When he said this is the way it was, you could go back over the mark-up notes, and that's the way it was. I never caught him. His memory was absolutely phenomenal. But poor old Howard. He could have done so much good; he just wasted the last part of his life.

Lifting the Veil

It is a marvel that Lockheed, TWA, and the vendors kept the Constellation project secret. By the time Lockheed found it advisable to announce the Constellation program, thousands of employees were directly involved. Yet, nothing leaked out during the years required for development. This is all the more remarkable because national security was in no way involved. This venture was perhaps the best kept industrial secret of all time.

The secrecy veil was lifted a few months before Pearl Harbor, when a visit to Lockheed from the War Production Board was imminent. Because Lockheed was obliged under law to show all work in process, with Hughes's consent it called a special press conference the day before the board arrived.

The announcement and photographs of the Constellation, which appeared in nearly every leading newspaper in the country, electrified the industry. Its long-range, high-speed, and high-altitude capabilities were clearly years ahead. It appeared that TWA would achieve a major lead on its competition because of the foresight of Hughes and Frye and the design genius of Hibbard and Johnson. Hughes was given great credit for his courage and willingness to put a fortune at risk by ordering the first 40 Constellations to the account of his wholly owned company. Without his confidence and determination, the program never would have materialized.

Pan American

Accounts of PAA's entry into the Constellation program are somewhat contradictory and fuzzy. Unfortunately, the principals involved—Howard

Hughes, Bob Gross, Jack Frye, and Juan Trippe—have long since died. Notwithstanding, I believe the following recollections of a number of contemporaries to be accurate.

Shortly after the Constellation program became public knowledge, Juan Trippe (PAA's chief executive officer) made clear to Bob Gross that he wanted PAA in the program. Nothing short of rights to an equal number of planes would do. Trippe was upset by Lockheed's having proceeded in secret with the Constellation after abandonment of the Excalibur project—a situation Gross was sensitive to. And, from Lockheed's point of view, getting PAA on board appeared to guarantee the commercial success of the program.

Gross discussed this matter with a reluctant Howard Hughes, who was finally persuaded to let PAA join the program on the condition that it operate overseas routes exclusively and was noncompetitive with TWA. This may have been Howard's ostensible reason for accepting Bob's arguments; however, it seems likely there was more to it.

Howard was an ambitious and remarkably astute businessman with a unique facility for visualizing future opportunities and leaving doors open for their realization. It seems highly probable that he thought of the possibility of expanding TWA into the international arena, for which Constellations would be well suited, even at that early date. Such gleam-in-the-eye considerations, had they existed, were likely outweighed in his thinking by pragmatic political considerations. For example, he may have believed that the Constellation program would be more likely to prosper during the oncoming period of heavy war preparations if PAA purchased a sizable fleet. (The greater national need was obviously for fighters and bombers and was certain to receive the highest priority). Whatever Howard's reasoning might have been, one can be absolutely certain that his decision to permit PAA to buy Constellations was arrived at only after exhaustively detailed study and painstaking evaluation of all aspects.

After Gross obtained Howard's acquiescence, PAA quietly ordered a fleet of 40 Constellations, matching the quantity ordered by Hughes in 1939. Not long afterward, John G. Borger was transferred to Burbank to serve under Bill Del Valle as PAA's chief expediter and liaison agent at Lockheed.

War Imperative

Not long after the Constellation program was announced, TWA assigned its rights to the 40 Constellations to the Army Air Forces because the production of commercial transports had been forbidden. TWA retained the right to repurchase the planes when they were no longer required in military service and obtained preferred delivery positions for new production units. The 40 planes on order were designated "C-69" transports and configured for carrying troops and cargo on long-range missions.

The Army initially increased the C-69 order to 50, later boosting it to 260 planes. Still later, when the end of the war seemed imminent, the order was cut to 73, then finally terminated after only 15 had been built. However, the Army agreed to accept 5 additional nearly completed aircraft. The Army had accorded low priority to the program, stopping production 17 times in favor of Lockheed's combat aircraft. Thus, 20 of the 40 Constellations Howard ordered emerged in olive-drab paint rather than polished aluminum and bright red TWA logo—that is, all except the first one, which sported TWA markings.

Howard Hughes had astutely worked out a deal with the Army giving TWA jurisdiction over the first Constellation until it was accepted by TWA, after which it was to be immediately turned over to the Air Forces. This arrangement permitted TWA to conduct acceptance shakedown flights. Hughes and Frye decided to fly such a flight while trying for a new transcontinental speed record, hoping to reap favorable publicity from the world's first real view of the plane.

They departed Burbank at 3:56 A.M., April 17, 1944, for Washington, D.C. Jack Frye was in command, with Howard as copilot. At exactly the halfway point to the minute by the flight plan, Jack and Howard changed places. Howard landed the plane in Washington 6 hours and 58 minutes after takeoff, setting an impressive new record.

Some of the Army officials, including Gen. H. H. ("Hap") Arnold, were reportedly chagrined and unhappy with the flight, especially because the plane had become a glamorous billboard for commercial publicity purposes, a circumstance deemed inappropriate considering stringent wartime conditions. Apparently, they also thought (probably correctly) that the intent, if not the letter, of the contract had been violated. Their frame of mind did not improve when Hughes and Frye spent several days demonstrating the plane to high government officials, including the entire Civil Aeronautics Board (CAB). The plane was painted in regulation olive-drab after the demonstration flights and turned over to the Air Forces.

The impact of the war on Hughes's grand game plan was devastating and tragic for TWA. The multiyear competitive advantages foreseen at program outset were very substantially lost because of the war. Indeed, TWA was unable to deploy Constellations in commercial services until February 1945—over one and a half years after I joined the company.

Notes

1. The Army Air Corps became the Army Air Forces in June 1941 and a separate branch of the armed services, the United States Air Force, in September 1947.
2. The original 307 wings were of identical design, but due to extraordinary diligence on the part of John Guy, the TWA inspector assigned to survey the construction of TWA's 307's at Boeing, microscopic cracks were discovered in the wing spar structural members prior to assembly—certain to have been troublesome, perhaps dangerous, in service. Because of John's discovery, such parts were eliminated from the TWA 307 wings, reducing the threat of postdelivery problems. Later, during the B-17 program, Boeing changed from 24SRT to 24ST aluminum alloy, which was less prone to cracking.
3. The following account is a composite of information given to the author by Tommy Tomlinson, Kelly Johnson, Hall Hibbard, Cyril Chappelet, John Guy, and Jack Franklin; and Constellation data contained in several publications listed in the bibliography.

Howard Robard Hughes, Jr., intrepid aviator and air transport entrepreneur. The plane is a Northrop Gamma. TWA Photo No. B2121, published with permission of Summa Corporation.

Howard Hughes by his record-breaking HR-1 Racer, c. 1935. Smithsonian Institution Photo No. B-13068.

The Rearwin Speedster after Rummel's redesign, which corrected spinning problems that had for years prevented certification. Rearwin photo courtesy of Royce S. Rearwin.

Robert W. Rummel, shortly after becoming chief engineer at Rearwin.

The Rearwin Cloudster, designed and engineered by Rummel in 1938 and produced in several models, was well known for its exceptional handling characteristics and spacious cabin. The instrument training model shown here was produced for PAA, TWA, Parks Air College, and others, including 25 for the government of Iran.

The Rearwin Skyranger, designed by Rummel in 1940. Skyrangers and Cloudsters were manufactured at a rate of one per day at peak production. Rearwin photo from Rummel memorabilia.

The original TWA management team. Left to right: Paul Richter, Tommy Tomlinson, Jack Frye, and Walt Hamilton. TWA Photo No. TW62-451.

Jack Frye, an inspired aviation pioneer and TWA president. TWA Photo No. 50730-1.

Paul Richter, TWA executive vice president, who added pragmatism and brought great executive ability to the company. TWA Photo No. TW-899-27.

TWA's pioneering Douglas DC-1 at the Grand Central Air Terminal, Glendale, California. Photo courtesy of TWA.

Joe Bartles (left) and Tommy Tomlinson before their record-breaking flight in the Douglas DC-1, May 1935. Photo courtesy of TWA.

Tommy Tomlinson by TWA's Northrop Gamma Experimental Overweather Laboratory after the plane had been modified for high altitude research flights. Smithsonian Institution Photo No. 1B-28827.

Frank Busch (left) and Tommy Tomlinson by the Gamma, c. 1936. Smithsonian Institution Photo No. 1B-28819.

The Boeing 307 Stratoliner, the world's first pressurized civil transport, was custom designed for TWA. Many Boeing B-17 bomber components were used. Photo courtesy of TWA.

Hall L. Hibbard (left) and Robert E. Gross by a TWA Constellation. Lockheed photo courtesy of Hall L. Hibbard.

Howard Hughes in the Constellation. Photo courtesy of TWA.

Benny Howard by one of his racing creations. Smithsonian Institution Photo No. 2B-10-12815.

The HK-1 "Spruce Goose" in Long Beach Harbor. Smithsonian Institution Photo No. 1B-7376.

Howard Hughes at the controls of the HK-1 "Spruce Goose." Smithsonian Institution Photo No. B-7360.

The Convair XC-99, developed from the B-36 bomber. The commercial version, Model 37, was to be the same size. Photo courtesy of General Dynamics Corporation.

The double-deck Lockheed Model 89 Constitution was developed for the U.S. Navy under the aegis of PAA. Two were built. Smithsonian Institution Photo No. 1B-15071.

The proposed commercial version of this plane, the Douglas C-74 Globemaster I, was the original DC-7. This design was given serious procurement consideration by Hughes and Rummel. McDonnell Douglas Corporation Photo No. C-20211-22, courtesy of Harry Gann.

The original DC-7 was withdrawn from the market partly as a result of the development of this plane, the Douglas Globemaster II, a double-deck version of the C-74. McDonnell Douglas Corporation Photo SM 214500, courtesy of Harry Gann.

A Constellation Model 049 in TWA logo. This was the first type of Constellation deployed commercially. Photo courtesy of TWA.

Howard's XF-11, in which he nearly lost his life. Smithsonian Institution Photo No. 1B-7461.

Howard in the cockpit of the XF-11. Smithsonian Institution Photo No. 1B-7458.

A jovial moment at dinner in a West Coast restaurant sometime before Howard's crash. Left to right: Jack Franklin, Lee Talman, Harry West, and Bob Rummel. Photo from Rummel memorabilia.

Howard Hughes (right) with John Collings in Kansas City during Howard's first stopover after the XF-11 crash. Photo courtesy of TWA.

Howard Hughes (right) discussing the installation of his newly developed Terrain Warning Indicator with Dave Evans, head of the Electronics Department of the Hughes Aircraft Company. Photo courtesy of TWA.

5.
1943—
Working
for TWA
and
Hughes

I was not sure what to expect. It was my first day of work at TWA, June 21, 1943. I was 27 years old, leaving a position of great responsibility in a small but substantial manufacturing enterprise to fill a new slot in a far larger organization. I rose at 6:00 A.M., ate a hearty breakfast, kissed Margie goodbye, and set out for work. I entered the Engineering Department at corporate headquarters, Municipal Airport, Kansas City, Missouri, promptly at eight o'clock, the daily starting time, to find nearly every office and desk already occupied with people hard at work.

My new boss, Jack Franklin, vice president of engineering, dropped what he was doing to greet me. He briefly discussed my forthcoming activities, assigned a desk to me, and introduced me to fellow engineering employees. This was all done in a snappy and efficient manner, leading me to believe, quite correctly, that I had joined an industrious and productive organization.

My desk was located in a bull pen in a cluster of four abutting desks with shared telephones—a far cry from the large private office I had long been accustomed to at Rearwin and Commonwealth. Most of the approximately 40 engineering employees were similarly situated—only three private offices existed in the entire department. All engineering employees except Franklin's assistant, Ted Thomsen; two engineering pilots; and me reported to the chief engineer, Ralph Ellinger, who had returned to Kansas City after his stint as TWA's West Coast factory representative. We four reported directly to Franklin.

My primary standing charge was—as I had hoped—to analyze the operational and economic characteristics of transport aircraft, recommend for procurement the numbers and types of planes that would best serve TWA, develop aircraft specifications, and organize and handle technical procurement negotiations. During the closing period of the war, many opportunities existed for acquisition of converted military transports or the development of brand new designs. Boeing, Budd, Curtiss Wright, Douglas, Fairchild, Lockheed, and Republic all had transport production programs underway. Consolidated Vultee (Convair), Martin, and North American had declared intentions of producing commercial transports after the war. Northrop, determined to do the same, sought to collaborate with TWA to best determine what type and size of transport it should offer. My work was cut out in spades.

Analyzing the sizable assortment of real and potential airplanes for TWA's use was sunshine and roses for me. I was happily part of an expanding industry whose primary working tools were perpetually being evolved from the forefront of technological advances in nearly all disciplines. Such aspects were regularly discussed with me by the engine and airframe manufacturers. I soon found I was close to the cutting edge, and I loved it.

It appeared that the air transportation industry was on the threshold of great expansion if flight safety, schedule reliability, and reasonable costs could be convincingly demonstrated. The massive fighter and bomber raids reported almost daily in the press and the general knowledge of routine over-ocean Air Transport Command (ATC) operations erased much of the fear of flying from an entire generation. It was obvious to me that the key to unlocking the inviting door of progress was to acquire and deploy new fleets of the right kind of aircraft.

The Equipment Committee

Soon after I joined TWA, Jack Franklin established the management Equipment Committee, the primary function of which was to recommend to Jack

Frye the number and types of aircraft TWA should purchase. Frye, whose rapport with Howard Hughes appeared to be excellent, cleared recommendations with him as appropriate. The committee proved to be an excellent vehicle for consolidating aircraft program considerations and finalizing recommendations. It consisted of E. Lee Talman, executive vice president (Paul Richter had resigned this position in January 1943 to join the Navy); John A. Collings, vice president of operations; Vince P. Conroy, vice president of traffic; John M. Lockhart, secretary and treasurer; and, of course, Jack Franklin. I supplied information and served as secretary.

I routinely provided written digests illustrating candidate aircraft, competitive airline fleet plans, and prospective TWA procurement timetables, and I developed numbers of new preliminary transport designs to illustrate concepts and generate interest. A fellow employee, Glen Scott, produced attractive isometric renderings of them in color, which, along with brief descriptive data, were sent to Frye and the committee. A few of these designs came to Howard's attention and captured his interest.

The committee took seriously its job of developing fleet procurement recommendations. Technical and business aspects of each potential program were debated at length. Due to the great volume of competing programs, achieving consensus was sometimes difficult and time consuming, but always interesting. My participation brought me into close contact with TWA's top management and almost immediately attracted Hughes's attention, a very special circumstance for a new employee.

The Back Room

The only way to reach Howard was through "the boys in the back room." The usual procedure was to telephone "the boys" and wait for a return call from Hughes.

Howard's operations center, at 7000 Romaine Street, Hollywood, was an unimpressive, two-story, off-white-stucco building on a corner lot. It contained offices for Noah Dietrich, Howard's financial management wizard; Thomas A. Slack, the Houston lawyer who was one of Howard's principal attorneys and who later became a member of TWA's Board of Directors, and still later, a principal Hughes antagonist; A. V. ("Vic") Leslie, who later became TWA's vice president of finance; Nadine Henley, Howard's personal secretary; Frank W. ("Bill") Gay, who handled confidential affairs and was in charge of the back room; and the boys.

73

I decided at the outset to try to keep all contacts with Howard direct and personal to avoid misunderstandings. While the majority of calls were initiated by Howard, numbers of occasions arose that required me to contact him. My conversations with the boys would start by my telling the answering voice that I needed to talk to Howard and would appreciate a return call. Invariably, the voice would say, "What do you wish to discuss with Mr. Hughes?" My response was also invariably, "That is between Mr. Hughes and myself. Please tell him I need to talk to him. He will know what it is about, and that I wouldn't disturb him if I didn't think it was necessary."

I did not mistrust any of the boys. They were carefully selected Mormons whose honesty and sobriety were without question and who could be trusted with confidential information. However, because many of the discussion subjects were technical or involved complicated business negotiations, I could not be certain that my words and thoughts would be accurately expressed to Hughes. Besides, issues needing resolution required direct discussion and debate to make certain that all bases had been covered and to assure common objectives. Too much was involved to risk distortions, however unintended they might be.

This approach usually worked. I would almost always get a return call from Howard, but sometimes not as soon as I wanted. In a few exceptionally urgent cases, when it proved to be absolutely impossible to talk to him, I bent and tried to pass the pending question or proposed position to him through the boys. They tried, but the results were almost always less than desirable.

I had occasion to meet with Bill Gay in his inner sanctum at the Romaine Street office. I was shown from the second-floor vestibule into the telephone answering room, which had multiple phone stations and spartan but adequate accommodations for the answering personnel. From there, I entered an unlighted broom and secretarial supplies closet, which had a second, hidden door behind a clothes rack. This opened into Bill's spacious and conveniently arranged office. An old-fashioned rolltop desk stood against one wall, and a large, fireproof steel safe was across the room, hidden behind wooden doors. Between them were several chairs and a table. Bill, as I always found him, was most pleasant and cooperative.

During the meeting a difference of opinion developed concerning an earlier conversation. Bill went to the safe and pulled out a stack of yellow, legal-size pads filled with shorthand notes. He read aloud verbatim the earlier conversation. This cleared the air and put me on notice that each of my

74

telephone conversations with people at Romaine Street had been and probably would continue to be recorded. I also learned that this practice was followed with all calls, including directives and requests Bill and the boys received from Howard. However, as far as I know, none of Howard's personal or business telephone conversations, which were transmitted directly rather than through the boys, was ever recorded. I am certain he would not have permitted this. But years later, during extended TWA-Hughes litigations, typed records of the telephone conversations that passed through the Romaine Street center were made available to and used by both parties.

Field Trips

Soon after I joined TWA, Jack Franklin arranged special familiarization trips to key manufacturers to introduce me, receive briefings on product development plans, and inspect aircraft. The contacts thus made were extremely helpful and enabled me to achieve reasonable job proficiency in good time.

The first field trip I made alone was in response to a request received from "the Principals" (Howard Hughes and Jack Frye) to evaluate the twin-engine, high-wing RB-1 Conestoga cargo plane being manufactured by the Edward G. Budd Manufacturing Company of Philadelphia. Budd's pioneering use of stainless steel throughout the Conestoga structure, consisting primarily of very thin spot-welded components, was of special interest. It gave promise of being less subject to corrosion, capable of long life, and lighter for large aircraft. I was anxious to learn about the design details and manufacturing processes.

I was met at the airport by a Budd executive and taken to the Philadelphia Athletic Club for one of the finest seafood dinners I have ever enjoyed. During dinner, he explained that Budd had sizable orders in hand for the Conestoga: 200 for the Navy and 600 for the Army. (These orders were subsequently reduced; only 25 were built.) He suggested a tour of the railway-car manufacturing factory the next morning, after which Benny Howard would take me for a flight in an experimental Conestoga.

Like most aviation enthusiasts, I knew of Benny Howard's legendary career. Benny had designed two fabulous small racing planes, *Ike* and *Mike,* which won most of races they participated in. I had witnessed one such victory when I helped time the 1936 National Air Races at Mines Field. His high-wing cabin monoplane, *Mr. Mulligan,* had won the Bendix

75

Trophy race between Los Angeles and Cleveland the year before. Benny had served as a test pilot for several manufacturers and was presently on loan from Douglas. I eagerly looked forward to meeting him.

Benny Howard was the kind of man one could meet and instantly feel at ease with. After examining the airplane, we sat in the cockpit to discuss the Conestoga. His first words were, "Bob, this thing is a crock. You won't want TWA to have them. It would be a mistake." Then, after a pause, "Despite what Budd promised you, I don't think the plane is ready to demonstrate, so I won't take you up today. I wouldn't feel right about it." Benny then explained in a very matter-of-fact and convincing way the reasons for his concern.

I appreciated his candor and from then on held special respect for Benny Howard. Our paths were to cross from time to time in the future. The last time was in San Diego in 1955 when he tried to convince me that Hughes should sponsor the development of a jet transport he had laid out. Each meeting with Benny, like our first on the Conestoga, was completely frank and fair. He was a real gentleman.

Another field trip arranged by "the Principals" was a special treat. I visited the Northrop factory in Hawthorne and had the privilege of meeting Jack Northrop, whose genius I had admired ever since the early record flights of the Lockheed Vegas, which he designed. The occasion for the meeting was to discuss the feasibility of adapting Northrop's revolutionary all-wing design concepts to civil transports. I had followed his earlier all-wing work; visited the old Northrop factory at Mines Field when the Gamma was in production, while I was a student at Curtiss Wright; and was familiar with the structural advances he pioneered.

The meeting, which occurred in Northrop's office, was most pleasant and informative. At the time, the piston-powered, all-wing bomber, the XB-35, was in the early stages of construction. Northrop discussed the aerodynamic and structural aspects of all-wing design and how this concept could be applied to future transports, with enormous improvements in operating efficiency. After our discussion, he showed me the shops and the XB-35 work in process. There, the great man climbed through jigs containing partly completed structures, pointed out features and details with enthusiasm, and continued to discuss the fundamental potential advantages of all-wing transports.

Despite the great potential payload-range advantages offered, I recommended, and Hughes and Frye concurred, that the inviting all-wing possi-

76

bility be put on the back burner until flight experience with B-35's permitted thoroughgoing evaluation of the operational aspects of this type of aircraft. Unfortunately, both the B-35 and YB-49 (its jet-powered successor) programs were canceled by the secretary of war, a vindictive, ill-considered act brought about by Northrop's refusal to merge with another airframe manufacturer. Except at Northrop, the all-wing concept was largely ignored until its recent reincarnation as the B-2, the controversial Stealth Bomber.

My introduction to the airframe manufacturers included becoming reacquainted at Lockheed and meeting other top executives, including Donald W. Douglas, Sr., and the Douglas staff; Isaac M. ("Mac") Laddon and Frank W. Fink of Convair; Wellwood E. Beall and Edward C. Wells of Boeing; and others. I also met a majority of the leading engineering executives of other airlines during these early days. Jack Franklin's efforts to help establish my credentials were helpful and much appreciated.

The Spruce Goose and the Giants

During the fall of 1943, Jack Franklin received word that Howard Hughes wanted me to examine the commercial potential of the mammoth Hughes flying boat, the HK-1, then under development in Culver City. I had not expected such an intriguing assignment, but I questioned the need because it seemed obvious that commercial operations would be impractical. To say the least, the HK-1 was oversized, and it could not land at any of the existing commercial landlocked airports. Notwithstanding, Jack asked me to proceed. Howard Hughes and Henry Kaiser had joined forces in August 1942 with the objective of producing the world's largest cargo planes for the U.S. military services. Kaiser was building "liberty ships" at the phenomenal rate of one per day and must have envisioned hundreds of the flying boats plying the skies in support of military operations. A contract was awarded by the War Production Board for development of a prototype to be constructed of nonstrategic material.

The HK-1, which proved to be politically controversial, was frequently derided by the press and, to Howard's extreme distaste, became known as the "Spruce Goose." After the design was underway, Kaiser became disenchanted and pulled out. Hughes continued alone. Finally, after years of delay and many millions of Howard's own money, the single prototype was completed and one short demonstration flight made, with Howard as pilot. It is presently on display in Long Beach, California.

The HK-1 dwarfed all other planes. Its immensity almost defied description. It had a wing span of 320 feet—20 feet longer than a football field—and a hull 218 feet long with a beam (width) of 24 feet. The span of the horizontal tail was 18.8 feet greater and its area 2.6 times that of the wing of a DC-3. From the waterline to the tip of the vertical tail was the height of an average eight-story building. It was constructed primarily of thin birch veneer—hardly any spruce was used—laminated by processes similar to those employed in the wing of the H-1 racer. It was an enormous but intricate woodworking marvel intended to be capable of transporting hundreds of troops and materiel on intercontinental runs. While large, the HK-1 had the sleek appearance of aerodynamic efficiency.

I suggested that evaluation of the HK-1 would be more meaningful if other giant aircraft then under development were included in the study for comparison and to learn if such aircraft could be useful to TWA. Accordingly, the Convair XC-99, the Lockheed Constitution, and the original Douglas DC-7 were included. Howard welcomed this approach and gave me a free hand to investigate.

All four planes were designed with the largest available piston engines—Pratt & Whitney (P & W) 4360's, rated at 3,000 hp each. The HK-1 had eight engines, the XC-99 had six, and the other two had four engines each. My preliminary review of performance data showed all except the DC-7 to be marginally powered for airline use. For example, the XC-99's all-engine climb at maximum weight was only 610 feet per minute, and the two-engine-out ceiling was only 9,500 feet, not enough to clear the western mountains.

In this exercise I supplemented the manufacturer's performance data by estimating performance for all except the DC-7 on the assumption that ''growth'' versions of the 4360's could eventually produce 1-hp-per-cubic-inch displacement, a power level of 4,360 hp, which seemed realistic as a measure of the ultimate power of the engines, but which seemed unlikely to be attained before such planes could be delivered. Then for comparison I projected performance of the three planes assuming the availability of 5,000-hp engines, which, after necessary empty- and fuel-weight adjustments, showed ample margins, thus indicating the extent of the initial power shortfall.

I knew 5,000 hp could come only from turbine engines, none of which would be available for an appreciable period. A strong military engine development program would have been required to produce such engines, but none was in the offing. It seemed to me that such a program, if one should develop, was unlikely to produce engines for commercial use because of anticipated low aircraft-production rates; certainly not in time for initial aircraft production. The only possible relief seemed anemic: reliance on power growth of the 4360's.

The power deficiency question was further complicated by inadequate federal performance standards. I firmly believed that the minimum CAA terrain-clearance standards for any transport having more than four engines must be met after failure of two rather than one engine. The federal standards were drawn for two-, three-, and four-engine transports and required compliance on assumption of only one engine failure at the most critical point in the takeoff path or while en route. Because of the disappointingly high piston-engine failure rates being experienced and the fact that the difference between all-engine and one-engine-out performance diminished as the numbers of installed engines increased, I did not think the rules provided ample flight margins for transports equipped with more than four engines. After all, the safety record established by the airlines through the years reflected for the larger part experience with all engines operating. I calculated performance with two engines out for the Hughes and Convair planes, but, following CAA standards, with one engine out for the Constitution and the original DC-7.

With preliminary data in hand, plans were laid for visiting Convair, Lockheed, and Douglas to review the latest technical data, discuss the power question, and inspect the planes under construction. The first meeting was at Convair, San Diego, with Mac Laddon, vice president and general manager, who had been responsible for development of the majority of Convair's highly successful military planes.

Convair's XC-99, two of which were being manufactured, was a double-deck transport version of the B-36 bomber, then being designed to fly round-trip missions from America to Europe. The B-36 was slated for high production, which, along with anticipated C-99 production, was expected to provide an economical base for producing the commercial version of the C-99, the Model 37, due to the great commonality of components. Even so, the variation in the estimated unit selling price of the Model 37 as a function of the numbers of B-36's and C-99's manufactured was in the millions. In contrast, at that time the projected purchase price of Constellations was only about one-half million dollars each.

The Model 37 could accommodate 307 passengers in "reasonable" comfort for flights of moderate length or 174 passengers in luxurious accommodations on long-range flights. TWA's 21-passenger Douglas DC-3's were puny by comparison. I described the size of the big planes to TWA's marketing people in terms of "DC-3 equivalents." Sometimes I could not tell if they had been overcome with delight or were crying with despair over the sales challenges they might face.

After a detailed briefing, during which the power question was discussed but not resolved, Mac Laddon, Jack Franklin, and I toured the Convair shops. We walked through both decks of the fuselage and inspected other XC-99 assemblies, which Mac described with justified pride. We paused in the detail parts fabrication shop while Mac related how one of the workmen had devised an ingenious tool for accurately drilling small 18-inch-deep holes through aluminum bars without drift in the drill bit—an impressive tooling accomplishment. I was curious about where such holes were needed and asked him. Mac said, "That was the problem. After the holes were drilled, he cut the bars into two-inch lengths. My first reaction was to fire him for wasting time, but instead, I transferred him to the tool shop, where his talents could be used under close supervision."

Before Jack and I left San Diego, Laddon enthusiastically discussed the fundamental advantages of turbine power for transports, which he was certain would become dominant as soon as suitable engines could be developed. He inquired of Howard's interest in turbines, pointing out that in time to come, large turboprop (propellers driven by turbines) engines would be ideal for succeeding versions of the Model 37.

I met next with Lockheed to review the Model 89 Constitution project. Willis M. Hawkins, who was responsible for the program, briefed me with great exuberance on the design and on Lockheed's production capabilities. We inspected the engineering mockup, looked at work in process, and attended briefings.

Lockheed had undertaken development of the Constitution in 1942. It was to be a high-speed, highly wing-loaded, relatively small fuselage design originated at PAA's request. When Lockheed applied to the military for permission to design such an airplane, permission was refused. Undaunted, Juan Terry Trippe, PAA's chief executive officer, pressed and finally succeeded in interesting the Navy, which drastically changed the concept of the airplane. Now it was to have an exceptionally large 174-passenger double-deck fuselage with lighter wing loading, and four turboprop engines. The order for turbine engines was subsequently canceled, and P & W 4360's were substituted. The Navy ordered 50, but only 2 were built.

The Navy wanted the plane designed to achieve high daily utilization (average hours flown per day) and low man-hour maintenance expenditures. It wanted practical airline experience reflected in the design and hired PAA to help achieve this goal. PAA's Bill Del Valle was on station, with Andre Priester, vice president of engineering, and John G. Borger, then his assistant, following progress at New York headquarters.

As was typical of Lockheed's transports, the Constitution had appealing lines, and, unlike the Constellations, the double-deck interior was unusually spacious and attractive. With more power, I thought, it could be a real winner, provided markets could support planes that large. TWA's interest in the Constitution continued well after my evaluation of the HK-1 and the other giants.

My next visit was to Douglas to learn more of the DC-7, a proposed commercial version of the C-74 Globemaster I transport, the design of which had been undertaken for the Army in 1942.[1] E. F. ("Ed") Burton, chief engineer, and Nathaniel Paschall, vice president of sales, arranged and participated in the factory tour and the briefings. They were anxious to sell Hughes and expand entry into the commercial market, wartime production restrictions notwithstanding.

The DC-7 was much better sized for most existing or forecast markets, although not as well sized as the Constellation. It had a tubular single-deck fuselage with a standard (four-abreast) capacity of 86 passengers and cargo. With apparently good economic usefulness and adequate performance, it could be either an asset or a significant competitive threat.

PAA placed an order for 26 DC-7's during 1944, according to a contemporary press release, for "its great Latin American expansion program." Perhaps so, but I was convinced that PAA intended to use the majority of them in transatlantic services. The first deliveries were expected in 1946.

As the design advanced, the unit price increased from an estimated $1,125,000 to nearly $1,500,000, and the empty weight increased to the point of seriously impairing payload-range performance. Because of these factors, plus the imminent availability of smaller transports, PAA canceled its order during October 1945. Douglas withdrew the DC-7 from the market because of the PAA cancellation and the development of the Globemaster II, a larger, double-deck transport scheduled to be produced in large quantities, which usurped available factory space and supplanted the Globemaster I in production. However, at the time of my investigation, the DC-7 was still a live project.

All of the giants presented challenging business enigmas. The question of flight frequency versus airplane size was just as pertinent and elusive then as today. Actually, then it was somewhat more so because the current limited availability of flight-schedule slots at major airports tends to reduce decision options and skew the frequency-versus-size decisions toward larger aircraft. How long would passengers wait to take the giants if smaller planes like the DC-4 or Constellation were available when they wanted to go? And considering the probability that only a small fleet of giants could be purchased, could the operating costs be kept low enough to justify the low fare levels believed necessary to fill the planes? In this regard, how much new traffic would be generated, and how much diversion from the smaller planes would occur? And if the ticket prices were significantly lower than TWA could afford for the smaller aircraft, which would still dominate its services, how would TWA make out financially overall?

Much of my investigation of the giants was amenable to mathematical analyses, but much had to be strongly tempered by intuitive judgments. The more complete my analyses became, the more obvious became the conclusion that the HK-1 had no commercial potential whatsoever, then or ever. I could not make any business or operational sense out of it. Deployment would have required construction of dedicated hangars, terminals, and water clearways at appreciable expense because, being a seaplane, the HK-1 could not land on commercial airfields, most of which were landlocked. To me it seemed obvious that the future belonged to land planes rather than seaplanes because passengers could be delivered directly to where they wanted to go rather than transferring. While all-cargo operations were marginally conceivable, the cargo market was entirely too small at that time to give this possibility serious consideration. And the HK-1 was grossly oversized for commercial marketing purposes, anywhere.

The other three planes were somewhat better sized. Of the four, moreover, the DC-7 was clearly the most realistic candidate for procurement consideration. I made no effort, however, to advance procurement recommendations at that time: Neither price nor deliveries could be finalized because of continuing war production commitments. I seriously questioned the wisdom of procuring at great cost a small fleet of oversized planes for relatively early postwar use when it appeared likely that large numbers of

82

Constellations and Douglas C-54's would be offered for early delivery at reasonable cost. I planned to follow each program closely, updating evaluations as appropriate, and I felt certain that Howard would agree that I should. He did.

The HK-1 comparative analyses were mine, and it fell to me to discuss the results with Hughes. I had decided earlier never to pull punches with him and always to present my findings faithfully. I thought it important to give him the best opinions I could develop, regardless of where they might lead; he was entitled to this. Nonetheless, it was with trepidation concerning his reaction that I undertook to review the study with him.

Howard spent hours on the telephone with me discussing my report in detail. His questions and comments were penetrating and on target. He wanted to know the facts and the reasons for judgmental conclusions. We discussed pros and cons. In the end, he seemed satisfied with my conclusions and did not challenge or reject them.

Later, when the HK-1 consisted mostly of subassemblies, Howard took three hours one afternoon to personally conduct me on a tour of the Culver City facility. Seeing was not believing. The size of the skeleton components was nearly overwhelming. For example, each aileron exceeded 70 feet in length and was about 5 feet thick. The wing-mounted floats, which appear quite small in photographs, were over 23 feet long and 7 feet deep. The wing sections looked like huge building trusses. Everything was immense. Howard exuded personal pride in all aspects of the design during our leisurely tour.

The last time I visited the HK-1 with Howard was early in 1946, shortly before it was moved to Long Beach Harbor. All major assemblies were complete and ready for final assembly at Long Beach. Howard and I climbed through the hull, which on the inside looked something like an ancient frigate, and spent time on the flight deck, where he described the complex control system and problems associated with managing eight engines. All surfaces exposed to the airstream were absolutely smooth, much more so than if the plane had been constructed of aluminum. When completely sheathed, the plane, while still enormous, looked smaller than it did in skeleton form. Howard seemed eager to get on with the job of flying the monster.

The HK-1 was a product of the Hughes Aircraft Division of Toolco, which should not be confused with the Hughes Aircraft Company. The Aircraft Division, after unsuccessful efforts to land major military contracts for the production of fighter and photoreconnaissance planes, developed and manufactured helicopters. Later, after it emerged as a major helicopter manufacturer and the name had been changed to Hughes Helicopters, the Aircraft Division was sold to the McDonnell Douglas Corporation and moved from Culver City to Mesa, Arizona. The Hughes Aircraft Company concentrated initially on the development of electronic units and integrated systems for the military and later expanded into the satellite design field. This enormously successful undertaking was sold during the 1980s to General Motors.

I had little to do with either company and then only on Hughes's instigation. Similarly, the executives and engineers of those companies had virtually nothing to do with TWA except for the peripheral involvement of some Aircraft Division experts in Howard's several plans to manufacture jet transports for TWA and other airlines, as discussed later. They did not, however, participate in any of our analyses of the suitability of proposed transports for TWA's use or in negotiations with the manufacturers for the development and procurement of the aircraft. That was not their responsibility; it was mine. Besides, TWA, not the Aircraft Division or Hughes Aircraft, had the years of accumulated operating experience so important in the design of the new transports and fully understood the dynamic airline competition situation. Howard was content to leave this as my personal responsibility.

Franklin Parties

My association with TWA might have been nipped in the bud except for the good humor and indulgence of Jack Franklin. Not long after joining TWA, Franklin invited engineering department personnel to a late Friday afternoon party at his home. I was late because of a telephone conversation with Hughes. Mrs. Franklin, who was most gracious, escorted me to the large living room, where everyone was seated. I sat in the only open chair in the room, a plain, straight-back polished piece. When an especially funny story was told, I reared back in laughter. To my horror, the chair broke into a dozen pieces, and I unceremoniously fell into the mess. The room became deathly still. I guess everyone in the room except me understood that the chair I had just broken was Mrs. Franklin's favorite antique. I apologized profusely and offered to repair the chair. I was quite good at woodworking, but, of course, Mrs. Franklin had no way of knowing that. She was stiffly polite and refused to even let me touch the pieces. She would not let me pay for it, or anything else. It was clearly an awkwardly closed subject.

Right after the chair was broken, the party moved outside, probably to preserve the rest of the house from Rummel. The chair may have had nothing to do with it, but that was the last time I ever knew of the Franklins' having the engineering personnel in for a party.

About six months later, however, the Franklins had an evening party at their home for TWA executives and their spouses. Margie and I were invited. She was pregnant and large with child. This was our first big TWA party, and it presented a good opportunity to become better acquainted with top Kansas City executives.

The Franklin home was unusual. It consisted of eight levels hugging a knoll. The party was held in the playroom, on the lowest level, at the bottom of an unusually long flight of stairs. The house was immaculate, and the floors were highly polished.

Margie started down the stairs in front of me. The floor was slippery. I started down and fell with my legs straddling hers. She fell, landing on me. I bounced all the way down with Margie on my lap. We gained considerable speed and slid halfway across the playroom in that position. What an entrance for our first big party!

The room was almost filled with executives and their wives. We were lucky not to collide with them. At first they had a look of surprise and amusement, which changed to concern when they noted Margie's condition. When I saw she appeared to be okay, my concern changed to embarrassment. Fortunately, the ride downstairs did not hurt Margie or the baby. But for a while, I wondered if my all-too-frequent mishaps would put an irreversible damper of my career at TWA.

Route Planning

Soon after I joined TWA, I became aware of Hughes's and Frye's interest in acquiring routes to Europe. TWA had been flying the Atlantic under ATC contracts for some time and was well poised to undertake early postwar commercial operations.

Around mid-1943 Jack Franklin said Jack Frye wanted me to meet him in his Washington office ''to discuss airplanes and routes.'' I had had a number of fairly lengthy phone conversations with Frye earlier, during which we discussed airplane design and performance, but had not yet met him personally. I enthusiastically looked forward to the meeting. I thought Jack Frye was a true aviation pioneer and an inspired, visionary leader who knew the score. Everyone I had met in TWA respected and admired him. When I started calling him "Mr. Frye," he said, "Bob, call me 'Jack,' like everyone else." He was a very considerate person and extremely easy to talk to. As the years passed during the period of Hughes's dominance of TWA affairs, a long succession of presidents was elected after Frye was forced out. Comparing him to them, I was to learn how truly great were Frye's contributions to the success and growth of the company. TWA had other good presidents, but none so innovative and hardly any so well liked.

In addition to Jack Frye and me, R. E. ("Bob") Lees and George A. Spater were present for the meeting. Lees was director of TWA's Economic Division and Frye's executive assistant for route development. Spater, a man with whom I would work closely on numbers of secret Hughes projects and who would one day become president of AAL, was TWA's chief outside counsel. The purpose of the meeting was to develop specific route objectives for TWA's prospective international operations and discuss route acquisition strategy. I was there to advise on aircraft operational capabilities and gain a better understanding of future fleet requirements.

Maps were spread on the floor so all could see. Jack Frye and the rest of us were soon on our hands and knees pouring over them. After the geographic areas to be served were identified, discussion centered on the nature of TWA's route applications. The principal service targets were the primary capitals of Europe, but Cairo and areas beyond were also discussed.

It was exhilarating to be involved in the planning stages of such an ambitious and pioneering venture. At that time, TWA's commercial services were being flown by only 28 Douglas DC-3's—a far cry from the extensive international operations foreseen in Frye's office. This, only one of many preparatory meetings that would eventually enable TWA to establish itself as a major international carrier, convinced me that I had joined the right company.

Note

1. The proposed DC-7 should not be confused with the smaller DC-7, produced in quantity beginning in late 1953.

6.
The First
"Connies"

How a Great Opportunity Was Lost

The TWA Constellation project was substantially on hold when I joined TWA in June 1943 pending the outcome of the war and resolution of when Lockheed could produce commercial planes. Hughes had retained rights to the 40 Constellations. When they might become available and whether they would be converted C-69's, new production planes, or both, was not known. Consequently, little work had been done at TWA to update contract specifications because of lack of program definition.

Lockheed correctly believed that the airlines were seriously short of flight equipment and that a large transport market would develop soon after the war. It was anxious to capitalize on the strong performance advantage of the Constellation and capture a major share of the market.

During the fall of 1944, it appeared that victory in Europe was imminent. While Lockheed's production capacity remained totally filled, it was keenly aware that when the war effort wound down the inevitable result would be sharp contract cuts and large-scale layoffs. Lockheed was not sure how well it would cope with this situation. It did not help to know that other manufacturers, including its chief commercial rival, Douglas, would face the same situation. The possibility of realizing a strong commercial Constellation program became a bright, shining star on Lockheed's horizon, worth every bit of nurturing the company could muster.

Lockheed needed numbers of critically important questions resolved to develop a firm commercial program for the postwar period. For example: Would the Army continue C-69 production after the war, and, if so, at what rate and for how long? When would Lockheed be released to undertake the detailed engineering necessary to develop a new postwar model or adapt the C-69 for commercial service? (The Army made changes to the C-69's that were not applicable to commercial services and required deletion. Further, new interiors, updated communication and navigation equipment installations, and numbers of other changes needed to be engineered and installed.) Would C-69's be declared war surplus, and, if so, when and at what price? When and under what cost formulae would military-owned facilities, jigs, and fixtures become available for commercial production? And, of course, when would Roosevelt's "unconditional surrender" goal be achieved?

Lockheed was also concerned whether Douglas might gain an advantage by receiving permission from the government to reenter the commercial business first. The DC-4, even though unpressurized, would compete for available airline dollars, and the pressurized DC-6, which was in early development (UAL ordered a fleet of DC-6's on September 11, 1944), gave promise of being a strong postwar competitive threat that could cost significant lead time advantage. If Douglas were to be released to manufacture commercial transports before Lockheed, Lockheed's situation could become even more difficult, and its decisions concerning the extent to which the Constellation would be further developed for the postwar market would be seriously affected.

Resolution of Lockheed's postwar Constellation program was of critical importance to both Lockheed and TWA, and it could not be expedited. Everything depended on the course of the war and military program decisions beyond the control of either party.

Shortly after joining TWA, I calculated the payload-range capability of the Constellation based on the latest information. To my horror, the plane could not even come close to complying with contract requirements. It was short by hundreds of miles! Substantial reductions in payload, or alternately, shorter flights, which would destroy planned schedules and nullify much of the Constellation's speed advantage, would be required. Both courses were completely unacceptable. The most plausible solution was for Lockheed to increase the airplane's permissible operating weight a commensurate amount.

This surprising news reverberated through the executive offices at TWA, with the result that Jack Franklin and I flew overnight from Kansas City to Burbank to discuss the problem with Hall Hibbard, Kelly Johnson, and M. Carl Haddon, the Constellation project engineer. It was daylight when Jack and I approached the Burbank Airport. However, it and the Lockheed factories were not to be seen because of camouflage. The streets and rooftops had been painted to make them look like part of the countryside. Chicken wire supported on tall poles had been stretched over low rooftops, parking lots, and other areas that might otherwise fix position for incoming enemy flights. The chicken-wire grid was covered with chicken feathers dyed in various colors to continue the overall pattern. It was effective. Even experienced airline pilots sometimes had difficulty in spotting runways.

Jack and I met Hall, Kelly, and Carl in a conference room in the engineering building. I had heard some of Kelly Johnson's arguments when I worked at Lockheed, and, even though the problem and design solution seemed beyond reasonable challenge, I knew that I should know any subject argued with Kelly inside out, upside down, and every other way if I were to prevail. I came armed with data and all the arguments I could think of.

To my surprise, when Jack expressed TWA's great concern over the deterioration in payload-range, Hall indicated that Lockheed had recently recognized the severity of the problem and planned to increase the maximum takeoff weight from 75,000 to 86,000 pounds, along with a proportionate increase in landing weight. My estimates confirmed the sufficiency of the weight increases, so I did not get to use my carefully prepared arguments. Excess power available from the four Wright 3350 engines permitted the weight increase without significant impairment of airplane performance. This change was the first of several yet to come, confirming the wisdom of Johnson's and Tomlinson's insistence on installation of the 3350's rather than the R-2600's during initial contract negotiations.

This was my first meeting with Lockheed as a TWA employee. It was pleasant and enjoyable. Jack and I had lunch in Lockheed's executive dining room, on the second floor of the old Burbank Air Terminal, where Bob Gross and his brother, Courtland E. Gross, joined the group. We briefly discussed Lockheed's postwar transport production plans, but, while Lockheed was outgoing, the many unresolved issues had prevented formation of specific programs. Notwithstanding, Hall urged that preliminary specification conferences be undertaken as soon as feasible to explore current airline requirements and help determine what Lockheed should build for the early postwar era.

A number of preliminary specification review meetings were held in Burbank following the Lockheed luncheon, including an early October 1944 meeting with Hall and several members of his staff, including Charles Thomas and William Beck. Our objective was to agree on design objectives for Lockheed's postwar Constellations and finalize plans for developing procurement specifications. Progress of the war in Europe indicated that new specifications would probably be needed by year's end.

Hall Hibbard noted that eventually three different specifications would probably be required: definition of the first "Connies" to be manufactured following the war; definition of a "gold-plated" model, which would embody the state-of-the-art improvements to counter Douglas DC-6 competition; and definition of a dream job Hibbard defined as the "ultimate" Constellation, either turboprop or jet powered, which could be either a glorified Connie or an airplane with entirely new lines. It was obvious that work on the dream job would be a waste of time. More urgent work, definition of early postwar Constellations, was at hand.

Hughes and Frye were anxious to obtain Constellations at the earliest feasible time, a viewpoint I enthusiastically shared. We recognized that in all probability the first planes would be either converted C-69's or brand new Commercial C-69's configured for airline services, manufactured as an efficient continuation of the C-69 production line.

I wanted such planes configured to eliminate troublesome problems encountered in ATC services and equipped with much more adequate cabin ventilation systems; new commercial interiors; and the latest navigation, instrumentation, and other system improvements needed to assure good operations. They would have to be certified for takeoff operations at no less than 86,000 pounds to ensure adequate range. Early deliveries were important, but I considered it more important to be able to demonstrate safe, reliable operations from the outset.

We saw Hibbard's "gold-plated" objective as an opportunity to press

Lockheed into developing an improved model for early postwar implementation. We believed such a design was needed to preserve and expand TWA's anticipated competitive advantage and substantially nullify anything Douglas could produce. This was especially important because Douglas had committed the bulk of its early production to TWA's arch rivals, UAL and AAL. We saw the gold-plated model as potentially the most luxurious, longest-range, best-performing plane in the skies and undertook with gusto to persuade Lockheed to develop it for early postwar production. Hall enthusiastically agreed to a joint specification development effort targeted toward early program implementation.

This was my first serious transport specification development activity. The Rearwin Cloudster and Skyranger models I had designed earlier— modern, well-performing planes with attractive upholstered interiors— were second to none in the light-plane business. By comparison, however, the Constellation, with its highly complicated systems, cabin pressurization, advanced instrumentation and power systems, and sheer enormity was a different world: an extremely demanding but exciting challenge. My own intuition and the good help of my proficient staff and experts from TWA's operating and marketing departments bridged the gap.

Lockheed called the gold-plated model the "Postwar 049." It was to be powered with much-improved, more powerful Wright 3350 engines; have vastly improved cabin air-conditioning, a plush interior with berths, and state-of-the-art design improvements throughout; and be capable of operating at a maximum weight of 100,000 pounds. There was no doubt that the plane we envisioned could be preeminent for years to come and give TWA the best possible operational and competitive advantages.

Our objective was to acquire a minimum number of Commercial C-69's—just enough to tide TWA over until the Postwar 049 could be produced—and a maximum number of Postwar 049's. Lockheed assigned all the engineering personnel it could muster under stringent wartime restrictions and proceeded with the preliminary design of both models to be prepared to act quickly and decisively as soon as war conditions permitted.

About the time our specification activities were well under way, on November 14, 1944, TWA and Lockheed, because of war exigencies, executed the special Conditional Purchase Commitment for 10 Constellations, constructed so as not to prejudice earlier delivery commitments. It was not known at that time whether the planes, the first to be delivered following the war, would be 86,000-pound Commercial C-69's, or

100,000-pound model Postwar 049's, or something in between. The agreement required Lockheed to notify TWA of price and delivery dates on or before December 31, 1944, in anticipation that a definitive contract would be executed before January 31, 1945. The time between receipt of government clearances and execution of the Conditional Purchase Commitment was to be used to reach final agreement on design changes, procurement specifications, and definitive contracts. On November 14, Lockheed expected to receive momentarily the necessary engineering and production releases from the government to engineer and manufacture commercial Constellations.

Definition of the Lockheed programs required correlating government release and airplane delivery dates. The longer the period between the government engineering release date and the production release date, the closer the features of the 86,000-pound version could match those projected for the 100,000-pound version. Only after the production release was obtained could Lockheed finally determine delivery dates, the detailed configuration of the aircraft to be manufactured in compliance therewith, and the purchase price.

To put this differently, if TWA agreed on a definitive specification and contract that contemplated airplane deliveries within a specified time and events transpired that moved the deliveries to later dates, TWA would have prejudiced its position by inadvertently closing out improvements that could have been made available. Thus, we could not close out specifications until the deliveries and purchase price were known; and Lockheed could not set a final price until the specification had been agreed to, nor could delivery dates be established until government releases had been obtained. The releases were not in fact obtained until substantially later, shortly after Japan accepted the Allies' Terms of Armistice on August 14, 1945.

While Lockheed saw the Constellation as a great star of opportunity, it remained acutely concerned with the stifling effect Howard Hughes's monopoly could have on its ability to capture a reasonable portion of the postwar market. It feared that by the time TWA's planes were produced, Douglas probably would acquire the lion's share, possibly reducing Lockheed's potential market volume to a level of questionable profitability. From Lockheed's point of view, ways *had* to be found to enable the timely delivery of Constellations to airlines other than TWA and PAA. As far as

Hughes was concerned, his 40-plane requirement was sacrosanct and non-negotiable.

During 1944, Bob Gross made numerous overtures to Hughes and TWA seeking contractual relief so Lockheed could sell early production Connies to other airlines. When this was refused, Lockheed adopted a disinterested, lackadaisical attitude toward the entire program, possibly because it became convinced that no substantial profit possibility existed under the circumstances. I thought Lockheed's position was mostly a hollow negotiating stance taken to improve its bargaining position, but one not entirely without merit. Even so, I was surprised when Lee Talman suggested TWA give serious consideration to recommending that the 40-plane stipulation be relaxed.

Lee wrote an interoffice memo to Jack Frye that stated in part: "Our position at Lockheed would be immediately strengthened, and we could get a better airplane more cheaply and more quickly, if we relaxed the (restrictive) provision to permit Lockheed to sell to anyone other than American and United. . . . The development of the DC-6 by Douglas, even though it does not appear to be as good an airplane as the Constellation, has discounted by a sizable percentage the competitive advantage which the provision originally gave us." In making this suggestion, Lee only recognized the changing realities of the market. Even so, the idea of giving up significant delivery advantages was disappointing and remained a subject of hot internal debate for months.

In the end, Lockheed won the relief it sought, primarily because of changed circumstances wrought by the war, and because a strong Constellation program was believed to be to TWA's best interest. As it worked out, TWA got nothing in return for surrendering its preferred position.

Continuing Negotiations

During the months following the Conditional Purchase Commitment, TWA and Lockheed continued to develop specification and definitive purchase agreements so the program could move forward expeditiously as soon as Lockheed obtained implementation permission from the government. Harry L. West, TWA's astute outside counsel, who specialized in aircraft procurement matters, and I were the primary negotiators for Hughes and TWA. Roger Smith, chief counsel for Lockheed, was an objective, entirely professional lawyer who repeatedly demonstrated a pleasant mastery for finding equitable solutions for difficult negotiating impasses. Leonard K. Schwartz, sales manager; and P. K. ("Kirk") Yost, Jr., a young, bright-eyed, enthusiastic salesman, were the other principal members of Lockheed's contract team. Hall Hibbard, Kelly Johnson, and Carl Haddon handled Lockheed's engineering negotiations.

Leonard Schwartz had direct responsibility for negotiating the contract. A bright, dapper, socially pleasant young executive, he was sometimes exasperating during negotiations. He had the extremely annoying habit of opening nearly every negotiating session with words to the effect, "I just talked to Howard and *here is your position.*" He would explain at length what he thought our position was on delivery, price, and any other key matter under consideration, as if we were completely uninformed. Then he would recite Lockheed's position in great detail, always being careful to explain that he had just discussed all this with Howard.

Harry and I were both in touch with Howard, and others as appropriate; we understood the Hughes-TWA objectives; we had authority to negotiate. Leonard's attempts to place us in the third balcony rather than in the front row of negotiations was not well received. Sometimes Leonard was well on the mark, and sometimes not. He did not realize the extent of, or chose to ignore, our close liaison with Hughes. I did not think he was being intentionally contumelious or malevolent, but his approach made negotiations awkward and difficult.

The majority of our efforts centered on the Postwar 049, however, the Commercial C-69 received its share of attention. Detail specifications and definitive contract work was completed for both models to the maximum extent that Lockheed's circumstances permitted.

Lockheed Engineering was beautifully cooperative. Hibbard, Johnson, and Haddon welcomed and agreed to the vast majority of TWA's requirements for both models. However, to assure early availability of the Commercial C-69's, TWA's design change requests were kept to a minimum compatible with safety and commercial acceptability. Even so, hundreds of design changes were advanced. It was a satisfying negotiation, despite Schwartz's irritating attitude.

Lockheed continued to enthusiastically embrace the Postwar 049 program and, like Hughes, Frye, and myself, looked forward to early program implementation. While final commitments had to wait on resolution of the war, Lockheed planned to implement this project at the earliest possible moment. Lockheed even found time to construct in a draped-off corner of the factory engineering mockups of the Postwar 049 power plant, cockpit, and passenger interior for TWA's acceptance so detail engineering could proceed apace after final project approval.

The majority of TWA's senior management attended the formal interior mockup approval meeting. Howard elected to inspect the mockup privately during late-night hours. The plush interior was beautifully represented. It looked like the real thing with finished seats, upholstery, carpets, working berths, and replica galleys. A first-rate job.

All went well except for the seats. Everything was wrong with them. No foot room existed under the seats, as if a wall had been erected; seat backs were high and thick, restricting knee room and making entrance difficult; the bottom cushions were so far from the floor that most women's feet could not touch the carpets; the arm rests were excessively high, causing shoulder discomfort; and the cushions were almost as hard as boards.

TWA's seat specification and our vendor liaison might just as well not have existed. The specification, which I had developed, strongly emphasized the need for ample shin and foot room, ease of access, and comfort— all of the things that were missing. I had relied on my engineers to work with the vendors to achieve the stated objectives, rather than taking time to personally inspect the seats ahead of time. The seats were a great embarrassment to me and my department, and we should have destroyed the monsters before the formal management approval meeting. I did not cause any heads to roll because I, too, was at fault, but we were never again caught by inadequate liaison and follow-through activities.

The Hiroshima and Nagasaki bombs closed the Pacific war much sooner than anticipated. Within days, the military sent contract cancellation notices to Lockheed and other war materiel manufacturers. By then, specifications and contracts for the Commercial C-69 and the Postwar 049 were virtually complete. All that remained was to close out a number of pending design changes requested by TWA, finalize a few equipment selections, and resolve airplane delivery schedules and purchase prices.

Plain Vanilla

Within one week after Japan accepted terms of armistice on August 14, 1945, Hall Hibbard urgently requested a meeting with Jack Franklin and me. Jack and I flew to Burbank the next day, expecting to receive proposals concerning resolution of the open contractual items and Lockheed's aircraft production schedules.

Hall opened the meeting with a bombshell. He advised that because of recent developments, Lockheed's senior management had "agonizingly reappraised" its postwar manufacturing plans. He explained that Lockheed could buy back government surplus tooling, parts, materiel, and five nearly completed C-69's, and continue the C-69 production line for the airlines with minimal disruption and expense. He said that Lockheed had taken a new look at the heavy expenditures and time required to engineer and produce the Postwar 049, and had "decided to cancel this project."

While I was still in a state of shock over hearing this, Hall explained that Lockheed had expected to be cleared to engineer the postwar model during the closing months of the war and to produce it much sooner than now appeared possible because the war had ended so abruptly. He said that Lockheed still planned to produce an improved model "some day" and repeated that this was "not in the cards for now." Hall went on to say that in the meantime, Lockheed would offer "plain vanilla" C-69's, which he called 049's—the original designation—with commercial interiors. In addition, if airline interest warranted, it would modify military C-69's if they became available.

Lockheed's cancellation of the Postwar 049 project was a bitter disappointment. Instead of obtaining a minimum quantity of Commercial C-69's and the maximum number of the greatly improved postwar model, as Hughes, Frye, and I wanted, it appeared that only C-69's would be available for an indefinite period.

Making matters worse, during the ensuing conversation Lockheed advised it intended to produce new C-69's for TWA and the commercial market exactly as they were being produced for the military, except for deletion of military navigation and communication equipment and the installation of minimal passenger interiors. Almost none of the carefully negotiated Commercial C-69 operational and maintenance improvements Lockheed had agreed to accomplish were to be incorporated, despite the critical needs evidenced by C-69 operations.

After further discussion, Hall conceded that Lockheed would "try" to incorporate "a few" improvements in the 049's if this could be done without impairing production, but he warned that extensive modifications such as improving the submarginal ventilation system were out. Further, the interior accommodations were to consist of only bare essentials, which

I knew would be far inferior to those of competitive DC-6's. Hall "regretted" these developments but considered it best for all parties, because Lockheed could produce Constellations more quickly this way than if any other course were followed.

Jack and I understood the compelling circumstances that faced Lockheed, but that did not make the news any more palatable. Howard Hughes, Jack Frye, and the Equipment Committee were immediately notified of this unsatisfactory development. At this point, the DC-6 looked better than ever before, but TWA could not afford to wait. Besides, Hughes and Frye were in bed with the Constellation.

The words that kept ringing in my ears were, "decided to cancel this project," "not in the cards for now," and "plain vanilla." I am afraid my disappointment and frustration over this development were not well hidden. We needed planes, but we did not need "plain vanilla." We needed good functional reliability, good operational economy, and good acceptance by the flight crews and flying public—factors that earlier negotiations had properly addressed, but which now appeared to be beyond reasonable reach.

Procurement of Civil C-69's

Shortly after Hall Hibbard's recital concerning Lockheed's reappraisal of its commercial program, TWA commenced negotiations with Lockheed for the conversion of military C-69's and acquisition of new production 049's. When the time for finalizing the C-69 conversion contract was close at hand, I met at the Hollywood Knickerbocker Hotel with Jack Franklin; Harry West; Ralph Ellinger; Robert C. Loomis, a crack TWA engineering pilot; and F. L. ("Lee") Spruill, TWA's factory representative at Lockheed. The purpose was to review the final draft specification and agree on a list of "Lockheed must do" predelivery modifications for consideration during a TWA senior management meeting scheduled later that day.

As Hibbard warned would be the case, the majority of TWA's improvement requests had been refused, except for urgent safety items, to maintain production with the least possible interruption. The group had little sympathy for Lockheed's position and recognized that many of the refused items would have to be accomplished, if not by Lockheed before delivery, then by TWA after delivery. Because of their reputations, I had hoped that when the chips were down Hall Hibbard and Kelly Johnson would convince Lockheed's senior management to alter its restrictive policy against making improvements. I do not know if they tried, but if they did, they certainly did not succeed.

Jack Franklin and I were anxious to obtain the support of TWA's senior management for making the purchase of the airplanes contingent on Lockheed's agreement to accomplish our "Lockheed must do" list. We doubted that Lockheed would budge very much but thought this was the only tactic left. We also thought it important to apprise senior management of the significant operational penalties that would inevitably result from not having the improvements, as well as the need for supplemental budgets to accomplish the changes after delivery in the event Lockheed continued to refuse our demands.

The Knickerbocker meeting started at 7:30 A.M. after a quick breakfast and continued to nearly 1:00 P.M. After nearly five and a half uninterrupted hours of developing consensus estimates of costs, flight delays, and passenger dissatisfactions that would likely arise during routine operations, I was overdue for a break. However, due to the press of time, we grabbed some candy bars and drove to the Beverly Hills Hotel for the meeting with senior management.

Lee Talman, John Collings, John Lockhart, and several others were waiting in Howard's hotel bungalow when we arrived. Jack Franklin opened the meeting by briefly reviewing the history of our technical negotiations, Lockheed's repeated refusals to accomplish the needed improvements, and the reasons therefor. He presented our rough estimates of incremental costs required to correct the problems and discussed the adverse impact the lack of Lockheed corrective actions would have on flight schedule reliability and operating costs. He urged management's support for one further effort to prevail at Lockheed and cautioned that if the deal moved forward as presently constituted, management should be prepared to receive sizable funding requests for post-delivery modifications. He made clear that under no circumstances would TWA accept anything believed to be unsafe. Safety was not the issue.

Jack then requested me to review our "Lockheed must do" list of design shortcomings. Examples of improvements demanded of Lockheed included control-wheel-actuated nose wheel steering, a redesigned flight deck pedestal to permit the captain to have full control of the engines (this duty had been assigned by design to the flight engineer), revised instrument arrangements, improved brakes, an engine-fire detection system far less apt to produce false warnings, resealed integral fuel tanks, a vastly improved cabin ventilating system, upgraded passenger accommodations, and numerous maintenance improvements. Even though tempered by our pressing need for aircraft and Lockheed's negotiating stance, our list was quite long. However, it reflected only the most compelling needs.

When I finished my review, Harry West reviewed open contractual items. Jack then concluded the presentation by again urging management's support for one further grand-slam effort to prevail at Lockheed before final procurement recommendations were decided and passed to Frye and Hughes for approval.

After lengthy discussion, senior management concluded that the penalties to be incurred from deferring or foregoing deliveries would outweigh the penalties that would be experienced because of the shortcomings. However, management agreed that one further effort should be made to convince Lockheed to incorporate the needed improvements or provide TWA with engineering and modification kits required for postdelivery installations.

This effort was made. Lockheed acceded to a few items, but the remainder of our "Lockheed must do" list took on a new, urgent meaning. It became a "TWA must do after delivery" list. Many changes were accomplished after delivery, but some of the most important, such as improved nose wheel steering and acceptable cabin ventilation, took years to implement. A few days after negotiations with Lockheed had been concluded and TWA management had provided Jack Frye with a final procurement recommendation, a contract was executed for a fleet of converted C-69's and new production 049's.

Lockheed was in the driver's seat throughout this negotiation. Our negotiating muscle was weak because of lack of acceptable alternatives and because of Hughes's and Frye's well-publicized association with the program, which placed us strongly in the Lockheed camp. And, despite their shortcomings, the Constellations were the best available planes for TWA, and Lockheed knew it.

In sharp contrast with his activities during the Postwar 049 negotiations, Howard Hughes did not participate in the technical aspects of the C-69 and 049 negotiations. He reviewed airplane delivery schedules with Harry West and me, but, except for final contract clearance, which Frye obtained, he adopted a detached, behind-the-scenes posture in all other respects. This recondite behavior was unwelcome and mystifying, but, as I learned, it would be repeated at unpredictable intervals in the future.

In lieu of TWA's initial intention of acquiring only a few C-69's until postwar Constellations could be produced, it finally acquired 39 C-69's and 049's, including the 10 planes committed November 14, 1944, but excluding an additional order for 18 049's, which was later converted to a succeeding model.

By November 1945, Lockheed had sold an aggregate of 89 049 Constellations to TWA, PAA, American Overseas Airlines, Panagra, KLM, and Air France. Lockheed's sales strategy was successful, and, except for the competitive threat of the Douglas DC-6, production of the 049's might have continued, despite unrelenting efforts by Hughes and me to persuade Lockheed to expedite the development of a true postwar model.

Early in 1946 Hughes telephoned me to advise that Lockheed had decided to move forward with development of the Model 649 Constellation, a true postwar model designed specifically for the commercial market—a market that would otherwise soon be dominated by the DC-6. He said Lockheed was sending specifications and a draft contract based on our Postwar 049 negotiations, and he requested early review toward commencing active negotiations.

The 649 was to be powered by more powerful Wright 3350 engines (2,500 hp versus 2,200 hp for takeoff) equipped with forged rather than cast cylinder heads, strengthened case, and other miscellaneous improvements. The plane was to have an entirely new, superior air-conditioning system, a plush interior, a revised flight deck, increased operating weights, and other changes TWA had requested during earlier negotiations. The 649 looked like a really fine, if overdue, model. Negotiations quickly culminated in TWA's converting its order for 18 049's, placed September 14, 1945, to 18 Model 649's.

Dinner with Bob Gross

During one of the times when negotiations with Lockheed became a bit sticky, Howard Hughes, Harry West, and I were invited to Bob Gross's Bel Air home for dinner. Courtland Gross, Hall Hibbard, Leonard Schwartz, and Kirk Yost were with Bob when Harry and I arrived. Howard, contrary to his general reputation, was nearly on time. The occasion was pleasant in all respects, except for a brief incident that occurred during the close of the cocktail hour.

Howard decided to use the phone in Bob's library, where we were talking. We all moved away so as not to hear or disturb him. After a few minutes, a visibly agitated Howard stopped talking and turned away from the phone. An embarrassed Courtland Gross rushed into the room exclaiming excitedly, "Howard, I wasn't listening. I wasn't listening. Honest! I was just going to make a call. I didn't know you were on the line. I'm so sorry. Please forgive . . . ."

This got everyone's attention. Courtland thought he had interrupted an important business call and that Howard thought he had been eavesdropping. Howard only grunted, mumbled something indistinguishable, and turned again to the telephone, saying, "Sorry, Honey, I was interrupted. Something has come up, and I won't be able to have dinner with you tonight. Will call you later. Bye, bye."

Or, I wondered, was this a quickly devised cover?

DC-6 Intrigue

During routine negotiations at Lockheed, I had the pleasure of introducing Jack Franklin to Howard. I was surprised when Jack casually indicated they had never met because I knew of Jack's involvement years before in the Constellation program-initiating conferences. Jack and I were in Ralph Ellinger's office in the Burbank Air Terminal, across the street from the Lockheed corporate offices. We had just freshened up after an all-night flight from Kansas City for a meeting with Hall Hibbard when Howard called me.

Howard explained that Nat Paschall, Douglas's vice president of sales; Jackson R. McGowen, the project engineer who would one day be president of Douglas; and J. O. ("Jake") Moxness, a well-known Douglas pilot and salesman, would bring the prototype DC-6 over for a flight demonstration. "Can you meet me in the Burbank terminal at Gate 5 at 12 o'clock sharp?" he asked.

I said, "Yes, Howard, I certainly can. Incidentally, Jack Franklin is with me and would like to meet you. Would it be all right to bring him along?"

"Who?"

"Jack Franklin, TWA's vice president of engineering—my TWA boss."

Howard exclaimed, "Oh! Yes, great! By all means bring him along. The more interest we show, the better. See you at 12."

Howard did not have a reputation for being on time, but Jack and I decided to be prompt, just in case. We showed up at Gate 5 exactly at 12 o'clock to see Howard approaching. Jack was a natty dresser, his necktie always carefully placed in the center, a carefully folded matching kerchief in his upper coat pocket, and every hair exactly in place. This time was no exception. I greeted Howard and said, "Howard, this is Jack Franklin. Jack, this is Howard Hughes."

Jack bowed politely from the waist, extended his hand, and said he was glad to meet him. Howard responded by extending his hand palm up, saying, "Jack, can you let me have a nickel? I want to make a phone call." Jack chuckled barely audibly, reached into his pocket, and said, "Here, Howard, have two." Howard took them and made a quick call in a nearby telephone booth.

The DC-6 arrived at Gate 5 a few minutes later. Gate 5 was immediately under the Lockheed executive dining room, which was on the second floor of the terminal, adjacent to a public restaurant. The Gross brothers, Hall Hibbard, Kelly Johnson, and other top executives usually convened at noon for lunch and palaver at a large round table by a picture window overlooking the gate.

It did not take long to figure out why Howard had selected Gate 5. Hughes waited near the gate, causing the Douglas men to approach and greet us in plain view of the dining room. After talking briefly, we inspected the exterior of the plane, always remaining between the plane and the picture window. This feature and that feature were pointed out and discussed. After about 30 minutes, we boarded the plane for the demonstration flight.

The takeoff, toward the terminal, was spectacular. It was also uncomfortable. Moxness flew with Howard in the first officer's seat. The airplane was lightly loaded. The takeoff climb appeared to be near the ragged edge of a stall at the highest possible angle of climb. I thought that if the Lockheed observers were as impressed with the performance of the DC-6 as I was, they would probably sharpen their negotiating pencils.

I expected and looked forward to a one- or two-hour demonstration flight, but instead, we flew directly across town to Clover Field and landed by the Douglas factory. One of Howard's Chevrolets was waiting by the plane. After we disembarked, Howard drove most of the group to a local country club for a late Douglas luncheon. He spent most of the luncheon period in a telephone booth, then drove the group back to the Douglas plant. On the way, he talked Nat Paschall out of a free tank of aviation gas for the Chevrolet.

Competitive face-offs between manufacturers were encouraged and normal in our negotiations, a circumstance that usually helped win our objectives. For example, the Lockheed Model 049 competed with the Douglas DC-4; the 649 with the DC-6; the 749, 749A, and 1049 with the DC-6B; the 1049G with the DC-7 and DC-7B; and finally, the Lockheed Model 1649A with the Douglas DC-7C. The DC-6 "demonstration flight" did in fact liven our 649 negotiations.

Inaugurals and Problems

The unequaled speed and "above-weather" comfort of TWA's Constellations were instantly popular with the flying public. The contrast of the high-speed, pressurized Constellation flights with lesser transports, which slogged through rough air strata thousands of feet below, placed TWA for a time in an extremely strong competitive position.

Jack Frye's efforts to acquire international routes for TWA had succeeded. Promotional and inaugural flights to introduce Constellation services in TWA's international and domestic divisions quickly followed delivery of the first Model 049 on November 14, 1945. Ten Constellations were delivered to TWA by year's end.

The first major promotion, a gala, New York-Paris round-trip flight, began on December 3, 1945. Red carpets were laid out all over the city to welcome TWA's honored guests during several days of festivities held in anticipation of the inauguration of scheduled services, flown in the *Star of Paris* by Capt. Hall Blackburn, February 5, 1946. TWA inaugurated the first U.S. airline service to Italy with great fanfare on April 2 and promptly extended the route to Cairo.

Howard Hughes flew the domestic inaugural in the *Star of California,* February 15, 1946, between Los Angeles and New York. Howard's 35 passengers included many top Hollywood celebrities, including Linda Darnell; Paulette Goddard; Cary Grant; Veronica Lake; Myrna Loy; Frank Morgan; Walter Pidgeon; William Powell; Tyrone Power and his wife, Anabella; Edward G. Robinson; Randolph Scott; David O. Selznick; and Gene Tierney. The press and two newsreels, *Fox Movietone* and *Para-*

mount News, recorded the departure and lauded the ahead-of-schedule arrival. The press compared Howard's 8-hour, 38-minute flight time with the 13 or 14 hours required for UAL's and AAL's competitive DC-4's. The national-headline-snatching publicity, just what Howard wanted, helped propel TWA into its deserved position of leadership.

However, the relatively short duration of TWA's exclusive Constellation advantage was a major disappointment. PAA flew its first transatlantic Constellation schedule, New York-Lisbon, January 20, 1946. UAL introduced transcontinental services with the Douglas DC-6, April 27, 1947. AAL began New York-Chicago DC-6 services earlier and was quick to follow UAL into the coast-to-coast market on May 20. Thus, TWA's anticipated competitive advantage was reduced to little more than a year in domestic services and to zero in the United States-Europe market.

Moreover, serious operational problems were encountered almost from the outset. Poor engine reliability, supercharger drive shaft failures, wobbling landing gear, cabin ventilation inadequacy, and extreme fear of engine induction system fires, along with the many items Lockheed refused to fix during negotiations, produced what I thought was considerably more than a fair share of new airplane problems.

Fear of engine induction system fires among flight crews and management erupted following the crash of an Air Forces C-69 near Topeka, Kansas, September 1945, after the outboard right engine caught on fire, could not be extinguished, and dropped off the airplane. While the exact cause had not been determined by the time of TWA's initial Constellation operations, conventional wisdom assumed the culprit to be an engine induction system fire, much like those reported from B-29 operations. Adding to our fears was our belief that induction system fires might ignite the magnesium engine cases. While hard to start, such fires would be impossible to extinguish due to the intense heat. Induction system fires had not been experienced, or at least not identified, during Lockheed's flight test program or during airline operations. Wright contended this was not a problem, but they could not sell the idea.

Two possible causes for such fires were believed to exist: ignition of fuel vapor in the induction system from engine backfires, or the high-speed blower rubbing on the magnesium case, an abnormal condition that tests showed could generate sufficient heat to cause ignition. Wright modified the design to avoid this possibility, and TWA developed precautionary engine operating instructions to minimize the possibility of engine back-fires. These steps alleviated but did not eliminate our concerns.

Shortly after the C-69 Topeka accident, Lockheed undertook an explor-atory flight test program to determine the Constellation's vulnerability to induction system fires and test a new engine fire extinguishing system. The risky flight tests were undertaken by Kelly Johnson; Rudy Thoren, Lock-heed's extremely capable flight test engineer; and Wright's Robert E. Johnson.

Repeated efforts to ignite induction system fires failed. A spark plug was then added to the induction system, and new tests, conducted at all alti-tudes, speeds, and fuel mixtures, again failed. Several loud and extremely disturbing explosions in the induction system were heard; however, no continuing fires or damage occurred. It proved to be impossible for them to set induction system fires, and, of course, the adequacy of the new fire extinguishing system could not be demonstrated.

The Lockheed tests were reassuring but did little to relieve operational concerns. I began to suspect our fears were ungrounded. Suspicions, how-ever, were insufficient; we needed hard facts.

The threat of engine induction system fires was finally removed by installing fuel injection systems. Direct injection systems (fuel injected directly into the engine cylinders) had been tested in a number of B-29's, but they had accumulated little experience when first installed in TWA's Constellations. Nonetheless, the systems operated well. Jack Franklin, recalling this situation over 40 years later, said, "We took every means to minimize the possibility of fires, but I didn't sleep very well during that period."

Only a few months after TWA and PAA inaugurated Connie services the right outboard engine—in the same location as the one that had failed in the Topeka accident—of a PAA Constellation bound for Europe caught on fire, June 18, 1946. It could not be extinguished and dropped off the plane. The PAA crew crash-landed in a grass field near Willimantic, Connecticut. Pending the examination of the wreckage, an induction system fire was assumed to be responsible.

Lockheed immediately dispatched an investigative team to Willimantic headed by Carl Haddon. Haddon's examination of the engine quickly pointed to the supercharger drive shaft as the suspect culprit, but this could not be proved because the shaft was missing. (The cabin supercharger, installed aft of the engine fire wall, was driven by an engine extension shaft.)

Andre Priester of PAA, Bob Johnson of Wright, and Kelly Johnson then searched Connecticut fields under the flight path and fortunately found the shaft. Examination showed that the shaft had failed and wobbled just enough to break the primary hydraulic line fitting at the engine-mounted hydraulic pump. The hydraulic fluid, under pressure, sprayed the engine accessory compartment and ignited. The resulting torch could not be extinguished.

Due to the similarity of the Topeka and Willimantic accidents, Andre Priester ran ads in the Topeka newspapers offering a $100 reward for the return of the C-69 supercharger drive shaft, which had not been found after that accident. After reading the ad, which included a picture of the drive shaft, a Kansas farmer returned it to PAA. He explained that, not knowing what it was, he put the shaft in his barn after finding it in a field. Examination of this shaft proved that the cause of both accidents was the same and had nothing to do with induction system fires.

The quick fix was simply to remove the supercharger and shaft and operate in the unpressurized mode. This solution was unacceptable over the long term because operating speeds and altitudes were severely penalized. Lockheed expeditiously designed for early retrofit a heavy cylindrical protective housing for the drive shaft, which came to be known as "the sewer pipe." Later, a mechanical drive shaft disconnect operable from the flight engineer's station and warning lights were also made available and installed in all of TWA's Constellations.

Wright 3350 C18 BA-3 engine operations were especially troublesome overall. The cast cylinder heads frequently overheated and required replacement, causing flight delays and unscheduled maintenance. False engine fire warnings were rampant, causing unnecessary and sometimes dangerous crew actions. And, worst of all, the time between engine overhauls was abysmally low. Forged cylinder heads and other Wright developed improvements were installed as time went on, but unfortunately the BA-3 never achieved acceptable reliability standards.

Several stories have been published explaining why it was necessary for Lockheed to install main landing gear drag strut dampers to avoid disastrous failures. For example, several flight crew members claimed Lockheed undertook this development as a direct result of incidents involving very hard landings, which broke the drag links loose from the wing spar. That is not how or why it happened.

During routine TWA aircraft flight acceptance operations at Lockheed, TWA pilots noticed a peculiar motion in an 049 during the roll following a routine landing. The airplane did not feel steady. Examination showed that although one of the main landing gear drag link wing spar attach fittings had worked loose, it still restrained the gear. (The drag links were diagonal assemblies that restrained the landing gears in the fore-and-aft direction.) Had the fitting become completely detached, the gear would have folded, causing extensive damage. All of TWA's Connies were immediately examined. Two were found with loose fittings. Thanks to the diligence and perspicacity of TWA's acceptance flight crew, two almost certain accidents were avoided.

Lockheed ran tests for several weeks to determine the cause of the failures. Strain gauges were fixed to the suspect components, and stress calculations were checked and rechecked. Everything checked out satisfactorily. All was normal. None of the design loads was exceeded. By all the rules, the fittings could not pull loose. But they did.

I called a Kansas City meeting with flight operations personnel to discuss this mystery. Capt. Gail A. Storck commented that the phenomenon might be related to wet runways. He had noticed that the planes had not felt quite right on wet surfaces.

After thinking this over, I telephoned Ralph Ellinger. Because none of Lockheed's taxi tests had been run on intermittently wet (puddled) runways, I suggested controlled tests on a runway that was intermittently wet and dry to simulate damp and puddled areas. "How?" asked Ralph. "How can Lockheed prepare such a runway? This is a damn busy airport."

I said, "If necessary, go somewhere else. Get fire trucks and spray the runways by short sections. Then taxi at various speeds to see what happens."

"Bob, I doubt if they can find enough hose to reach that far. The runways are awfully long."

"Ralph, I know that. Use tank trucks. Since this hasn't been tried, and the project seems to be on dead center, talk Lockheed into it. If you don't have any luck, let me know, and I'll call Hall Hibbard."

Several days later, Ralph called back and explained that a reluctant Lockheed had conducted the tests, and the mystery had been solved. At certain speeds and degrees of runway wetness, dynamic loads were generated in the drag strut at a frequency that matched the natural frequency of the strut-wing linkage. This condition multiplied the strut loads and caused the failures. He said Lockheed believed the obvious solution was to install shock links in the struts designed to dampen the dynamic loads, and that such a project was now under way. This proved to be the correct solution. Dampers were installed as standard production items and retrofitted to all delivered 049's as quickly as possible.

Problems were also encountered with astrodomes during early operations. Plexiglas bubble astrodomes were mounted topside forward to permit celestial navigation sightings during overseas flights. On March 11, 1947, a tragic failure occurred during sighting operations by Navigator George Hart. The dome failed, and escaping cabin air blew him from the plane over the Atlantic. The initial fix was to provide the navigators with a cumbersome body harness bolted to the structure and replace the single-ply domes with three-ply laminated ones. The final fix, which came considerably later, was to remove the domes and substitute periscopic sextants.

Early commercial operations also confirmed our worst fears concerning poor passenger acceptance of the submarginal ventilating system. The planes were insufferably hot and stuffy on the ground on summer days, and most of the time in the air. Much greater air circulation was needed during ground operations, and more fresh air was sorely needed during flight.

The 049 ventilation system inadequacy was never fully corrected. However, installation by TWA of a large blower on the forward bulkhead near the ceiling, which moved air the length of the cabin, provided much-needed supplemental circulation. A few passengers complained of the draft, but this "crutch" substantially reduced the total number of complaints.

Also, during late 1956, 10 years after TWA introduced Constellation services, TWA's Maintenance Engineering Department designed an 049 cabin refrigeration system with individual "eyeball" outlets for the passengers and crew. This design, which provided some much-needed relief, was installed at great expense in all of TWA's 049's during routine overhaul operations.

Accomplishing airplane modifications to correct deficiencies and finding solutions to maintenance problems proved to be a continuing challenge. When Lockheed considered it feasible, it cooperated by making new designs and parts kits available. In other cases, TWA designed and manufactured parts, keeping Lockheed and the CAA advised. The Constellation may have been troublesome, but it was not the only transport with problems.

Dinner at Howard's Place

Howard kept in close personal touch with all these developments, but he seldom participated in the detailed negotiations. He was regularly on the telephone with me on the safety questions and other critical issues. I and members of my staff were routinely in touch with Lockheed and the other manufacturers. During a routine West Coast safari, Bill Gay called me at the Hollywood Roosevelt Hotel and inquired if Harry West and I would like to join Howard for dinner at "Howard's place." Of course, we accepted. "Howard's place" was a well-kept white house with a gabled roof on the south side of Sunset Boulevard, not far from the old Trocadero. The exterior was unmarked, giving no clue as to its function, which was to serve strictly as a restaurant for Hughes's special dinner guests.

We were cordially received and offered a drink by the butler, who ushered us from the vestibule to a large combination lounge and dining room overlooking the valley, where a half dozen of Howard's guests had convened. The room was furnished tastefully but not extravagantly. The butler advised that Howard was due to arrive in about 15 minutes. About an hour later, the chef appeared and explained the menu for the evening. He said Howard would be "a little late" and suggested that we start dinner without him.

The dinner was relaxed and thoroughly enjoyable, except for Howard's absence. Just as we were enjoying coffee following desert, the chef appeared again. After receiving our plaudits, he said he had just talked to Hughes, who offered his profound apologies for his absence. Then he read a note from Howard: "Please forgive me, but something arose unexpectedly, and, despite my best efforts, I simply could not break loose. Notwithstanding, I hope you found the evening enjoyable."

After coffee, several of us talked on the patio before taking leave. One man, a top movie executive, said, "This is the fifth time I've eaten here during the past two months. Each time, it's the same story: Howard doesn't show up. I really need to see him." I sympathized, but wondered if he was part of the problem.

Another guest, a well-known movie director, asked me if Howard could really fly an airplane and if "he was good at it." I was surprised that he had never heard of Howard's record-breaking flights, but I responded by assuring him that Howard was an extremely thoroughgoing aviator, his flight-training activities were exhaustive, and, indeed, he was a competent if somewhat unorthodox pilot.

He then asked if Howard were an engineer. I indicated that he had a fine, largely self-acquired engineering education, that the world's experts were as near to him as the telephone, that he delegated responsibilities extensively, and that in my opinion, he was quite capable of judging the validity of most technical-economic recommendations.

The director then said, "I've known Howard for many years and have closely followed his movie career. I consider him a genius in this field. I've talked to others who say he has a cagey legal mind. And he certainly understands business. Now, you say what amounts to the same thing in aviation. Isn't it remarkable that one man can excel in so many fields?"

I responded, "Howard is a man of many accomplishments. I certainly agree." I privately thought that it also was an extraordinary accomplishment to arrange gatherings of this kind and then stand everyone up.

7.

Year of
Distress

Devastating events in 1946 left TWA scarred for years. Expansion plans
were put on hold; aircraft procurement programs were seriously impaired;
the corporation drew dangerously close to bankruptcy; Hughes reconstituted the Board of Directors and forced Jack Frye out.

The first disaster was the crash of Howard Hughes in his experimental
fighter, the XF-11. Hughes was close to death for weeks, suffered a slow
recuperation, and was unable to actively participate in TWA affairs. The
second blow was the grounding of TWA's Constellation fleet following a
tragic crash near Reading, Pennsylvania. The third misfortune was a TWA
pilot's strike, called almost immediately after the Constellations were returned to commercial service following the grounding. The fourth disaster
was Howard's repeated refusals to permit TWA to capitalize. Finally,
during early 1947, Hughes relieved the immediate financial pressure by
investing some additional money in TWA, packed the Board of Directors,
and discharged Jack Frye, the highly respected president who had been
responsible to a major extent for TWA's emergence as one of the world's
preeminent airlines.

Howard's XF-11 Crash

A group of TWA executives including Lee Talman; Jack Franklin; John Lockhart; Harry West; Paul Goldsborough, TWA's technical representative in international affairs; and I flew to San Diego on July 6, 1946, to tour Convair's production facilities, inspect their twin-engine DC-3 replacement prototype aircraft, the Model 110, and learn more about Convair's current offering. TWA, with Howard's concurrence, had already executed preliminary agreements with the Glen L. Martin Company for the purchase of competitive Martin 202's and 303's. Notwithstanding, Howard and I considered it good tactics to continue discussions with both manufacturers until final contract execution.

After a short night's rest at the El Cortez Hotel, the group set out early Sunday morning for a prearranged fishing trip in Pacific waters southwest of San Diego. It was my first such trip: a wonderful treat that included landing several good-size, extremely feisty barracuda. That afternoon we drove across the Mexican border at Tijuana, then south to Rosa Rita Ranch, where we enjoyed an early dinner and excellent Mexican music. We returned to the El Cortez Hotel around 11 o'clock for a good night's rest before meeting with Convair Monday morning.

Lee Talman was met at the door with an urgent telephone message from Jack Frye, who had relayed terrible news: Howard had just crashed in his XF-11 and was near death. Jack had left word before leaving Washington for Beverly Hills to be with Howard, indicating he would advise Lee of more details as soon as possible.

The TWA contingent collected in Lee's room to commiserate and discuss the possible impact Howard's death or long recovery might have. It was obvious to all that this was not an appropriate time to undertake negotiations or seek major financial commitment authority. We concluded it would be best to only tour Convair's facilities, inspect the 110, and briefly review its latest transport proposal.

The next morning we met with Mac Laddon; Frank Fink; and Ralph L. Bayless, Convair's outstanding designer and highly respected engineering executive, in Laddon's office on the second floor of Convair's experimental factory—the only office with windows. Lee advised them of our position. Laddon and his associates were entirely understanding and stood ready to assist Howard in any way possible. But nothing could be done by any of us except wait. After our abbreviated activities, the TWA group marked time in San Diego an extra day waiting for further news of Howard's condition. It was all bad. Then we returned to Kansas City.

Howard's XF-11 was an all-metal, twin-engine, photoreconnaissance plane developed under Army contract at Hughes's Culver City factory. It had a centrally located, gracefully contoured stub fuselage extending forward of the wing, with the empennage mounted on slender booms extending aft of the wing-mounted engine nacelles. The XF-11 was equipped with Hamilton Standard contra-rotating propellers (two four-bladed propellers mounted on each engine that turned in opposite directions) to convert the power of the P & W engines into efficient propulsive thrust for superior performance. It was a sleek, attractive design, similar to Howard's all-wood D-2 forerunner, which had been produced as a promotional venture.

The Hughes Aircraft engineers involved in the development of the XF-11 included, among others, Carl Babberger, Stanley Bell, Rae A. Hopper, Warren Reed, Kenneth F. Ridley, and Louis Tribett, some of whom I had worked with as an engineer on the H-1 Hughes Racer. Ken Ridley had been Hughes's chief engineer during the HK-1 boat project. Later, after his career ran its course at Hughes Aircraft, Noah Dietrich insisted on orders from Hughes that I hire Ridley as a member of my TWA staff even though his salary was excessive by TWA standards and he was better qualified for airframe manufacturing. Howard wanted him within easy grasp, and not employed by any non-Hughes interests.

Howard had personally made all the test flights in the XF-11. His takeoff from Culver City on July 7, 1946, was routine. He checked landing gear retraction and made other flight checks. About 1 hour and 20 minutes after takeoff, without warning, the XF-11 violently yawed (turned), pitched, and immediately went out of control. Howard said later, "It was like a giant hand grabbed the plane and threw it out of the sky."

Howard regained partial control but found it impossible to maintain altitude. He had no choice but to descend over a populated area, and he rejected the idea of bailing out. He was able to wrestle the plane toward the Los Angeles Country Club but could not make the fairway. The plane crashed through the roof of one house, ricocheted, tore through a wall of a second house, demolished a garage, and came to rest, twisted and torn. A badly burned and battered Howard Hughes was pulled from the wreck-

113

age and taken by ambulance to the Beverly Hills Emergency Hospital. After receiving emergency treatment, he was moved to Good Samaritan. The doctors gave him only an even chance for survival.

It was hours later when Howard regained consciousness—long after Jack Frye had arrived at the hospital. Howard said the right propeller was the likely cause of the accident. Examination of the wreckage confirmed that it had malfunctioned and gone into reverse pitch. The resulting high drag and disrupted airflow rendered the airplane virtually uncontrollable. It seemed miraculous that he was able to approach the country club.

Howard remained in the hospital for five weeks but required months longer for full recovery. While suffering excruciating pain, he complained about the inconvenience of needing nurses to adjust his bed. He requested his engineers to design motor-driven jacks for the bed so it could be adjusted by merely pushing buttons. They produced what is believed to be the first motorized hospital bed. It arrived at Good Samaritan shortly before Howard was discharged and was not used.

Howard's accident could not have occurred at a worse time. Heavy expenditures involved in expanding TWA's domestic operations, establishing its International Division, and introducing Constellation services in both areas had all but drained TWA's resources. The postwar business recession only made matters worse. Several times that year, high-level concerns were expressed privately regarding the issuance of paychecks. It was an ominous, yet promising period. TWA was well positioned for dramatic growth, but the inviting gains could only be realized if adequate funds were available.

TWA's marginal financial reserves did not result from lack of management foresight or effort. TWA's Board of Directors had created the Finance Committee on April 26, 1945, to recommend a program for raising funds through the sale of stock. Market conditions were favorable, with TWA stock in the $50 range. (Between September 1945 and year's end, the stock ranged between $47 and $79.) This committee recommended that $20 million be raised through the sale of common stock and that serious consideration be given to raising an additional $25 million through the sale of preferred stock. However, the recommended capitalization plan never reached fruition because Hughes, who owned 46 percent of TWA's stock, would not agree.

Because of favorable market conditions, PAA sold $43 million of capital stock in 1945, and AAL sold $40 million of cumulative preferred stock in

1946. TWA, unable to capitalize, succeeded in borrowing $30 million from the Equitable Life Assurance Society of the United States (Equitable) on November 30, 1945.

Market conditions deteriorated rapidly during the first quarter of 1946, and TWA stock dropped to the $20 range. TWA's stringent financial straits were relieved somewhat on May 10, 1946, by Equitable's purchase of an additional $10 million in sinking-fund debentures. This cash infusion helped but did not fully satisfy TWA's needs. Unfortunately, the company's cash problems were to get much worse.

Reading

A few days after Howard's crash, on July 11, 1946, an International Division Constellation on a routine training flight crashed approximately one mile northeast of the Reading, Pennsylvania, airport with a devastating impact on TWA and other Constellation operators. The plane was demolished. Capt. Richard F. Brown was the only survivor of a crew of six. Captain Brown, who was in command, had noticed a faint odor, like that produced by burning insulation, at about 3,000 feet altitude. He asked the flight engineer to investigate in the main cabin. He looked over his shoulder as the flight engineer opened the cabin door. The main cabin was a raging inferno, a mass of flames and black smoke swirling from floor to ceiling. The carbon dioxide hand extinguisher was obviously useless. With the door quickly closed, Dick instantly headed for the Reading airport, only a few miles away.

During the brief instant the door was open, a veil of smoke penetrated the flight deck. A crew member, intending to clear out the smoke, unlatched and pulled open the exterior crew exit door, forward of the left inboard engine. When Dick heard the door being unlatched he turned and shouted, "Don't open that door!" But, most unfortunately, it was opened anyway.

The opened door created a strong suction, which instantly pulled dense, choking smoke and intense heat through the cabin door grill into the flight deck. Everything—instruments, controls, windshield—was instantly blacked out. Outside vision was impossible. The searing heat made Dick feel as if he were inside a blast furnace. With sight of the airport lost, and on belief that he would quickly lose consciousness, Dick had no choice but to crash-land as soon as possible.

115

Immediately after the smoke and heat permeated the flight deck, Dick unbuckled his safety belt, leaned forward over the control yoke, opened the oblique window (between the windshield and side window), and put his head out to get oxygen and to see. This made it possible for him to control the plane until shortly before touchdown. When the plane was about 100 feet in the air, he had to sit back in the blinding smoke to pull the yoke back to get the nose up. He landed entirely blind, with flaps retracted and gear up.

The left wing contacted two electric power lines about 25 feet above the ground, impacted scattered rocks, and struck the base of a large tree. The aircraft rotating to the left as it skidded about 1,000 feet across a hay field with fuel tanks exploding, causing disintegration of the left wing. The plane then plunged through a row of trees and telephone poles lining a road bordering the field. It came to rest in a pasture with the empennage and all four engines torn off.

Nearby farm workers who saw the plane descend trailing smoke drove a truck to the scene, arriving about one minute after the crash. They observed Dick Brown walking away from the wreckage. Dick believes he was catapulted through an opening somehow created when the plane struck the trees. He remembers going through an inferno and ending up several yards ahead of the nose of the Connie. He rolled on the ground to put the fire out on what clothing remained. Miraculously, he then got up, walked toward the truck coming across the field, and got in, holding his arms out in front of him because sheets of skin were hanging loosely. When the truck driver reached across Dick to close the door, his arm contacted Dick's wristwatch, searing his skin.

Dick retained consciousness for a short time after walking into the Reading hospital. He sat bolt upright on the gurney and recited in detail exactly what happened. Then he lost consciousness except for brief periods for nearly two months, during which he hovered between life and death. His recital greatly aided the accident investigation, which, without his input, might have taken months, during which other similar accidents would likely have occurred.

Dick Brown recovered to enjoy a good family life and a useful career as a TWA executive; however, his recovery was slow and painful. He lost one arm and suffered severe burns over much of his body. Three years later, in 1949, while recuperating from a lengthy series of plastic surgery operations, Dick Brown met and married a beautiful young lady, DeLys D.

Herbert. Three fine children were born of this union. When Dick was able, he accepted a position in TWA's Flight Operations Department. He soon demonstrated unusual capabilities and excelled as TWA's chief of liaison in international technical and operational affairs. Later, he was made a staff vice president and placed in charge of flight planning for the entire system. Great credit is due Dick Brown for surmounting circumstances that would break many men and for the constructive TWA career that followed.

Dick is convinced that opening the exterior door caused the death of the five crew members, his own injuries, and loss of the Constellation. Had the smoke and intense heat not been quickly sucked into the flight deck, he would have had an excellent chance to land successfully at the Reading airport.

Immediately after the accident, Jack Frye voluntarily grounded TWA's Constellation fleet pending determination of the cause and implementation of suitable corrective actions. TWA also promptly advised all parties—the CAB, Lockheed, and other airlines—of all known aspects of the accident. Jack always put safety first. While this was as it should be, Jack's deliberate grounding action was especially commendable considering TWA's weak financial condition and the critical impact this action would produce if the cause of the accident could not be quickly determined and services expeditiously restored.

The CAB was required by law to conduct the formal accident investigation. With the investigation barely underway, on July 12, 1946, the day after the accident, without warning or discussion, the CAB ordered all Constellations grounded, including TWA's, without ever acknowledging Frye's prior action. This angered Frye and many of us who felt strongly that as a matter of courtesy the CAB should have advised Frye of its intentions and given him the opportunity to formally announce TWA's grounding action before the CAB order was issued.

The CAB grounding quickly produced damaging newspaper innuendoes and allegations of "questionable" airline maintenance and Lockheed design practices, which, along with the accident itself, all but destroyed public confidence in the airplane.

The cause of the Reading accident proved to be faulty through-stud bolts, which carried main line electrical power from the engine-driven generators through the fuselage skin into the pressurized zone. Three through-studs were located on each side of the fuselage in the forward below-deck baggage compartment area. This arrangement functioned sat-

117

isfactorily as long as the connections were tight. However, due to differential expansion of the aluminum and other materials used, the connections could loosen. When this occurred, increased electrical resistance and dangerous heating resulted. In Dick Brown's case, electrical arcing burned through a hydraulic line under 3,000 pounds of pressure. The resulting torch quickly spread the fire.

Immediately after the through-studs were suspected, TWA inspected all Constellations in its possession. To our horror, the through-studs in several planes evidenced signs of severe distress. They were accidents waiting to happen.

Lockheed expedited corrective engineering to the maximum possible extent. The new design, which according to Raymond M. Dunn was originated by Raymond North of TWA, entirely eliminated the through-studs. (At that time, Ray Dunn was responsible for maintenance and overhaul operations at TWA's Intercontinental Division, but he would one day become a senior vice president and system general manager.) Additionally, copper electrical cable was substituted for aluminum in the main leads, and vulnerable hydraulic lines were moved.

The Reading accident investigation, like most, confirmed the need for making design improvements not related to the cause of the accident. Included were heavier-gauge alcohol tanks, which Lockheed then had under development; increased nacelle ventilation aft of the fire wall, also under development; strengthened engine exhaust collectors; and a few other such improvements.

In addition to requiring that the cause of the accident be corrected, the CAB required that all such peripheral items be corrected prior to ungrounding the planes. While all these changes were advisable, they should not have been made a requirement for ungrounding because imminent safety risks were not involved. TWA would have expeditiously installed such improvements as soon as they became available during routine maintenance operations, thus avoiding unnecessary delays in returning the planes to commercial service. Indeed, prior to the accident TWA had been planning to accomplish most of them. Even elimination of the through-studs was not immediately necessary because similar accidents could be avoided through frequent inspections and shielding the hydraulic lines, precautions that would have effectively avoided overheating and arcing until permanent fixes could be installed. I considered the CAB's ungrounding requirements to be outrageous and punitive.

During the extended grounding period, TWA reassigned some of its Douglas C-54's from domestic to international operations to help fill the Constellation flight schedule gap, but international schedules remained terribly weak. Withdrawal of the C-54's from domestic services pitted TWA's DC-3's against UAL's and AAL's more attractive C-54's and made the lack of domestic Constellation services more acute. Gross revenues fell drastically, and because many of TWA's costs were fixed or could not be reduced by commensurate amounts, TWA's financial condition became critical.

Pilot's Strike

One month after TWA Constellation services resumed, about the time passengers began to return to the airline, at midnight, October 21, 1946, TWA's pilots went on strike. If a single root cause could be ascribed to this belligerent action, it would be failure of both management and the Air Line Pilots Association (ALPA), the pilot's union, to cope rationally and in a timely manner with technology-bred issues raised by Constellation operations. The increased payload-range capabilities, speed, and allowable operating weight of the Constellations, all of which had been known for an extended period, generated questions concerning fair levels of crew compensation that required resolution. My impression was that the strike was the direct result of eleventh-hour intransigence on both sides of the table. Neither side would yield, possibly in the belief that the other would fold at the last minute. That is the kind of uncompromising bullheadedness that wars are made of.

While I had no part in the negotiation, I believed that a strike was inadmissible and entirely avoidable, especially under the financial circumstances that existed. All the airline pilots I had ever met seemed to be intelligent, competent individuals. I could not believe that when the chips were down they would permit the union to take advantage of TWA's weakened position, especially when TWA so desperately needed to rebuild public confidence and gain much-needed revenue. And I did not believe management, which I also held in high respect, would permit the strike. I was confident the potpourri of union demands concerning compensation, work rules, and fringe benefits would be resolved and that management would likely work out some method of deferred compensation, payable as soon as the company regained sufficient financial strength. I could not have been more wrong. My confidence in management and pilots alike was utterly naive.

It appeared likely that a strike would force cancellation of undelivered Model 049 (C-69) Constellations. When this was explained to the pilots, they took it as a humorous ruse, as if Howard's money well were bottomless and could be easily tapped for TWA's benefit. Before the strike was over, TWA was forced to cancel 8 undelivered 049's. Later, all 18 Postwar 649's, planes considered vital for maintaining TWA's competitive position, met the same fate.

The strike continued nearly five weeks until November 15, 1946, when TWA and ALPA agreed to binding arbitration. The strike left a wake of bitter feelings, suspicion, and discontent that lasted for years. In addition to forcing cancellation of 049's and 649's, the strike and other 1946 disasters, including Hughes's unwillingness to capitalize, curtailed all growth plans and severely impaired TWA's competitive position.

Financial Nemesis

A serious cleavage developed between Hughes and Frye during 1946 over the financing of TWA, which led to Frye's dismissal in early 1947. Frye contended that the sale of securities was the best way to raise the considerable capital required for the purchase of new TWA aircraft fleets and other corporate needs, whereas Hughes preferred debt financing and rejected all of the several plans put forward by Frye. There was, however, more to the dispute than this.

The excellent working relationship between Hughes and Frye, which had produced the Constellation and built TWA into an international carrier, was irreparably eroded by Hughes's chief financial watchdog, Noah Dietrich. Dietrich had been highly critical of TWA's management for an extended period, contending that TWA carried a disproportionate share of expensive pioneering for the industry—perhaps true, but both Hughes and Frye considered this essential to enhance TWA's competitive position and build the airline. Dietrich, aided and abetted by some Toolco cohorts, also insisted that TWA's costs were out of hand, and it and other airlines were overequipping. Dietrich had the unrealistic notion that the U.S. airlines should have relied on the military services to bear the costs of developing new commercial transports and on leasing rather than purchasing them, and TWA and the other airlines should have in the meantime bought only war-surplus Douglas C-54's. He persisted in this wrong-headed view even after TWA's principal competitors announced the purchase of Douglas DC-6's, vastly superior to the C-54's. Dietrich's concentration on the lower investments required to purchase war-surplus planes revealed an intensely myopic vision of aviation's future. Smart men sometimes make blockbuster mistakes. This was one of his.

TWA's financial circumstance as the end of 1946 approached was critical. Stockholder's equity had decreased from $18,665,483 on June 30, 1945, to $4,177,158. Short-term debt was $4,340,000, long-term debt was a whopping $38,947,124, and TWA's net loss for 1946 was approximately $14.5 million. TWA was broke, and unless additional planes were promptly ordered it would be critically short of the capacity needed if it were ever to recover. Frye had little choice except to try to expeditiously resolve TWA's financial predicament.

The financing plans Frye put forward in 1946 included a $150-million line of credit through the Export-Import Bank and the Reconstruction Finance Corporation (RFC), probably contemplating some infusion of equity; a $100-million plan with $80 million of bank credit through the Bankers Trust Company and $20 million in equity financing; and a $100-million underwriting plan through the First Boston Corporation.

All such plans aborted because of Hughes. He owned 100 percent of Toolco, a veritable money fountain, which owned 46 percent of TWA. This gave Howard effective control of TWA management (as opposed to legal control of the company). Toolco was Howard's alter ego. It acted in his name and at his command. Hughes personally made all major decisions. Toolco executives such as Noah Dietrich and Raymond M. Holliday, executive vice president, although in a position to advance recommendations and influence Hughes, were powerless to act in major financing matters without Howard's specific approval.

Frye's insistence on following a course independent from Hughes flew in the face of one of Howard's two inviolate precepts—his personal approval of plans to finance—and was certain to be considered an affront. I was appalled by the possibility that Howard and Jack might break up and fervently hoped they would find common ground. Knowing Howard, I could not imagine Frye's winning unless Howard concluded this would be to his best interests. Knowing Jack, I could not question his motive of obtaining adequate financing for the company. The handwriting on the wall was frightening as year's end approached.

121

Frye's plans to issue large quantities of stock were contingent on TWA's amending its Delaware charter, which required approval of the holders of a majority of shares. Hughes's 46 percent (owned through Toolco) gave him the controlling hand; because the rest of the shares were widely scattered, his approval was essential. Frye called a special meeting of the TWA board on November 8, 1946, in Washington, D.C. He recommended that the number of authorized shares be increased from one million to four million and that consideration be given to the issuance of preferred stock in amounts sufficient to raise not more than $25 million. He advised the board that five weeks would be required to satisfy necessary regulatory and legal aspects associated with issuance of the stock and proposed to set the machinery in motion to amend the charter, increase the authorized shares, and call the necessary shareholders meeting.

Before acting, the directors invited Noah Dietrich and Palmer Bradley, counsel for Toolco, to join the meeting to discuss the proposed financing program. The record does not show what position Dietrich and Bradley took, but the directors agreed that common stock should be increased in an amount necessary to support any security convertible into common stock and to provide common stock for issue in accordance with the numerous corporate plans under consideration. It was also agreed that an increase in authorized common stock up to three million shares would be desirable. Accordingly, formal resolutions were adopted to this effect, and the necessary stockholders approval meeting was set for December 23, 1946.

Dietrich and Bradley requested that a special board meeting be held on December 18 to consider a revision proposed by Equitable in the outstanding Equitable Life debentures, which they had discussed with the representatives of Equitable—no doubt at Hughes's suggestion or at least with his concurrence. The full board considered the Equitable proposal "desirable," except it did not take into account the $40-million credit then being discussed with RFC. Dietrich and Bradley then requested a recess to permit them to meet informally with all of the nonmanagement board members present—many of them Toolco nominees. When the full board reconvened, counsel outlined a management reorganization plan the outside directors had agreed to. It included the designation of a new senior vice president, responsible directly to the board, who would serve as the chief financial officer of the corporation with direct authority over the treasurer; the abolition of the Finance Committee; and the designation of an Executive Committee to act between meetings of the board. The board adopted this plan and stipulated that the officers were to work with Dietrich and Bradley to develop a financing program that included establishment of a line of credit with the RFC, revision of the Equitable loan, and $10 million in common stock. The board also resolved that Frye would continue as president, Gen. T. B. Wilson as chairman, and Richter as executive vice president of TWA. At this point it did not require a psychic to see that Dietrich had prevailed and that Frye, Wilson, and Richter had a limited future at TWA.

The special meeting of the stockholders was held on December 23, 1946, as previously planned. Hughes surprised management by electing to withhold Toolco's proxy, so there was no quorum. Consequently, the change in bylaws to increase authorized shares did not pass. It became apparent that Hughes had no intention of permitting the bylaws to be so amended because he continued to withhold Toolco's proxy during a series of special stockholders meetings, which adjourned successively to December 28, December 31, and January 6, 1947, whereupon the meeting was again adjourned to January 13, but never held.[1]

A special meeting of the board was held December 27, 1946. Noah Dietrich discussed a new financing proposal described in a Toolco letter of the same date. Toolco offered to immediately loan TWA $5 million and an additional, like sum on or before June 1, 1947, in the form of demand notes subordinate to Equitable. Toolco proposed that it have the option of converting the loans into common stock at any time during the life of the loans after additional shares could be legally issued. The proposed basis for conversion was $19 per share or, at Toolco's option, a price to be determined by the average of the closing market price for 10 days preceding the date upon which Toolco exercised its option to convert.

Jack Frye reacted quickly to the Toolco letter by responding in writing the same day. He pointed out, among other things, that the Toolco proposal did not provide sufficient working capital required for financial stability and that it made no provisions for the $40-million loan contemplated from the RFC. The board meeting adjourned late that evening to the following day, when Toolco presented a revised proposal. It satisfied most of the questions expressed by Frye except that funding beyond the $10 million was left for future resolution. The board decided to adjourn the meeting until Monday, December 30, to permit further discussion and made the unusual request that representatives of Equitable, the RFC, and the chairman of the CAB be invited to attend. The meeting was not held until January 9 to accommodate the invited guests. Habitually, Howard Hughes avoided meetings, preferring to deal by telephone. However, this one was especially important, so he elected to attend along with Dietrich and Bradley; A. V. Leslie; Chauncey Y. Dodds of the RFC; and James M. Landis, chairman of the CAB.

The January 9 meeting was decisive in the affairs of TWA. A new Toolco proposal was presented, which provided that upon delivery of the first $5 million to TWA, the Board of Directors would be reconstituted so that a majority of directors would be nominees of the Hughes Tool Company. To allow time for consideration, the meeting was again adjourned to the following day. Just as the meeting was well under way, a hand-carried letter was delivered to the TWA board from Thomas I. Parkinson, president of Equitable. It read:

In view of certain statements which have appeared in the press within the last few days regarding the financial plans of TWA, and of Equitable's status as a holder of $40,000,000 in principal amount of your Company's bonds, we wish to advise you as follows:

First, that no application is now pending with the Equitable for a further loan to your company, and if such an application were made, it would have to be declined.

Second, in view of what we understand as to your Company's present financial condition, it seems to us that you are subjecting the interests of your stockholders and creditors to serious risk in continuing to preserve a situation which results in the company's being unable to obtain additional funds which it needs promptly in order to carry on operations. So far as our holding of bonds is concerned, we intend to hold those responsible strictly accountable for any loss which may arise from this continued inaction.

The Parkinson letter was greeted with indignation, but the threat of personal financial responsibility for any loss by Equitable had a chilling effect on the board. This letter, a final shot in the vendetta that torpedoed Frye, was largely engineered by Noah Dietrich by his own admission.[2]

After the letter was discussed a few minutes, the board received word that Hughes would like to enter the meeting and meet with the nonmanagement directors. Accordingly, Frye, Richter, and TWA counsel withdrew. Hughes said that he did not seek the resignation of any present members of the board at that time but merely desired to have representatives of Toolco added to the board, and that he had no present intention of

124

disturbing the executives of the corporation whose status was of concern to the board. Later during the meeting, Hughes advised that he wanted Frye, Wilson, and Richter to remain in the service of the corporation in any capacity that might be agreed upon, "at least until the annual meeting," and, if they should leave the service of the corporation on or before July 1, 1947, they should receive 12 months' salary at present rates.

The board accepted Toolco's $10-million loan offer, formally arranged to pay Frye, Wilson, and Richter as requested by Hughes; established an Executive Committee of the Board of Directors with full authority to act for the board between board meetings; elected 13 new Hughes appointees to the Board of Directors, giving Hughes clear control of the board; and determined that Frye, Wilson, and Richter would remain in office until the annual meeting, April 24, 1947. Richter resigned a few days before the meeting. On April 24, Frye and Wilson were "not reelected."

Jack Frye testified before the CAB two years later. His forthright testimony about the man who had fired him is, I think, to his great credit. In response to a question by CAB counsel concerning Hughes's contributions to the progress and welfare of TWA, he said in part:

One thing about Mr. Hughes that interested me, and I enjoyed—caused me to enjoy working with him over a period of years, is that he did have an understanding of the airplane. In fact, the airplane is not a developed field of transportation as yet. It has many years yet to go before it will be there, and in the meantime if it was attempted to be treated by either the Government or the airlines, or a combination of them, as any other fully developed business is, it will be very, very slow in ever attaining its growth and development. Air transportation may be a great business some day, as, if and when it can be operated safely and dependably, and on schedule, but until it gets there a great deal of money has to be spent and people who have understanding of the technical problems involved will have to devote time and effort to solving those problems. . . . Now, Mr. Hughes is one of the few people in the industry that has any of that kind of understanding.[3]

Frye's overall opinion of Hughes was well summarized in the CAB examiner's 1950 report of the 1949 hearing: "Except for his differences with Mr. Hughes over the manner in which the carrier should have accomplished its financing for the post war period, Mr. Frye is still of the opinion that the relationship of Mr. Hughes and his company [Toolco] to

TWA is one of substantial public benefit to both the carrier and the industry.''[4]

Shortly before Frye's departure, during March, TWA was forced to cancel its order for 18 Model 649 Constellations, the greatly improved postwar model Lockheed had under development in compliance with TWA specifications. I considered this a compounded disaster. First, Lockheed refused on the eve of contract execution in 1945 to develop the Postwar 049. When this project was resurrected as the 649, 18 were ordered for TWA, only to now find the company in the position of competing against AAL's and UAL's Douglas DC-6's with its relatively inferior 049's for an indefinite, extended period—a bleak outlook indeed.

During January, when Howard agreed to loan TWA the $10 million, talk in the halls of TWA was to the effect of, ''What a wonderful thing Howard did for TWA! He put in his own money and saved the company.'' I agreed it was good to have the $5 million in hand with another $5 million promised, but I was disturbed because the much larger capital sums under negotiation seemed to have evaporated out of corporate reach. When it became clear that Frye had been frozen out of active management, I was even more concerned as to who and what the new management would consist of, and when we could get back on track building the airline. It seemed obvious that fleet expansion plans would remain seriously curtailed while major competitors continued to add aircraft and expand services. It almost always costs more and takes longer to earn business back from worthy competitors than to generate it in the first place.

My feelings about Howard were mixed. The fact of his expanded control was not unwelcome, particularly in light of the close association I had come to have with him, but I did not like the way it happened, and I was disillusioned and disappointed over Frye's departure—a poor reward indeed for an aviation pioneer and inspired leader whose genius had been substantially responsible for TWA's emergence as a major international airline! Nearly everyone at TWA respected Jack Frye and, like me, did not want him to leave the company, but I do not recall a single word of criticism of Hughes—only words of appreciation for the $10 million.

An event that helped boost company morale after it had hit a new low following the meeting that placed Frye on ice was Howard's flight demonstration of the Terrain Warning Indicator (TWI) system. He personally demonstrated the TWI to aviation writers on three hair-raising Constel-

126

lation flights in the Los Angeles area, flying into canyons at low levels with cliffs looming menacingly ahead. When the 2,000-foot alarm sounded, and the cliffs less than five seconds away, he rammed the throttles full forward and made abrupt, steep climbing turns, barely clearing the canyon walls. The flight garnered an enormous amount of extremely favorable publicity because of its daring and the promise of preventing premature contact with the ground during routine operations—always a sensitive subject, but especially so then because of several recent aircraft accidents.

Dave Evans, head of the Electronics Department of Hughes Aircraft Company, had developed the TWIs from surplus military equipment. A contemporary TWA News Bureau publicity release described them this way: "The equipment, which weighs only 16 pounds installed . . . warns the pilot whenever a plane comes within a 2,000 foot radius of a building, mountain peak, another aircraft, or any other obstruction, regardless of darkness or weather conditions." Hughes offered to make the units available to the industry at costs and pointed out that all of TWA's transports would be so equipped. Howard's interest in safety, like mine, was sincere, but he also relished the publicity.

The firing of Jack Frye and TWA's acceptance of Howard's money did not end the 1946–47 financing story. Howard's maneuvering continued. Two years later, he offered to convert the $10-million loan to common stock at $10 per share even though the conversion price calculated according to the formula set by the agreements was $15.80 per share. (He first offered $5 per share, but even a Hughes-controlled board could not swallow that!) The board agreed to accept the $10 offer, and Toolco acquired an additional 1,034,423 shares, more than the total amount of TWA common stock then outstanding. Howard had finally permitted his stock to be voted at a special stockholders meeting on August 10, 1948, authorizing the issuance of the additional shares. With this conversion, Howard's interest in TWA increased from 46 percent to approximately 76 percent. It later rose to 78 percent. Because of persuasive arguments, carefully planned procrastination, outright disagreements concerning financing, and rights acquired only after the corporation was forced to the verge of receivership, Howard had acquired a major share of TWA stock at below-market prices, bringing his stock ownership to well above the 66⅔-percent level needed under Delaware law to carry out any major corporate restructuring. Besides installing his personally approved new senior management, he had also gained legal control of the company.

Notes

1. Hughes explained his position during a 1959 CAB hearing concerning the control of TWA: "My position was . . . debt financing was very attractive. Interest rates were low, and interest could be paid out of basic earnings before taxation. Equity financing, to leave a satisfied stockholder, probably should have returned something between 7 and 10 percent, and that would have been required to be paid out of earnings after taxation." Equity financing also quite obviously would have made it more difficult for Hughes to increase his percentage of ownership and gain legal control of the corporation. "Trans World Airlines, Inc., Further Control by Hughes Tool Company: Decided October 6, 1950," Docket No. 2796 (E-4701), *Civil Aeronautics Board Reports* 12 (12): 223.
2. Dietrich, Noah, and Bob Thomas, *Howard: The Amazing Mr. Hughes* (Greenwich, Connecticut: Fawcett Publications, 1972), pp. 224–31.
3. "Trans World Airlines, Inc., Further Control by Hughes Tool Company: Decided October 6, 1950," Docket No. 2796 (E-4701), *Civil Aeronautics Board Reports* 12 (12): 200, n. 17.
4. Ibid., p. 223.

8.

Howard's New President

LaMotte T. Cohu, Howard's new president, had a good reputation and a rich aviation background when he joined TWA. He had the appearance of a tough-minded, penny-counting, no-nonsense manager who understood the business. Cohu's association with TWA had begun with the company's predecessor, TAT, as an early member of the Board of Directors and Executive Committee. He had been president of American Airways (now AAL) and the American Airplane and Engine Corporation. He had served as a director of North American Aviation and as a member of the board of Eastern Air Transport (now EAL). During 1939 he became chairman of the board and manager of Northrop Aircraft, a position held until he was elected president of TWA.

One could hardly hope for a more experienced man. While I had lingering doubts that anyone could fill Frye's shoes, I thought he should at least come close. I eagerly looked forward to my first meeting with him and for an opportunity to review the Lockheed and Martin situations. The latter was at a critical contractual stage, having been on hold since Howard's XF-11 accident.

My high hopes were soon dashed. Cohu was quick to issue decrees that I thought ran strongly counter to the welfare of the corporation and infringed on the responsibilities I had been assigned by Jack Franklin—and Hughes. It was as if Cohu did not want to hear anything about aircraft procurement. Trying to work with him proved to be an unpalatable, frustrating experience. He was almost always unavailable either to me or Franklin, even to discuss urgent matters. When he was visible, he was always in a group, making discussion either inappropriate or unwelcome. He proved to be a hard man to reach, and certainly one who was difficult to know.

One of the first things Cohu did was to disband the Equipment Committee. When I tried to find out why, I was told, "Cohu said it isn't needed." An effective management coordinating function was wiped out, and no substitute was provided.

The next thing to go was the Engineering Laboratory. Jack Franklin had established the "Lab" shortly after I joined the company. It occupied a two-story garage on Third Street, Kansas City, Missouri. The upper floor was used primarily for passenger cabin and cockpit mockup purposes, and the first floor was used by Eve De Marino to develop frozen food techniques and test galley equipment for TWA in-flight use. De Marino's pioneering in this new field led the air transport industry by a large margin in anticipation of capturing an important competitive lead. (After the Lab was discontinued, UAL picked up the experimental ball for its exclusive benefit. However, De Marino's good work did permit TWA to move forward expeditiously later on.) The prevailing management view, until Cohu spoke, was that the Lab was a valuable asset that had repetitively proven its worth.

Cohu gave the same reason for the discontinuance of the Lab: "It isn't needed." Everyone would have accepted this decree more gracefully if he had said something like, "I understand the Lab has proved to be worthwhile and that its continuance would probably pay over the long term. Notwithstanding, TWA must cut every cost possible for near-term health, and for this reason, it must forgo the laboratory, at least for now." Instead, only, "It isn't needed."

Shortly thereafter, Cohu made clear to Jack Franklin and me his view that airlines had no business negotiating airplane design changes and improvements, which he called "supposed improvements." He said the manufacturers knew how to build airplanes and did not need airline inputs—

that airline design changes only increased the price of the planes. According to him, such changes could not be important anyway because the airlines did not "agree on requirements." The fact of the matter was that the majority of differences in airline requirements reflected differences in routes, scheduling practices, and operational environments, not capricious or arbitrary positions. Cohu then declared that the manufacturers built good airplanes, adding, "In the future TWA will have to buy whatever the manufacturers offer."

A terrible mistake was in the making. I tried to point out the value of past airline contributions to design and the continuing need for incorporating improvements born of bitter operating experience. He listened for a moment and then sharply cut off any possibility of debate or further rebuttal. Jack and I had our sailing orders, and the matter was closed.

But the subject could not be closed that simply. I knew that other airlines that had participated in the development of transport aircraft through the years would never accept the Cohu philosophy and that all U.S. transport manufacturers wanted the constructive relationships to continue. I was convinced that the practice of injecting the lessons of experience and airline needs into new designs—a practice more effectively accomplished in the United States than anywhere else—was a key reason for the preeminence of U.S. transports. It would continue with or without TWA.

I did not believe that Cohu's aircraft procurement philosophy reflected a change in Howard's views. Building better airplanes was in Howard's blood. Our frequent discussions of needed improvements, along with his standing directive to me to obtain airplanes that complied fully with TWA's requirements, left no room for doubt: Cohu had to be standing alone.

This serious dichotomy between Cohu and Hughes placed the two on a collision course. I wanted the differences resolved, not only to eliminate conflicting directives concerning my work, but also to avoid future problems between the two principals. It was also obvious that the demise of the Equipment Committee and Cohu's directive on aircraft procurement practices eliminated a significant part of my responsibilities. I, too, might be "not needed." I might have lost sleep over this, but I knew it would not help, and besides, Howard had not indicated even the slightest dissatisfaction with my work.

I decided not to mention Cohu's directive to Howard because my motives could be misunderstood and because new airplane development activities were at low ebb at that time. I thought the best thing to do was to sit down quietly with Cohu to review Howard's directive to me and explain my concerns—a delicate matter, but I did not see any reasonable alternative. I tried to get with Cohu several times to do this, but all I got was the closed-door treatment. Indeed, I do not remember ever having had a single private discussion with him, and very few group meetings.

I wished I were a horseman. Cohu loved to ride. Not long after he became president, nearly all of the officers suddenly became expert horsemen. A few, such as Frank E. Busch, who was in charge of Flight Operations, really were, but the majority had ridden seldom, if ever. Still, they talked about horses during coffee breaks or at lunch, or whenever they could attract Cohu's attention. Being invited to ride with him on weekends came to be accepted as an indication of corporate status. I then knew little about horses, had no interest in them, did not want to take riding lessons or buy any part of a riding habit. I definitely was not part of Cohu's horsey entourage.

Along with Cohu's election came other management changes. Warren Lee Pierson replaced General Wilson as chairman; Lee Talman was not reelected; Jack Franklin waited until September 15 to take a leave of absence to join Jack Frye, who had been elected president of General Analine and Film Corporation. Frye never came back. A. V. Leslie, a Hughes-Dietrich man, was elected treasurer and a member of the board on October 1, replacing John Lockhart. Shortly after Cohu took office, Paul Richter was persuaded to return to TWA for an interim period to help Cohu. Other senior people left that summer, but by and large, personnel in the primary operating departments—Marketing, Maintenance, and Operations—were not affected.

The Senate Hearing

Following Cohu's election, Howard was almost completely out of touch for months. I became concerned lest he had turned over the entire affairs of the corporation to Cohu, including aircraft procurement matters, but that was not the case. He was completely immersed in trying to save his HK-1 flying boat and the second XF-11 development contracts; fighting Juan Trippe's "chosen instrument" policy, which advocated only one U.S. international airline; and preparing for Senate hearings on the propriety of his handling of the war contracts. There simply were not enough hours in the day for Howard to handle all of his interests.

The HK-1 contract had been canceled earlier, but it had been reinstated by President Roosevelt, who interceded in Hughes's behalf over the recommendations of numerous prominent aviation experts. The XF-11 fighter contract, which expired after Howard's crash, was renewed to develop a photoreconnaissance version for the Air Force on the recommendation of Eliot Roosevelt, the president's son, despite the objections of Gen. O. P. Echols and other Air Force officers.

This was all great fodder for publicity-seeking Senate Republicans, who were especially anxious to tarnish the Democrats because of the coming presidential election. The Special Senate Committee to Investigate the National Defense Program scheduled hearings concerning the Hughes contracts to begin August 5, 1947. Sens. Ralph Owen Brewster, Maine; and Homer Ferguson, Michigan, played key roles in the Washington hearings, which *Newsweek* referred to as "the biggest circus that had pitched its tent in Washington in many years."[1] Hughes had a lot at stake. He could lose the HK-1 and XF-11 contracts, and if Trippe's chosen instrument policy became law, TWA would be relegated to domestic service only or be forced to merge with PAA.

Hughes fought adroitly with press releases, including a published letter charging, among other things, that Brewster had agreed to call off the hearing if Hughes agreed to merge TWA with PAA. Brewster denied such charges, but the fact that he was strongly beholden to Trippe and biased against Hughes became transparent. By the time the hearings started, daily headline press accounts of charges, countercharges, and denials by Hughes and Brewster generated intense public interest. By the time the hearings were over, Hughes, cast by Brewster as a wealthy playboy who squandered federal funds, had completely turned the tables on Brewster and was acclaimed a national hero.[2] The Hughes contracts were saved, the chosen instrument policy idea was dropped, and a disgraced Senator Brewster shortly retired from public life.[3]After Howard's highly successful handling of his Washington problems, he found time to again become active in aircraft procurement matters.

Again, the Postwar Connies

After trying without success for weeks to discuss with Cohu critical equipment matters, which required his personal attention, I met with Paul Richter, hoping he would open the door to Cohu's office for me or obtain needed decisions. He listened sympathetically, explained he was not authorized to act in equipment affairs, and said he would call Cohu's attention to the problem areas. I am sure he did, but I never heard back.

I took the occasion, however, to explain in confidence my concerns about the apparent collision of directives between Cohu and Hughes. Paul volunteered that continuation of our past airplane procurement practices was entirely appropriate and advisable, concluding, "Bob, it will all work out." I hoped he knew something I did not.

Then I discussed the current Lockheed situation. Lockheed had virtually stopped work on the 18 649's TWA had canceled because of inability to sell them, and it was currently planning to upgrade the planes by increasing payload and range capabilities to make them more salable to international operators, redesignating them 749's. I noted that the upgraded planes would be capable of effectively competing against DC-6's in both domestic and international services and reminded Paul that the 649's themselves had been developed in substantial conformity with TWA specifications.

I then offered the same suggestion I had made earlier to Jack Franklin. I proposed a "bootstrap" plan, saying, "TWA can't afford to buy the airplanes now, and Lockheed apparently can't afford to complete them. They are just sitting there, expensive piles of unproductive, useless hardware as long as they remain unsold. The required incremental investment to complete them—I don't know exactly what the amount is—has to be small compared to the sunk funds. What is wrong with the banks' advancing Lockheed money for completion so TWA could put the planes to work to return the investment? We need the competitive edge they would provide, and they should easily pay their way. If satisfactory financial arrangements—perhaps simple leases—could be worked out, TWA could get moving again." I made the same suggestion to Leonard Schwartz of Lockheed later that week, making sure that Leonard understood that I was not expressing formal interest on behalf of either TWA or Hughes.

During late August, Jack Franklin dropped by my office with surprising but happy news. He said that Cohu wanted procurement papers drawn for TWA's canceled 649's, now upgraded to 749's, to enhance international operations. He said that Lockheed had proposed to Cohu a "bootstrap" type approach that might permit TWA to acquire as many as 12 749's. I exclaimed, "Holy God! Jack, that's wonderful! But doesn't that sound familiar to you?" All he said was, "Yes. Can you get to work on this right away?"

I inquired if Cohu's earlier directive to buy airplanes "as is" was still effective. If so, I suggested that a lot of time could be saved by simply accepting the Lockheed offer without taking time to confirm that the planes still had the features and details TWA negotiated prior to canceling the initial order, and not worrying about whether our latest operational requirements had been satisfied. I said I could not recommend this approach, hoping I could proceed in the normal manner. I added that if the as-is approach were selected, it should be made clear to TWA's pilot, maintenance, and traffic personnel, who had participated in the tedious development of our requirements and who would rightfully expect to take part in specification negotiations, why they were being excluded. After hashing this over, Jack directed me to proceed as I thought best, knowing full well what I would do.

Shortly after the 749 project was underway, Jack Franklin took his leave of absence, never to return as an employee. Louis R. Koepnick, who had never met Hughes or had any contact with him, replaced Franklin. He was given the title of chief engineer rather than vice president because Cohu considered this title to be sufficient. Lou was well liked, competent, and deserving of this promotion. I reviewed the Cohu as-is policy and Franklin's permissive directive with him. Lou said Cohu's position was unrealistic and endorsed my method.

Our specification negotiation should have been smooth and easy. However, to my consternation, instead of starting with papers that described the planes that were actually being manufactured, Lockheed insisted on use of a "standard" specification as the basis for negotiations. The standard specification described minimally equipped planes that Lockheed by its subsequent admission would never have been willing to manufacture. It omitted many features already incorporated in the planes and many of the items Lockheed had agreed to incorporate in TWA's 649's, all of which I had been led to believe were part of the deal. Lockheed was willing to incorporate most such items but proposed to negotiate the price of each of them separately. Lockheed's reason for proceeding on this basis was clearly to raise the airplane purchase price quoted to Cohu. This situation was especially galling because Lockheed made it clear at the outset that none of the incrementally priced features already incorporated in the planes could be removed.

Persistent table pounding finally produced essential design changes, an acceptable specification, and a compromised purchase price, which, although higher than I wanted, totaled about half of the sum of Lockheed's opening requests. I thought Cohu might balk at the price increase, but he did not. I never learned whether Cohu thought we were actually following his directive by buying as-is planes because they were under construction when they were reordered, or whether the attractiveness of the bootstrap deal caused him to suppress his "buy whatever the manufacturers offer" views. When the papers were finally ready, however, execution was unexpectedly delayed, pending Howard's approval.

A Surprising Meeting with Hughes

During early October, Bob Loomis and I were summoned to meet with Howard at his Culver City factory, where the HK-1 flying boat was being built. I flew overnight to Los Angeles from Kansas City and met Bob at the airport. After taking time for a much-needed haircut, I joined Bob for a flight in one of TWA's cargo DC-3's to Culver City, where we were driven to the meeting in one of Howard's Chevrolets.

Within a minute or two of our arrival, Hughes showed up. He wanted to know all about the payload, performance, and projected operating costs of the 749's and how TWA planned to use them. He directed all of his questions to Loomis and me, even though several Hughes employees were present at the meeting. As usual, his questions were penetrating and to the point. He wanted to know if TWA really needed the planes.

I cited the position of TWA's Traffic Department, which was strongly in favor of acquiring the planes. Howard was unsatisfied and continued to examine how TWA could profitably use the planes. After nearly an hour of cross-examination, during which he was becoming visibly annoyed (perhaps because repetitious questions got repetitious answers), he paused, grew very stern, and exclaimed, "Look, I hear you. But, what I want to know is whether Cohu is trying to ram these planes down TWA's throat."

After waiting a moment, hoping Loomis would respond, I picked up the ball and told Howard that I certainly could not speak for Mr. Cohu, but I would be glad to summarize what I knew of the 749 project. He listened intently, then asked whether I personally thought TWA could make good use of the planes. I told him I was convinced the necessary traffic could be generated, and that if TWA did not provide the services, the competition probably would. However, I could not comment on the overall acceptability of the undertaking with regard to its financial impact on TWA. Howard

136

seemed satisfied with this answer and closed the meeting, after which the three of us chatted cordially about aviation affairs.

Bob and I returned to Kansas City that evening. The next morning, we met with John Collings, then vice president of domestic operations, to review the meeting—including Howard's comment about Cohu. John cautioned against discussing the comment with anyone, indicating he would personally let Cohu know the results of the meeting.

A few days later, after receiving clearance from Hughes, Cohu executed the contract for 12 749's on October 18, 1947. All 12 were delivered during 1948 and flown primarily in overseas services. They did pay their way.

Cohu's Big Meeting

During the following spring, scuttlebutt had it that not all was well between Cohu and Hughes. I made it a point generally to pay little attention to rumors, but in this case, I knew good foundation for them might exist.

During April, Cohu announced arrangements for an unusual Hollywood meeting with Hughes. His top corporate officers, together with Harry West, Lou Koepnick, and me—possibly 12 in all—were requested to be available for the meeting. Cohu made no effort to apprise us of the specific subjects to be discussed so we could come prepared; we knew only that we were to be there. We suspected that long-range financial plans and the future of TWA would be the principal topics of discussion. Vic Leslie, TWA's new treasurer, who had worked extensively with Hughes and Dietrich at 7000 Romaine Street, had developed a number of financial plans at Cohu's request, but none had moved off dead center.

We met at Cohu's home in Beverly Hills the morning of the scheduled meeting. Shortly before our arrival, Howard's boys in the back room at the Romaine Street communications center called Cohu, indicating that Howard would be delayed and that he would call as soon as possible. Cohu was requested to please stand by. We sat around Cohu's living room for several hours, then moved to the patio and lawn, waiting for Howard's call. Cohu tried several times to reach Howard through the Romaine Street office without success. Around noon he received further word from Romaine Street that Hughes had just called. He was still tied up and would probably not be available for several hours. Cohu was again requested to stand by.

On receiving this message, LaMotte became very flustered, rushed across the lawn without saying a word, jumped on his motor scooter, and took off down the street. He raced back and forth for possibly 10 minutes, passing in front of the house at the highest possible speed, hunched over the handlebars. Then he turned in, got off, and said with poorly disguised anger, "Howard just told the boys we should wait." Then he disappeared into the house. Around one o'clock, he came out and suggested we grab a bite at a nearby restaurant and return in an hour or less, "Just in case he calls." We did, and we continued to wait. Around five o'clock, a visibly annoyed and embarrassed Cohu said he still had not heard from Howard. He said he would wait another day but that the rest of us should return to Kansas City, or wherever our TWA business required.

I did not care for Cohu's executive style, but I felt sympathy for his personal situation that afternoon. He had assembled TWA's top brass for a palaver with Howard, only to be embarrassed. This evasion was unquestionably deliberate on Howard's part, who obviously did not elect to be confronted en masse. On June 1, 1948, after only slightly over 13 months in office, Cohu resigned. The man picked to replace Jack Frye had not made the grade with Howard. I was not sorry to see him leave, and I hoped that this time Howard would find a more consensus-minded and sagacious president.

Notes

1. Charles Barton, *Howard Hughes and His Flying Boat* (Fallbrook, California: Aero Publishers, 1982), p. 171.
2. Detailed congressional accounts of the hearing make fascinating reading.
3. William P. Rogers, chief counsel for the Senate investigative committee, was approached by Howard immediately following the hearings and thanked for his fairness. This was the same William Rogers who was to become secretary of state for President Richard M. Nixon and who would serve President Ronald Reagan as chairman of the Presidential Commission on the Space Shuttle Challenger Accident. It was my privilege to work with him as a member of that commission. Incidentally, Rogers and Charles C. Tillinghast, Jr., who became president of TWA in 1961 and played a prominent role in the subsequent Hughes-TWA litigation, had worked together as young lawyers for New York District Attorney Thomas Dewey, who may be best remembered for his early New York gang busting and the unexpected trouncing he received while governor of New York in the 1948 presidential election.

9.

Quest
for the
Twins

Our quest to acquire twin-engine transports to replace Douglas DC-3's spanned nearly eight years instead of the usual three or four for the U.S. commercial transport industry and did not turn out the way any of us thought it would. At first, it appeared that this project would be orderly and finished on time. We could not have been more wrong—nearly every aspect was a surprise. Three program cancellations were encountered: one by the airline, two by manufacturers. Three successive TWA presidents had a hand in it, a fact not conducive to project stability; and, worst of all, we were not able to buy the planes we wanted.

TWA's timely acquisition of twins for short- to medium-haul services was competitively important, but our first objective following the war was uncontested and clear: to equip the domestic and newly acquired international routes with long-range aircraft to satisfy route franchise obligations, establish a strong competitive presence, and build financial strength for the future. It was simply good business to take care of TWA's principal bread-winning routes first. Besides, there were not enough dollars to do everything at once, and acquisition of the twins had to be accorded lower priority.

TWA's fleet of DC-3's (including converted C-47's) served well but could not match the speed and comfort of the prospective new twins. We planned to retire a large part of the DC-3 fleet after acquisition of replacement aircraft and relegate the rest to all-cargo and passenger services on city-pair segments subject to minimal competition. This happened, but only after we were forced to operate DC-3's against tough competition years longer than planned.

Landing DC-3 replacement contracts had become a Holy Grail quest by aviation manufacturers. Competition was keen. We gave serious consideration to seven new types of aircraft offered by six U.S. manufacturers. Boeing introduced its high-wing Model 417 design, which it finally sold to Fokker; Convair offered to refine its Model 110; Curtiss Wright refined the C-46 Commando and adopted the original CW-20 model designation; Douglas promoted the original DC-8 Allison-powered transport version of the XB-42 propeller-in-tail Mixmaster; Lockheed offered its high-wing Saturn; and Martin offered 202's and 303's. In due course, our studies narrowed the field to planes offered by three manufacturers: Convair, Curtiss Wright, and the Glen L. Martin Company (Martin).

Curtiss Wright

An aggressive Curtiss Wright did not wait for the war to end. It first offered updated C-46 Commando transports, CW-20's, in 1943 for early postwar delivery.

In a sense, the 36-passenger Model CW-20 was a glorified DC-3. Even in 1943, the design seemed out of date because cabin pressurization was lacking and a tail wheel rather than a tricycle-type landing gear was incorporated. While these features were undesirable, they did not disqualify the CW-20 from receiving full TWA consideration because of early availability and somewhat greater cruising speed than the DC-3.

The CW-20 had been designed as a commercial venture by George Page in 1936, years before the transport (T) category rules had been promulgated by the CAA. (Page offered me an engineering position on the original CW-20 project in 1937, shortly before I joined Rearwin.) Later, it emerged as the C-46. The postwar performance of the CW-20 was such that under the T category rules, TWA would have been required to limit operations to areas east of the Rockies. In contrast, Kelly Johnson had anticipated the new rules when designing the Constellation a few years later in 1939 and took a strong lead in forging them during Washington meetings held in 1938, which I was privileged to attend as an industry representative.

After negotiations with Curtiss Wright and thoroughgoing internal reviews, I wrote a letter to Jack Frye on September 22, 1944, which recommended that TWA acquire a minimum number of additional C-47's to tide it over rather than order CW-20's and wait for development of the then prospective Convair or Martin twins, the availability of which appeared to dovetail nicely with our anticipated Constellation program with regard to probable competitive needs. The letter pointed out that the revenue-generating capabilities of the DC-3 and CW-20 fleets would be about equal; the investment required for a CW-20 fleet would be nearly 4½ times as great as for DC-3's; operations and maintenance would be expensive; and the CW-20 was not apt to find a large niche in the transport market and become a significant competitive threat. I explained: "On transcontinental and Chicago-New York schedules, for example, they cannot compete with the larger, pressurized airplanes. On other schedules where frequency is necessary and the air traffic has not been developed to the point to justify both frequency and large size, it is our belief this airplane will not prove as profitable as the DC-3." The letter carried a penned notation by Jack Franklin: "I agree."

After Frye confirmed agreement, I advised Curtiss Wright that TWA would forego procurement of CW-20's. Notwithstanding, Curtiss persisted for several years in its efforts to sell CW-20's to TWA, no doubt because of TWA's lack of firm commitments for any of the new twins. We continued to review the new proposals Curtiss Wright tendered from time to time, but this only reconfirmed our 1944 decision.

Convair

Mac Laddon, Convair's vice president and general manager, was extremely anxious to establish Convair in the commercial transport business. During the closing period of the war, when Convair was in full military production, he directed Frank Fink, Convair's chief engineer, to establish a small

DC-3 replacement project group out of sight in a loft in the factory. Tom Hemphill was placed in charge, and all of Convair's technical groups were available as necessary.

This project was a closely held secret, intended to gain a march on the competition. Airlines did not take part, and even vendor participation was minimized. For example, the plane—the Model 110—was designed for pressurization, but the system was not installed because doing so would have required bringing in another vendor.

Laddon's strategy appeared to work. The 110 was the first of the new U.S. postwar twins to fly and might have been the first into production except for airline-instigated redevelopment, which produced the Model 240. The 110 was a 30-passenger, low-gull-wing transport with P & W R-2800 engines. The Model 240 was configured to carry 40 passengers.

AAL was the dominant airline in the development of the 240. The principals were William Littlewood, AAL's well-known vice president of engineering; R. Dixon Speas, Littlewood's assistant and director of research and development; and Franklin Kolk, an aerodynamicist Speas had recently hired from Martin. Speas, with typical enthusiasm and seemingly limitless energy, took the initiative in convincing Convair to redevelop the 110 to comply with AAL's requirements.

Discussing the 240 program, Speas recalled:

While the competition between the manufacturers was on, I suggested we summarize the competitive designs in a brochure ballot and let AAL employees vote. Bill Littlewood and C. R. Smith [Cyrus Rowlett Smith, the president of AAL] agreed, but with considerable trepidation. The ballot described six designs with artists' conceptions of each plane. We sent ballots to all employees. Believe it or not, Convair won the poll, so everybody was happy.

AAL insisted that nearly every external dimension of the 240 be different from those of the 110. Ralph Bayless, Convair's designer, reminisced:

American wanted everything changed, even a little. We reluctantly made such changes because we wanted American's order to start the program. For example, they insisted on a three-inch-smaller-diameter fuselage for no good reason. Forever afterward, we regretted making this change because this really made the fuselage too small. Many years later, Frank Kolk, who had carried on at Convair for AAL after Speas had been promoted, told me he didn't want any part of the 110; he wanted an entirely new airplane with no leftovers from the 110.

142

I suspect this was an oversimplification of Kolk's position. The idea of making changes for the sake of making changes or possibly to claim design origination was never admissible during my tenure at TWA, and unlikely at American. I insisted that every design change request be soundly based and thoroughly justified with regard to weight, cost, and other significant aspects. Indeed, the departmental analyses that justified changes were retained in my engineering files for years. This was only sound departmental discipline and good business practice.

Dixon Speas recalls the 240 development situation somewhat differently:

American wanted the best possible short-haul planes and didn't want the single 110 prototype to necessarily govern the detail characteristics of the 100-plane 240 fleet American had in mind. Thus, parametric specification negotiations were conducted from ground zero. For example, sectional mockups of several diameter fuselages were constructed and inspected. The smaller diameter was selected by American to enhance short-haul operational efficiency on belief that passengers would find this acceptable. Other dimensional changes evolved for various reasons, with the overall result that nearly everything was different.

American launched the 240 program by ordering 100 aircraft at a price of only $190,000 each less engines, with a price-escalation clause of little consequence. An excellent bargain. Ralph Bayless commented years later that the airplanes were sold to AAL at about half the cost to build them. When production was in full swing and the first 240 neared completion, a concerned Mac Laddon came to C. R. Smith and asked if he would be willing to cancel the program if Convair gave American all of its money back. Laddon explained that by doing so, Convair would lose less money than if it were to build 100 planes at $190,000 each. After thinking a moment, Smith said, "No. A deal is a deal. However, I will agree to cut the order to 75, so you can sell the remaining 25." Convair accepted the revised order and sold the 25 planes, Dixon Speas recalled, "for about $500,000 each."

The first Convair 240 was accepted by AAL on February 28, 1948. TWA was still over two years away from executing a firm contract for twins.

Martin

Martin, faced with a substantial loss of military business following the war, was also anxious to reenter the commercial market. Finding ways to quietly sandwich commercial design work with military projects, it offered two similar twin-engine models: the 202, and the speedier 303, named the "Mercury." Both were 36-passenger, low-wing planes with fuselage diameters three inches greater than that of the Convair 240, the same diameter as that of the 110. The Mercury had a smaller wing than the 202, was 20 mph faster, had more powerful engines, and was pressurized. The unpressurized 202 was designed to comply with the CAA 80-mph maximum stalling speed rule. The Mercury, which could not comply, reflected Martin's assumption that this inconsonant rule would yield, which it ultimately did.

Martin's sales drives emphasized the Mercury, but Northwest Air Lines (NWA), EAL, and several other airlines preferred the 202. The reasons given included earlier delivery, avoidance of the complexity and expense of pressurization on short-haul services, and fear that the 80-mph rule would be retained.

Martin's commercial sales campaigns were managed by William K. Ebel, vice president of engineering; and George B. Shaw, the exuberant and indefatigable vice president of procurement and chief sales executive. A majority of U.S. airlines placed orders. NWA received the first group of 202's and inaugurated services during November 1947, three months before Convair delivered the first 240 to AAL. NWA's 202's quickly established a good reputation for fast, comfortable, and dependable services.

We closely followed NWA's 202 operational experience and continued to evaluate Martin's and Convair's procurement proposals. But with regard to ordering twins, we could only mark time until financial circumstances improved.

Early Evaluations

Our early evaluations of the Convair and Martin twins occurred while Jack Frye was still president and showed on balance that, while the competing designs would produce remarkably close bottom-line results for TWA, the Martins had a slight advantage.

The proposed contracts were something else. Martin offered to reserve delivery positions on execution of a letter of intent with virtually no money down and easy customer outs. The letter was only a loose agreement to agree. It was to be followed by execution of a contract within a specified time following Martin's assurance that the program had become firm, contingent on the firm sale of a minimum number of planes and their obtaining clearance from the Navy to use its production facilities to produce commercial aircraft. Harry West confirmed that execution of the Martin letter would obligate Martin to hold specific delivery positions if the program moved forward, but it would not bind TWA to purchase the planes.

In contrast with Martin's unorthodox contractual approach, Convair required firm and binding commitments, including a substantial down payment and heavy progress payments. Convair representatives scoffed at the Martin approach, explaining that Convair could not give even the slightest consideration to anything less than firm commitments, or it would be impossible to justify the heavy expenditures entailed in the program. They claimed the Martin letters of intent were meaningless and continued to vigorously pursue sales to the airlines that reserved Martin delivery positions.

Because our evaluations continued to show advantages to a Martin fleet, albeit marginally so, TWA, on concurrence of the Equipment Committee and Jack Frye, who presumably obtained clearance from Hughes, executed the one-sided Martin letter of intent for a small fleet of 202's and a sizable fleet of Mercurys. This action was taken in good faith to secure favorable delivery positions and on assumption that TWA's financial problems would be solved in a timely manner. We were entirely candid with the Martin executives and made clear our intention to continue to evaluate the Convair 240. They accepted this and expressed confidence that our final choice would be Martin.

Our Cohu Dilemma

The Martin letter of intent required TWA to execute firm contracts within a specific period after receipt of formal notice from Martin that the program had become firm, if TWA in fact elected to procure the planes. The stipulated penalty for not purchasing the planes was inconsequential. The formal Martin notice was received when Howard was jockeying for control of the board. It was impossible under the circumstances to obtain authority to undertake final negotiations with Martin, and it would have been inappropriate to even suggest to Martin that we would, in fact, procure the planes. After Frye had been put on ice, Martin painfully bided its time until after Cohu's election.

Cohu's insensitive, enigmatic disregard of all aspects of aircraft procurement became evident soon after he joined TWA and continued throughout his tenure as president. I repeatedly tried to discuss this contractual go-no-go issue directly with him and indirectly through Jack Franklin and John Collings. No matter how hard or often any of us tried, no response was forthcoming.

Because I could not reach Cohu, and Hughes remained out of touch, I suggested to George Shaw that he write to Cohu to briefly summarize the history of the affair, explain Martin's pressing need for a formal go-no-go decision, and to urge an early response. He did so and sent me a copy, but he heard nothing from Cohu. Shaw tried to phone Cohu without success and wrote several follow-up letters. Still, no response.

Martin's need to know whether or not TWA would place 202's and Mercurys on firm order became acute because other airlines wanted TWA's reserved delivery positions, and Martin faced increasingly critical production lead-time requirements. Martin could have walked away, but it was reluctant to close out a major potential customer.

About one week after Shaw's last letter to Cohu, I finally telephoned Harry West and said, "Harry, this Martin fiasco has got to end. Whether we have authority or not, Martin has got to somehow be advised that TWA simply cannot proceed with the deal under existing circumstances. If Cohu had the even slightest intention of proceeding, we certainly would have heard. Anyway, we're wasting too damned much time on this project. It's time to cut it off. What's the best way to legally do this?"

Harry agreed as he had before that action was needed, but he suggested that one more effort be made to contact Cohu. I thought this would be a waste of time but finally acquiesced when he insisted because I did not have a reasonable alternative. We both tried and failed.

About one week later, Cohu's executive secretary excitedly called Harry and said, "I found something by accident I know will interest you. When I was going through the files, I ran across a long letter from George Shaw of Martin [his first] and noticed a penned notation in the margin. It's in Mr. Cohu's hand, underlined, and reads,'This plan is out.' It's dated the day after Shaw's letter was received. I don't know how it got in the file or why you and Bob weren't advised."

A flabbergasted Harry West immediately called me and said, "Holy crap! Bob, here we've been breaking our butts trying to get a response, and it was in Cohu's file all the time. I don't know why in hell Cohu couldn't have passed the word along, or at the very least responded to our queries. We certainly aren't mind readers. Damned if I understand it.''

I was numb for a moment, then I asked Harry if Cohu's position had been cleared with TWA's board or Hughes. He said, ''No, I don't think so. All I know is what she said about the notation. She's sending the letter. As you know, I found nothing pertinent in the minutes of the board and Executive Committee meetings when I checked previously.''

We concluded the conversation by agreeing that Harry would contact his boss, George Spater, TWA's chief outside counsel, to review the latest development and, if necessary, arrange for board ratification. George, possibly by magic, got to Cohu and explained the situation. Within a few days, I was cleared to advise Martin that the deal was off and that Martin would be so advised formally in due course. I did so, expressing sincere appreciation on behalf of TWA for Martin's patience.

Cohu's refusal to discuss the Martin situation or make his position known remained an enigma. His handling of the whole affair, or lack thereof, seemed nonsensical, in character for him but completely out of corporate character for TWA.

NWA Disasters

On August 29, 1948, a NWA Martin 202, Flight 421, crashed near Winona, Minnesota, killing all 37 passengers and crew members. The plane had penetrated a severe thunderstorm area when the left wing broke off near the fuselage.

Examination of the wreckage clearly revealed the cause of the accident. A structural failure occurred in the left forward spar cap (a principal span-wise structural member) where the wing panel and center section joined. Minute, telltale waves in the fractured metal surfaces proved the culprit to be metal fatigue caused by stress concentration. Abrupt changes in the cross section of the stair-step spar cap joint caused uneven deflections of the material under load, which imposed severely concentrated stresses in the inside corners of the steps. After repeated exposure, a tiny crack developed in one of the corners, which gradually spread until not enough sound material remained to carry the heavy tension loads encountered in the storm.

The fatigue crack was only about ⅞ of an inch long by 3⁄32 of an inch deep. Martin's choice of 75ST material (in lieu of commonly used, more forgiving 24ST), which had high allowable tensile strength but low fatigue resistance at high stress levels, made the joint more prone to failure. The design of the wing was clearly at fault, a fact that Martin was quick to acknowledge.

Martin had added a wedge in the wing spars to increase the wing dihedral angle after initial flight tests showed the need for greater lateral stability. The Winona failure occurred in the lower front wedge area after the plane had accumulated only 1,321 flight hours.

About an hour after the accident, another NWA 202 flew through the same severe storm area. Then it flew to Duluth and back to Minneapolis, after which a mechanic noticed a discontinuity in the right wing surface. The plane was inspected, and to everyone's horror, spar cap separation had occurred in the same area as in the Winona accident. Only a brief period, perhaps minutes, had kept the plane from disaster. Complete inspection of NWA's fleet of 19 202's showed 5 had fatigue cracks in the front spars, 3 in both wings, and 2 in one wing.

Prior to certification, Martin had subjected a 202 wing to cyclical load tests to establish its fatigue resistance. After 1,885 cycles, the wing was visually inspected. No sign of failure was found. After the Winona accident, the same test wing was again examined. This time the zinc chromate primer was removed, and the spar caustically etched and microscopically examined. Inspection showed cracks in the same area as those that had caused the accident. The evidence of impending doom was there all along, masked by the primer.

The sobering realization that little additional flight exposure would have produced several additional catastrophic failures produced headlines, finger pointing, and condemnation of the design. The press made hay with this situation for weeks. Virtually overnight the term *Martin 202* became synonymous with *perilous*.

Adding fuel for the press was the fact that NWA had suffered two 202 accidents prior to the Winona disaster. Both planes suffered heavy damage but no loss of life. Also, on the day of the Winona crash, a NWA 202 flying near Spokane, Washington, lost its forward cargo door. The door hit the fuselage, wing, and tail, causing extensive damage, but the plane landed safely. Later on, NWA was to suffer eight additional 202 accidents, including four destroyed and four substantially damaged aircraft. Each time a 202 accident occurred, the press recapitulated all of the prior accidents, frightening prospective passengers and driving business away.

Many of us thought the CAB would quickly ground all Martin 202's, but this did not happen. NWA voluntarily grounded its 202 fleet while minor modifications were made, but then the airline kept right on flying 202's.

The CAB Bureau of Safety Investigation accident report, released June 30, 1949, states:

At the present time the wing root fittings on the Martin 202's are being given frequent and thorough inspections for the development of fatigue cracks, and the operating speeds have been reduced 10%. In addition, the front center section spar flange has been modified so as to include five steps in vertical increases in thickness to avoid any radical change in cross section. The radius in the fifth step fillet has been increased from ⅛ of an inch to ¼ of an inch; two bolts have been added; and all parts have been polished. In general the above constitutes present corrective action approved by the Administrator of Civil Aeronautics. It is to be temporary in nature, but sufficient for safe operation until 3,000 hours of flight. After 3,000 hours of flight have been accumulated on the aircraft or before, the airplane will be modified at the Martin Company with a permanent correction which involves extensive structural changes to the wing.

The CAB's technical approach seemed rational and satisfactory, in sharp contrast to the severity of its earlier action in abruptly grounding all Constellations following the Reading accident.

The major modifications required to permanently correct the structural deficiency were made in all operational 202's at Martin's Baltimore factory. Substantial sections of the wing and center section required disassembly and remanufacturing in special jigs to replace the 75ST spar joints with redesigned 24ST joints. This time-consuming operation was done without equivocation at great expense to Martin, whose cash reserves were rapidly depleted.

Confronted with the real possibility of bankruptcy, a flood of canceled airline orders, and no sales prospects, Martin canceled the 202 and Mercury programs. At this time the first Mercury was nearing completion and was cut up into small, irretrievable pieces. Martin was suddenly out of the business of manufacturing twins.

The Convair 110, the first of the U.S. postwar twins to fly, turned out to be only the prototype for the Convair 240, a popular transport. Photo courtesy of General Dynamics Corporation.

The Convair 240 over Balboa Park, San Diego. Nearly every dimension was different from those of the Model 110. Photo courtesy of General Dynamics Corporation.

The Martin 202A in TWA livery: a fine plane, but TWA's second choice. Smithsonian Institution Photo No. 1B-19810.

The Convair 340. Specifications for this Model were 90 percent in common with
the Super 240 configuration Rummel negotiated for procurement by Hughes, but
which LaMotte T. Cohu withdrew from the market at the last minute. Photo
courtesy of General Dynamics Corporation.

The Lockheed Constellation Model 749A in TWA livery: one of the best Constellations ever produced. Photo courtesy of TWA.

The Douglas DC-6B was one of the finest planes in the business. McDonnell Douglas Photo No. SM 112981, courtesy of Harry Gann.

TWA's Constellation Model 1049 over the Grand Canyon. This was the first of Lockheed's long-body models and the first transport to provide regular nonstop coast-to-coast schedules. Photo courtesy of TWA.

The DC-7 was the Douglas answer to Lockheed's 1049. McDonnell Douglas Corporation Photo HG-79-64, courtesy of Harry Gann.

TWA's Super G Constellation, the most successful type of Constellation ever produced, was the direct result of Hughes's and Rummel's labored negotiations. Note the wing-tip fuel tanks. Photo courtesy of TWA.

The Douglas DC-7C's, stretched versions of the DC-6B equipped with the same basic engines as the Lockheed 1049G's, proved to be formidable competitors, just as expected. Hughes elected not to seriously consider this plane for procurement for TWA despite repeated recommendations that he do so. McDonnell Douglas Corporation photo, courtesy of Harry Gann.

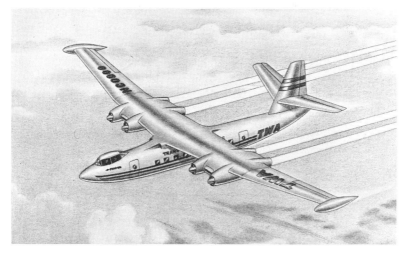

Rendering of Rummel's New York–Chicago jet design of 1946. Photo from Rummel memorabilia.

Lockheed's Model 1649A started life on paper as a turboprop, but when engine difficulty was encountered, it evolved into a conventional piston-powered transport. A beautiful plane, it set new comfort standards but lived up to Rummel's worst economic expectations. Photo courtesy of TWA.

Jim Floyd holding a model of the AVRO Jetliner. A. V. Roe Canada photo, courtesy of Jim Floyd.

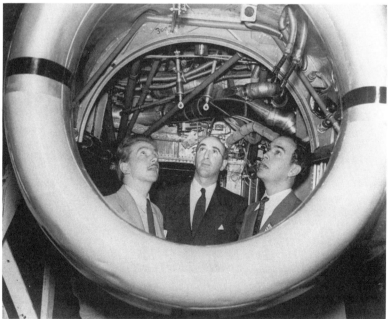

Visual inspection of the Jetliner nacelle. Left to right: Jim Floyd, Joe Morley, and Dixon Speas. A. V. Roe Canada photo, courtesy of Jim Floyd.

Howard Hughes by the Jetliner in Culver City, April 1952. Howard was well taken with the plane. Photo courtesy of Don Rogers.

The Jetliner at Malton, Ontario. A. V. Roe Canada photo, courtesy of Jim Floyd.

The 10-engine Convair B-36 intercontinental bomber. Photo courtesy of General Dynamics Corporation.

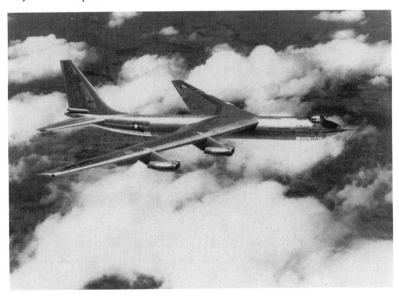

Convair's YB-60 developed from B-36 parts in only eight months. Floyd Odlum wanted Hughes to purchase transport versions for TWA's use. Photo courtesy of General Dynamics Corporation.

A. V. Roe Company's Vulcan delta-wing bomber. Transport versions were proposed and considered. Photo from Rummel memorabilia.

Vickers-Armstrongs Viscount for Capital Airlines. Hughes agreed to buy 15 for TWA, only to have TWA turn its back on the deal. Smithsonian Institution Photo No. 1B-46010.

Vickers-Armstrongs Viscount production line, Weybridge, England. Smithsonian Institution Photo No. 1B-46060.

Ralph Shepard Damon, one of TWA's great presidents. Photo courtesy of TWA.

The house Convair 880 in company logo. Photo courtesy of General Dynamics Corporation.

Charles Sparks Thomas, TWA president when Hughes withheld Convair 880's purchased for TWA. Photo courtesy of TWA.

The Convair 990, an 880 derivative design. Photo courtesy of General Dynamics Corporation.

Ernest R. Breech, trustee and chairman of TWA from 1961 to 1969. Photo courtesy of TWA.

Charles C. Tillinghast, Jr., president of TWA following Hughes's loss of control. Fabian Bachrach photo, courtesy of TWA.

10.

Twins at Last

Damon—Not Just Another President

Ralph Shepard Damon was elected president of TWA on January 25, 1949, after a rich and successful aviation career. He had been president of the Curtiss Airplane Company, Republic Aviation, and American Airlines, and he was well liked throughout the industry. Ralph agreed to join TWA after becoming disillusioned at AAL.

Ralph wanted AAL in the transatlantic market. During the course of the CAB North Atlantic case, he successfully negotiated with John Slater, president of American Export Airlines, for the purchase of that airline. The CAB awarded routes to the northern tier of Europe to American Export on June 1, 1945, and approved the merger between AAL and American Export the same day. A few months later, American Export's name was changed to American Overseas Airlines (AOA).

Damon was proud of the good progress AOA made under his leadership. Much to Ralph's disgust, and against his strong recommendation, C. R. Smith sold AOA to PAA. Hughes, who had tried earlier to interest Damon in joining TWA, saw this as an opportunity and again approached him. This time he succeeded.

Ralph, like Jack Frye, understood aviation thoroughly. He knew instinctively how to improve TWA's competitive posture and the bottom-line importance of deploying adequate fleets of fully competitive aircraft. He described air transportation as "a race between technology and bankruptcy," and it certainly was. Ralph was wonderful to work with. His door was always open; he was easy to talk to and welcomed suggestions; he had a keen understanding of aircraft design and appreciation of technological opportunities; he was entirely candid and fair minded.

TWA had no president from June 1, 1948, when Cohu resigned, until January 25, 1949, when Ralph Damon was elected. This was only one of several periods between the five presidents who held office during Hughes's period of control when there would be no president. "Acting" heads or executive committees were usually appointed, but no matter how capable they might be, their temporary status precluded the enthusiastic and cooperative response among executives so necessary for success. In TWA's case, the all too frequent lack of a president spawned the development of strong, independent department heads, who sometimes tended to operate their functions as if they were separate companies rather than parts of a common enterprise. This was not good, but it was not all bad. The strong departments that emerged at least provided stability when the corporation was leaderless.

Damon, however, quickly forged TWA into a cohesive team, demonstrated good working relations with Hughes, and rebuilt the confidence of the financial community in TWA. Before long, our new aircraft procurement activities were renewed at Convair and Lockheed.

New Interest

During early 1949, shortly after Damon became president, I received word from the Romaine Street boys that Howard wanted to meet me at RKO Studios, which he had recently purchased from Floyd Odlum. I was in Hollywood with Lou Koepnick on a business trip.

As was usual on trips to the Los Angeles area, I was provided the convenience of a Hughes Chevrolet. I drove with Lou to the RKO main gate and was directed by a lone watchman to the building occupied by Hughes. As I drove past studio buildings, not a single person was to be

152

seen. It was as if the property had been abandoned, which was virtually the case. One of the boys motioned from a doorway for me to stop the car. He said, "Howard is on the throne, but he said to come on up."

Lou and I passed through a narrow hall to an enclosed staircase, which led to a large, second-floor room sparsely furnished with several straight-back chairs and a single table. After about 20 minutes, Howard entered.

After I introduced Lou, Howard said he wanted to discuss current aircraft projects. I reviewed the Convair, Lockheed, and Douglas development programs and discussed how the current offerings might be improved. Lou was uncharacteristically quiet and essentially out of the discussion from the beginning because Howard elected to direct his comments to me and looked to me rather than him for responses. Lou soon drifted off to talk to the boy, possibly thinking that Howard wanted confidentiality. After the meeting, I volunteered summary information to Lou.

My discussion with Hughes centered on the Convair 240. I advised that while the 240 was a good plane, the time was right technically for the development of an improved, higher-powered model with increased passenger capacity. I urged that when conditions warranted, he authorize me to undertake exploratory discussions with Convair in his behalf.

I made a similar pitch for increasing the range of the Lockheed 749, noting that Lockheed was already giving consideration to this possibility to surpass the Douglas DC-6 and enhance sales to international carriers.

The meeting with Howard lasted nearly four hours, during which he inquired exhaustively into nearly every design and operational aspect of planes currently being offered by the three manufacturers. Even though he was noncommittal, I felt certain this exchange would help pave the way for renewed technical discussions with Convair and Lockheed as I had recommended. At the first opportunity, I privately mentioned the meeting to John Collings and Ralph Damon and briefly discussed the same design improvement possibilities.

The discussion at RKO Studios was typical of the unique personal relationship that existed between Howard and me—a relationship that no one else at TWA shared. That August, Lou resigned from TWA to return to his former work with the Air Force. Mrs. Koepnick had not been content in Kansas City and longed to return to the ambiance of Wright Field. On August 10, 1949, I was appointed chief engineer.

Not long afterward, Howard telephoned me at home and said, "Bob, I want you to develop the best damn engineering department in the business." He explained that he wanted "the safest, most competitive, and most economic transports, second to none, for TWA." He said he would look to me to see that this was done.

I was elated. This is what I wanted to hear and what I wanted to do. I assured Howard I already had a good engineering department but would do all possible to build even a better one. After discussing potential projects, I mentioned the need for an adequate budget and fully competitive engineering wages. I also suggested raising the prestige of the department by changing my title from chief engineer to vice president, as it had been under Jack Franklin.

Howard said he was reluctant to become directly involved in TWA budgets and titles, concluding, "Anyway, TWA has plenty of prestige, and I'm sure Damon will be reasonable."

I resolved to meet Howard's objective as soon as possible but to do so without fanfare or claims that my department would become "the best." I thought it better to let progress it speak for itself. As the years went by, I would recall Howard's request when I heard quite frequently, especially from the manufacturers, that "Rummel has the best damn engineering department in the business."

The Super 240

I received clearance from Hughes to undertake secret negotiations with Convair shortly after the RKO Studios meeting. My objective was to sell Convair on developing a Super 240, much as discussed with Howard.

By this time, Floyd Odlum's Atlas Corporation had purchased a controlling interest in Convair, and LaMotte T. Cohu, who had said, "In the future TWA will have to buy whatever the manufacturers offer," was president of Convair. I was concerned with the negative attitude Cohu had expressed and thought Floyd Odlum and his assistant, Rocky Rockefeller, my old friend from Hughes Racer days, might be aces in the hole I could call on if necessary.

Convair was clearly in the negotiating driver's seat because Martin's withdrawal left little reason to build a better plane, especially with Convair's production lines full. Also, it seemed likely that Convair would be reluctant to put substantial funds into a new model because it claimed to have lost a great deal of money on the 240 program. It was a long shot, but it was the only show in town.

My first meeting with Convair on this project was with LaMotte Cohu, Frank Fink, Ralph Bayless, and several other Convair executives. Harry West was with me. I declared our interest in the development of a much-improved version of the 240 and briefly described the plane I had in mind: a heavier, more powerful, increased-capacity 240 with a greater wing span to reduce stalling speed and improve aerodynamic efficiency. Frank and Ralph, who apparently had already pushed preliminary pencils, supported the idea but carefully avoided making commitments, pending some signal from Cohu. After about two hours of discussion, the Convair executives withdrew to prepare for a follow-on meeting.

Harry and I met with Cohu and Fink the next afternoon. Cohu was hurriedly preparing to leave for an extended trip to Europe. To my surprise and delight, he approved proceeding with the definition of the plane. He stipulated that the purchase price and delivery dates would be contingent on agreeing on the specifications—an entirely customary qualification. With Cohu's approval to proceed, spirited configuration discussions ensued, and plans were laid for expedited negotiations.

Several weeks later, after Convair had time to develop preliminary specifications and a proposed contract, secret negotiating sessions were held in the old Constance Hotel on Colorado Boulevard in Pasadena. Frank Fink and Ralph Bayless represented Convair in all sessions, along with specialists when required. I headed a small TWA group whose makeup varied depending on the subject matter. Harry West sat in all of the meetings to provide legal guidance for the TWA group and acquire background for contract discussions.

It was a pressure-cooker operation. In addition to negotiating with Convair afternoons and some evenings seven days a week, Harry and I negotiated with Lockheed during the mornings every day except Sunday for the purchase of 20 749A Constellations—749's with increased range and other improvements, much as Howard and I discussed at RKO Studios.

We stayed at the old Knickerbocker Hotel on Vine Street in Hollywood. After a quick breakfast we would drive to Burbank, negotiate with Lockheed, then drive to Pasadena, grabbing a sandwich en route, meet with Convair, and return to the hotel during the evening. This left precious little time for studied review, liaison with my experts, handling other TWA matters that would not wait, and sleep. Absolutely no time was available for relaxation, and barely enough for dinner.

Sleep was frequently interrupted by long calls from Howard. Harry's room was directly under mine. When Howard asked to be transferred to Harry, I stomped on the floor to alert him, an act other hotel guests probably did not appreciate. He returned the favor by whacking on the pipes.

After three weeks of this marathon, I felt a little like a suppressed explosion ready to blow. I telephoned Margie and asked her to come out. Harry followed suit and called Janet, his wife. Margie must have sensed that I needed her. She lined up babysitters and arrived the next day. She was wonderful. She saved my sanity, gave me strength, and restored my perspective. My schedule was not fair to her, but she accepted it without even a hint of a complaint.

When our negotiations were nearly complete, Convair asked for permission to find another customer to justify the venture. Howard, who wanted to maintain secrecy as long as possible, discussed the project with Eddie Rickenbacker of EAL. Shortly thereafter, Charles Froesch, EAL's chief engineer, telephoned me for further information. The upshot was expedited negotiations between EAL and Convair, with occasional commonality meetings between Charlie and me. Eastern looked like the second customer Convair needed for program go-ahead.

A New Martin Offer

While we were busy at Convair, Martin declared its intention of getting back into the commercial business. It offered 404's, described as extensively redesigned, pressurized 202's, and the completion of 12 unpressurized 202A's from structurally revised components left over from the disastrous 202 program.

Martin pressed the case that the proposed program could solve TWA's "acute need" for modern twins much faster than Convair because the 202A's could be turned out rapidly. Martin also offered 404's to EAL, which had no interest in 202A's. The Martin proposal was greeted at TWA with only lukewarm interest because the Super 240 was clearly superior, and the NWA 202 accidents might have irreparably tarnished the name "Martin" in the minds of travelers.

After extensive independent negotiations, TWA and EAL elected to procure Super 240's. Contracts for fleet purchases were readied for joint execution in New York. Lavish preparations were completed for a joint drumbeating press conference with Convair following contract execution and a festive affair that evening with prominent guests.

Cohu returned from Europe, where he had been since approving the Super 240 negotiation, only a few days before the TWA-EAL contract execution was scheduled. With no warning whatsoever, Ralph Damon and Captain Rickenbacker received identical letters from Cohu, formally withdrawing both offers. Convair was unwilling to proceed!

The Cohu letters explained that the production 240's would be more than adequate for TWA and EAL services, 240's were performing well for the airlines, and Convair would be willing to produce standard 240's in lieu of the Super 240's. Cohu's "buy as is" philosophy, perhaps backed by the comforting thought that Martin could not successfully reenter the market, overcame what should have been his better judgment.

Damon and Rickenbacker were flabbergasted and angry. To have the rug pulled out at the last minute, after months of good-faith negotiations, was entirely unconscionable. TWA and EAL had every right to believe that the senior management of Convair, with whom both airlines negotiated, would not have drawn final papers without Cohu's approval, and indeed, that of Convair's board because large sums and a new model were involved. TWA's and EAL's reaction to the Cohu letter was predictable and identical. We abruptly turned from Convair and seriously negotiated with Martin.

Fly-off Tests

Martin enthusiastically undertook renewed sales efforts, and Convair, stung by our concentration on Martin, mounted a vigorous new sales campaign to sell Cohu's 240's. TWA's evaluation of the Convair 240 and Martin 404 showed the planes to be, on balance, nearly equal, with Martin having only a slight advantage. However, both planes were suspect with regard to the adequacy of one-engine-out airport and en route performance, especially in TWA's mountainous western region.

Surprisingly, TWA's management jumped the gun by announcing on March 7, 1949, its "intention" to purchase 30 40-passenger, pressurized Martin 404's and lease 12 unpressurized 202A's for early delivery and interim operations pending delivery of the 404's. This announcement was made primarily to garner favorable publicity and enhance TWA's competitive posture, notwithstanding that execution of firm Martin contracts was understood to be months away. This action did not help my negotiating position at Martin. Convair ignored the announcement and continued aggressively to try to sell 240's.

157

As the competition intensified, both manufacturers claimed better and better performance, frequently by sharpening predictive pencils rather than making improvements. This merry-go-round produced derogatory and vitriolic comments from the salesmen, who scathingly declared that the competition could not possibly perform as claimed. It was impossible to keep our analyses up to date and know who was correct. When I had enough, I called Howard.

Arrangements were made under Howard's aegis for comparative flight tests of Convair's house 240, and a Martin 202 at Hughes's Culver City landing strip, September 1949. Both manufacturers were required to agree on the test procedures, engine power settings, operating weights, and other pertinent aspects for the planes. Each was required to have representatives on board each aircraft on every flight. And both manufacturers were obliged to agree before the tests started that they would accept the test results for both planes, with the understanding that any dispute that might arise would be settled by additional flights. Impartial Hughes employees operated the ground-based recording equipment.

Bob Loomis, who left TWA to join Convair during August 1948, served as pilot on the 240 and observer on the 202, which was configured to match the 404. Captain Rodney of Martin was pilot on the 202 and served as observer on the 240. Other crew members also flew on both planes.

Debriefings, attended by all participants, were held each day after flight tests. Generally, the entire sequence went smoothly, and only a few tests had to be rerun. The test report, dated October 4, 1949, was jointly prepared and signed by the principal Convair and Martin participants.

These tests, the results of which were never made public out of deference to the manufacturers, put to rest for a considerable period the war of claims and counterclaims that had been waged so vigorously. Now we were in a reasonable position to make a rational choice between Convair and Martin—that is, as soon as contract negotiations could be completed. This required nearly five months.

Finally, a Contract

When continuing negotiations with Martin became sticky and strained, Glen L. Martin, president, Glen L. Martin Company, invited Harry West and me to lunch. I did not know if the luncheon were intended to be purely a social occasion or if Martin planned to lower the negotiating boom in controversial areas. Just to make certain we were adequately prepared, and hoping for an opportunity to make a few points of our own if the occasion seemed right, Harry and I made a special late-night review of open items. I had met Martin on a number of previous occasions, held him in high regard, and looked forward to the luncheon, which was in a private dining room near his office.

Martin was most gracious. To my surprise, at no point did he mention the 202A and 404 programs. He spent the entire luncheon period talking about ducks, duck blinds, the migration habits of ducks, the historic and current duck population; really, all about ducks. It was interesting, and clearly not the time to discuss pressing problems. I decided this was just as well because to do so might have unduly agitated Martin's negotiating team.

Howard had been active for some time and was thoroughly conversant with the Martin and Convair offerings and my fleet evaluations. Ralph Damon, John Collings, Vic Leslie, and other TWA principals were also appropriately informed. The earlier announcement notwithstanding, all reviewed the current evaluations and agreed that the Martin 202A-404 combination was best for TWA.

With Howard's approval, contracts for a fleet of 12 202A's and 30 404's were executed February 22, 1950, by Ralph Damon and C. C. Pearson, president of Martin. The 202A's were leased with TWA rights to terminate individual leases after the combined fleet totaled 32 planes, that is, 202A's could be turned back to Martin on a one-for-one basis when the twentieth and subsequent 404's were delivered. At that time, we planned to eventually operate only 404's. Later on, TWA ordered 10 additional 404's, and still later, instead of canceling the 202A leases, TWA elected to purchase the 10 planes rather than invest more substantial funds in additional 404's, thus producing a combined fleet of 52 modern twins.

Not long after TWA's February 22 order was placed, EAL ordered 60 404's. Martin was emphatically back in the business of manufacturing twins.

Howard ordered one 404 for himself through the Hughes Tool Company and requested me to implement the contract and treat his airplane as just another TWA plane. We did not know which one of the 41 404's Howard would select—the Toolco contract did not specify the serial number—until a few weeks before delivery. Even then, we were not certain because he danced around the selection question, requiring time-consuming, repetitive, exhaustive reviews of construction inspection reports, acceptance flight test information, and the like. Howard's 404 was one of the last to be accepted.

Floyd Odlum's Review

A few weeks after contract execution, Howard called and said Floyd Odlum had recently handed him a Convair engineering report. He explained that this report, "Comparison of Convair 240-16 and Martin 404," dated March 13, 1950, was a severe critique of Martin's representations and showed the 240 to be the better plane. Howard asked, "Will you please review it and provide Ralph Damon with any comments you might develop?" The report arrived in my office the next day.

I assumed that Odlum wanted to convince Hughes that a terrible mistake had been made that could only be rectified by canceling the Martin order and buying Convairs. I also assumed that Howard, by directing my comments to Ralph, wanted Ralph to review the Convair report and my comments preliminary to direct discussions with him.

The Convair report was based on a superseded Martin 404 specification and contained many of Convair's critiques discussed ad nauseam during negotiations. I addressed every claim in the report—a few were valid—in a 19-page critique, covered it with a single-page summary letter, and sent them with the report to Damon.

The summary letter, dated March 24, 1950, stated that the Convair report was in part based on incorrect information; that many of its conclusions were invalid; and that it did not invalidate TWA's final aircraft selection analyses or conclusions. In short, TWA's choice of the 404 was prudent. After reviewing the data, Damon asked for clarification of a few items, but other than that, nothing happened.

About three months later, Howard telephoned me early one morning at Ralph Ellinger's office in the Burbank Air Terminal. He asked if I could meet him at Gate 7 at 11 o'clock "to take a little ride." I of course agreed.

Howard almost always knew how to reach me, even when I was not obliged to check in. At times, I wondered who besides me was keeping the boys in the back room advised. One time, I changed hotels on arrival at the airport without calling in and without canceling the original reservation (I wanted to look the new hotel over before doing so), only to have a call from Howard waiting when I arrived at the new hotel.

Howard taxied to Gate 7 a few minutes past 11 in a converted Douglas B-23, a pot-bellied variant of the C-47. I boarded with the engines running and was invited to sit in the first officer's seat. Howard immediately took off and headed for San Gorgonio Pass near Palm Springs. He did not offer one word of explanation for the trip.

Howard was always his own man, but especially so while flying. He relished being in the air, exuding confidence and the complete sense of freedom that is so much a part of flying. On the way he demonstrated some unusual flight characteristics of the plane while engaging in small talk. We passed the San Jacinto peaks and landed at Palm Springs Airport, where one of the boys was waiting with a Chevrolet. Jackie Cooper happened to be standing beside his airplane and came over to greet Howard. Howard introduced me as "Bob Rummel, *the* airplane designer." While I had designed planes, I certainly did not expect to be introduced as "*the*" airplane designer. I guess he thought he needed to build me up.

Howard drove the Chevrolet and seemed deep in thought. Suddenly, he said, "We're meeting Odlum to talk about the Martin deal."

"Holy God!" I thought, "so that's what it's all about. Could Howard possibly be considering canceling the Martin contract? Why hadn't he given me warning so I could collect my thoughts? Does he understand how far along Martin really is? What is Odlum up to?" Just then, before I had time to collect myself and advise Howard of the current status of the Martin program, we arrived at a large white house surrounded by palm and eucalyptus trees.

Floyd Odlum had the reputation of being an inconsiderate, steel-eyed, ruthless plunderer who made his fortune early on by buying and mercilessly liquidating corporations. He was chairman of his highly successful Atlas Corporation, chairman of RKO when it was purchased by Hughes, and chairman of Convair. I had met him on several occasions with Howard and, contrary to his reputation, always found him to be friendly and considerate, but I had never been involved with him in eyeball-to-eyeball clinches.

When Howard and I entered, Floyd Odlum and a contingent from Convair consisting of Rocky Rockefeller; Frank Fink; Ralph Bayless; B. J. ("Bernie") Simons, project engineer; J. G. ("Jack") Zevely, vice president of sales; and a few others were waiting in the living room. Howard and Floyd took chairs at one end of the room, facing the group.

Floyd said he would like to know why Howard and TWA decided to buy

Martins rather than Convairs. Rocky and Frank ably and accurately reviewed in detail the extended negotiations for the Super 240, including Convair's authority to make formal offers to TWA and EAL, Cohu's abrupt withdrawal of the Convair offers shortly after his return from Europe (neither of them knew of the Cohu withdrawal letters until after they had been sent), TWA's and EAL's negotiations for the standard 240 that followed, the comparative flight tests, and Convair's diligent efforts to sell 240's to both airlines.

Then, after being asked the same question by Odlum and Hughes, I confirmed what they had been told and explained that TWA and EAL had selected the Super 240 and planned to execute fleet buy contracts when Cohu withdrew the offers. I said both airlines thoroughly reexamined the subsequent 240 and 404 offerings and decided the 404 was best. In other words, the Super 240 was first choice, the 404 second choice, and the standard 240 last in preference. I made clear that serious negotiations for the 404's were not undertaken until after Cohu had pulled the rug from under the Convair deals. I also mentioned the months that had been spent in configuring the Super 240's, and Damon's and Rickenbacker's displeasure on receiving the Cohu letters, an unfortunate situation exacerbated by lack of warning or prior discussion.

At that point, Rocky emphasized that the Cohu letters were the turning point and that both airlines had finalized arrangements for joint contract execution before the Cohu letters were sent. There were no unpleasant words or recriminations; just straight talk.

Howard and Floyd then exchanged views and agreed that Convair would have won both contracts had it been willing to produce the Super 240; and, had this occurred, Martin would most likely not have been able to reenter the commercial transport business.

Shortly thereafter, Howard and I drove back to the B-23. We arrived in Burbank at sunset after an uneventful flight. Howard invited me to have dinner with him in the restaurant on the second floor of the terminal building. We were met at the door by an elderly hostess who led us to a secluded booth. I thought he might have made special arrangements for his food, but he ordered a regular meal from the menu. After a pleasant meal and discussion of aviation safety and the fleet plans of TWA's competitors, I offered to pick up the check, thinking he might prefer to have TWA pay for it. He smiled and said, "No, this is on Uncle." Altogether, it was a good day.

Within two months of the Palm Springs meeting, LaMotte T. Cohu was relieved of his duties as president of Convair. He was made vice chairman of the board and headed one of the board's committees. After that happened, some of my Convair friends indicated that Cohu had little voice in the affairs of Convair.

Not long afterward, Floyd Odlum, realizing that Martin was a strong competitor that intended to remain in the business, decided Convair should offer an improved version of the 240. The Super 240 specification, developed during negotiations with TWA and embraced by EAL, was adopted as the.appropriate vehicle for negotiations with interested airlines. UAL became the prime target for Convair's new sales campaign.

UAL had enjoyed excellent success with its 240's, and needed somewhat larger, longer-range twins. The Super 240 seemed to have been made to order. This design, after nurturing by UAL negotiations, became the 340. The 340 was rushed to completion and first flew October 5, 1951.

The Super 240 seemed to have been made to order for UAL. This design, after nurturing by UAL negotiations, became the 340. The 340 was rushed to completion and first flew October 5, 1951.

The first TWA 202A was accepted at New Castle, Delaware, on July 14, 1950. The last of the 53 Martins was delivered to TWA during September 1952, nearly eight years, three TWA presidents, and three program cancellations after our first studied evaluations of the prospective twins.

TWA's Martin services were well received. Our fears that the earlier NWA crashes might deter passengers proved to be unfounded, or, at least, not identifiable. TWA's Martins earned an enviable safety record throughout their years of service. They were finally sold after turboprops and jets made them competitively unattractive. The last TWA 404 flight, from Baltimore to St. Louis via Washington, Columbus, Dayton, and Indianapolis, took place April 29, 1961.

11.
Determined
Manufacturers

Douglas versus Lockheed

Howard Hughes opened competitive negotiations with Douglas for improved DC-6's, and with Lockheed for improved 749's during early 1949, not long after Ralph Damon became president. Each manufacturer, aware that an order for as many as 25 planes might be involved, undertook intense negotiations with enthusiasm, ingenuity, and a firm resolve to win the competition.

We sought models that could fly the Atlantic nonstop in both directions against severe winter winds to reduce trip time by eliminating stops and improve schedule reliability. The 749's obtained during the close of Cohu's presidency were more capable than the 049's, but they fell considerably short of this goal. Neither Howard nor I thought full attainment was in the cards, but we wanted to make as much progress as possible. We finally obtained planes with good nonstop capabilities, but not until after several more negotiations.

This negotiation, like the others, involved working with some of the truly great aviation pioneers—the entrepreneurial innovators and designers who helped advance air transportation beyond the threshold of trepidation into the age of nearly universal acceptance.

The involved Lockheed principals were as before: Bob Gross, whose intentions and integrity were always above question; Hall Hibbard, the brilliant, forthright, and firm leader responsible for all of Lockheed's technical undertakings; Kelly Johnson, the determined and confident design genius; Carl Haddon, whose solid engineering capabilities did well for the industry; Willis Hawkins, whose vision helped shape the future; and Leonard Schwartz, whose sales efforts were probably well intended but too often employed to frustrate goals the engineers on both sides agreed on.

The Douglas principal was Donald Douglas, Sr., the innovative airplane design pioneer, who ran the company. No major decision was made without his personal approval. The Douglas board listened to him and acquiesced. He was respected everywhere that airplanes flew. I knew him as a friend and a helpful and dedicated but conservative executive who earnestly sought Howard's transport business, popular accounts to the contrary notwithstanding.

The other Douglas principals we worked with included Ed Burton, the prolific and innovative designer, who listened carefully to customers; Carlos Wood, my old friend from early days; Jackson R. McGowen, the realistic and proficient project engineer, who later became president of Douglas; Nat Paschall, the engaging vice president of sales, who knew how to try to please customers and smooth negotiations; J. O. (''Jake'') Moxness, an experienced pilot who thoroughly understood the business; James K. Clyne, crack salesman and engineer; and Donald W. Douglas, Jr., who learned the business from the ground up by successively working in various departments throughout the company.

I do not remember a single engineering executive at any of the companies who did not want to build the best possible planes. However, just what constituted the best and what could be economically produced were frequently the subject of intense debates. Firm convictions did not always yield to persuasion. The arguments sometimes became heated, but tempers remained in check.

Flight safety was always front and center. All of us searched for designs that would reduce the probability of encountering any flight condition or malfunction that could become hazardous. When Carl Haddon was project engineer for the Constellation he drove seven miles to work every day through a residential area. He would ask himself, ''Do I know anything about the Constellation that would prevent me from putting my family on a flight today?'' If he could think of any suspect element he would introduce a special corrective project on arriving at the office. That kind of dedication was typical. We did not need lawyers or federal rules to motivate us. We did it because it was right.

At the outset of the negotiation, Lockheed offered production 749's. However, in line with my discussions with Howard at the RKO Studios, an improved, longer-range version, Model 749A, was soon on the table. Lockheed proposed a 5,000-pound increase in operating weight, increased fuel capacity, improved brakes, engine air intakes less susceptible to icing, and other improvements.[1] Our reviews showed the 749A to be superior to the Douglas DC-6 and capable of serving TWA's domestic and international routes well.

Active negotiations with Douglas followed the discussions that produced Lockheed's 749A proposal. Almost immediately, Douglas, driven by knowledge of the 749A, discussed increasing the standard DC-6 fuselage length six feet to accommodate from six to eight additional passengers, an 8,000-pound increase in operating weight, and the installation of more powerful P & W R-2800 engines. This concept became the DC-6B. Douglas did not want to yield any part of the market to Lockheed. It was anxious to sell Hughes: a fine prize indeed, which would send advantageous signals to the entire industry.

Douglas was provided with additional incentives to stretch the DC-6 by the military and several all-cargo carriers, who frequently found payloads limited by the volume of the DC-6-size fuselage when carrying low-density cargo. The DC-6A, considerably longer than the DC-6 but somewhat shorter than the DC-6B, was proposed for them.

The principal Douglas spokesman in Howard's and my negotiations was Donald Douglas, Jr., who endeavored to sell Hughes on the West Coast and me in Kansas City. Douglas technical teams, armed with reports comparing the DC-6B with the 749A, descended frequently on my office. They and Lockheed representatives, who were doing the same thing, would pass each other in the hallways.

My preliminary analyses showed the DC-6B to be extremely attractive and an effective competitor to the 749A. It had good performance and the potential on TWA's routes for producing seat-mile costs significantly lower than those of the 749A. The calculated cost differences were large enough to more than offset the estimated commonality benefits that would accrue from operating a combined fleet of 749's and 749A's.

Operating costs became a controversial issue. Lockheed produced reports proving major operating cost advantages for a TWA fleet of 749A's, Douglas produced reports proving just the opposite, and neither agreed with my independent studies.

Hughes, somewhat to my chagrin, when confronted with three conflicting cost studies, asked Vic Leslie, TWA's vice president and treasurer, to analyze the studies and give him an ''independent'' opinion. After spending three days in Kansas City, Vic advised Howard that the expenses incurred from operating a fleet of 749A's would be more than offset by operating a fleet of DC-6B's—exactly what I had been saying.

By the time final negotiations were close at hand, my personal choice was the DC-6B because of its relative simplicity, straightforward passenger accommodations, and good economic and operational characteristics. I emphasized to Howard the advantages that would accrue from the purchase of a fleet of DC-6B's but, in fairness, also advised him that a fleet of 749A's could also do a creditable job for TWA. Ralph Damon preferred to deal with Lockheed and so advised Howard.

After exasperatingly detailed telephone reviews, including several all-night telephone sessions, Howard agreed that the DC-6B's would be best for TWA. He said he liked the idea of a new model, was favorably impressed with the performance and cost projections, and commented that a mixed fleet might cover the market better because customers could have their choice. To keep the manufacturer's feet to the fire, we agreed not to reveal our preference for the DC-6B's to them until the last detail in our negotiations had been settled. By mid-April 1949, only a few items remained to be negotiated.

About this time I received a call from Howard in Ralph Ellinger's Burbank office to review recent meetings with Douglas and Lockheed. Toward the conclusion of the conversation, because I knew of Damon's and Leslie's concern over the large associated debt burdens, I said without really thinking, ''I wonder if TWA is really in a financial position to buy these airplanes.''

Howard's reaction was explosive: ''What? What did you say? Listen, Bob, you are not to concern yourself in any way with financial matters concerning this program. That is not your job. This area involves my interests and me personally. It is not your business. Your job is to see that the planes fully comply with mission guarantees and TWA's requirements. I thought we understood each other on that." Then he repeated himself before I could get a word in.

When he paused, I said, "Jesus, Howard, all I said was—"

Howard interrupted, "I know exactly what you said. Now, listen carefully, Bob, you are not, I said *not*, to become involved in financial matters concerning this program. Now, are you entirely clear on that?"

I replied, "Yes, Howard. I hear you loud and clear. I won't even let myself think about it."

Confrontation

During early May, Howard, Ralph Damon, and I met at Douglas with Nat Paschall and Jake Moxness to resolve a few remaining issues. After brief introductory exchanges, Ralph raised the question of the adequacy of the Douglas postdelivery product support program. His highly critical comments on this important subject touched off an intense argument with Howard. Howard defended Douglas with words of assurance. The more he did, the more Damon criticized Douglas, giving examples of his experience at American with poor parts availability and bad service. Damon became somewhat flushed and exasperated. Howard was calmer, but just as intense. It was eyeball to eyeball. Howard said Douglas had improved in recent years. Ralph disagreed. Howard thought Douglas would do a better job in the future. Ralph did not.

Nat and Jake just sat and listened with their mouths open, making no effort to defend Douglas, which was probably wise. It would have been difficult to get words in, and they probably would not have helped their cause. I elected not to jump into the argument unless called upon.

When the futility of continuing to try to resolve the argument became apparent, Howard turned to Nat and said, "Well, Nat, I guess we have a few things to settle internally. Why don't we get back to you later?" With that, the meeting broke up. We did not get back.

Howard and Ralph were entirely cordial immediately after the meeting. We were together another hour, during which the two airplane deals and other aviation affairs were discussed, but neither of them brought up the Douglas product support matter.

I was not surprised to hear some divergence of opinion between Hughes and Damon—every person worth his salt has a mind of his own—but the fact that such an intense argument occurred in the presence of the Douglas executives seemed incredible. I wondered if the argument had been staged, possibly to help Howard out of some sort of moral commitment at Douglas; however, I tended to dismiss this theory because if Howard wanted to buy Constellations, the baby he and Frye conceived, such a charade should have been unnecessary. He had the final say, and everyone knew it.

Shortly after the Douglas meeting, on May 31, 1949, while I was still negotiating the Super 240 with Convair, TWA executed a contract for 20 Lockheed 749A's for delivery in 1950. Later, the contract was amended to add 5 749A's for early 1951 delivery. Three more manufactured for Delta in compliance with TWA specifications were acquired by TWA in 1951.

Damon's choice had prevailed in the first major equipment decision after he was installed. Or had it? I wondered if Hughes had leveled with me concerning his preference for the DC-6B's. I could never be certain of Howard's position until final decision time. In any event, Damon never won such an argument again.

Consequences

TWA's 749A's proved to be excellent airplanes. They served well for 17 years in domestic and international operations and were among the last of TWA's Connies to be retired. At retirement they were still good mechanically and most likely could have provided many additional years of service. But, not surprisingly, the jets pushed them aside competitively.

The 749A's were also good for Lockheed. The TWA order provided continuity of production at a crucial time, and in doing so enabled Lockheed to develop the stretched Constellation, the Model 1049.

The Douglas DC-6B program also proved to be highly successful for Douglas, far more indeed than the 749A's for Lockheed. DC-6B fleets were ordered by UAL, AAL, and many other airlines around the world. The all-cargo version, the DC-6A, was ordered by Slick Airways and several other airlines. It had two above-floor cargo doors, a strengthened floor, and an automatic cargo-compartment cooling system designed to protect perishables. Military versions were also built in large quantities: C-118A Liftmasters for the Air Force, and R6D-1's for the Navy. The stretched DC-6 designs were winners. The part played by Hughes and myself in initiating the stretched DC-6 programs and the technical contributions made thereto, like the part we played in the Convair 340 program, went by virtually unnoticed, perhaps because of Howard's demands for secrecy and the fact that in the end we bought other types of airplanes.

We always welcomed, indeed encouraged, direct competition between manufacturers, rather than working exclusively with a preselected winner, because it always produced better aircraft and better deals. However, we became concerned about this practice because our Convair 340 and DC-6B negotiations produced aircraft purchased by TWA's competition, eroding its competitive position. We wanted better planes but, except for matters of safety, which were routinely discussed with competitors, had no interest whatsoever in helping our competition.

We had numbers of discussions on this subject but always came to the same conclusion: long-term corporate interests demanded obtaining the best possible planes, and competitive negotiations best assured obtaining the desired results. The possibility that losing designs could ultimately benefit our competition was important but secondary. Moreover, it was not a one-way street. TWA also occasionally benefited from developments fostered by our competition.

Howard's 749A

Howard ordered one TWA-type 749A through the Hughes Tool Company only a short time after the 20 were ordered by TWA. He asked me to handle customer inspection and acceptance activities for Toolco and treat his plane just like the other TWA 749A's.

After the plane was ready for flight tests in Burbank, Hughes, without giving any notice whatsoever, placed it under 24-hour armed guard notwithstanding that it was on Lockheed property and contractual acceptance had not occurred. It made no difference to him that he did not have Lockheed's permission or any legal right to do so. Absolutely no one was allowed to approach the plane, and all progress stopped. Howard must have wanted to buy time, possibly for financing reasons.

Because the plane's location interfered with normal Lockheed operations, Bob Gross tried without success for weeks to get Hughes to remove the guards and permit the airplane to be towed aside. Gross continued to press; Hughes continued to procrastinate. One night about 2:00 A.M., Howard, probably annoyed by Lockheed's persistence, showed up at the Burbank airport with a flight engineer. After carefully warming the engines, he taxied the plane toward a designated parking area near a blast fence. The flight engineer suddenly shouted, "Brakes! Reverse! Reverse!" Howard jumped on the brakes and abruptly stopped. The leading edge of the left wing was only six inches from impacting a tall metal floodlight stanchion anchored in concrete.

Because towing gear was not available at that hour, the easy way out of the predicament was to use reverse thrust to back up just far enough to swing the wing clear. Howard balked, probably for fear of overheating the engines, although little danger existed that this would have occurred or that engine warranties would have been invalidated.

Howard left the plane in that position and again posted guards. He refused to permit Lockheed to move the plane, insisting that the light pole be moved because, "By God, it shouldn't be there." After several days of haggling, Howard won. Lockheed moved the pole, and he permitted the plane to be towed.

Several years later, Howard sold the still brand-new plane, which he had never flown, to the British at a nice profit.

Note

1. One such improvement was the installation of jet stacks—short engine exhaust pipes designed to enhance performance, improve engine cooling, and reduce maintenance costs—which Lockheed had set out to develop in early 1949. At the time of our negotiation, the Lockheed program was not far enough along to permit Lockheed to make a firm contractual commitment to install the jet stacks before delivery; however, it promised to do its best. Lockheed was finally able to make good on its promise, with the result that the cruising speed of TWA's 749A's was increased by from 5 to 8 mph, depending on altitude, with a commensurate increase in range. Later, the 749's that had been delivered in 1948 were similarly equipped. Because of the success of this program, I arranged under a contract of bailment for a TWA 049 to be placed in trust to Lockheed on April 13, 1951, to permit the development of jet stacks for that model. The plane was returned on May 20, after which all of TWA's 049's were modified, a program that Hughes wholeheartedly applauded.

12.

Progress
and
Disaster

The Long Bodies

Lockheed's proposed Model 1049, the first of the long-body Constellations, was an attractive design that offered lower seat-mile costs and greater range capability than the earlier Connies: features that could clearly strengthen TWA's competitive position against UAL's and AAL's Douglas DC-6B's. I was convinced that a fleet of these fine planes would do well for TWA, and happily, Hughes's position at Lockheed virtually guaranteed first deliveries to TWA.

I had followed Lockheed's 1049 gestation period closely, keeping Howard and Ralph Damon advised. On the day Lockheed advised of the 1049 program go-ahead during late 1949, I called Howard to report this and seek authority to negotiate specifications.

Lockheed had urged me to work with them toward the development of mutually satisfactory specifications, not only as a necessary step toward procurement, but also to inject airline requirements during the formative stages of the design, when compliance could be best achieved. This appeared to be a great opportunity to help configure the planes to TWA's liking.

Try as I might, I could not raise Hughes. He was not answering phones. His Romaine Street Mormons repeatedly passed the word along, but Hughes would not respond. Bob Gross and Leonard Schwartz also tried without success. It was almost as if he had never been born. Unfortunately, this lasted for months.

During this period I met with Hall Hibbard, Kelly Johnson, and Carl Haddon numbers of times for briefings and to inject TWA's thinking into the design. Lockheed listened, but because Howard had not expressed procurement interest or authorized me to undertake technical negotiations, my power of persuasion was limited, and desirable items fell by the wayside.

Development of long-body ("stretched") Constellations had been under intermittent consideration for years. The first stretched version I am aware of was discussed with Jack Franklin and me in 1943, when Lockheed tentatively proposed a 13-foot fuselage extension. This possibility was abandoned during the preliminary design phase because of inadequate engine power. Lockheed proposed a 12-foot extension in 1948, but this too was dropped for the same reason. Finally, during late 1949, Lockheed undertook development of the 1049, with an 18-foot fuselage extension.

Lockheed's action was triggered by its need to compete more favorably with Douglas DC-6B's and by the availability of more powerful engines. No doubt the company was also motivated by a sobering belief that Howard had nearly bought DC-6B's instead of 749A's.

Lockheed needed an experimental plane to expedite development of the 1049. The original prototype Constellation, Serial 1961, which had been used extensively for experimental purposes, had been declared surplus and disposed of by Lockheed when it no longer appeared to be useful. Hughes had purchased this plane from the war surplus market for about $25,000, parked it, and never made use of it. I was prepared to argue against TWA's undertaking to modify the 1961 to our standard 049 configuration because of high costs and the extended disruption it would cause TWA's engineering and production schedules. However, Howard did not pursue this course. He sold the 1961 back to Lockheed for the 1049 program at a handsome profit.

Lockheed added cylindrical sections to the 1961 fuselage ahead of and behind the wing to represent the 1049 and permit evaluation of taxi and

174

flight characteristics. Even though operated in severely restricted modes because of lack of power (P & W R-2800 engines had been installed in lieu of the Wright 3350 for experimental purposes) and structural limitations, the tests saved considerable development time and confirmed the need for numbers of changes, including larger vertical tail surfaces.

Ralph Damon enjoyed excellent relations with Hughes but was reluctant to countermand Howard's standing directive that TWA not undertake negotiations without his personal approval. I think he probably would have done so had he considered technical participation as timely and important as I did.

Howard's standoff behavior, which was never explained, may have been on advice of counsel. Hughes had personally testified at a CAB hearing during October on his further control of TWA, resulting from the conversion of Toolco's note into stock and raising his ownership to about 76 percent. The hearing was held over the opposition of Hughes and TWA, which considered it inappropriate and unnecessary. A similar hearing had been held in 1944, culminating in the CAB's approval of the degree of ownership that existed at that time.

CAB public counsel did not have an easy time interrogating Hughes. Hughes seemed to deliberately misunderstand nearly every question, blaming his well-known hearing problem. He answered the questions by telling counsel what he wanted the CAB to hear—in effect, virtually taking control of the hearing. This did not go down well with public counsel. This was the last time Howard ever appeared in a public hearing. Thereafter, until the CAB ruled favorably in his favor on the control issue about one year later, Howard's stewardship of TWA was under nearly constant attack by the CAB public counsel. Because of this, Hughes may have felt it best to hold back from the close personal involvement in TWA fleet procurement affairs that had been his trademark.

Whatever the reason for it, Howard's unavailability seemed unnatural because of his intense interest in new aircraft developments. It was also unfortunate because it prevented negotiations, which undoubtedly would have produced 1049's in much closer compliance with TWA's requirements. Notwithstanding, Lockheed agreed with me to voluntarily hold good delivery positions for TWA, pending a direct expression of interest from Hughes in a reasonable time.

EAL was the first to buy 1049's. After brief negotiations by Eddie Rickenbacker and Charlie Froesch, 10 were ordered on April 24, 1950.

The order was increased later to 14 planes. The first was delivered November 26, 1951, eight months after UAL placed its first DC-6B in passenger service.

Finally, after continuing efforts, Leonard Schwartz succeeded in contacting Hughes four months after EAL placed its order. Howard called me at home. After months of total inaccessibility, he suddenly wanted papers for procuring 10 planes negotiated overnight. He explained Lockheed was almost out of the production lead-time required to make good the early delivery positions being held for TWA. Howard said, "Bob, Leonard insists that the planes be built in strict compliance with Eastern's specifications with absolutely no TWA changes and that the deal be concluded within days. Get Harry West and review the papers on a top-priority basis."

With some pride, Howard said that Leonard, despite his uncompromising stance, had agreed to incorporate a number of changes, which he enumerated and then repeated. Disappointingly, Howard's changes were entirely standard items, expected and included in every contract as a matter of course to suit the customer's desires. For example: TWA was to select instruments, the interior color scheme, the exterior logo, and the like. Howard had agreed to limit our demands for improvements to only those few items to preserve the favorable delivery positions.

Howard's directive to me left virtually no room for negotiations. His agreement with Schwartz tied my hands, contrary to his standing charge that I obtain transports in full compliance with TWA requirements. The Lockheed can't-do attitude, encountered during our Civil C-69 negotiations, appeared to be alive and well.

This situation was intensely frustrating. TWA also expected me to obtain airplanes that met its requirements. I knew perfectly well that when operational difficulties were encountered after delivery, citing the ground-rule restrictions that surrounded these negotiations would be totally inadmissible and imprudent. It could appear to be irresponsible excuse-making—tantamount to blaming Hughes. Besides, my really important challenge was to find ways to incorporate the needed improvements before delivery despite Howard's directive (which I hoped to change), a feat that appeared to be impossible.

I phoned Leonard Schwartz to get the papers. He reminded me that he had personally tried for months to activate Howard without success, and he had persuaded Lockheed to preserve good delivery positions for him.

176

Leonard added, "Now that so much time has gone by and Lockheed is in a tight box schedule-wise, you of course understand, Bob, time will not permit any deviation from the specifications. But we can still deliver the airplanes Howard wants." My only comment was that I would look the papers over and see what might be required. He sent the EAL specifications and draft contract to Kansas City on the next plane.

The specifications were even more disappointing than I had anticipated. For example, the air-conditioning system was totally inadequate, the passenger interior was spartan, the flight-deck changes were insufficient, and desired maintenance improvements were largely lacking.

Lockheed had retained the 749A air-conditioning system to save development cost despite the need to accommodate 30 more passengers. After universally poor experience and all the haggling and fighting over the ventilation deficiencies of the 049's, it was hard to believe that Lockheed was willing for TWA and its passengers to suffer a similar fiasco. Ground rules or no ground rules, I simply could not accept another inadequate environmental system.

The spartan EAL interior, designed to cater to its dense, north-south East Coast markets, was totally unsuited for TWA's long-range, east-west routes, particularly because our customers were accustomed to and liked the relatively plush 749's and 749A's. Unfortunately, Schwartz understood his agreement with Howard to mean that Lockheed would only change the color of the upholstery, carpets, and sidewalls. Everything else was to be exactly like EAL's interior, an obviously unacceptable plan.

Lockheed's agreement on cockpit changes was also too restrictive to satisfy TWA's flight operations personnel. A few instruments could be changed if they fit the same holes and connections, but that was all. And adding to the negotiating challenge was the need to satisfy numerous maintenance needs previously discussed with Lockheed, which were not addressed in the specifications, as well as those I knew perfectly well would develop during specification review sessions.

I was prepared to press for the desired cockpit changes by bending the ground rules because Lockheed's position was so unreasonable, but I was not entirely unsympathetic to Lockheed's resistance to change. Flight-deck change requests were quite frequently an enigma to me. While I accepted as normal changes requested because of new Air Traffic Control System requirements, demonstrated equipment deficiencies, or advantageous new instrumentation developments, I was bothered by requests that only re-

177

flected capricious crew opinions. When I objected to changes falling in the latter category, I was almost always overridden by Jack Franklin or John Collings, TWA pilot opinion at that time being considered entirely sacrosanct.

TWA's primary cycles of flight-deck change requests coincided with changes in Flight Operations leadership. Sometimes instruments would be interchanged, only to be put back in the original positions by the following regime. This merry-go-round of fickle changes did not end until jets were acquired. From that time onward until his retirement, Capt. Gordon Stanley Granger stabilized flight-deck requirements, and I had a firm and decisive grip on associated expenditures. We limited changes to those that were necessary to accommodate technological advances or to correct deficiencies.

Review of the EAL specifications produced a long list of desired changes, which could not be achieved or even seriously discussed under Howard's agreement with Leonard. I placed a call to Howard to review this situation and persuade him to relax his directive so I could try to sell Lockheed on accommodating more TWA requirements.

Howard promptly returned my call and heard me out—the conversation lasted about four hours—but he concluded that I would have to essentially live by his agreement with Leonard. He did, however, approve negotiating for an adequate environmental system. He also relented slightly by agreeing that if Lockheed could make minor changes without adversely affecting delivery dates or purchase price, he would have no objection. He "regretted" placing me in an awkward position vis-à-vis TWA and said it had been "absolutely impossible" for him to act earlier, when the program was being formulated. He said I would just have to do the best I could within the guidelines and as discussed, and that I should keep him advised. E. Z. ("Oz") Cocke, TWA's vice president of traffic, insisted on the installation of upper berths and refused to accept the fact that the Hughes-Schwartz agreement ruled them out. He would not accept no as an answer and insisted that I at least discuss the subject with Lockheed, repeatedly saying, "Bob, what harm can it do to at least *talk* to Lockheed?" Because I knew of no good reason why Lockheed could not install berths just as they had done in earlier TWA planes, I raised this issue and pressed for berths, believing that if Lockheed agreed, Howard would not object. This was a mistake. The next thing I knew, Howard called me with one clear, crisp message: "Drop TWA's requests for berths. Berths are out. Don't even use the word *berth* when talking to Lockheed.'' Leonard, or someone else, had complained to Howard. We did not get berths and many other desired improvements.

It was my feeling throughout this negotiation that the Lockheed Sales Department should have much more aggressively promoted TWA's interests within the Lockheed organization. They should have tried harder to produce the design changes TWA wanted, especially those that would have made future sales easier for them. It seemed as if Sales automatically said no to almost everything in compliance with a Schwartz policy directive, rather than as a result of internal consultation with Lockheed's Engineering, Procurement, and Production departments to determine what really could be done. Thus, they rode roughshod over most change requests, no matter how minor, rather than demonstrate serious intent to satisfy TWA's needs.

However, thanks mostly to Hall Hibbard's engineering organization and despite the Schwartz-Hughes agreement, Lockheed agreed to incorporate more improvements than I had a right to expect. Lockheed Engineering, which had always performed at the leading edge of technology, clearly saw the advisability of correcting deficiencies and incorporating operational improvements. Engineering went to bat with Production and found ways to bend the ground rules to accommodate numbers of requests when convinced the changes were needed. It was not easy. We had heavy and spirited arguments, but considering the ground rules, I felt quite good about the success of this negotiation. Nevertheless, quite a few of TWA's flight operations, maintenance, and marketing personnel were understandably disappointed.

The increased capacity air-conditioning system was particularly difficult to achieve, partly because the 749A design accepted by EAL was already committed to production for the 1049's at the time of our negotiation. When I asked my friend Charlie Froesch, Eastern's no-wool-over-the-eyes vice president of engineering, why EAL accepted such an inadequate system, he said Rickenbacker insisted on early deliveries and ruled out all improvements that might cause delays.

After Howard's interest in the 1049's became known, Douglas renewed its efforts to sell DC-6B's. Because the 1049 appeared to be clearly superior and Howard's ''deal'' with Schwartz appeared to foreclose negotiations, I listened to the Douglas representatives but made no effort to bargain.

179

About this time, Howard again demonstrated his pertinacious and un-compromising nature. Months earlier, I had committed to deliver a technical paper at a meeting of the International Air Transport Association (IATA) in Puerto Rico. The presentation came due during 1049 negotiations, requiring me to burn a great deal of midnight oil to finish the paper on time. At the very last minute, I flew to New York on my way to Puerto Rico with several hundred distribution copies in hand. I planned to return to Burbank the next evening to continue negotiations with Lockheed, foregoing four days of IATA meetings.

On arrival at La Guardia, an urgent phone call was waiting for me. It was Howard. Even though he had known of my trip to Puerto Rico for months and had not objected, the man absolutely insisted that I return to Burbank immediately to continue negotiations. He said, "Bob, what in hell are you doing at La Guardia? You have been *personally* involved and understand all aspects of this negotiation, and *naturally* I assumed you would remain in Burbank and *personally* handle this to a conclusion."

I explained I had briefed my staff on pending matters, that they were fully competent to handle everything in my absence, and that if anything unexpected came up, I would be as close as the telephone. He responded, "I have every confidence in your staff, Bob, but we just can't risk changes in direction or misunderstandings. I'd deeply appreciate your returning to Burbank on the next flight to *personally* handle these matters to a conclusion. If you will just do this, I'd be eternally grateful. Bob, an awful lot is at stake, and after all, continuing with this deal the way we discussed it is a damn sight more important than IATA." Howard spent 40 minutes discussing this—just enough for me to miss my flight. Nothing would do except for me to return immediately to Burbank, even though a few days away would have made absolutely no difference in the outcome.

I called Russell K. Rourke, head of my economics section, a proficient engineer with a background in banking and economics, whom I would later appoint to the position of staff vice president of technical development, and who still later would become a full vice president. I requested him to drop everything and rush overnight to Puerto Rico to deliver my paper. He had not read the paper prior to boarding for this trip, but he did a fine job. Such were the vagaries of Hughes.

Shortly before finalizing the 1049 contract, Lockheed offered a choice of engines. They offered to install either standard Wright 3350 CB-1's or the new, higher-powered "turbo-compound" version. The turbo-compounds were essentially standard CB-1's with three exhaust-driven blow-down turbines arranged as an assembly, inserted in the engine like meat in a sandwich, to supply additional power to the propeller through shafts and gearing. With little military and no commercial operating experience, they were extremely complicated, expensive to buy, appeared to be excessively costly to maintain, and would delay airplane deliveries. Little advantage could be gained from the installation of turbo-compounds because of Lockheed's inability to increase the 1049 structural operating weight limits, and the turbo-compounds would only slightly increase speed at cruising altitudes.

I concluded TWA would be better off with the standard CB-1's and reviewed this position in detail with Howard, who concurred. This choice did not exist in later Constellations. By then, the maximum operating weights had increased, making the additional power of the turbo-compounds mandatory.

As usual, bad news came at the worst possible time. Just as we were preparing to wrap up the contract in Burbank, I received an urgent telephone call from Margie. She had just received word from her doctor that recent tests, taken because of a lethargic condition, showed she had polio. This was frightening, not only for her welfare, but also because of the children. Alarmed, I returned to Kansas City on the next flight after leaving word at Howard's Romaine Street office. Howard called the next morning to express sympathy and did not raise questions about my return to the Lockheed firing line. I thanked him and reassured him that my staff and I would do all possible to satisfy his goal of having the contract executed by year's end.

This nightmare turned out to be a false alarm the next afternoon. Someone had put another patient's test results in Margie's report. Of course, we were greatly relieved, but not enough to accept this inexcusable error without making an issue out of it. Anyone can make mistakes, but cases of this type should be double-checked. When it appeared certain that Margie's condition would quickly improve, I returned to Burbank to complete the 1049 deal.

Ralph Damon and Bob Gross executed a contract for 10 1049's on December 5, 1950, well before Howard's year-end deadline. After delivery in 1952, considerable carping was directed toward me from the operating departments, but because I had included departmental representatives in the negotiations, it was fairly short lived.

181

One year later, in December 1951, Douglas announced its DC-7 development program along with the sale of 25 DC-7's to AAL, with deliveries to begin late in 1953, somewhat over one year after TWA would receive its 10 1049's. They were to be long-range, stretched versions of the DC-6B, equipped with Wright 3350 turbo-compound engines, somewhat more powerful than engines scheduled for installation in TWA's 1049's.

The DC-7 was the Douglas answer to Lockheed's 1049. It was smaller overall than the 1049 and gave promise of being considerably faster at a time when speed was a dominant passenger drawing card. Once again the fascinating game of technological leapfrog was being played. The DC-7's were a serious competitive threat that we somehow had to meet head on. The importance of taking full advantage of the performance capabilities of the 1049 was crystal clear.

However, TWA did not do so, that is, not until the competition forced its hand. Despite my pleadings, TWA did not introduce nonstop transcontinental service until October 19, 1953, only briefly before the competition, and then only because the competition planned to do so. Although it may be difficult to believe, TWA's Traffic Department insisted that flights stop in Chicago, arguing: "The passengers want to get out and stretch their legs. No one wants to fly nonstop. Nine hours is just too long to be confined." I was absolutely convinced that nonstop operations would be a major drawing card, but I could not convince our traffic people.

I learned years later that Hall Hibbard also sought early TWA nonstop transcontinental Constellation operations. He, like me, was convinced that passengers wanted the shortest possible flight exposure, would relish the convenience of nonstop services, and that a golden opportunity was being missed. He approached Bob Gross, hoping Bob would swing his cudgel of persuasion toward TWA's Traffic Department: "Bob, you know we're not getting all the benefits from the Constellation that we should. The DC-6B's can't match the Connie now, but before long the DC-7's will catch up. Why can't we push TWA to fly nonstop? It would help our sales and help TWA at the same time."

Bob responded, "Hall, don't you realize that people can't sit that long? They want to get out and stretch their legs. Besides, another meal would have to be served and probably extra crew members carried. It just isn't the thing to do."

Without Bob's support, Hall elected to drop the issue. My reaction on hearing this story from Hall was that Bob had somehow been conned by TWA's Traffic Department.

This was only one of several disappointments through the years that led to my private conclusion that airline marketing people as a lot, while fine people, were not very imaginative. The belated nonstop services proved to be extremely successful. Soon after this was demonstrated, TWA's Traffic Department was the first to enthusiastically insist on more such flights. It was tragic that TWA did not take advantage of the inherent capability of the 1049's earlier.

Project Dynamite

The more we learned of the speed advantage of AAL's DC-7's, the greater our concern. Performance calculations showed the DC-7 to be sufficiently faster than the 1049 to permit AAL to advertise the fastest coast-to-coast flight schedules—probably within the long-sought eight-hour elapsed-time advertising panacea. Conventional wisdom had it that if a 20-minute advantage existed, travelers would choose the fastest service. If this were true, TWA would lose a great deal of valuable business to the DC-7's.

I requested M. B. (''Marcy'') Fannon, a bright young aerodynamicist who reported to Russell Rourke and who was later to become a valuable assistant to me at New York headquarters, to make a detailed study of this situation. Fannon's early 1951 report defined the magnitude of the problem and reconfirmed my worst concerns.

I apprised Collings, Damon, and other key people in TWA and placed a call to Howard. I knew Lockheed also had to be concerned and recommended that an expedited program be undertaken to develop speed improvements, which could be applied to TWA's 1049 fleet before delivery, or, in case that proved to be impractical, retroactively after delivery. It appeared that usual refinements such as improved propeller efficiency, better aerodynamic fillets, reduced air leakage, and the like could only produce a few miles per hour gain and would be collectively insufficient to match the DC-7's. I expressed the hope that discussions with Lockheed would produce some sort of an unexpected breakthrough.

Howard authorized pursuit of this program and said that some time before my call he had considered equipping a DC-6 with two auxiliary jet engines. He asked, ''Why wouldn't that be a good idea for the 1049's?''

183

The result was the establishment of a project at Lockheed to explore the feasibility of installing jet engines in wing-mounted pods. From the first, Howard insisted that this project be wrapped in complete secrecy. He tabbed it "Project Dynamite."

Lockheed examined the feasibility of installing two Westinghouse J-34 jet engines, one to be mounted on each wing tip, and agreed to investigate a slate of drag-reduction possibilities. In the interests of conservatism and safety, I proposed that the jet-equipped 1049's be certified at maximum weights without taking the thrust of the two auxiliary engines into account because flight experience with the jet engines was minimal. Thus, the power of the jets would provide a margin of performance in event of loss of main engine power, and loss of either or both jets would not adversely affect legal minimum terrain-clearance margins. I thought this approach would have the further advantage of expediting certification by avoiding many knotty questions concerning operations with six engines. Lockheed agreed.

The idea of the 1049 jet-piston hybrid was superficially inviting. It would be the fastest transport in the business, significantly surpassing AAL's DC-7's, unless, of course, auxiliary jets were also added to that plane. However, even if that were done, TWA would have over one year's lead-time advantage because of Lockheed's earlier deliveries, possibly more if Howard's secrecy ploy worked. However, as more information became available, I seriously questioned the advisability of installing the wing-tip engines, finally recommending a loss-leader approach to Hughes and Damon—that is, installation provisions would be made in all 10 1049's, but jet engines would be installed initially in only a few planes for advertising and prestige purposes. I was concerned with predicted high operating costs, the impact of certification tests on airplane delivery, excessive flight crew work loads, noise around airports, range limitations, and the fact that the jets had little operational experience. I argued that if and when operational experience justified, jets could be installed in the rest of the 1049's. They somewhat reluctantly agreed this was sound and approved this approach.

Subsequent Lockheed engine tests showed the jets to be considerably thirstier than anticipated, which would result in hopelessly inadequate range. Because the need for making en route stops would have nullified the potential reduction in elapsed flight times, Howard agreed to drop Project Dynamite provided Lockheed expedited its work on the other speed improvement items. Lockheed did so, and some gain resulted, but not nearly enough to offset the speed advantage of the DC-7's.

The Kansas City Flood

In July 1951, record downpours lasting nearly two weeks caused the levels of the Missouri and Kansas rivers to quickly rise, raising serious flood concerns. Kansas City Municipal Airport (MKC), near the confluence of the two rivers, was the center of TWA's operations. TWA's overhaul base was across the Missouri River at nearby Fairfax Airport. Both airports were protected by dikes, which had only recently been raised and strengthened by the Army.

Words of assurance from the mayor of Kansas City and other officials that little danger existed changed to shrill cries of concern as the flood approached. The day the crest neared Kansas City, the radio stations were virtually one big drumbeating alarm. By noontime, the streets were almost gridlocked by dismissed employees, rubberneckers, convoys of National Guard personnel, and what normal traffic remained.

John Collings, Frank Busch, several others, and I conferred in Collings's office at MKC. Word was received that the city manager planned to evacuate and close off threatened city areas, including MKC, and issue passes to permit only a selected few to pass through the precautionary antilooting National Guard lines he intended to establish. The principal concerns expressed in Collings's office centered on how to maintain flight operations at MKC and get materiel and employees to the Fairfax overhaul base under this restriction. At one point, Collings tried to call the city manager to request special handling provisions for TWA passengers and employees.

I was uncomfortable with the tenor of these discussions because they presumed flood damage would be nonexistent or inconsequential. When living about 10 miles from the Mississippi as a boy in Morrison, Illinois, I had observed recurrent springtime floods and knew of the terrible resulting damage. This was before most of the existing flood-control dams had been constructed. We would drive south a few miles on Route 78 and see backed-up Mississippi floodwaters, which must have been at least 12 miles wide. Later, after the waters receded, we would drive through ravaged towns and see destroyed buildings and homes. I never forgot.

I gave a short speech urging that the worst be assumed and that all

185

precautionary steps be taken in case the dikes, which had never been put to the test, did not hold. This seemed like cheap insurance in case the Army engineers were wrong.

Soon afterwards, the group made a DC-3 survey flight over the suburban area and west over the Kansas River Basin, which clearly was the main threat. We were appalled. The extent of the flood was far greater than any of us had been led to believe. It seemed obvious that the only prudent action was the precautionary closing of MKC and Fairfax, and the evacuation of aircraft, materiel, and employees. On landing, Collings and Busch diverted incoming flights to Grandview Airport (renamed Richards-Gebaur Air Force Base in 1957), on high ground south of the city, and ordered the precautionary evacuation of Fairfax, only to find that Ray Dunn had already started.

Every effort was made to fly planes and move equipment to safe ground. With few trucks on hand, employees carried what they could in their cars and pickups. Unfortunately, partially assembled planes, engines, and major accessories could not be moved, and most spare parts, tooling, and the like had to remain because of the limited time available for evacuation. The dikes at both airports held, just as the Army predicted, but water entered Fairfax through drainage grills, which could not be located and closed after the water rose.

Ray Dunn and Pat Gallup, management pilot responsible for maintenance flight tests, were the last people to leave Fairfax. They flew without a flight engineer in the last flyable Constellation. Water was already over nearly half of the runway at the start of their takeoff roll. Gallup hit the water near takeoff speed, which prolonged the roll, but with uncommon adroitness and perhaps some overboosting of the engines, he managed to attain liftoff speed. They landed at Grandview.

In only a short time the overhaul base was covered with as much as 12 feet of water. The Phillips refinery was nearby, and a film of oil and gasoline quickly covered the water, creating an extreme fire hazard. The areas surrounding the airport were quickly closed to minimize the threat of conflagration. Inside the overhaul base, solvents, plating solutions, petroleum, and river water mixed, adding to the threat of fire and widespread corrosion. With the flood unlikely to abate for some time, the outlook was bleak.

The evening of the flood, Dunn called an emergency meeting of key maintenance personnel. He appointed A. E. (''Al'') Jordon ''Mr. Inside'' and Jim Davis "Mr. Outside." Al was responsible for rehabilitation of the overhaul base, and Jim was responsible for arranging contracts for all outside work required to keep the airline flying while the base was down.

A critically important need was to maintain maintenance records and quality control of outside work so the eventual transition to in-house work would be smooth and efficient. Selected TWA engineers and foremen worked at the vendors to assure compatible records and product quality. Engines went to the engine manufacturers for overhaul, except for the C-54 R-2000's, which went to Airwork, New Jersey. TWA line stations did most of the DC-3 and Constellation maintenance, and the C-54's went to Temco. The plan worked well. Ray Dunn said later, "It was only through the dedication of the good working people at the base that we managed to keep the airline flying in spite of the flood, which wiped us out completely."

When the water started to recede, Ray Dunn and J. A. ("Jim") Shaunty, vice president of purchasing, met on the Fairfax dike shortly after sunrise. They had obtained permission from the National Guard to inspect the overhaul base. They placed all smoking and other personal articles on the dike, muffled the oarlocks with rags on a small wooden rowboat to minimize the possibility of generating sparks, and set out. It was highly risky business. The water was still covered with oil and gasoline, which could easily have become a raging inferno.

They slowly approached the giant overhaul facility. After rowing about halfway around the building, they found one of the hangar doors open just wide enough for the boat to enter. Their worst fears were confirmed. Everything was a shambles. Debris and muck were everywhere as they rowed around half-submerged planes and through the shops.

The true scope of the damage became clear only after the waters receded and rehabilitation work was fully assessed. Many airplane parts and accessories could not be salvaged and had to be scrapped at great loss. Considerable tooling, jigs, work stands, file cabinets, and furniture had to be replaced. In one case, a wooden desktop warped and curled up so much it slid off the desk. Scarcely anything escaped damage or destruction.

Soon after the water receded, wet record files were removed and submerged in local swimming pools until the papers could be removed and individually pressed dry with ordinary household electric irons and mangles. Numbers of TWA wives pitched in and helped. In this manner the majority of vital records were reclaimed.

It is hard to think of anything good that came out of the flood. However, a spirit of camaraderie and teamwork surfaced throughout TWA, together with the kind of resolute determination that makes corporations great.

TWA was short of Constellations because of the flood. On October 9, 1951, I wrote to John Collings, suggesting that TWA make arrangements to use Howard's 749A, which was still under armed guard at the Burbank Airport, "in view of our engine and airplane shortage arising from the flood situation." I expected John to ask me to try to work out a short-term lease with Howard, but instead he said, "It's unlikely Howard would agree," and closed the subject.

The flood had a devastating impact on Howard's TWA, one that far outlived the time required to restore the base physically. It seriously impaired flight operations for an extended period, generated extraordinary costs, and impaired TWA's standing in the financial community. Capital investments, including those required for new transports, had to be severely curtailed. A record gap of almost three years developed between transport orders.

Yet during this period, Howard's interest in aircraft development did not waver or diminish in the slightest. The early jet age was dawning. Attention was given to a turboprop-powered version of the Martin 404; the de Havilland Comet was considered; Lockheed's proposed jet-powered L-193 was examined; I made technology survey trips to Europe to learn about the remarkable progress being made in turbine-powered aircraft design; and Howard again asked me to build "the best damn engineering department in the airline business." He was deeply concerned about the flood, but this did not affect his interest in TWA fleets to come.

To my best recollection, Howard had no words either of criticism or of commendation concerning TWA's handling of the disaster or its rate of recovery. Praise from Hughes for jobs well done was rare; he expected the best and accepted good work as a matter of course.

13.
The Performance Race

The 1049C

Lockheed developed a series of long-body Constellations with impressive results following the 1049 program. Nine additional models—1049A through 1049H, followed by the 1649A, equipped with an entirely new wing—were developed for Lockheed's military and commercial markets.

Throughout this period, Lockheed's response to military requirements produced design features that, combined with background military experience, greatly aided the development of the commercial planes. And, balancing the scale, commercial experience produced improved designs, which significantly helped the military programs.

To my delight and surprise—TWA had barely started recuperating from the flood—Howard authorized full-scale specification negotiations for Lockheed Model 1049C's in 1952, during the initial project formation, when TWA's requirements could be injected into the design at the most opportune time. Perhaps he had remembered the disappointments generated by his delay in authorizing the 1049 negotiations.

The Lockheed 1049C was essentially a heavy, longer-range, turbo-compound-powered, luxury version of the 1049 developed from Lockheed's A and B models, the latter developed to perform long-duration radar picket and combat intelligence missions for the Navy. The long-range capability of the 1049C was especially attractive, although Lockheed had not taken full advantage of "building block" designs, which were available with minimal rework from its military programs. Even so, the new Lockheed, undertaken to compete more favorably with the DC-7, clearly merited serious procurement consideration.

As many as 30 1049C's were discussed for procurement, a number that would whet any manufacture's appetite. In sharp contrast with my 1049 negotiating experience, Lockheed was cooperative and adopted many TWA-requested design changes as standard for the production configuration.

When the specification and contract development work was well advanced, Hughes was suddenly unwilling to commit and elected to abort the negotiation. On close examination, possibly on Noah Dietrich's insistence, he deemed that financing of a fleet of 1049C's was untimely and imprudent because of TWA's heavy debt burden and fragile financial health following the flood. I had assumed that if necessary Howard would use the resources of Toolco to float the deal, but he did not. His decision to abort was a disappointment.

Fleets of 1049C's were subsequently ordered by Air France, Air India, EAL, Iberia, KLM, Qantas, Trans Canada, and other airlines. Seventy had been ordered by the time of the first flight, February 17, 1953.

The 1049E versus the DC-7B

During early 1953, Hughes again activated negotiations with Lockheed, this time for a fleet of 1049E's. The 1049E's were 1049C's with the structure upgraded sufficiently to permit the installation of turboprop engines sometime after delivery, if such should become available. I did not consider engine substitution to be a realistic possibility but thought the strengthened structure might permit worthwhile future weight growth.

By the time our 1049E negotiations were undertaken, Avianca, Cubana, Iberia, and LAV had changed their orders of C's to E's, and new orders for E's had been placed by Lufthansa, Northwest Orient, Thai Airways, and

VARIG. These circumstances tended to set the design firmly in concrete and severely limited our ability to achieve design objectives.

Our primary negotiating goals were still the attainment of transatlantic nonstop range capability against severe winter head winds and speed parity with the DC-7's, an important objective since the advent of the DC-7 program. Each prior negotiation had taken us one step closer to this long-standing range goal, and now for the first time true transatlantic nonstop capability appeared to be within grasp.

I was convinced that installation of the new turbo-compound engines, wing-tip fuel tanks, and the strengthened structure would permit attaining the range goal, but I was less certain that the speed of the DC-7 could be exceeded or even matched. It was with considerable enthusiasm that I undertook to convince Lockheed, with Howard's approval and moral support, that it would be to its own advantage to revise the design of the 1049E accordingly, and that it should do so. It seemed obvious that this would be an uphill battle with Lockheed, and it was.

From the outset, Lockheed made clear that it was unwilling to undertake extensive redevelopment of the 1049E for the following primary reasons: Its good sales success to date with the 1049C's and 1049E's made such incremental investments unnecessary; it appeared that Lockheed's heavy production backlog would not abate for an appreciable period; there was a strong possibility that introduction of major design improvements would delay production; and prospective customers might choose to wait for the new model rather than procure current production aircraft.

The fact that Lockheed's unwillingness was understandable did not make its position palatable. I doggedly tried without success to convince Schwartz, Hibbard, and Johnson to satisfy our range and speed requirements. They agreed that attaining our objectives could be advantageous for Lockheed over the long term but insisted that Lockheed could not justify undertaking such work at that time.

When Douglas learned serious discussions were under way at Lockheed, it was quick to offer DC-7 proposals: exactly the spark needed to increase Lockheed's interests in satisfying our requirements, but not enough for them to accede to our range and speed goals. Because the DC-7 also lacked the desired nonstop transatlantic range capability, I pressed Douglas to find ways to meet the same objectives.

The 1049E speed issue was given impetus by new Fannon studies, which showed the block speed (average speed measured from the time the wheels start to roll at the boarding ramp until they stop rolling at the disembarkation gate) of the DC-7 to be from 12 mph to 17 mph faster than that of the 1049E, depending on trip distance. This factor might have convinced us to buy DC-7's, except for the somewhat superior range and operating cost characteristics predicted for the 1049E in international services.

Lockheed aerodynamicists estimated that as much as 10 mph might be gained by reshaping the blow-down turbine hoods, and further gains could be achieved by submerging antennas and reshaping the wing fillets. Because Lockheed could not make a test airplane available for the required extensive flight tests and still meet its heavy delivery obligations, it set aside over our objections these potentially beneficial speed-improvement possibilities.

Douglas responded to my range pleas by proposing a new model, the DC-7B. This was the standard DC-7 with the fuel capacity and operating weight increased sufficiently to permit 500 miles additional range. This proposal clearly improved the odds for Douglas to win Howard's order and caused Lockheed to review its position. However, Lockheed still did not budge on the range and speed issues.

At this point in our negotiations, the activities of the Lockheed and Douglas sales personnel deteriorated into the same kind of derogatory and caustic criticism of their opponent's claims that led to the Martin-Convair fly-off. Reports issued by both manufactures were repeatedly superseded by new reports containing performance claims made without changes in either design or operating limits. It became impossible to keep up with the constantly updated performance documentation.

When Howard became a bit annoyed with repeated changes in my comparative studies, I explained this situation. He agreed this absurdity had gone far enough and called Nat Paschall and Leonard Schwartz to arrange for a meeting between responsible Douglas and Lockheed performance experts in my Kansas City office for the sole purpose of requiring them to jointly agree on the performance capabilities of the DC-7B and 1049E.

Both manufacturers sent their top performance experts. I explained the situation to them and requested they remain closeted in a nearby conference room until they could present a unified opinion on the performance of both aircraft. I was not sure they could or would. After remaining closeted two full working days, they emerged with a jointly signed handwritten report showing full agreement on performance. I doubt that this ever happened before or that it has happened since. That ended the fiasco, at least for an extended period. After that, claimed performance improvements were usually backed up with specific design changes and convincing technical presentations.

About the time I felt certain that Hall Hibbard and Kelly Johnson would bend and agree to meet our range objective, and considerably before detailed specification negotiations had been concluded, Schwartz lowered the boom by convincing Howard that if he did not order 1049E's at once, the delivery positions Schwartz had reserved for TWA would have to be sold to a competing airline, and the next open positions would be at least one year further downstream. Schwartz was in a position to do this, but I did not think he would sell Howard short, especially because at this point, production lead-time was in no way critical.

To my extreme distaste, Howard undercut my negotiating position and solved this crisis against my recommendation by accepting Leonard's position. Thus, despite the fact that the specifications were far from complete, Lockheed formally submitted to TWA on July 10, 1953, for early execution a definitive contract for the purchase of 20 1049E's, the principal terms of which Howard had accepted.

I had urgently advised Howard that the 1049E as defined did not meet our agreed-on range objectives, that design building blocks existed at Lockheed that should permit expeditious compliance with our range requirement, and that both Lockheed and Douglas engineers were actively exploring additional ways to improve, respectively, their 1049E and DC-7B offerings. I said in effect, "By committing now, we will arrest the development of a true international nonstop plane that can put us well ahead of the competition, and there is a good reason to believe that Douglas will soon offer DC-7B improvements. It could be a serious mistake to close out either possibility by contracting now with Lockheed."

I went on to say that it could be worthwhile to wait a few months and insist in the meantime that Lockheed do everything possible to increase the 1049E fuel capacity and certifiable operating weight. Production lead-time was not critical, and I did not believe Lockheed would accept the risk that he might buy DC-7B's by giving his delivery positions away. I recommended that instead of signing up then, we make one further major effort to prevail on the range issue.

Howard listened, discussed various aspects, and said he would think it

193

over. I guess he did, but not for long. The very next day he told me of his decision and asked me to expedite review of Lockheed's submission toward early execution of the contract. Not long afterward, Ralph Damon called and said Howard had made the same request through him.

Lockheed, per its usual practice, insisted on use of an outdated "standard" specification for negotiations rather than taking the expeditious course of updating the 1049C specification agreed on between us during the time-consuming 1952 negotiations. As far as I was concerned, this unconscionable practice only prolonged negotiations and provided Lockheed with an arguable basis for increasing the purchase price.

Lockheed and TWA technical functions literally worked night and day but found it impossible to conclude the revised standard detail specifications by the stipulated contract execution date. The date was extended by mutual agreement several times. After three months had gone by, Hughes, who had become unduly concerned over Lockheed's ability to deliver planes on time, joined by Schwartz, insisted that the contract be executed whether or not the papers were ready.

Howard almost always went through the motion of asking for TWA senior management's final concurrence with his equipment decisions immediately before contract execution. Ralph Damon, who earlier on had urged purchase of 749A's in lieu of DC-6's, did an about-face and recommended Howard forego Lockheed 1049E's and authorize the purchase of Douglas DC-7B's because of speed superiority and in belief that Douglas could improve their range still more. However, while he stuck to his guns, he chose not to make this a do-or-die issue. My position, which I reiterated as forcibly as I dared to Howard and Ralph, was that Lockheed be required to increase the range of the 1049E's, which I insisted they were quite capable of, but in event they continued to refuse to do so, that DC-7B's be purchased. The difference between Damon and Hughes was quickly settled by Hughes. TWA ordered 20 1049E's on September 12, 1953, for 1955 delivery, conditioned on mutually acceptable resolution of the open specification items by a specified date.

The best time to negotiate is obviously before and not after deals are closed. TWA's cost for contract changes agreed to after contract execution totaled nearly $3,400,000—approximately $1,500,000 less than Lockheed's initial asking price for the changes. I am sure much more would have been saved if Howard had allowed a few extra weeks before contract execution to complete negotiations and that Lockheed would have acceded

194

to more TWA change requests. Even so, we were able to obtain quite a few detailed improvements, including, for example, the installation of RCA AVQ-10 weather radar, the first radar installed in any civil Constellation.

A month or so later, to get a current measure of potential competition from the DC-7B, I requested Marcy Fannon and Russ Rourke to develop updated comparative performance studies of it and the 1049E to take into account improvements offered by Douglas after Howard's buy decision. Fannon's original report had showed the 1049E to be superior in international service and the DC-7B to have operating cost and speed advantages in domestic operations.

The new report was a shocker. It showed the updated DC-7B to be much more capable. It also indicated operating cost advantages for the DC-7B in both areas of operation and greater payload capability in long-range international services. The summary conclusion in the report read: ''The DC-7B now appears to be a better system [domestic and international] airplane than the 1049E.''

I apprised Hughes and Damon of this situation and emphasized the adverse long-term competitive implications of the DC-7B's, especially the customer appeal of greater speed. They were not happy to hear such news so soon after contract execution but were only complimentary of the part played by my department and me in the recent drama.

Speed Improvement and the Super G's

American Airlines inaugurated DC-7 Mercury services on the New York-Los Angeles route, November 29, 1953, in direct competition with TWA's until-then highly successful 1049 Ambassador services. As anticipated, AAL ran full-page adds announcing eight-hour coast-to-coast DC-7 services as the fastest in the business, which they were. AAL's adds were effective, especially with the valuable repeat-business travelers. The TWA Ambassador flights soon lost a significant share of passengers, a loss that increased as additional DC-7's were placed in service. This circumstance was especially alarming because our performance projections showed that TWA's forthcoming 1049E fleet would also suffer a speed disadvantage. The speed game TWA had successfully practiced so many years was working in reverse and would likely continue to do so much too long.

TWA managed to curb somewhat AAL's advertising campaign by statistically proving that the eight-hour claim was unrealistic, especially for westbound flights. After complaints were formally registered, AAL changed its westbound schedules to 8¼ hours, but AAL's advertising had already made its mark, and the DC-7 marketing advantage remained.

Hughes, who only a year before had cut off my efforts to convince Lockheed to make full use of available design technology to increase the range and speed of the 1049E's, now insisted on an all-out campaign to accomplish these same ends. The only course open to offset the DC-7 speed advantage, other than upgrading services (which was done), was to convince Lockheed to increase speed through the development and incorporation of design improvements without sacrificing the desired range capabilities. This could be done only by increasing the aerodynamic and/or propulsive efficiency of the 1049E's.

Now supported fully by both Hughes and Damon, I met with Hall Hibbard, Kelly Johnson, and Carl Haddon to press for urgent action. Now appreciating the need for matching the DC-7's on TWA's account as well as Lockheed's, they directed Lockheed engineers to expedite formation of a speed improvement program.

The comprehensive program that emerged included numbers of potential improvements requiring flight tests. Lockheed Engineering wanted to undertake the program, but Bert Monosmith, who was in charge of production, supported by Lockheed's Sales Department, refused to make an airplane available for flight test purposes because to do so would have caused Lockheed to default on a 1049E delivery commitment.

I wrote to Ralph Ellinger, who was still our plant representative at Lockheed, on March 23, 1954, requesting him to press Lockheed to obtain permission from another airline to release an airplane for the flight tests. The letter read in part:

It is essential that everything be done by Lockheed to improve the cruising speed of our 1049E's as well as the 1049's presently in service. Our competitive position is demanding and seems to grow more critical every day. It is, therefore, important that you, as well as the rest of us, continue to push Lockheed for productive action. . . . Urge them to take immediate steps to do something concrete about two very important facets: (1) speed improvement . . . and (2) expedite [solution of] the gross weight problem so that all LD-111 aircraft [1049E's] will be delivered for initial use at 137,500 pounds maximum takeoff weight.

After Lockheed was unsuccessful in convincing other airlines to accept a delay in delivery to make a flight test airplane available, the flight test impasse was resolved by my arranging to bail a TWA 1049 to Lockheed for a 54-day test period beginning April 24, 1954. The fact that John Collings and Ralph Damon agreed to removal of 10 percent of TWA's 1049 fleet from service during its busy summer season attests to the importance attached to this program.

The test program narrowed but, as expected, did not eliminate the speed advantage of the DC-7. Lockheed incorporated as many of these speed-improvement refinements as practical before airplane delivery; TWA installed the rest as soon as possible afterward.

My continuing negotiations, however, reinforced by Lockheed's keen awareness of the popularity of the DC-7's and Howard's direct interest, finally paid off. Lockheed offered by "Contract Change Order" a series of major 1049E improvements, which I had been seeking from day one of the negotiations. The improvements included an increase of 4,500 pounds in maximum operating weight, raising it to 137,500 pounds; installation of wing-tip fuel tanks and more efficient propellers; and the substitution of Wright DA-3 engines for DA-1's.

The DA-3's produced 400 hp more METO (maximum except takeoff) power, an especially significant increase because under the civil rules, METO power limited the certificated maximum weight in the one-engine-out, second-segment-climb condition. Flight tests in the bailed TWA 1049 had confirmed that the 4,500-pound weight increase could be certified.

The wing-tip fuel tanks, similar to those installed on the Navy's R7V-1's (1049B's), carried 1,200 gallons of fuel (the wing was already chocka-block with fuel), which, combined with the added 4,500 pounds of allowable weight, provided 700 miles additional range—a major improvement I was confident all along that Lockheed could produce.

Due to the number and magnitude of the changes, including inevadable improvements such as strengthened landing gear, Lockheed designated this model the 1049G. Howard was quick to authorize the additional cost, and TWA's 1049E order was converted to 1049G's.

TWA's 1049G's were superb planes. They were capable of flying the Atlantic nonstop in both directions most of the time, even against winter head winds. In domestic operations, they could fly nonstop coast to coast in all weather conditions, while AAL's DC-7's were frequently forced to stop for fuel when encountering high head winds. TWA's luxurious sleeper interiors set new standards of comfort. The pleasing ambiance was enhanced by more effective soundproofing, engine shock mounts, and improved cabin air-conditioning systems. Except for the now minimal cruising speed advantage of the DC-7's, the 1049G's were superior planes. They came to be known throughout the industry as the "Super G's."

As was invariably the case, problems developed during construction of the Super G's, but one was particularly memorable. Ralph Ellinger called me one evening to report an unacceptable berth problem. The upper berths were nearly impossible for either Ralph or Paul R. Strohm, his assistant, to raise and lock in the closed position. Ralph explained, "Bob, it can be done, but it's damned hard. Our hostesses could never manage. The funny thing is, during the official demonstration two Lockheed girls were able to raise the berths without any trouble."

I interjected, "Ralph, we can't assign two attendants to raise berths. Our specification clearly states that only one—"

Ralph interrupted, "Oh, Bob, I know that. What I mean is, each girl was able to raise the berths by simply flicking a wrist. They took turns. The berths just snapped into place. But when I tried it, they just wouldn't move worth a damn. There's something screwy here and I don't know what it is." Ralph was a large man and certainly did not lack strength. I did not know what to say except to recommend a repeat test.

Ralph telephoned a few days later. Paul Strohm had discovered while talking to shop friends that the two Lockheed employees who so easily raised the berths were professional female wrestlers Lockheed had recently added to the payroll. One was in fact the champion of San Fernando Valley. He said that Lockheed, confronted with this discovery, had agreed to strengthen the lift springs, which would permit ordinary women to do the job with ease.

The Super G's proved to be popular everywhere they were flown. Lockheed produced more of this model than any other civil Constellation. When it was first announced, numbers of airlines that had ordered 1049E's switched to the G model.

TWA introduced Super G domestic services on April 1, 1955. On September 25, the first multiple-class services (first-class and coach cabins on the same airplane) in the United States were introduced, which produced the first nonstop coast-to-coast coach services in the industry. On October 30, TWA inaugurated California-Europe through-plane service on the Los Angeles-London-via-New York route, a service no other airline could produce because of TWA's route structure and the great range of its Super

G's. TWA's Super G's quickly became industry pace-setting aircraft, worth every minute of the needlessly extended negotiation.

Howard and Courtland

Shortly after the 1049G negotiation, R. L. ("Bob") Adams and I arrived at Mines Field at 11:00 P.M. after a pleasant Constellation flight from Kansas City for a routine meeting with Lockheed the next morning. Bob was one of my well-recognized, highly qualified electrical and communication systems experts.

One of Howard's Romaine Street Mormons was at the gate. He said he had a Chevrolet available for me to drive to the Hughes Aircraft Company for a meeting. The participants were waiting for my arrival. This was news. He had no idea what the meeting was about and had changed our hotel reservations on Howard's instructions from the Hollywood Roosevelt to the luxurious, "more convenient" Beverly Wilshire Hotel.

Bob and I arrived at the Hughes Aircraft vice president's office around midnight. The vice president, his chief of structures, and the chief of structures for Convair, who had flown in earlier that evening for the meeting, were the only others present. The vice president explained that Howard had requested the meeting to discuss a current problem and develop recommendations for handling the matter. He said Howard wanted my opinion, but because Howard had bound him to complete secrecy, he regretted that he could give me only limited information.

The vice president continued, "Bob, this boils down to appraising the consequences of a nick in a box. How it got there is unimportant. The problem is to understand the effect of the nick, and the question is what to do about it."

I waited for him to continue. When he did not, I asked questions about what kind of a box (which I assumed was part of an airplane), where it was used, its construction, the materials used, its stress levels, and the dimensions and location of the nick, and asked to see drawings or photographs. He only talked around the questions and failed to produce drawings or pictures, explaining that these aspects were all secret.

I became exasperated by this silly situation, looked him squarely in the eye, and said, "You haven't told me anything. Nothing at all. Look, I know that you know perfectly well, and I'm sure Howard does too, what I need to know to develop a meaningful position. I assume Howard thinks

199

this is important, or I wouldn't have been asked to come here at midnight. If you can't give me the details, I can't develop an opinion.''

The vice president responded quite soberly, ''Bob, I know you need to know these things. I'm sorry to say again that all I am authorized to tell you is what I have said.'' This did not make any sense. I thought the vice president must have misunderstood Howard's instructions. I glanced at Bob Adams, who was sitting on a nearby sofa with a bemused, incredulous look on his face.

The conversation then turned to probing several general engineering considerations, which I assumed somehow applied to the box question. The subjects included metal fatigue, structural life expectancy, design load factors, and structural repair techniques. It would have been interesting at almost any other time.

Howard called the vice president at around 3:00 A.M. All the vice president said was ''yes'' and ''no,'' no doubt on instructions from Howard. After about 20 minutes, I was told Howard wanted to talk to me. He expressed his ''deep appreciation'' for what I had done, saying that it was most helpful, and when we were through talking, I would be free to go to the hotel and get a good night's rest. A good night's rest? It was nearly 3:30 in the morning and the hotel was an hour away.

I said, ''Howard, I appreciate the words, but I haven't done anything. In order to develop a meaningful solution to whatever the problem is, I must have the details. I'd be glad to give it a good try, but as matters now stand, I can't have an opinion.''

Howard responded by again expressing appreciation and closing with, ''You have done more than you know, and I am grateful.''

I turned in some frustration to the vice president and said, ''Now that my part of this affair is apparently over, can you tell me what this is all about?''

He said he was not supposed to, but he would give me the background story. While Howard was recently visiting the Constellation production line with Courtland Gross, he had conceived of a much more efficient way to handle final assembly operations. His plan involved hoisting and moving nearly completed Constellations over other Constellations in Lockheed's final assembly area. Courtland, who was in charge of production, was skeptical. He did not want to risk moving the planes that way. After a long discussion, Howard said, ''Court, why not at least try my plan? After all, they're my planes.'' With that, Courtland agreed.

200

A few days later, Courtland and Howard were in the shop directing the experiment. A Connie hoisted in jury-rigged slings was being moved across the factory over other nearly completed planes when the plane suddenly shifted position. One wing crashed down on a major assembly fixture, damaging the wing box spar. The damage was the "nick." Fortunately, no one was injured. That ended the experiment.

"Howard doesn't want the word to get out," explained the vice president. "He thinks it might lead to ridicule, possibly in the gossip columns, and for that reason demanded extreme secrecy."

I told him without enmity that secrecy in my case was inappropriate and made no sense whatsoever—I had been regularly involved for years in Howard's secret undertakings, most of them "a damn sight more important than this," and as far as I was concerned the evening was a complete fiasco.

I wondered on the way to the hotel whether I might have been an innocent pawn of sorts. Possibly, through peripheral discussions, I had unknowingly set the character of or confirmed repair plans, or perhaps I had inferred acceptance of them on subsequent delivery of the plane to TWA. Because neither possibility seemed very plausible, I decided I should dismiss the handling of this affair as just one of Howard's human idiosyncrasies. The matter was never referred to again.

14.

The Last
of the
Constellations

The piston and jet eras overlapped. During 1952–54, when the last of the piston transports were being developed, the design technologies available in the United States were insufficient to permit the development of acceptable turbine-powered transports. The state of the art of turbine aircraft design was moving forward rapidly under the aegis of the military, a circumstance welcomed by TWA and those U.S. manufacturers who had sporadically invested modestly in exploratory but abortive efforts to develop commercial turbine-powered transports since the mid-1940s.

In contrast, the British had developed a significant turbine aircraft technology lead, which it had been quick to apply to commercial aircraft development. By then, the moderate-range Vickers Viscount turboprop had been extremely well received by the travel market, as had the de Havilland Comet, which British Overseas Airways Corporation (BOAC) introduced on its London-Johannesburg route on March 2, 1952. Additionally, the long-range, turboprop-powered Bristol Britannia prototype had flown during August 1952 and had been accorded great expectations.

The British commercial turbine age had dawned, but it was still in gestation in the United States.

I had followed progress and had pressed hard for advancing as rapidly as possible the state of the art of jet engine and airframe design, and in fact had developed a number of preliminary jet aircraft designs for TWA sponsorship (see Chapter 15). The principal technical deterrents encountered in all such cases was excessive fuel consumption, which too severely limited range for TWA's long-haul operations, and lack of proven engine reliability. I had become convinced during late 1952 as a result of extensive personal technology survey trips in the United States and England that the United States would soon catch up with the British and have well in hand the capability to produce excellent jet transports. I thought such transports could be produced by the late 1950s. I so advised Hughes and TWA management and recommended that only that minimum number of additional piston transports absolutely required to serve TWA's routes be purchased and that Hughes give top priority to procuring jet transports. Hughes disagreed and pushed TWA into acquiring a fleet of piston aircraft that were obsolescent before delivery: the most serious equipment blunder that occurred during my 35 years at TWA.

The Lockheed Turboprop versus the Douglas DC-7C

The Lockheed 1049G project goaded Douglas, pressed by PAA, to develop the DC-7C: an excellent long-range airplane and a potent competitive threat to TWA. Douglas announced the DC-7C about mid-1954, and PAA shortly thereafter confirmed its order of 15 for transatlantic operations. PAA's initial deliveries were scheduled for the second quarter, 1956, in time for the prime summer travel season. From TWA's point of view, this was entirely too soon after its expected inaugural of 1049G services the preceding spring.

DC-7C's were long-range versions of the DC-7B's. They were stretched one seat row and equipped with a larger wing, capable of carrying more fuel than the 1049G's. The span of the wing center section was increased 10 feet, which moved the engines and propellers outboard half that amount. This arrangement provided the space for the fuel and gave promise of producing markedly quiet interiors. The DC-7C's had more powerful turbo-compound engines than the 1049G's and appeared capable of carrying economical payloads nonstop on the Paris-New York route three hours faster.

Because the new Douglas plane had the potential for drastically altering

TWA's future competitive situation, I thought it important to contact Hughes to make certain he was fully apprised. I tried repeatedly without success. This was another of those times when Hughes simply could not be reached. Even the Romaine Street Mormons could not raise him.

I wrote a confidential letter to Nadine Henley, his private secretary, on July 12, 1954, asking her to advise Howard I had "urgent matters" to discuss with him. When I did not hear, I wrote Howard directly on August 3, stating, "The DC-7C appears to be a major competitive threat." I apprised him of the PAA order and the comparative performance of the two planes. Nadine assured me the letter had been sent on to Howard, but I did not hear from him for a considerable period.

I met with Nat Paschall and Jake Moxness at the Douglas Santa Monica factory for DC-7C briefings soon after the announcement. Douglas had sold half of their capacity of four planes per month to PAA. Paschall offered to hold the remaining open positions for Howard and invited me to work with Douglas "so the DC-7C's will more nearly meet TWA requirements, in event Howard decides to procure them."

This seemed like a good idea, at least to the extent of preserving delivery positions while studying the design. I agreed to advise Howard as soon as possible and to keep Nat posted. I met with Nat and his associates from time to time to remain current and maintain the delivery offering, with the hope that Howard would soon respond.

During the summer and early fall, 1954, rumor had it that Lockheed was working in secret on a "thin wing," turboprop-powered Constellation that would have more range and be faster than the DC-7C. Lockheed's Kirk Yost telephoned me and confirmed this project, which I reported by letter to John Collings and Ralph Damon on September 2, part of which follows:

I have been advised by a confidential but reliable Lockheed source that:

1. Lockheed has definitely decided to proceed with the development of a new, larger area thin wing for the Constellation.
2. Lockheed is endeavoring to sell the Navy this improvement so the $14,000,000. [development expense] can be shared between the Navy and commercial customers.
3. Lockheed has attempted to advise TWA's Principal [Hughes] of this development but has not been able to contact him.
4. The thin wing version should be slightly faster, it is claimed, than the DC-7.

My letter concluded by suggesting that John Collings or Ralph Damon contact Bob Gross to express interest, rather than continue to wait for Howard to reply to my earlier efforts to contact him. I was deeply concerned with Howard's unavailability during such a crucially important project formation period and considered it a disservice to wait any longer.

Damon set up a briefing session with Gross, Hibbard, and Johnson for September 30. At that time Lockheed advised that the new plane, the Model 1449, was to be essentially a heavy Constellation equipped with an impressive new 150-foot-span wing—a whopping 27 feet greater than the 1049G—powered by four P & W T-34 turboprop engines, each rated at 5,500 hp.

The proposed use of turboprops was of great interest because of the prospective increase of 100 mph in cruising speed and the success of turbine aircraft operations overseas. Contrasting sharply with the situation in England, there was a general lack of meaningful nonmilitary operating experience with turbine engines designed in the United States. The T-34 was a new design slated for experimental installation in a variety of military transports, including two Navy R7V-2 (1049B) Constellations. The first R7V-2 had made its maiden T-34 flight on September 1 and was delivered to the Navy on September 10. The Lockheed sales people had glowing reports of the Navy flights during the September 30 meeting, but little hard data.

Our operating cost studies showed that the fuselage Lockheed proposed for the 1449, the same as that of the 1049G, was far too small to be economical: 100-percent-capacity payloads could not cover predicted operating costs, at least not without exorbitant increases in fares. The T-34's and the proposed wing had sufficient power and lift to justify a substantial increase in fuselage capacity and seemed like an open invitation to improve Lockheed's offering. Consequently, I urged Hibbard and Johnson to design a larger, constant-cross-section fuselage, commensurate with operating costs and performance. They refused, saying doing so would be tantamount to designing a new plane, which simply "wasn't in the cards." Then I pressed for adding cylindrical sections to the fuselage. This was also refused. When it became clear after several such efforts that continuing the debate would do more harm than good, I decided to return to the subject later.

About that time Howard became active. He made no mention of where he had been or why he had not responded earlier. It was as if he had picked up on a conversation of a few moments before. I was relieved he had called and did not think it was appropriate to question him.

During several long telephone calls and one direct meeting that followed, Howard reviewed the DC-7C and 1449 projects, including performance and estimated operating costs, and my evaluation of both designs. I gave the DC-7C high marks and advised him the 1449 unmistakably needed a larger fuselage to avoid becoming a serious economic liability; four-wheel, bogie-type main landing gears to reduce runway loading, which was already critical for the Constellation at many TWA airports; and other improvements, which I enumerated. Howard listened, did not agree or disagree, and, contrary to my recommendation, elected not to authorize further exploratory discussions with Douglas.

Ignoring my warnings concerning the economics of operations, Howard seemed ebullient over prospects of using 1449 turboprops, probably because of the promise of outperforming AAL's and PAA's DC-7's. Soon he ordered "expedited" resolution, "at the utmost speed," of procurement specifications and a contract for 25 1449's. Deeply concerned, I was more circumspect.

I cleared the decks for this job by placing Russell Rourke in charge of the Kansas City office and departed for what I thought would be a month's work at Lockheed. S. L. ("Sam") Higginbottom and Norman R. Parmet, new members of my staff added to help build "the best damn engineering department in the business," remained in Kansas City about one week to prepare for the Lockheed meetings before joining me in California. Sam Higginbottom, who had a fine engineering background in aircraft structures and systems, would one day become president of EAL, and later president and chairman of Rolls-Royce, Inc. Norm Parmet was an expert aircraft power plant engineer who joined my department to pursue the exciting field of turbine engines. Later, Norm would hold in succession a number of TWA staff vice president positions.

Ralph Ellinger rented at my request a good-sized apartment overlooking the beach in Santa Monica, which I planned to use as headquarters for the TWA negotiating team. Because I would be alone the first week in California, Margie and the four older children joined me. The second afternoon in the apartment, Howard called with a bombshell. It was urgent, he said, that I proceed at once to San Diego to meet with Convair on the Southern Comfort project!

Southern Comfort was the code Howard gave to a Convair jet transport development project we were formulating, which had been the subject of

207

conferences—secret, of course—between Howard, Convair representatives, and me over a period of many months. Howard added, "Naish [J. V. ("Jack") Naish, Convair's executive vice president, later president] and Zevely are in a hot sweat to define the plane and wrap up a deal. Bob, we should take advantage of their frame of mind and show good faith, so I've arranged for you to meet with them in the morning."

I thought, "In the morning? What about Lockheed? Only a few days ago, nothing was more important than the 1449. Why ants in the pants over Convair? Why can't Convair wait a few weeks?" I said, "Howard, I'm up to my eyeballs in the 1449. Can't this wait a few weeks until I'm further along here?"

He said, "No. I've put them off as long as I can. I don't know how you're going to do it, but you will just have to divide yourself in two and get both projects handled."

That same evening, just as we were becoming settled in the apartment, Margie, the four kids, and I quickly packed, piled into a rented station wagon, and drove to San Diego. This did not help my relations with Lockheed, especially because secrecy prevented telling them my whereabouts. After a week, during which I saw almost nothing of my family because of the Convair project, Margie and the children, who had thoroughly enjoyed San Diego's attractions, returned to Kansas City. Until late December, I commuted between Convair and Lockheed, but I was occasionally able to come home for a weekend. Home seemed like a shining oasis in the wonderfully complicated and unconscionably busy world of Hughes and TWA. Around mid-December, Howard made it clear that he intended to place an order before year's end for 25 1449's to the account of the Hughes Tool Company—not TWA.

We were not ready. My diversion to Convair plus the time required for Lockheed to examine TWA's engineering requests were too much. And Howard's great interest in the plane led Lockheed to believe a deal was a foregone conclusion: an unwelcome conviction, which did not help my negotiating position and tended to prolong discussions. Lockheed steadfastly refused to enlarge the fuselage, provide the bogie-type landing gear, and make numbers of other needed improvements. Such refused items became known as the "Hell No!" list.

When Howard insisted on contract execution by year's end, our expedited specification effort accelerated into a crash night-and-day marathon. Even so, the specification was not ready on December 22, 1954, when we convened at the Beverly Hills Hotel for contract execution.

It remained my conviction, shared by Ralph Damon, that the 1449 turboprop was uneconomical and poorly timed. Howard's 1449 deliveries were scheduled only one year before Boeing jets were apt to be available. I recommended to Howard that he skip the 1449's, substitute a few 1049G's or DC-7C's to satisfy interim traffic needs, and undertake active dialogue with Boeing toward obtaining priority jet transport delivery positions.

In summary (see Chapter 18 for a thorough discussion), my reasons for wanting dialogue undertaken with Boeing were: The Convair Southern Comfort program was not definite and should be hedged; Boeing's experience with the B-47, B-52, and the prototype 707, along with my review of preliminary Boeing specifications, indicated the 707 would be an excellent design; and it seemed certain that Boeing could deliver jet transports well ahead of Douglas or Convair.

This viewpoint, reemphasized with some trepidation on the eve of contract execution, did not make a hit with Howard. My persistent opposition to the 1449 program had annoyed him. Several times, I thought he was on the verge of firing me.

The contract closing was attended by Leonard Schwartz, Kirk Yost, Walter J. Wayman, B. F. ("Ben") Brundred, and Roger Donaldson for Lockheed; and Raymond A. Cook, Micky West, Harry West, Ralph Ellinger, and me for Hughes. Ray Cook and Micky West were Toolco lawyers from Houston. Ray, who proved to be a good friend, participated in Howard's aircraft procurement activities throughout the remaining period of Hughes's control of TWA. Micky was a highly regarded tax specialist.

It was not my practice to make written records of Howard's activities. Just the opposite. I even avoided using his name in correspondence, referring to him as "Tool," "the Principal," "an authoritative source," "the West Coast," and the like. I made the 1449 closing an exception because Howard's insistence on the purchase of patently uneconomical and incompletely defined planes was inappropriate and out of character. I wanted to be able to establish my position after history proved the planes to be uneconomical, which it did in spades. The record dictated immediately following the closing was never used for that purpose, but it surfaced during proceedings associated with the two lawsuits filed against Hughes by TWA in 1961. Excerpts follow:

> I have steadfastly maintained and pointed out to TWA management, which has concurred . . . and to Mr. Hughes, as well as to Lockheed representatives, that I believe the airplane as proposed to be an unsound project, primarily because of overall economic aspects. I . . . pointed out ways this condition could be rectified by LAC [Lockheed]. . . .
>
> I explained . . . why any present deal should be made contingent upon final resolution [subsequent to contract execution] of specifications satisfactory to both parties. . . . [T]he Contract LD-111 [for 20 1049G's] was handled in this manner. . . . [T]his handling resulted in saving $1,500,000. . . . [M]uch more would likely be saved [in this instance] if the same procedure was followed. . . . Lockheed's willingness to go along with this condition was confirmed by Kirk Yost following the signing. He stated that LAC had approached Hughes several days earlier urging that no papers be signed until specifications were agreed upon and that Mr. Hughes turned this down.
>
> Leonard Schwartz . . . advised that Mr. Hughes was on the line. . . . I pointed out [to Howard] again, as I had done that morning, that the airplane specification . . . was not sufficiently complete . . . for use as a contractual instrument and that I felt the most practical way to proceed was to make the deal contingent on agreement [on the specifications]. . . . Mr. Hughes flatly rejected this proposal on the basis that he trusted Lockheed, that he believed Lockheed would do a good job, and that he believed Lockheed would be fair.
>
> I pointed out to Mr. Hughes that Lockheed intended to exclude the "Hell No!" list of items, the accomplishment of which I thought was vital to building a successful airplane. . . . Howard said he thought Lockheed would be willing to consider these items and that they would be fair in their evaluation. He also stated he thought Lockheed would cooperate fully.

Howard must have appreciated that Lockheed most likely would not accede to the Hell No! list, no matter what. His insistence on closing without contingencies before the papers were ready was extraordinary. I considered his attitude uncharacteristically naive and inappropriate. But Howard usually knew exactly what he was doing and was in no sense a flibbertigibbet. Several of my involved legal friends were convinced that year-end tax considerations had governed his actions. Toolco was Howard's highly profitable personal holding company, and they believed that the drastic penalty tax on undistributed profits made it desirable that Toolco incur substantial contractual obligations before December 31.

The 1449 contract, LD-138, was ratified by the Hughes Tool Company board on December 23, 1954, the day after it was executed at the Beverly Hills Hotel.

Transition to the 1649A

When the 1449 contractual ink was hardly dry, January 7, 1955, Kelly Johnson telephoned me with electrifying news. The T-34 engine-propeller combination in the Navy R7V-2's was in serious trouble.

Kelly explained that the lateral motion of the engine, which had a single plane mount, was excessive, that the oil system was not functioning properly, and that the three-bladed propellers induced serious vibration throughout the engine and nacelle. He said substitution of a four-bladed propeller was doubtful because of ram loss in the engine air-intake duct. (*Ram* is a measurement of the dynamic pressure of air under motion). Kelly estimated "there would be a change in ram of an undetermined nature, but probably ⅓ of the loss from the three-bladed prop due to one more blade passing in front of the compressor. A percent change in ram is ½-percent or ¾-percent change in fuel consumption."

He continued, "Bob, P & W is redesigning the engine case to retain failed compressor blades, which will add 1,000 pounds per airplane. You start adding all of these things up and it is possible you can run yourself into a trap for as much as from 3,000 pounds to 5,000 pounds." He explained he had received this information during a P & W conference only the day before. He was not sure if the problems could be corrected or how long that might take. "I'm sorrier than you can imagine to tell you this at this stage of the game," he concluded. "It is a hell of a note."

The impact of what I was hearing about an airplane already considered economically submarginal was horrible. Kelly and I agreed to postpone postcontract specification completion conferences until Lockheed could sort this out.

On January 13, Kenneth Gordon, Boeing's commercial sales manager, handed me a production notice contract for Model 707 jet transports. Ken said a copy had just been given to PAA and that Boeing was anxious to discuss specifications and contract terms with TWA. I discussed the Gordon meeting with Hughes and sent copies of the draft papers to him, Collings, Damon, and Leslie. Boeing's timing seemed fortuitous; the 1449 appeared to be in trouble. I was especially anxious to undertake discussions with Boeing, who confirmed that jets could be produced in 1958. However, agreement from Howard to do so was not forthcoming.

Within a few months after Kelly Johnson learned of the T-34 shortcomings, P & W withdrew the T-34 from the market. Lockheed's 1449 was suddenly a design sans engines. Because of precautionary, exploratory work undertaken after initial T-34 difficulties were discovered, Lockheed fairly quickly proposed alternative power plants.

The Model 1549 was proposed with four single Allison 501 turboprops, using essentially the same nacelle installation as Lockheed's YC-130 Hercules cargo planes, the first of which had flown the preceding August. Other possibilities investigated and dropped included the twin Allison, which was too large; the Bristol Proteus, which was too late; and the Napier Eland, which lacked operational experience.

Continuing Lockheed and independent TWA studies confirmed that the best alternative was not to substitute the Allisons but to install advanced Wright 3350 EA-2 turbo-compound piston engines driving slow-turning, increased-diameter (17-foot) propellers. The Douglas DC-7C could not match the exceptional range capability of such planes, which Lockheed optimistically claimed would fly at the same block-to-block speeds. The engine change improved the outlook for achieving lower operating costs, but not enough to substantially change the dismal economics. Lockheed designated this model the 1649A and undertook to formally amend the Toolco contract.

I met with Schwartz, Yost, and Wayman on March 1, 1955, to discuss the 1649A situation only to discover that Howard had independently decided to plunge ahead pell-mell with installation of jet pods on TWA's 1049G's for 1956 summer operations. Prior to this meeting, neither Damon nor I (nor anyone else in TWA, as far as I ever knew) knew of this secret project, which Howard called "String Bean." Schwartz told me because Howard had requested him to ask me how many G's should be equipped with jet pods and because Lockheed, which needed to order the Westinghouse J-34's that same day, had to know how many installed and spare engines to purchase. Schwartz had been happily up to his old tricks of dealing directly with Hughes.

I told Leonard I could not commit TWA to the program without internal consultation, and I would let him know as soon as possible. I apprised Collings and Damon of this situation by telephone and recommended that if Howard insisted on this course of action, installation provisions—fittings, plumbing, and other items required for the subsequent installation of jet pods—be made in only eight planes, the minimum number required for scheduling purposes. My plan was to install the pods and engines only if Lockheed flight tests unexpectedly showed them to be worthwhile. They agreed.

Finally, Howard reluctantly agreed to drop this project. The additional Lockheed studies, like earlier TWA studies, established once more that J-34 jet pods would not be worthwhile. I never understood what possessed Howard to independently press forward with 1049G pods after earlier work in which he was involved showed this to be a mistake. This was the second time we wasted engineering man hours on hybrid piston-jet power. But it was not the last.

Howard's next request for jet pods made more sense. He asked for 1649A pod studies. It appeared that the larger wing and higher operating weight might be sufficient for medium-length flights with auxiliary jet thrust, albeit at substantial operating cost penalty. The scheme we agreed on was to equip 10 planes with pods, which would produce the fastest services in the business, and to operate the other 15 planes without pods, which would produce the longest-range nonstop services available anywhere, such as the West Coast to Europe. Thus, if pods proved to be feasible, TWA would have the fastest and longest-range transports in the world.

A supplemental agreement to Contract LD-138, dated March 29, 1955, changed the 25 1449's to 1649A's. Unfortunately, deliveries slipped because of the engine change. Instead of having 7 planes at the beginning of the busy 1957 season, TWA would have only 1. Another supplemental agreement on the same date called for complete provisions for jet pods on 10 planes. However, in the end, pods were never installed. Operational economics and the fact that they would so soon be eclipsed by jets ruled them out.

I was completely surprised on April 6, 1955, when Lockheed sent a wire to Toolco canceling the contract and the 1649A program! When Ray Cook told me, I could hardly believe that Lockheed wanted out after their painful and desperate efforts to resurrect the 1449 with new engines. My immediate reaction was relief because of the early probable availability of jets and my undiminished concern about high 1649A operating costs. I checked with Jake Moxness the same day to determine if the DC-7C delivery positions Nat Paschall held earlier were still available. They had been sold, ruling them out as a viable alternative.

This seemed like a golden opportunity to turn to the jets, which I hoped Howard would now do. However, Ray Cook called again the next day. Howard had refused to accept Lockheed's cancellation. (Tax problems would have resurfaced even more seriously had Howard accepted the cancellation.) A wire insisting that Lockheed live up to terms of contract had just been sent from Houston. Lockheed tried for several days to persuade Howard to accept cancellation. When this failed, Lockheed reluctantly agreed to continue with the program.

I thought the persistence of my arguments with Howard against the 1449 program might have tarnished our working relationship. This did not happen. Howard requested and cleared with Ralph Damon that I take charge of all technical and business aspects of implementing Contract LD-138 on behalf of Toolco, except for changes in aircraft delivery and mission guarantees, which required his approval. Additionally, I was to "make sure the airplanes comply with all of TWA's requirements," an impossible charge in light of the restrictive nature of precontract negotiations.

Procedurally, Lockheed sent all formal contract notices to Toolco and me. Responses were issued from my office; Toolco never responded directly except after consultation and made no attempt to exercise independent technical or business judgment. Lockheed and equipment vendors also worked through my office, and Howard became involved only in matters of his personal choosing. This unorthodox arrangement was followed for all except one of TWA's subsequent flight equipment programs, until Hughes lost control of TWA at the end of 1960. It worked well except for procurement of buyer-furnished equipment and spare parts, which was quite another matter (see "No TWA Rights," this chapter).

Hollow Aluminum Propellers

Hughes usually reserved for himself the right to choose propellers for TWA's transports. The 1649A was no exception.

The usual procedure was for my department to analyze the available options in collaboration with the manufacturers and develop procurement recommendations based on design, performance, and cost considerations. I discussed all aspects with Howard, who of course had the final say, but I do not recall any disagreements on propeller selection.

214

Propellers for the 1649A were offered by the Hamilton Standard Division of United Aircraft Corporation and the Propeller Division of Curtiss Wright. Hamilton Standard initially offered "hydromatic" (hydraulically controlled) propellers with solid aluminum blades, the same type design that TWA and other airlines had used successfully for many years. After TWA's preference for Curtiss Wright's electrically controlled propellers equipped with hollow steel blades became evident, Hamilton Standard offered lightweight, hollow aluminum blades, which were still under development.

I was leery of hollow blades of any kind, notwithstanding excellent industry experience with the Curtiss Wright hollow steel blades. Because months of downtime would be required for blade changeover if new blades had to be manufactured from scratch following unsatisfactory service experience, I decided not to recommend hollow blades unless the manufacturer agreed to keep immediately available a supply of solid aluminum blades for quick installation in event serious service problems were unexpectedly encountered.

Compliance with this tough demand not only required the successful vendor to manufacture and keep on hand a sufficient supply of solid blades to permit field changeover after airplane delivery with minimum impairment of scheduled flight operations, but it also required Lockheed to duplicate propeller certification tests at extra expense, which I suggested be borne by Lockheed or the propeller manufacture. I proposed that the cost of producing the backup blades be borne exclusively by the propeller manufacturers but expressed willingness to absorb a fair pro rata share of the standard purchase price of the hollow blades based on hours of use and to purchase the solid blades in event their installation proved to be necessary.

Harold H. Warden, general sales manager for Curtis Wright; and George W. Brady, director of engineering, agreed to comply except for investing in backup blades. I preferred Curtiss Wright propellers but saw no way for TWA to justify purchase of standby blades. After all, sound design and warranty aspects were the responsibility of the manufacturer. Their refusal to alter their position centered our negotiations on Hamilton Standard.

The principal Hamilton Standard participants were Erle Martin, chief scientist; John F. Burridge, sales representative; and A. M. ("Al") French, West Coast representative. They were extremely anxious to establish lightweight, hollow aluminum propellers in the airline market and reluctantly agreed to my demands, including bearing most of Lockheed's added propeller certification costs. After extended negotiations with Hamilton Standard, Howard and I agreed that the hollow-aluminum-bladed propellers would be best and so advised Lockheed.

The propeller contract change order first submitted by Lockheed was weasel worded and unsatisfactory. For example, it stated Lockheed would install hollow blades "at its sole discretion, if they should become available." Straightening out the order required nearly two months.

During this period, Lockheed sold a small fleet of 1649A's to Lufthansa, who selected Curtiss Wright propellers. Lockheed then advised that because it was obligated to certificate Curtiss Wright propellers, it could no longer certificate the Hamilton Standard solid aluminum backup blades due to lack of available flight test time. This rankled Howard. Lockheed finally bent and agreed to conduct the tests "at the earliest possible date." I wished later that Lockheed had flatly refused to install the hollow blades rather than accommodate us.

With the emergence of an acceptable contract change order, I reviewed the entire propeller selection matter in detail with Howard on August 8, 1956. Selection of the Hamilton Standard hollow-bladed propellers was reconfirmed and the approved order returned to Lockheed with the following covering letter:

The enclosures have of course been executed by us on the understanding that Lockheed will proceed with all due diligence to effect full certification of LD-138 airplanes, equipped with Hamilton Standard 43H60 propellers with 6993-4 solid aluminum blades, in any event and at the earliest possible date to the end that such propellers and blades shall be immediately available for replacement of the 43H60 propeller with HA171A3-4 hollow aluminum blades, should such replacement at any time become advisable, either prior to or subsequent to Airplane delivery. This backup program has from the outset been fundamental and basic to the whole situation, and this is to memorialize that complete implementation will be consummated.

I insisted on this precaution because of lack of extensive operational experience with the hollow aluminum blades, not because I anticipated serious operational problems. We certainly would never have purchased them had that been the case.

TWA's 1649A operations commenced during 1957, when Carter Burgess, who had taken no part in any of the 1649A negotiations, was president. Initially the hollow blades performed well. Then it happened. A 1649A inboard propeller lost a blade tip on a transatlantic flight from Paris. The tip penetrated a lavatory, slightly injuring a passenger. The engine was immediately feathered (shut down) because of extreme vibration. Shortly after this, on a routine flight to St. Louis, abnormal engine vibration was encountered in another 1649A, causing the captain to feather the engine and land as soon as possible. Inspection showed a badly bulged blade tip, presumably near separation.

The cause of both incidents was failure of the bond that attached the porous blade stuffing to the blade. When failure occurred, centrifugal force pushed the stuffing toward the blade tip, causing imbalance, bulging, and failure. Hamilton Standard had used the best cement available and had no way to improve the bond. All stops were pulled to expedite the installation of the backup solid aluminum blades.

The CAA permitted TWA's 1649A operations to continue during the transition to solid blades because the bonding failures were progressive and could be located before they became dangerous by tapping a coin on the blade surfaces (separated areas sounded something like tapping a watermelon) and because of the early availability of the solid backup blades. As a precaution, TWA's 1649A's were temporarily withdrawn from international service and operated exclusively within the United States because of the availability of a greater number of alternate landing sites and the fact that closer surveillance was possible.

Hamilton Standard had the full quota of blade forgings on hand for the entire program but had finish manufacturing only those backup blades required to reequip most of TWA's delivered 1649A's. They immediately went on a 24-hour, three-shift factory schedule to expedite production of the remainder. Shortly afterward, I visited the Hamilton Standard plant without warning one night about 1:00 A.M. to show interest and to be assured that all that could be done was being done. John Burridge scurried over to the plant to conduct the factory tour. We inspected all work in process; it appeared that Hamilton Standard was essentially on schedule. The next day, word around the plant was that Howard Hughes had personally inspected the factory the night before!

Several months were required to complete the installation of the solid blades, after which we all breathed easier. The special contractual solid-blade backup provisions I had negotiated saved the day. Without them,

TWA's 1649A fleet downtime would likely have approached one year, possibly longer, because of the time required for tooling, production, certification, and installation of replacement blades. I do not remember receiving a single word of personal commendation from anyone except Hughes for having the foresight and determination to arrange for the backup blades. I do remember overhearing one TWA board member comment to a small group following a meeting: "What a wonderful thing Carter Burgess did to arrange for the backup blades. He saved the company."

No TWA Rights

Howard declared at the outset, "TWA has no rights" to the 25 1649A's that Toolco ordered by his direction. This was probably true legally, but I had no doubt that the planes were intended for TWA. They had been ordered to satisfy TWA's competitive needs and were being manufactured in compliance with TWA specifications. The contract permitted Howard to assign the planes to TWA without Lockheed's consent. I assumed that Howard would make them available to TWA in due course, and so did TWA's senior management.

Because the contract was between Lockheed and Toolco, it was Toolco's responsibility to provide the considerable funding required for spares provisioning and buyer-furnished equipment (BFE)—spare parts, communications equipment, galleys, passenger seats—just as it was to make the required progress payments. After discussing this matter with Ray Holliday and Ray Cook, Toolco's attorney, I provided Toolco with estimated capital requirements and commitment schedules and recommended that Howard authorize TWA to buy the necessary items in the name of Toolco as the only practical way to get the job done. This did not happen. In fact, nothing happened for all too long.

Lockheed became unhappy because of missed dock dates (dates when BFE should have been on hand at Lockheed) and started making noises about Toolco's being close to defaulting. After this situation became critical, Howard authorized Toolco to place the BFE purchase orders in compliance with TWA's requirements on my personal approval as its "Agent," *provided I cleared major vendor selection with him.*

. The personal approval aspect was awkward internally because TWA had a separate, entirely competent provisioning function within the Purchasing Department. It was a normal function of my department to establish associated technical requirements, help negotiate with key vendors, and usually to chair the vendor selection processes. But what I did not do was issue and formally approve the purchase orders, and TWA was not in the habit of clearing vendors with Howard.

Following Ralph Damon's passing on January 4, 1956, the TWA board had appointed John Collings chief executive officer. On March 24 I was elected vice president of engineering without any change whatsoever in my portfolio or salary, but I was pleased nevertheless with this recognition and the fact that the title Cohu ruled out in 1947 had been restored.

I reviewed Howard's instructions with John Collings, who said complying with them was okay, but I would have to keep my approval of the purchase orders secret to avoid jealousies and organizational problems. I objected to this demeaning and unnecessary complication. It would be a simple matter to have the purchase orders handled through me for approval as a "Special Agent." My department was already involved in the selection process, and, because the planes were on order by Toolco rather than TWA, this procedure could have been easily explained and should have been acceptable to all concerned. John was adamant. His final words were, "Handle it, but don't let the provisioning people or anyone else know you are required to approve the purchase orders."

The more I thought about it, the more I considered John's instructions repugnant and insulting. The special responsibilities Howard had assigned to me should have been recognized as an aid to discharging my duties. I swallowed my pride with some difficulty, met with the purchasing and provisioning heads, and explained that all BFE purchase orders would be prepared by TWA, placed by Toolco, and sent to Toolco through my office. This permitted my personal, private review. They accepted this as a Hughes quirk and agreed to the procedure. Then I called Vic Leslie, now senior vice president of finance, and requested a special work order to permit identification of associated TWA costs so Toolco could be charged for the service.

The purchase orders were prepared and then held because I could not reach Howard to clear the vendor list. Howard's reluctance to provide direct authority for the purchase of BFE not only added considerable work, but also threatened to delay airplane delivery. I tried repeatedly without success to reach him to obtain approval of the key vendors so the delayed orders could be released. I also requested Ray Cook and Bill Gay to try to contact him to explain the urgency of the situation.

Bill Gay finally got through to Howard, who said, "If Bob feels that this is the advisable thing to do and it is to our advantage to do so, why then by all means let's do it. Bob can send the vendor lists and costs at his convenience. However, the orders must be placed out of Houston by the Hughes Tool Company.'' Bill's call broke the logjam, but Howard's response was so casual that it suggested he had forgotten the emphasis he had placed on his instructions to clear vendors with him, or perhaps he did not understand the bind the BFE delay had caused at Lockheed.

The purchase of spare parts was also a major problem because of lack of commitment authority. The TWA board could not offer relief by authorizing funds because TWA had ''no rights'' to the planes, and, because the board was Hughes controlled, it would not have done so anyway without prior clearance from Howard. Finally, with no time remaining for receipt of spare parts before the first plane was delivered, Ray Cook received clearance from Howard for the spare parts provisioning purchase orders to be placed by Toolco, provided they were cleared with me. There were times, and this was one of them, when I thought I was the most underpaid person at TWA.

1649A Deficiencies

Hall Hibbard advised that instead of matching the speed of the DC-7, the 1649A was going to be about 18 mph slower than predicted, and the planes were overweight. Hall thought that some improvement in speed might become available, but weight reduction programs would be effective only on future production aircraft. He advised that Kelly Johnson, Carl Haddon, and Rudy Thoren were formulating wind tunnel and flight test programs to recoup as much speed as possible.

Hall's news, given only six months before delivery of the first plane, was a bitter, unexpected pill. The speed loss would clearly undercut TWA's anticipated competitive position, and payloads would be substantially reduced on long-range flights.

By early January, Lockheed claimed the speed could be increased by 10 mph through aerodynamic refinements. Kelly estimated that performance in the final delivery configuration would likely miss the low end of the speed guarantees by only 3 mph. I could see endless contractual arguments looming.

Howard, displeased and concerned about the continuing speed superiority of the DC-7's, as we all were, asked Harry West and me to develop a legal bill of particulars and see that nothing was done that could undermine his ability to refuse delivery of the 25 planes. I wrote a confidential letter to Ralph Ellinger with internal copies to others on January 9, 1957, which stated in part: "I have been requested by higher authority to direct you and others to do nothing which would in any way detract from our ability to refuse delivery of the Constellations . . . making certain at the same time, however, to do nothing which would deter Lockheed from meeting scheduled delivery commitments."

A complete list of 1649A deficiency claims—not just performance and empty weight, but everything that did not meet the exact letter of the specifications—was developed and sent to TWA's and Toolco's lawyers for review, and then on to Howard. It appeared that Howard was preparing to refuse delivery and sue Lockheed. This distasteful development provided heavy pressure on Lockheed to correct the deficiencies, which was part of Howard's strategy. My impression, however, was that Lockheed's engineers did not need extra pressure. Surprised, keenly disappointed, and perhaps a bit embarrassed with the speed deficiency, they were collectively doing their utmost to correct this and other problems at considerable extra expense. However, I was not so sure about Lockheed's bean counters and sales people.

The most difficult problem we faced in establishing a sound position for refusing delivery was proving noncompliance with the speed guarantees. Lockheed was the only party with 1649A's, and had control of all flight tests. Further, even if a 1649A had been available for independent flight tests, proving incontrovertibly that the plane missed minimum guarantees by only 2 mph or 3 mph would have been next to impossible. And, even if proven, establishing damage from future loss of revenue stemming from such small differences in speed would have been difficult and would, I think, have kept lawyers busy quite a long time. Additional costs to be incurred from higher fuel consumption, maintenance deficiencies, and other design shortcomings were relatively easy to compute and were included in the bill of particulars.

In the end, Howard did not sue and agreed to accept the planes provided Lockheed settled all claims to "Rummel's satisfaction." Lockheed finally settled our claims, but not until two more TWA presidents had been elected and Howard had lost control of the company.

221

Howard's 1649A

During the latter part of 1956, Howard instructed his lawyers to obtain the CAB's approval for transferring 1649A's to TWA. However, someone made a mistake. The CAB approved the transfer of all 25 planes, but it was Howard's intention to keep one for himself.

Ray Cook wrote Noah Dietrich on November 14: "A possible conflict may arise between Hughes and TWA as to the disposition of one of the 25 1649A Lockheed airplanes in production for delivery commencing next spring . . . since this runs counter to transactions which have already been consummated with CAB approval." Ray reviewed the history of the deal and suggested that perhaps the best way to accommodate Howard would be to order a 26th airplane rather than seek to alter the recently granted CAB approval.

Howard did not pursue either course, but he did not give up the idea of having a 1649A for his own use. This situation came to an unfortunate head during Carter Burgess's short regime as president. A hands-on, direct-action executive, Burgess was elected president on January 23, 1957. He had served as Jack Frye's assistant in 1946 and early 1947, was close to Jack's problems with Hughes and Noah Dietrich, which had cost Jack his job, and must have known what he was getting into.

Howard telephoned me within a few days of Carter's election and said he and I would continue to handle fleet procurement matters and that Carter would run the rest of the airline. I hoped that Howard had made this clear to Carter. Negotiations, some secret, were then underway for the possible acquisition of several types of turboprops and jets. I suggested to Howard that Carter be apprised of such activities as a matter of courtesy. Howard said the projects did not involve TWA at that stage, he would handle this with Burgess when the time was right, and I was to maintain absolute secrecy. It was clear that life would not be smooth under Carter, and trouble did in fact develop in many areas.

Lockheed delivered the first 1649A to TWA on May 4, 1957. During June Howard helped himself to one of TWA's few delivered 1649A's at Los Angeles. He simply showed up at the TWA hangar with Bill Gay and Johnny Meyer, a well-known Hughes associate; borrowed a TWA captain to serve as copilot; and took off for Montreal, Canada.

The plane was badly needed the very next day for route-proving flights (flights required by the CAA before start of commercial service). The loss of this plane, even for a few days, was serious because it threatened the advertised start-of-service date. However, the plane was not gone a few days; it was gone for months. After Montreal, Howard flew it to Nassau in August, then back to Los Angeles during October, and he did not return it until late December.

Howard had not bothered to talk to Carter Burgess at all about using the plane, which understandably inflamed Carter. In fact, Carter got damned mad and repeatedly left word for Hughes—Howard never could be reached directly—that TWA needed the plane, and he wanted the plane back. Hughes was not given to acceding to angry demands, and this was no exception. Confronted with fruitless calls, Carter asked Bill Gay; Lee Flanigan, TWA pilot and operations executive, and a friend of Hughes; and me to intercede. I mentioned to Howard by telephone how strongly Carter felt about the return of the plane. He grunted his annoyance and mumbled a few expletives but elected not to discuss the matter. After waiting a few moments, I introduced another subject, knowing that if Howard returned the plane, it would be only in his own good time.

The real importance of having "Howard's" 1649A returned to TWA diminished as the fleet grew during the summer months. Indeed, my earlier concerns over inability to turn a profit with 1649A's proved to be justified. Even when completely filled, the 1649A's could not carry fully allocated expenses, although a few flights did contribute to overhead. As the fall season approached, I could not see the importance of adding one more loser to the fleet and was surprised at Carter's persistence.

In an effort to attract 1649A payloads, Carter ordered the installation of fully reclining, widely spaced "siesta" seats. In this reduced-capacity configuration, TWA's 1649A's were undoubtedly the most luxurious, comfortable, and longest-range transports flying. While they were loss leaders for TWA, passengers considered the 1649A's the queen of the skies.

The return of the plane Howard "borrowed" became a consuming challenge with Carter, as if its absence somehow was an affront to his personal honor. The more Carter pressed, the more Howard dug his heels in. After Howard returned the plane to Los Angeles during October, he placed it out of Carter's reach under armed guard until late December. During November, Hughes and Burgess had a confrontation about a planned purchase of Viscount turboprops (see Chapter 17). Carter Burgess tendered his resignation on December 31, 1957.

"Vacation" in Europe

Margie, the three older children, and I had planned for months to take a three-week trip the summer of 1957 to England, France, Italy, and Spain. The girls were excited, conjuring up visions of intriguing places, and could hardly wait for their first trip to Europe. I looked forward too—it was to be my first real vacation in 14 years with TWA. I planned to do absolutely nothing but enjoy the trip except for brief business meetings in England and France and courtesy calls at a few TWA offices. I suppose I knew better, but I counted on nothing interfering with our carefully laid plans, which included 24-hour babysitters for Bobby and Diana. Luck seemed to be with us because the scheduled departure date arrived shortly after the hollow propeller problem was safely under control, and other projects showed no sign of imminent crises.

Two days before the scheduled departure from New York, Carter Burgess summoned me for management meetings, which was not unusual. I assured Margie not to worry—Carter had approved of the trip to Europe and would not interfere.

Immediately on my arrival in New York, Bill Gay called and said Howard had an extremely urgent project for me that could not wait on my return from Europe. He said Howard knew of my trip plans and certainly would not ask me to postpone the trip, but circumstances beyond his control were forcing his hand. He would "deeply appreciate" my remaining available. Bill said Howard would call "right away" and explain, but he had wanted to make sure I was immediately available to handle this matter for him.

This did not go down at all well. I explained that my wife and three girls were on their way to New York to join me for the trip to Europe and that I would have to know a whole lot more about Howard's project before agreeing to disappoint them. He repeated that Howard would call and explain. I said, "Okay, Bill, fine. As matters now stand, I plan to leave for England tomorrow morning and will be at the Lexington Hotel tonight. If Howard doesn't call before I leave, I'll leave a trail so he can reach me anytime in Europe. If you will explain my reason for going ahead, I'm sure he will understand."

That afternoon Carter Burgess called me into his inner sanctum (Carter had made the president's office a conference room and taken over a small, adjacent private secretary's office for personal use) and led me to believe that Howard had called him with the request that my trip be postponed. It was unusual for Howard to call Carter, and I wondered why he had not called me directly. When I asked why Howard wanted the trip postponed, Carter said there was not time during the call for detailed explanations, but Howard considered the matter of extreme importance. Carter recommended I postpone the trip and said he would appreciate it if I did.

Here were both the president and the principal owner asking me to postpone a special family trip to Europe without explaining themselves. After agonizing several hours waiting for a call from Howard, I reluctantly decided that prudence required me to wait in New York for Howard's call, even if it interfered with our trip. I also decided that if I did not go, I would insist that Margie and the three girls go ahead as planned. I would join them as soon as possible.

Margie and the girls joined me at the Lexington that evening. I did not tell them I might not be able to go, hoping to change Howard's mind if he called, and because I thought Margie might not go if I told her ahead of time. I did not hear from Howard, which did not help my frame of mind.

The next day on the way to the airport, I gave them the news. At first they thought it was one of "Daddy's jokes." When Margie realized I was dead serious, she absolutely refused to go. However, through gentle persuasion and some insistence on my part, she changed her mind by boarding time so as not to disappoint the girls.

It proved to be a great adventure for them to be on their own in strange lands. They were entertained everywhere by business friends and given every courtesy, including the use of two Rolls-Royce limos—they could only use one—waiting by the plane on arrival in London, their first stop. They saw the sights, did the shops, and sampled good food everywhere they went. It was a great introduction to Europe for the girls and a long-remembered trip for Margie.

As for Howard, I waited in vain for his call for over two weeks despite repeated attempts to reach him. When it came, Howard did not know why I had been trying to reach him. When I explained what had happened, he indicated there must have been some "horrible misunderstanding." He had asked Bill Gay to locate me to so he could discuss the latest Bristol Britannia turboprop delivery offer. He was "deeply sorry" for my personal inconvenience and regretted the unintended "screw-up" of my plans. Howard's call revealed that he had not called Carter, but Bill Gay had called both Carter and me with the same "urgent" message! When I confronted Bill, he said he was sorry, but he had understood Howard exactly as he had put it to me.

The 1049H Fiasco

TWA's acquisition of Lockheed Model 1049H aircraft followed a splintered, freakish negotiating imbroglio. Lockheed manufactured planes without customer orders; Hughes put unowned planes under armed guard; TWA made elaborate plans to operate planes that neither TWA or Hughes purchased or provisioned; and, on Howard's direction, planes that were to be leased were parked instead. It was an unpredictable, screwed-up, crazy affair.

By 1957, when Carter Burgess became president, Oz Cocke had developed a considerable case of hot pants for a fleet of 1049H's for transatlantic, high-density, "austerity" passenger services, like those TWA's competitors planned to introduce the following summer, and for expanded cargo operations. The 1049H's were configured essentially like the 1049G's except they were tailored for all-cargo services and rapid conversion between cargo and passenger operations. Oz pressed Carter, Ray Cook, Bill Gay, me, and anyone else who would listen to sell Howard on acquiring H's. For several months, Leonard Schwartz had been up to his old tricks of trying to land a commitment directly from Howard.

Carter ignored Howard's instructions that Howard and I handle aircraft procurement matters and assigned Jack L. Weller, vice president of planning and coordination, to handle the 1049H program. Jack began wheeling and dealing with Lockheed and undertook negotiations with National and other airlines for the joint seasonal use of several planes. Because I was out of the negotiating loop, I called Carter's attention by letter of March 4 to the need for me to be involved. Carter responded by requesting me to apprise Weller of anything pertinent to the H's. This was something like a kick in the teeth.

Around March 15, Ralph Ellinger called me and said Lockheed was manufacturing as many as nine 1049H's on speculation. Leonard had sold Bob Gross on the idea, claiming Howard would buy them, but because Howard had not done so, Bob was unhappy with Leonard. Ralph also reported that Jorge E. Carnicero, senior vice president of California Eastern Aviation, who was serving as agent for Resort Airlines, was trying to place the two H's acquired earlier for that airline.

Howard called in early July and requested me to arrange for the standardization of the two Carnicero planes in TWA's shops for early operations "to the absolute minimum acceptable extent." Because our shops were saturated with peak summer-season work, I advised Howard it would be impossible to do so without impairing commercial operations. Howard commented that TWA could do a better job cheaper than Lockheed, which was true, and advised that one of the planes would shortly arrive in Kansas City. He elected, however, not to impair summer operations and asked me to make interim storage arrangements. He spent nearly a full half hour emphasizing that he wanted the plane on TWA property, but not where it could become the center of attention. He wanted 24-hour armed guards posted with strict orders that no one other than me was to approach the plane. Howard concluded, "Don't you see, Bob, I don't want the mechanics gawking and commenting every day on the way to work." He asked me to review the 1049H specifications that Schwartz was sending. I advised Weller and Burgess and took charge of technical negotiations.

The second Resort H was flown to Kansas City early that fall, modified in Ray Dunn's shops, and placed in pilot training operations. It still sported the Resort logo. During November, the plane I had placed under guard was also modified. By this time neither Hughes nor TWA had contracted for a fleet of 1049H's, nor had CAB approval for use of the Carnicero planes been sought. Notwithstanding, Lockheed continued to invest more millions in H's for Hughes. After some of them were ready for flight tests, without any right to do so, Howard placed them under armed guard at Lockheed's Burbank factory. No explanation was given, but I assumed this had to do with lack of financing.

Neither TWA nor Toolco could authorize the purchase of BFE because neither had ordered the planes—the same kind of problem encountered in the 1649A program. A considerably vexed Leonard Schwartz called me on December 16, advised that Lockheed was unwilling to buy the BFE, and insisted that TWA do so right away. He proposed that Lockheed buy back the BFE and pay associated TWA costs if TWA did not use the planes. (I had suggested to Leonard months earlier that if he was convinced TWA would use the planes, Lockheed should buy the BFE to our specifications and sell it to us if and when TWA purchased the planes.) Leonard said his management was convinced that if TWA agreed to buy the BFE, Howard would agree to purchase the planes. My rejoinder was, "They incorrectly evaluate the man and the situation. The best pressure that can be brought to bear is for you to get Howard and say, lookee, order these damned things.'' A few days later, Lockheed reconsidered and decided to purchase TWA-specified BFE for the planes.

Hughes authorized the purchase of nine 1049H's on December 31, the very day that Carter Burgess resigned. Two were delivered the same day, and the two Carnicero H's were soon returned. Cocke got the airplanes he wanted and put them to good use. By procrastinating (although this may not have been his intention), Howard was not required to make the customary down and progress payments, and he avoided incurring major financial commitments during the difficult period following his March firing of Noah Dietrich (see Chapter 19).

Leonard Schwartz shortly left Lockheed's employment and was hired by Hughes. Howard explained that Leonard would be concerned primarily with the financial and programmatic aspects (whatever that meant) of our equipment programs. I was to continue as usual and should make information available to Leonard as appropriate. After my hassles with Leonard at Lockheed, it was not the best of days.

As for Carter, at times he made my work and my position difficult, and he must have considered my association with Howard a grating corporate anomaly. Still, I was sorry to see him leave TWA despite his unwillingness to abide by Howard's directive concerning aircraft procurement. He shook up the organization and was melding it into an efficient team with focused efforts. I thought he could be good for TWA if he would only work well with Howard, as Ralph Damon had done. But that was not to happen.

End of an Era

The transports of the Constellation era were powerful instruments for forging bonds of commerce and friendship between world communities. Airline routes expanded until nearly all major traffic generating areas in the free world were linked. Passenger services improved, embryonic all-cargo services gained respectability, the airline business boomed, and major U.S. airlines finally went off federal subsidy. The fine transports of that era set the world's stage for the next great advancement in transportation: the magnificent jets.

Lockheed's Constellation production line ended not long after delivery of the last 1649A, a circumstance largely generated by the airline rush to reequip with jets and turboprops (in which propellers are driven by turbines) and the inability of the last pistons to cover their costs. The turbo-prop Electra program, however, quickly established Lockheed as a dominant manufacturer of turboprops.

Piston transports continued to ply the airways and serve the public effectively for years after the jets were introduced. However, their economic obsolescence was certain and predictable due to the superior speed and comfort of the jets. Jets and turboprops finally pushed them aside, even on short-haul services.

For me, the Constellation era was exciting, challenging, and gratifying. The transports that emerged were good for TWA and the industry and, on average, produced acceptable corporate results. The public and most people in industry—even many at TWA—knew little or nothing of the hectic problems and disappointments encountered and usually mastered during our aircraft development programs. Certainly, the gestation problems of the 1049G and 1649A programs were never aired in public. Nothing would have been gained, and only doubts raised by ventilating such things.

For TWA overall, the Constellations, while not always my first choice for procurement, were effective tools for building the corporation. Each succeeding model pressed operational frontiers forward and justified expanded services. Of all the Constellation models, TWA's 749A's and 1049G's were, in my opinion, the very best. The attractive lines of the Constellations graced TWA skies for over 21 years. During this period TWA's Constellations flew popes and presidents and were accepted by the flying public as superb, high-speed, pioneering airliners. The Constellations, which Howard always elected to purchase even when competing Douglas DC's were clearly superior, helped forge TWA into a leading domestic carrier and one of the world's preeminent international airlines, which in the end made Howard a great deal of money. However, that was only after the jet era was well established, and after TWA, driven to the very edge of bankruptcy by his increasingly irresponsible actions, had escaped from his control.

15.
Jets—
The Early
Promise,
1944–1949

The jet age was only a vague, beckoning vision in 1943 when I joined TWA. Early jet fighters portended the doubling of transport speeds and cruising altitudes, thus signaling an enormous potential for achieving unparalleled advances in transportation efficiency and comfort. It seemed certain that such gains awaited only the development of suitable engines, compatible airframes, and an essential background of operational experience. The inviting vision strengthened with passing time, but realization remained beyond the pale of reasonable expectations for years.

The inherent capability of turbines to generate great power with little vibration contrasted sharply with the vibrating piston power plants, which clawed and shook their way through the atmosphere despite the best available damping mechanisms. Even the best soundproofing could only reduce the ear-stressing racket to barely acceptable dissonance. Complete elimination of the usual cyclical crescendo of fuselage side wall drumming became possible with the omission of propellers, and the simple rotating power components of the turbines appeared to be a maintenance man's dream.

231

Nearly every aspect of jet transportation appeared inviting. The ability to fly at high altitudes through the smooth air reaches, reduction in flight times and exposure to risk by nearly half (many people still considered flying unsafe), and the prospect for achieving striking increases in passenger comfort seemed certain to dramatically expand the travel market. Frye's and Tomlinson's goal of true over-weather flight, a goal shared by Hughes and myself, appeared to lie within the misty reach of the rapidly evolving technology.

Howard, Jack, and the Jets

Hughes's and Frye's intense, aspiring interest in turbine transports was evident from the time of my association with TWA. Their interest and my youthful enthusiasm became a common bond between us and justification for my continually probing and evaluating this promising field.

By early 1944, embryonic jet technology began to bear striking results. The British Gloster Meteor had demonstrated its unique performance capabilities by destroying German V-1 "Buzz Bombs" over England; General Electric was manufacturing I-40 jet engines developed under British license; the Bell Aircraft Corporation XP-59 Airacomet and the experimental Lockheed pursuit, the XP-80 *Lulu Belle,* had flown.

At that time, the British led the world in jet technology. The British government, in compliance with recommendations of the Civil Aviation Committee on Post-War Transports, known as the Brabazon Committee, had established policies designed to place England in the strongest possible civil transport world marketing position in the early postwar era. The policies worked. New British transports were in full-scale development soon after VE day, while the resources of the United States were still devoted to winning the war in the Pacific.

I developed numbers of original jet transport designs to better understand the inherent advantages and limits of turbine power. At my request, a fellow employee, Glen Scott, made artist's renderings of them to illustrate design concepts and help develop management interest. Jack Franklin forwarded two such renderings by "secret" letter to Jack Frye and Lee Talman on April 13, 1944:

Attached are sketches of two "dream jobs" by Bob Rummel using jet propulsion. They are based on the best information we have available on jet equipment.

Lockheed is very enthusiastic over jet propulsion possibilities in airplanes in the relatively near future. They are laying out a jet propulsion installation for the Constellation (which would involve a new wing).

Other manufacturers seem to feel that the gas turbine driving a propeller is something to be expected in the relatively near future, but that jet propulsion is farther off, based on their belief that necessary fuel economy cannot be obtained.

I vividly remember being in Lockheed's executive dining room on the second floor of the Burbank Terminal with Hall Hibbard, Kelly Johnson, Carl Haddon, and Jack Franklin watching for the first time the remarkably performing P-80A's take off toward us. The eight or nine jet takeoffs we saw contrasted sharply with the interspersed, relatively sluggish piston aircraft. Each time a P-80A took off, Jack and I watched through the picture window. It was exciting. The obvious acceleration, dramatic speed, and impression of sheer power as they thundered past at high angles of climb, shaking the building with undamped exhaust roar, was absolutely spectacular.

During the following December, I drafted letters to the presidents or senior engineering officers of seven major U.S. airframe manufacturers with whom Franklin and I had had discussions concerning jet aircraft: Wellwood E. Beall, Boeing; Donald Douglas, Sr.; Mac Laddon, Convair; Bob Gross, Lockheed; Glen L. Martin; Alfred Marachev, Republic Aviation; and J. H. ("Dutch") Kindelberger, North American Aviation. The letters were labeled "Secret and Confidential" and read in part: "You will recall our conversations regarding recent jet and turbine [turboprop] developments. In our opinion sufficient progress has been made in developing power units of these types to permit predicating aircraft of new designs on them. . . . We should like to discuss with you the development of a long range, high speed, passenger and cargo transport utilizing power plants of these types."

The letters, reflecting internal discussions with Frye and Talman, carried Franklin's signature and were sent through Lee Talman for final clearance with Hughes. Clearance never came. Word was that Jack Frye approved, but he was unable to obtain clearance from Hughes. Whether Howard wanted to reserve the prerogative of making formal contacts for himself; whether he thought such contacts to be technologically premature (they probably were, but it was not too early to sort out the possibilities); whether he characteristically decided to hold the matter in abeyance while he

233

thought it over; or whether some other circumstance blocked clearance was never made clear. Thus, my first attempt to place TWA in the forefront of commercial turbine transport development, for whatever reason, was stonewalled by Hughes.

During March of 1945, when it appeared that Germany would soon capitulate, Jack Frye wrote an internal "personal, confidential, and secret" memorandum expressing interest in exploring the development of a "jet propulsion airplane" capable of transcontinental, nonstop, all-mail operations with 10,000 pounds of payload, or alternately, with 6,000 pounds of payload 4,000 miles. Airmail contracts were quite lucrative and were usually awarded to the airline providing the fastest service. Frye's strategy was to acquire just enough planes to give TWA top priority and lock out the competition for a meaningful period.

In response to Frye's interest, I laid out a single-engine (the engine was under development by P & W for the Navy), high-wing plane with a 70-foot wing span. The cockpit was located forward, with the engine air scoop just aft and on top of the fuselage to minimize ingestion of destructive ground debris. The mail compartment was between the cockpit and the engine, which was buried in the fuselage aft of the wing carry-through structure. Two JATO (jet-assisted takeoff) retractable rockets were located aft to enable high-altitude airport or short-runway takeoffs. Most of my design data were developed during evenings at home to maintain secrecy. It was a nice-looking plane, even by today's standards.

After reviewing my design, Jack Frye reconfirmed his interest by telephone, indicating he had sent a copy of the data to Howard. Jack made a number of design suggestions, including two engines rather than one to increase schedule reliability, full- rather than partial-span wing flaps, thermal wing deicing, and space for a navigator or radio operator. He raised good technical questions such as how to slow such a clean airplane during descent.

The plan for implementing this design was to contract for detail engineering and construction with a selected manufacturer (Lockheed seemed like an ideal choice) as soon as war priorities permitted, if continuing exploration proved the project to be feasible. After Japan surrendered in August 1945, it was necessary to spend virtually all of our time acquiring war surplus C-47, C-54, and C-69 transports on a top-priority basis to build as soon as possible Howard's equipment-starved airline. By the time the peak of these efforts was behind us, stringent financial circumstances required putting the jet mail plane on "temporary" hold. The outlook gradually worsened, and implementation prospects faded into oblivion.

Jack Frye wrote another "personal, confidential, and secret" letter early in 1946, this time expressing interest in the development of a 24-passenger "turbojet or turboprop" transport capable of New York-Chicago nonstop services. Frye wanted TWA to dominate this important, rapidly growing repeat-business market. Achieving this goal required weaning satisfied passengers from AAL and UAL—not an easy task. Frye believed and I was convinced that jets would provide a commanding equipment lead and be the right marketing solution, a viewpoint experience would prove correct. I laid out such a transport to be powered by four General Electric TG-180 jet engines. Like the mail plane, most of the detail work was done at home. After considerable preliminary work, I submitted drawings, performance estimates, and descriptive data by letter of June 13, 1946.

I proposed a moderately swept high-wing plane (high angles of wing sweep would have cost too much weight and raised serious stability questions) with engines mounted in two under-wing nacelles faired into the lower wing surface. Wing-tip fuel tanks were provided because of limited capacity in the relatively thin wing. The cockpit had tandem seating and was to be covered with a streamlined canopy. I predicted a maximum speed of 540 mph and an average speed of 505 mph for a 750-mile trip with full payload and ample fuel reserves. Such speeds would have cut flight times in half and made feasible daily business trips between New York and Chicago.

Jack Frye and Howard Hughes expressed serious interest. Hughes immediately demanded absolute secrecy for this already secret project. Frye wrote a number of comments concerning my design on a three-view drawing, which I still have. He suggested, among other things, a longer fuselage, power boosts for the control system, full-span flaps, single-wheel in lieu of double-wheel main landing gears (I disagreed), and shock-mount engines. He also asked that I consider seating the pilot further ahead, with the copilot seated higher, permitting him to view the pilot's instrument panel as well as his own. Howard also discussed numbers of design aspects with me and requested continuing study and preparation of paperwork for

●

discussion with prospective manufacturers. This was extremely encouraging for a relatively new employee, who thoroughly appreciated the attention and recognition accorded his design.

A week or so later, on July 7, 1946, Howard crashed in the XF-11. Dick Brown's Reading accident occurred four days later, followed the next day by the Constellation grounding. Then, on October 21, TWA pilots went on strike, which finished the jet transport project and all but finished the airline.

During the following December, Ralph Ellinger, then TWA's West Coast factory representative, met in Santa Monica with Ed Burton, Nat Paschall, and Carlos Wood of the Douglas Company. They advised Ralph that Douglas proposed to develop, at its own expense, a 20- to 23-passenger jet transport powered by three or four Westinghouse 24-C engines capable of New York-Chicago flights. During the second week of January 1947, Ed Burton telephoned Jack Franklin and confirmed the Douglas project. Burton proposed construction of a prototype to fly in mid-1948, with production deliveries "probable" during 1949. Franklin relayed this information to Jack Frye and Paul Richter by letter of January 16, with the following comment (this was seven days after Howard and the TWA board stripped Frye of presidential authority preliminary to the April 24, 1947, annual meeting, during which he was "not reelected"): "It is interesting to note that the Douglas proposal, which I will discuss with Ed Burton later this week, almost exactly parallels Bob Rummel's design. . . . Ed Burton indicated that he would like to talk to us about this airplane first [before talking to any other airline]." Franklin included a brief tabular comparison of the Douglas and my designs.

I met with Ed Burton later that week in Kansas City. We compared designs and concluded that a solid technical foundation existed for collaboration on and furtherance of the 24-passenger project. As engineers, Ed and I were enthusiastic, but TWA's adverse financial circumstance and fragile management situation put a heavy damper on thoughts of a cooperative venture.

It became crystal clear soon after Cohu's election as president of TWA on April 24 that any possibility of selling him (Hughes was out of touch during most of this period) on the idea of sponsoring the development of any airplane, let alone a jet, had about as much chance for success as I would have climbing Mount Everest wearing only jockey shorts. The

•

disasters of 1946, Frye's departure, and Cohu's election killed what might have been an exciting pioneering venture.

The Douglas project also aborted because the engines lacked operational experience and proved to be too thirsty. A great deal more time and research would be required to design jet engines with higher compression ratios and more efficient turbines, so essential to the development of acceptable commercial transports.

Bomber Conversion Proposals

The far-seeing U.S. Army Air Forces, under the able leadership of General Arnold, had been quick to understand the inherent potential advantages of jet propulsion and pressed jet engine and aircraft design technology from 1941 onward. About the time I joined TWA in 1943, the Air Forces solicited proposals for the development of jet bombers. Four companies responded: Boeing (XB-47), Convair (XB-46), Martin (XB-48), and North American (XB-45). Initially, all the designs submitted had straight, nonswept wings. Consolidated and North American proposed planes with four jet engines, the others with six.

About the time Germany collapsed, Dr. Theodore Von Karman, California Institute of Technology; Dr. George S. Schairer, Boeing; and Dr. William R. Sears, chief of aerodynamics for Northrop, now Professor Emeritus in the Aerospace and Mechanical Engineering departments of the University of Arizona, were flown to Germany in a C-54 to inspect available aeronautical research. And available it was. The Germans had stacks of data neatly arranged in piles on tables, as if they were anxious for the Americans to have it.

One data stack was on swept-wing research. After quick review, Schairer contacted a key Boeing associate in Seattle, Bob Withington, and requested wind tunnel tests. Bob "cobbled up" an existing straight-wing model by sweeping the wings 30 degrees forward, and then 30 degrees aft. The tests were rough but conclusive. Wing sweep dramatically reduced high-speed drag.

Boeing then undertook extensive revision of its bomber design, including the development of a highly swept wing. This caused Boeing to be about one year late and put it out of contention for the initial contract award, which went to North American for 100 B-45's.

Ed Wells, George Schairer, Bob Withington, and others at Boeing were convinced that the Air Forces would ultimately order the revised B-47 design because of pronounced performance superiority. They continued the XB-47 development program without interruption. They were right! In the end, over 2,000 were built.

The severely swept wing; sleek, underslung, wing-mounted engine nacelles; and overall geometric configuration of the B-47 represented a major advance that earned undisputed world leadership in military aircraft and strongly influenced jet aircraft design throughout the world. Not many planes merit this distinction. In my opinion, the only piston aircraft clearly falling in this category were the Northrop Alpha, the Douglas DC-1, and the Boeing 307 Stratoliner.

The four manufacturers received permission from the Air Forces to develop preliminary transport versions for discussion with several key airlines, including TWA. Convair, Martin, and North American did so. Boeing elected to concentrate on the B-47, which it did not consider suitable for redevelopment for transport usage. The three manufacturers visited my office frequently to brief me on plans for the transport versions. None was seeking firm airline development or production contracts at that time, but each planned to do so if they won the production contract. All three informally requested TWA to voluntarily express serious interest to the Air Forces: an obvious move to garner political support.

The designs were intriguing. Because the three manufactures wanted maximum commonality between their bombers and transports, the proposed transport versions were essentially identical to the bombers except for enlarged fuselages, designed to provide space for the passengers. Detailed review indicated more extensive redesign would have been required to comply with CAA design criteria, install civil equipment, and provide essential systems redundancy for commercial operations. Obvious operational problems like stopping on wet or icy runways without reverse thrust or propeller drag were not effectively addressed. Such considerations, plus an insufficient background of operational experience to support the manufacturers' economic and performance estimates, led me to conclude that, no matter how intriguing, none of the proposed transports would be suitable for airline use. Accordingly, after internal discussion, we elected not to express interest to the Air Forces. I do not recall clearing this position with Hughes or whether Frye did so. Later on, when I reviewed the conversion proposals with Howard, he was not critical of our handling and agreed that one of our primary standing objectives must be to encourage and, when feasible, foster the development jet transports suitable for TWA's use.

Boeing

Boeing's development of the swept-wing B-47, which seemed to open up new design possibilities for jet transports, was of intense interest. When Ed Wells, Boeing's chief engineer, invited me and other airline representatives to visit Boeing's Wichita facility on November 20, 1946, to inspect its DC-3 replacement offering, the twin-engine, high-wing Model 417, I jumped at the chance it might afford to privately discuss jet transport design.

Ed was most gracious. We met privately for nearly three hours during the late afternoon before a group dinner at the stockyards. I summarized this meeting in a letter to Jack Franklin dated December 3, 1946, the highlights of which follow:

1. It was agreed [between us] that the development of commercial jet transports should logically precede the development of turbine-propeller powered transports. . . .

2. Mr. Wells is convinced that a 30 to 40 passenger turbojet transport with a cruising speed of 600 mph, and a range with appropriate reserves from New York to Los Angeles, can be successfully manufactured in the not too distant future. He looks forward to substantial improvements in specific fuel consumption. . . .

3. Mr. Wells believes the jet transport to be superior direct cost wise to reciprocating engine transports. This checks with our studies.

4. Swept back wings reduce the gust effect to an amount that Mr. Wells believes will be acceptable for high altitude, high speed operation with passengers.

My letter also advised that Boeing was considering negotiating with the Army for the design of a troop-tanker transport to be developed from the B-47 design. Ed believed that such a project should logically precede the development of a commercial transport because of economics. This was done considerably later. The new design incorporated lessons learned from the B-47 and B-52 programs and quickly evolved into the Boeing 707.

Ed Wells proposed that Boeing submit early in 1947 three jet transport proposals for TWA's review to crystallize design objectives for an anticipated Boeing commercial transport program. I liked Ed's approach. He wanted to collaborate with TWA toward achieving a design that would best meet airline requirements.

I could not conceive of Howard's not approving of this activity because it appeared to place us in the forefront of Boeing's evolving jet transport program and would likely place us in an excellent negotiating position. Because the activity was exploratory rather than a negotiation, I indicated without checking with Howard that TWA would be glad to review Boeing's proposals and assist in the establishment of Boeing's civil transport design objectives.

Boeing followed through by submitting new designs based on B-47 technology tailored to the commercial market, making no effort to standardize with the B-47. Numbers of Boeing-TWA design review meetings were held in my Kansas City office notwithstanding Frye's departure and Cohu's negative attitude concerning participation in new airplane projects.

The joint Boeing-TWA efforts were of great interest and technically helpful to both parties but premature with regard to program formation. Although sound airplane design concepts emerged, detailed development proved to be years away, primarily because of lack of efficient engines.

Later on, after Hughes became active toward the end of Cohu's regime as president of TWA, I advised Howard of this project and briefly discussed Boeing's proposed designs. I thought he would be pleased, even complimentary, that Boeing elected to collaborate with me on this project, but all I heard was a bland indication that this activity was okay and a stern reminder that I was not to undertake negotiations with Boeing or any other manufacturer without his consent.

Lockheed

Lockheed, like other manufacturers engaged or interested in the production of transports, from time to time investigated jet and turboprop civil transport development possibilities. Hall Hibbard and Kelly Johnson took occasion during the periods of our Constellation negotiations to discuss such possibilities. The first such discussion, in early 1944, concerned the possible development of a jet-powered version of the Constellation. This soon proved to be infeasible. However, Hibbard and Johnson remained ebullient but circumspect about the ultimate use of turbine power in transports.

Hall Hibbard discussed an entirely new preliminary jet transport design with me in early May 1948. When I could not reach Howard by phone, I sent him a sketch and brief description on May 18 because of his great interest in new aircraft design and his desire to be kept up to date. My letter stated in part:

Lockheed is proposing a four-engine jet transport design that has commercial possibilities. This transport is in many respects similar [except for engine location] to the design I laid out some time ago and discussed with you and Mr. Franklin during July 1947. The attachment lists salient points of Lockheed's design.

Due to the DC-6 grounding and time spent on the now dormant DC-9 project, Douglas profess to have done little jet transport work since our meeting with Donald Douglas and Ed Burton last July.

The Lockheed design was offered to the military, with the hope that it could also find a commercial market. It was a 40-passenger, low-wing, four-engine, V-tail plane with uniquely placed engines. Two were shown under the main-deck cargo floor in the forward portion of the fuselage with P-80-type intake air scoops on each side of the flight deck and tail pipes extended to the area beneath the wing center section. The other two engines were in the aft part of the fuselage with similar side-mounted air scoops. Power from the four General Electric TG-180 engines was expected to lift the 11,000-pound payload 2,100 miles at 550 mph.

On March 7, 1949, Bob Gross presented in Kansas City sketches of three versions of a new jet transport Lockheed was considering offering to the airlines: 30-, 36-, and 40-passenger planes with gross weights ranging from 60,000 to 75,000 pounds. All of them had very thin, low-aspect-ratio (relatively narrow-span, wide-chord) wings with moderate leading-edge sweep, straight trailing edges, and extremely large wing-tip fuel tanks. The four engines were aft of the passenger compartment below a large, above-deck cargo compartment near the conventional empennage. All passenger seats were ahead of the trailing edge of the wing. The predicted flight range varied from 1,000 to 1,600 miles at about 500 mph. They were slick designs that never emerged as serious proposals.

241

During early 1950, the year that Douglas quietly began studies culminating in development of the DC-8, Lockheed forwarded preliminary plans for a new model, the L-193 Global Jet Transport, and solicited comments on the design from several airlines, including TWA. A revised L-193 preliminary proposal emerged several months later, partly as a result of airline comments. It was to have a 2,700-square-foot wing, a maximum takeoff weight of 220,000 pounds, and a maximum landing weight of 144,000 pounds. Each of the four jet engines near the tail was expected to produce with moderate afterburning 16,500 pounds thrust by delivery (I thought airport noise with afterburning would be intolerable). The predicted cruising speed was close to the speed of sound.

The L-193 was an advanced design, such as one might expect from Johnson and Hibbard, which Lockheed continued to evolve for several years. We revisited this project from time to time as appropriate; however, neither it nor any other civil Lockheed jet transport emerged until the L-1011 trijets of 1972.

Technology Survey—Europe

Our continuing investigation of turbine-powered transport design posed many configuration and operational questions that required timely answers if TWA were to attempt to pioneer the commercial jet age. I undertook, with Hughes's concurrence, an aggressive campaign to find the needed answers by on-site examination of state-of-the-art turbine engine and aircraft designs and related operational experience in Europe. England, which was far ahead of the United States, was my most important target. My quest was not only inviting; it was necessary. With flight safety and millions of dollars to be ultimately involved, no room for mistakes existed. Besides, while Howard expected me to work at the cutting edge, it was extremely important to leaven my conclusions and recommendations with hard-nosed realism. I felt review of operational experience was absolutely essential, because only experience could provide a realistic evaluation of design.

One of the important questions was whether the advantage then enjoyed by the British would increase, decrease, or perhaps remain static compared to prospective U.S. transports that might emerge during the next five to seven years. Specifically: How would *future* American and British ships compare? Important corollary questions were: Should I encourage Howard

242

to give serious consideration to a large-scale purchase of British planes, or perhaps buy a small fleet for familiarization purposes? Or would it be better to bypass the British entirely and wait for U.S. jets?

The development of turbine-powered aircraft experienced a fateful year in 1952. Boeing's prototype B-52 bomber first flew on April 15; BOAC shattered speed records and established a reputation for "no-fatigue" flying shortly after it began scheduled services with de Havilland Comets on May 2; Douglas, without fanfare, established a special DC-8 projects office in June; Boeing announced that it would develop a jet transport with its own funds during August, the same month that Bristol's Whispering Giant turboprop, the Britannia, first flew and the new Viscount Model 701 made its maiden flight.

The press of business required my trip to England to be deferred until October 1952. I requested Paul S. Fredrickson, TWA's chief pilot, to accompany me to lend further insight into the significance of our findings. We visited British European Airways (BEA), BOAC, A. V. Roe & Company,[1] Bristol Aeroplane Company, de Havilland, Handley Page, and Vickers-Armstrongs.

At the de Havilland Hatfield facility, F. H. M. ("Frank") Lloyd, commercial sales manager, briefed us on the Comet program, which had been underway since March 1943, when specification activities commenced. Two models, Mark I and IA, had been manufactured. Production was being changed over to the Mark II version, engineering for the Mark III was in process, and plans were being crystallized for development of the Mark IV. The Mark IV was to be an entirely new, larger Comet designed to be fully competitive with or surpass any aircraft that the United States could offer the world market by 1959–60. It was to be powered by Rolls-Royce Conway ducted-fan engines.[2] This project reflected Britain's strong determination to continue to excel.

By American standards, de Havilland's production tooling seemed meager and rudimentary. Except for an improved mating fixture, the wing and final assembly tooling was constructed of wood and essentially the same that I had seen in 1951. Wings were being constructed in an inefficient horizontal position over pits rather than with the wing chord (the line between the leading and trailing edges) vertical, as was customary in the States. Production was very slow. Only nine Mark I's had been delivered. De Havilland planned to establish additional production lines at Chester and Belfast rather than expand the Hatfield facility. Frank Lloyd explained that this would make use of existing factory facilities. It was necessary to move the work to the workman rather than the opposite because of the housing shortage and the extreme reluctance of workmen to move. He said, "They refuse to leave their homes, which in many cases have been in the family for generations."

United States certification of the Comet was considered a major problem. Lloyd said de Havilland wanted complete reciprocity to permit automatic certification in the United States without need for the aircraft design to comply with U.S. Civil Air Requirements (CAR). This viewpoint was also expressed by Vickers and Bristol representatives in subsequent meetings. While Britain and the United States had agreed to reciprocal certification during the 1944 Chicago Convention, which resulted in the formation of the International Civil Aviation Organization, the United States held the view that this was limited to piston aircraft only because U.S. turbine aircraft certification requirements had not then been written and, indeed, had still not been written by the time of my visit. I volunteered that automatic certification was an unrealistic expectation, and it would be more constructive for de Havilland and the British authorities to assist the CAA in establishing appropriate U.S. turbine-powered aircraft certification requirements. I indicated that these requirements would most likely have to be fully complied with in any event.

I considered the Comet program to be a superb pioneering venture that quite obviously required pressing the state of the art of airplane design in nearly all significant technology areas to achieve the barest minimum acceptable overall efficiency. In the earlier models this produced marginal structure, minimal operating weights, and borderline performance. For example, the thin fuselage skin of the Comet had been stretched during manufacturing to increase strength at the expense of ductility; every pound of empty weight was critical re payload or range; higher-thrust engines were clearly needed. The limited range, sluggish takeoff at high rotation angles, and the ability to stop after landing on slippery runways were also important concerns.

Except for the lack of reverse thrust, I did not think any one of the marginal conditions ruled the airplane out, but the combination of them gave me serious pause. I thought it likely that the anticipated march of progress could lessen or erase these concerns in succeeding models, possibly in the Mark IV, which was years away.

I had evaluated potential TWA Comet operations several times and recommended each time to Hughes that none be procured because of borderline design and performance or because of program timing with respect to the clearly superior U.S. jets. My early negative recommendations, which Howard accepted, generated considerable high-echelon TWA criticism after BOAC's initial operations proved the extreme popularity of the Comet. One TWA board member even commented, "Bob, you could have been a hero." Soon, however, BOAC experienced a series of tragic accidents involving the total loss of aircraft and all on board. Determination of the cause—burst fuselages from fatigue failures of the structure— required months, during which all Comet production ceased pending redevelopment. PAA, who seemed to order every new type plane that appeared to be coming down the pike, had ordered six but canceled them due to program delay following the accidents. I did not predict the fatigue problem per se, but I had recognized the overall marginal nature of the design. Recommending against the Comet was not easy for me because of my nearly overwhelming conviction that jets were the right answer.

Our principal contacts at the Vickers Weybridge facility were with Sir George R. Edwards, Christopher Clarkson, and Derek J. Lambert. In addition to discussing the Viscount, which earlier in the year we had seriously considered but rejected (see Chapter 17), Edwards reviewed plans for developing commercial jets derived from the Valiant bomber design. He said he expected the commercial Valiants to compete successfully with not only the Comet Mark IV, but also any American jets that might be produced for the British and European markets. He added, "Of course, we're glad you are here and would be glad to invade the American market as well." The commercial Valiant was to be an entirely new design, not just a converted bomber. Two versions were envisioned: one intended for domestic routes, and a heavier model with added fuel capacity to be provided by unique "slipper-wing," leading-edge tanks for carrying 100 passengers from Paris to Gander and serving other international routes.

Commercial Valiants, however, were never manufactured. The Valiants discussed with Edwards finally gave way to the Vickers VC-10, powered by four rear-fuselage-mounted jets, and undertaken in earnest in 1958.

In Filton, Fredrickson and I met with W. R. Farnes, sales manager; and Bill Pegg, chief test pilot for Bristol. At that time the prototype Britannia, equipped with Proteus II turboprop engines, had accumulated only about 150 flight hours. The production prototype, powered by Proteus III engines, was scheduled to fly in June 1953.

The Britannia was of conventional design except for the turboprop engines. Bill Farnes offered both short- and long-fuselage versions, with "standard" seating capacity—roughly equivalent to first class—ranging from 63 to 110 passengers. The large, essentially constant cross section fuselage appeared appropriate for either cargo or passenger use—a somewhat sensitive consideration for me because of the interior constrictions imposed by curved Constellation sidewalls, which I fought for years.

Overall, the Britannia looked quite attractive but required substantial additional testing prior to airline use. (Later, icing proved to be a major problem for the Proteus III, the correction of which required considerable time and seriously disrupted production schedules.) I thought the Britannia would be a major step forward vis-à-vis piston aircraft but that it could not compete successfully head-on against the faster, smoother jets I expected to become available only a few years later.

Perhaps the most fascinating parts of our 1952 survey were the meetings with BEA concerning the pioneering operations with the Viscount and Rolls-Royce-powered Dakotas (C-47's), and BOAC's early operations with the Mark IA Comet. The information so freely made available during meetings with Sir Victor Tait, Charles Abell, and Capt. M. J. R. Anderson of BOAC and with Peter G. Masefield and K. G. Wilkenson of BEA helped ensure realistic appraisal of prospective turbine planes and provided background information that was very helpful later on in planning TWA's jet implementation programs.

My conclusions concerning the general course of action TWA and Hughes should follow with respect to the development and acquisition of turbine-powered transports are recorded in a report I authored entitled "British Progress in Turbine Transport Aircraft," dated November 17, 1952. My principal conclusions, abridged from the report, follow:

1. American jet transport aircraft can be as good as, and possibly better than, any aircraft the British can produce. The existing British lead will be materially lessened the next several years and will all but disappear by late 1960.

2. If U.S. manufacturers will begin development soon, say by early 1953, prototype aircraft could be flying in 1956, with production units by 1958. This would be virtually contemporary with the new British designs, which are intended to be fully competitive.

3. Practical exigencies will militate against realizing sizable fleet operations

with U.S. jets before 1959 or 1960. [U.S. jet transports were in fact introduced in 1958 and flown in fleet quantities in 1959.]

4. American rather than British turbine-powered aircraft should be procured for TWA except on a short-term, limited-quantity basis if forced by the competition or to acquire direct-flight operations experience with turbine-powered aircraft.

So I recommended that Hughes bypass the British jets, except possibly by acquiring a few for learning purposes, and wait on the American jets, which I was convinced would be superior. Hughes seemed to agree and decided to leave all negotiating doors open for future trading purposes as I had recommended. He may have considered this a hedge against the possibility that the American jets might not be developed as I anticipated, but in fact, they were.

Europe Revisited—1954

Jet aircraft technology evolved rapidly during the early 1950s, especially in the turbine engine field. While I was comfortable with the conclusions derived from my 1952 survey trip, I considered it only prudent to carefully evaluate the pertinent developments that followed to measure European progress and determine if my conclusions remained valid. Accordingly, an expanded survey trip with Norman R. Parmet, supervisor of engine development at TWA, was taken in 1954. The same companies were visited, along with Bristol Aero Engines; D. Napier and Son; Rolls-Royce of England; Hurel Dubois, near Paris; and Sud Aviation, near Toulouse, France.

I renewed acquaintance at Bristol with Stanley G. Hooker (later, Sir Stanley), technical director, whom I had met in 1951 during the Brighton Anglo-American Technical Conference. Hooker was a brilliant mathematician who had a natural bent for engine design and developing practical solutions for complicated mechanical-thermodynamic problems. He worked with Frank Whittle (later, Sir Frank) during early jet engine days, had spent several years with Rolls-Royce, joined Bristol during January 1949, and was already known internationally for his technical achievements.

Hooker spent several hours with us reviewing the fundamental advantages of jet propulsion, explaining why he was convinced most future transports would be powered by turbine engines, and promoting interest in Bristol engines. This meeting, of intense interest, was only the first of many times our paths would cross in the future.

We met with Adrian Lombard, chief engineer, and his associates at Rolls-Royce, Darby. Lombard, who had had no formal technical training, had demonstrated his design genius early as a motor car engineer at Morris, then Rover. He joined Rolls-Royce in 1943, went on to become technical director of all of Rolls-Royce, and so served until his untimely death in 1967.

Lombard discussed the Avon and Conway projects with obvious pride and considerable enthusiasm concerning transport applications. Because of my work with Convair, I expressed interest in the Conway, and suggested that it might be worthwhile for Rolls-Royce to expedite production of the commercial version because the production plan Lombard presented appeared to rule this engine out of contention for installation in early American jets. He appreciated my viewpoint but offered no encouragement that this could be done. After the briefing, Norm and I were shown the development and production shops.

A year later, during a private meeting with Lombard at the London Hilton after Howard began to move on the Boeing program, I indicated willingness, perhaps eagerness, to seriously consider the installation of Conway engines in the Boeings I expected Hughes to order, provided Rolls-Royce could expedite production to accommodate Boeing's on-dock dates. This proved to be impractical for them. The upshot was that because we could not accept delays in airplane delivery—PAA and AAL already had captured a significant lead—no further consideration was given to Conway engines in Hughes's Boeings.

After a brief meeting with Napier executives and two days at BOAC and BEA to learn more about turbine aircraft operations, Norm and I left England with a suitcase full of data, and more to come by mail. We flew in a BOAC Comet from London to Paris. While we were being seated, considerable excitement among the cabin crew became evident. The celebrated boxer, Sugar Ray Robinson, and his entourage entered, filling the remaining seats in the compartment. He clearly was a valued BOAC customer. The short, comfortable trip that we shared with him to Paris strongly reinforced my interest in obtaining suitable jets for TWA at the earliest practicable time.

The Hurel Dubois Company had developed two small demonstration planes with high-aspect-ratio wings (narrow chord, great span) and forwarded data to me in Kansas City on a proposed transport version. Norm and I inspected the larger of the two planes, were briefed on the features and the remarkable cruising efficiency claimed for the proposed transport, and enjoyed a superb soufflé luncheon in a nearby country restaurant. On leaving, I indicated I would much appreciate being kept advised of progress of the transport project. For whatever reasons, however, the plane was not developed.

We were the first U.S. airline representatives to visit Sud Aviation. Our purpose was to obtain sufficient information to enable evaluation of the Caravelle for airline use. We were also interested in inspecting Sud's workmanship and observing its manufacturing processes—I sent John Guy over later to further evaluate this aspect—because I was not very familiar with the French aviation industry.

The Caravelle was a new breed. It was being designed as an innovative, medium-range plane with two jet engines mounted at the rear, capable of hauling about the same payload as the Vickers Viscount, but at higher speeds. The prototype was in the early stages of development.

Pierre Satre, in charge of technical matters, was our host. The first evening was spent in a private room at Maté's downtown restaurant, where the dinner choice consisted of rare hare or ortolan. I did not want rare hare, so I ordered ortolan without knowing what it was—noneviscerated meadowlark roasted to a dark, shoeleather brown, served with the little legs and beaks still in place. I felt guilty eating four-inch innocents that had been trapped in high nets strung on poles between trees, but did not want to be rude to our new Sud Aviation friends by refusing both entrees. Actually, the ortolans were not bad at all, but I offered the little heads to one of the Frenchmen, who ate them with great relish.

The next two days were spent in briefings, touring the factory, and becoming better acquainted. The more I learned, the more I became convinced that the Caravelle would likely prove to be an excellent airline plane. I thought it needed reverse thrust and greater power, and it would deserve thoroughgoing evaluation as the program progressed. We followed the Caravelle program closely during the years that followed, evaluating for procurement several succeeding models, including one tailored specifically for TWA's use. It was not purchased, however, due to TWA financial reversals experienced as an aftermath of Hughes's untoward actions during the later years of his control.

My European survey trips were most worthwhile. They generated lasting personnel contacts and invaluable information that helped put American progress in correct perspective and led to the formation and adoption of sound TWA policies and transport procurement programs. Although my resulting action recommendations to Hughes were timely, implementation of the programs was delayed at great cost to the company by Howard's subsequent digressions.

Notes

1. There were two A. V. Roe companies: this one, in England; and A. V. Roe Canada (AVRO). Both were part of the old Hawker-Siddeley group.
2. Ducted-fan, or bypass, engines are designed so that part of the air flowing from the fan passes around rather than through the turbines.

16.
Jets—
Early Possibilities,
1950–1953

The AVRO Jetliner

The jet project that first came closest to manifesting my conclusions—which Howard ultimately shared—was essentially a product of British technology, but it was developed on this side of the Atlantic, although not in the United States. The Jetliner, the first jet transport produced in North America, was an advanced, medium-range, 450-mph plane that first flew an amazing eight years before Boeing's 707. This extraordinary achievement is all the more remarkable considering that it was the first product of a new company in a country not dominant in the development or construction of aircraft. The design, developed by A. V. Roe Canada (AVRO), was conspicuously ahead of any competitive transport. The program represented a giant bite for any company to chew in 1946, when the project was undertaken, no matter how extensive its resources or how well qualified the individual participants.

J. C. ("Jim") Floyd, AVRO's chief engineer, was responsible for the design. He had contributed to the design of many famous aircraft produced in England by the parent company, and he transferred to Canada when the project started. Jim's overall design goal was to achieve the best compromise between the conflicting requirements of short-runway and high-speed operations without sacrificing reliability and maintainability. The prototype Jetliner was a distinctive-appearing, low-wing, 30-passenger design with four engines mounted in two double nacelles faired smoothly into the wing leading edge, and with the horizontal tail mounted halfway up the fin. Its exceptionally clean lines gave the impression of aerodynamic efficiency.

The project was beautifully timed and appeared to have a rosy future. By the time of the first flight, August 10, 1949, the Convair and Martin twins were underway; the first Vickers Viscount had not yet entered BEA's experimental service; and all of them except the de Havilland Comet, which had flown a few weeks before, lacked the sparkling performance and exceptional comfort of the Jetliner.

Early on, Trans Canada Airlines (TCA) executed a letter of intent of its own construction for the conditional purchase of an undisclosed number of Jetliners. The conditions were tough. TCA was to furnish AVRO with detailed specifications for the design; the first plane had to be delivered within 30 months; a low estimated purchase price was stipulated with rebates to TCA from sales to others. AVRO, anxious to land its first customer, accepted TCA's demanding terms.

AVRO's deal with TCA began to unravel after Floyd's design was well under way. TCA had insisted on the installation of Rolls-Royce AJ-65 engines, and AVRO had inexplicably acquiesced notwithstanding unconfirmed availability. When E. W. Hives, later Lord Hives, of Rolls-Royce made it emphatically clear that the AJ-65's were on the military's "secret" list and could not be made available commercially for many years, extensive redesign was undertaken to install Rolls-Royce Derwent-5 engines at considerable cost and schedule penalty.

It became apparent as the design progressed that the purchase price stated in the TCA letter of intent was unrealistic and required adjustment. AVRO proposed an increase in price along with modification of a number of letter-of-intent obligations it considered onerous. The upshot was that TCA wanted out. A keenly disappointed AVRO acquiesced. After that unfavorable event, design of the prototype continued, but at a slower pace.

AVRO continued its efforts to sell TCA. In early 1948, after the design had congealed and construction was underway, TCA suggested compliance with sweeping new design objectives, including a substantial increase in design speed. Acceding would have required complete redesign. Jim Floyd said later, "It would have been easier to convert a cow into a crocodile than to comply with TCA's new objectives."

The final act, which completely unraveled all prospects of TCA's becoming the launching customer, was Gordon R. McGregor's statement shortly after his election as president of the company: He did not want TCA to be the first airline in North America to operate jet transports. With that, development work was sharply curtailed.

As soon as the test program permitted, a series of record-breaking demonstration flights were made in Canada and the United States. The flights generated lavish praise in the press and captured for weeks the attention of the world aviation community. Buoyed by this success, the construction of a second Jetliner was undertaken.

With the loss of TCA as the first customer, it was clear that AVRO needed to mount an effective sales campaign quickly if the venture were to succeed. Attention was turned toward the United States. Among others, C. R. Smith, then president of AAL, was invited to visit Toronto to inspect and ride in the Jetliner. Smith accepted and brought along his assistant, R. Dixon Speas, who was captivated by the plane. Dixon was offered and accepted a position with AVRO as U.S. representative. Speas, on a year's leave of absence from AAL, with the help of Joe A. Morley, AVRO's sales and service manager; and Gil Dunkin, its sales engineering representative, brought the Jetliner to the attention of the key executives of all major U.S. airlines.

Dixon was soon able to report to Joe Morley that key engineering and operations executives at AAL, Capital, EAL, TWA, and UAL were favorably impressed with the plane's performance; and that George T. ("Ted") Baker, president of National Airlines, was prepared to negotiate a contract for 4 of the aircraft at $1 million each with an option for 6 additional planes. The Jetliner was also demonstrated to the U.S. Air Force and U.S. Navy. The Air Force was so favorably impressed that it considered ordering 20 for high-altitude navigation training. Ralph Golt, then head of sales for the Allison Division of General Motors, called Dixon Speas later and informed him that the Air Force deal was on with Allison engines, and one of the engines was being prepared for shipment to Toronto for tests. This serious U.S. military interest, along with airline interest, suggested that the Jetliner program was about to take off in a big way.

By this time the United States and Canada were heavily involved in the Korean conflict. AVRO was manufacturing in quantity twin-engine CF-100 fighters for the Royal Canadian Air Force but was behind schedule. The fighter program had top priority and had usurped personnel from the Jetliner program—a fact that almost stopped the design and construction of the second Jetliner.

The Right Hon. C. D. Howe, the Canadian minister responsible for such matters, was requested to approve an increase in manpower for the Jetliner program. Instead, he unequivocally ordered the project closed until AVRO got the CF-100 program back on schedule. Fred Smye, the general manager of the Aircraft Division, responded by terminating the Jetliner project and made Jim Floyd plant manager. In a last ditch effort to save the program, Dixon Speas maneuvered himself into a seat beside C. D. Howe at a Massachusetts Institute of Technology alumni affair in Toronto and endeavored to persuade him to review his program closure decision. Failing to persuade Howe during the dinner, Dixon slipped into the limousine driving Howe to the airport and continued his sales efforts. Just as they reached the airport, Howe turned and said, "Speas, haven't you ever heard of someone having too much on their plate? Well, AVRO has too much on its plate. We are committed to going forward with the fighter, so the Jetliner must go on the shelf—and that is that."

Howe's turndown appeared so definite that Dixon resigned from AVRO, but instead of returning to AAL started his own consulting business. With this development, despite strong airline and serious military procurement interest, this promising program became entirely dormant, a victim of the Korean involvement and improvident political thinking. AVRO knew the clear lead it held in jet transport design in this hemisphere was a perishable advantage that would disappear with passing time if the project could not be quickly resurrected.

I had kept Hughes advised of the merits of the Jetliner and program progress. Shortly before Howe's conversation with Speas, he had discussed with me in confidence his desire to manufacture jets for TWA and other airlines.[1] He asked for my opinion concerning the suitability of the Jetliner for airline use and my recommendations concerning design changes that might enhance utility. Without revealing Howard's interest in manufacturing, I undertook studies of several design variations of the Jetliner with the cooperation of Jim Floyd and Dixon Speas.

Howard and I debated at length the merits of the study designs. Capacities ranged from 40 to 52 passengers. Power was to be provided by four Rolls-Royce Derwents or "cool" (reduced hot-section temperature) Nenes, or by two P & W J-57 engines. The 48-passenger Derwent and the 52-passenger cool Nene versions appeared capable of carrying excellent payloads at good operating costs on New York-Chicago and Chicago-Kansas City segments. The twin appeared capable of economic operations on the Chicago-Los Angeles segment, but the annual average performance of the twins would have been undercut somewhat by the higher CAA weather minimums (airport ceiling and visibility limits for takeoff and landing operations) required for two-engine compared to four-engine aircraft. We tentatively decided in favor of the cool Nene version, partly because it required less investment and could be produced considerably earlier than the twin.

Howard had a wonderful facility for selecting the most opportune times possible to express interest in potentially attractive ventures. This was no exception. When he heard the program was headed for oblivion, he adroitly jumped in with a double objective: the production of jetliners on his own behalf and the sale of Hughes Aircraft's MG2 armament fire-control system for AVRO's CF-100's.

It appeared the Jetliner might well serve both ends. First, the Jetliner seemed like an ideal test vehicle for the MG2 system because of its high-altitude capability and ample fuselage space for test equipment. Secondly, use of the jetliner by Hughes Aircraft would provide an excellent opportunity for Howard to fly the plane and study production feasibility. So, early in 1952, use of the single prototype Jetliner to test the MG2 system was suggested.

Crawford Gordon, Jr., AVRO's president and general manager; and Fred Smye were especially pleased with the prospect of demonstrating the plane to Hughes. They saw this as a great opportunity to work out a rescue operation for the precarious Jetliner project, if Hughes could be persuaded to produce them under license for TWA. At the first opportunity, Smye broached this subject with Hughes, which was exactly what Hughes wanted. Don Rogers, AVRO's chief test pilot, flew the Jetliner to Hughes's Culver City facility on April 8, 1952. Jim Floyd, Joe Morley, and a few others were on board. Fred Smye and Crawford Gordon had arrived in the Los Angeles area a few days earlier for opening discussions with Hughes.

Hughes inspected the plane soon after its arrival, spending most of his time on the flight deck. The next day, after only one takeoff and landing by Rogers, Howard flew the plane, making numbers of landings. Almost from the first, he was completely at ease with the plane. After landing, he complimented Floyd on the plane's good handling characteristics.

During the next few months the AVRO executives played Hughes's customary waiting game, during which Howard made numbers of additional flights. Floyd and the other AVRO representatives were on call anytime night or day throughout this period. Floyd was initiated into the fairly exclusive club of all-night palavers with Hughes.

I flew to Los Angeles to inspect and make a flight in the Jetliner with Howard. We spent about an hour on the ground at Van Nuys Airport discussing and visually examining the plane, after which Howard put it through its paces for nearly two hours with Rogers as copilot.

The flight was smooth and exhilarating and reinforced my enthusiasm for jet power. During the flight, I made voluminous notes and sketches concerning detail design, the interior, noise and vibration levels, apparent ventilation rates, and other items of interest. I was standing in the center of the flight deck behind Howard and Don, hanging on to the backs of their seats, when Howard made the landing approach to Van Nuys Airport. The plane approached much too low at too high a sink rate near subminimal speed. Not a happy situation. Don abruptly but with a smile applied full throttle to increase the speed and stretch the glide. Howard did not object and landed at the very end of the runway.

After a few minutes on the ground with Don, Howard and I drove in one of his Chevrolets through Laurel Canyon to Hollywood with a side trip on Mulholland Drive, where we parked several hours to talk. We discussed the plane and my design studies, which I had summarized and mailed April 29. I gave the plane high marks but recommended further exploration of the use of engines manufactured in the United States to enhance sales, and the development of a stretched, high-speed version as soon as the market warranted. Then he dropped me off at the Hollywood Roosevelt Hotel.

Howard opted to manufacture the Jetliner and took exploratory actions. Because the enormous Hughes Culver City facility was jammed with flying boat and other pressing work, Howard turned to Convair, with whom we had had numbers of recent conferences concerning the development of long-range, turbine-powered aircraft. He suggested to Floyd Odlum a contractual arrangement between AVRO, Convair, Hughes Aircraft, and

TWA, which, contingent on CAB approval, would permit the early construction of Jetliners for TWA and ultimately for other airlines. Odlum responded by requesting Convair, which he controlled, to examine its ability to produce and sell Jetliners.

Convair did so, but the company was only lukewarm. It preferred to manufacture larger, longer-range, higher-speed aircraft of its own design. Convair, like me, thought that the largest initial market for jets designed in the United States would be for long-range planes, and that soon after long-range jet services were introduced, services on the shorter segments would be upgraded by long-range piston aircraft displaced by the jets, thus limiting the market for Jetliner-type aircraft. On the other hand, Convair realized the manufacture of Jetliners would offer the exceptional long-term advantage of entering the jet transport market early. The Convair exercise required several months for completion, during which intermittent discussions continued between AVRO and Hughes.

Howard's plan to manufacture Jetliners dragged on a while but finally did not work out—not because of Convair's lack of enthusiasm, but because U.S. military authorities were unwilling to permit use of Convair's factory space for commercial projects. I suspected that in addition to the usual factors, the military's position reflected high-level political considerations involving relations with Canada. Both the United States and Canada were manufacturing equipment for the Korean conflict. Thus, while Howard's plan to produce Jetliners in the United States did not succeed, he did manage later on to sell the Hughes Aircraft fire-control systems for AVRO's fighter program.

The Jetliner was used in AVRO's CF-100 development program for three years following Howard's flights. Finally, after its last flight, on November 23, 1956, Jim Floyd was placed in charge of ignominiously breaking it into small pieces, ending forever what had initially been an extremely promising future for the plane.[2] This had to be a heart-wrenching experience for Jim.

Hughes, Odlum, and the YB-60

In early 1953, Hughes developed a consuming interest in exploring the feasibility of redesigning Convair's YB-60 experimental jet-powered bomber into an airline transport. This was soon after the demise of the

Jetliner project and during the most intense and hectic part of early negotiations with Lockheed, which ultimately produced the 1049G Constellation.

Convair's YB-60, which had been constructed in only eight months and
had flown only a short time before, was an 8-engine, swept-wing experimental bomber designed to use many major Convair B-36 components.
The B-36 was a huge, 10-engine (6 piston engines and 4 jets) intercontinental bomber that Convair was manufacturing in quantity for the Air
Force.

The YB-60 was designed to win the Air Force competition then underway with Boeing's B-52 for the final source selection, notwithstanding that
Boeing had been awarded a series of small incremental production contracts and was well positioned. This competition was Convair's last chance
to remain in the intercontinental bomber manufacturing business, which
had been the primary bread and butter for Convair's Fort Worth plant for
years. The stakes were high.

Howard explained that Floyd Odlum was extremely anxious to sell
commercial versions of the YB-60, the climate was right for negotiations,
and I should meet in Fort Worth with Convair's experts "during the next
few days" to examine and evaluate the transport design.

During the next few days? No way, I thought. I was up to my eyebrows
pressing Lockheed to design a nonstop intercontinental Constellation. Negotiations were at a sensitive stage, so I suggested to Howard that YB-60
project be deferred a few weeks. He said no, he had already promised
Odlum I would be available the next few days, and while it might be
difficult, I should keep the Lockheed project hot but give immediate priority to the YB-60. Howard also explained that Odlum wanted maximum
commonality between the military and commercial versions so both could
be manufactured on the same production line, and the construction of
transports was contingent on Odlum's winning a major production contract
for B-60's.

Howard, who envisioned the huge jet transports flying at high speeds
coast to coast and to Europe, relished the prospect of draining passengers
from the competition. So did I, and I was equally if not more anxious for
TWA to acquire jet transports. But I wanted good planes. I thought that
just about everything was wrong with the idea of developing commercial
B-60's. It seemed obvious that it was not the right design: The wing was
much too large for the passenger capacity and therefore would be excep-

tionally inefficient; eight engines would produce excessive operational and maintenance complications; the mid-wing arrangement split the passenger cabin in half, which appeared to require multiple cabin crews; TWA's hangars were too small; runways lacked strength at several airports; and CAA rules for the certification and operation of eight-engine transports had not been written.

Boeing had announced the preceding August it would invest $16 million of its own money in the development of an experimental jet transport, the 367-80, which was initially targeted for the military market, but which appeared to have great promise as a commercial transport. Douglas had a jet transport in early development but had not announced its intention to build a prototype. However, I had no doubt that it would do so. And we had jointly undertaken preliminary jet transport investigative work with Convair, a program later known as "Southern Comfort" (see Chapter 18). I thought our attention should be focused in these areas, not on the YB-60.

Compared to the outsized commercial YB-60, the Boeing 367-80 was a beautiful dream. It was being optimized throughout as a transport, and it made the B-60 look so bad by comparison that I wondered if Howard could be serious. Surely he must know better.

It dawned on me when I was mulling this over that part of Odlum's motivation almost had to be to create a situation that could be used to generate political support in Washington to improve Convair's chances of winning the bomber production contract. A contract to manufacture commercial transports with great parts commonality on a common production line could arguably provide a lower cost base or other advantages and influence Washington's contract award decision. I wondered if Howard might be playing footsie with Odlum.

I decided that regardless of possible political ramifications or any other consequences that might result, I could only give Howard my best professional opinion, as I had always done. I thought life was much too short and complicated to do anything less and arranged for an early trip to Fort Worth to determine the facts.

I will always be grateful to E. B. ("Red") Maske and his Fort Worth associates for their candor and no-holds-barred behavior. Design, performance, certification, and production aspects were reviewed in detail. When requested data was not immediately available, it was expeditiously provided. They could not have been more cooperative.

Review of the data showed, and Convair's representatives agreed, that redeveloping the YB-60 would not be a simple, low-cost, quick undertaking. It would require extensive redesign throughout the plane, including systems and considerable primary structure. It would, in fact, be an enormous, time-consuming, expensive undertaking that would require being subsidized or written off over a substantial number of planes.

Several fuselage designs were considered. The one involving the least work would accommodate about 136 passengers and little cargo. With additional tooling the capacity could be increased to about 156 passengers. A canoe-shaped passage below the fuselage under the wing was proposed to permit access between passenger compartments. When I complained about the fuselage-wing mismatch, Convair's engineers showed me an entirely new double-deck fuselage design, commensurate with the size of the wing, that would accommodate approximately 180 passengers. Because development fell outside Odlum's ground rules, they could not promote it.

The only conditions under which Convair was willing to manufacture the planes were: The planes had to be built in the Fort Worth plant; government approval for the project had to be obtained because the government owned the plant; the planes had to be ordered promptly; all work had to be done on a cost-plus-fixed-fee basis, the same as other work in the plant; commercial production had to fit military production plans by filling valleys in the military production rates to keep overhead low and to benefit from the B-36 learning curve (production manpower efficiency); and the engineering work had to be done by other than Convair engineering because of military commitments. As far as I was concerned, the last three conditions, unless changed, ruled out any possibility of purchase.

Instead of requiring a few days, the YB-60 investigation took several months, largely because of the time required for Convair to provide supplemental information. During this period, I took every opportunity to apprise Howard of the virtues of the Boeing jet, hoping to turn his principal attention toward that option. This did not happen.

During the course of the YB-60 investigation, Boeing advised it was confident it could produce its first commercial jet transport by mid-1955, and 10 by mid-1957, if an order were placed no later than August 1953. Boeing requested that I pass this information on to Howard and urged early conferences. I left a call for Howard and phoned Ralph Damon, who was spending a few days at the Boca Raton Hotel, Boca Raton, Florida, because he wanted to be kept up to date concerning Boeing's jet. When

Howard returned my call and heard the news, he acted interested but elected not to authorize detailed discussions.

Bill Gay called me in Kansas City a few weeks later and said Howard was anxious to hear my report on the Convair project and wanted to know when I would have it ready. I said I could discuss it anytime, thinking Howard would telephone me. Instead, I received another call requesting me to meet Howard a few mornings later at the Burbank airport.

Howard picked me up in his B-23, flew to Palm Springs, and drove us to Floyd Odlum's Indio ranch in one of his Chevrolets. I was anxious to explain my position before meeting with Odlum, thinking it important for Howard to be apprised of several proposed contractual items I considered completely unsatisfactory and my conclusions concerning the suitability of the design for TWA's use. However, he was more interested in talking about almost everything else. When I persisted, he said my report could wait until we met with Odlum.

So there I was, about to tell Hughes and Odlum that development of a commercial B-60 was a hopelessly lousy idea, understanding fully the importance to Odlum of a positive recommendation and not knowing the real extent of Howard's involvement. I was not sure how best to proceed but decided against blurting out my position. The day was sparkling, but I did not notice it until later.

We conferred with Floyd on the patio by a large, heated swimming pool, which he used to relieve a severe arthritic condition. As always, Floyd was most cordial. After pleasantries, Howard turned to me and asked me to report my findings.

I started by telling Floyd how helpful and cooperative his Fort Worth people had been, that it had been a pleasure to work with them, and that every bit of requested information had been made expeditiously available. Then I summarily reviewed the scope of the undertaking, explaining in some detail the extent of redesign that would be involved; the resulting noncommonality between the B-60 and the transport, which was much greater than Odlum had been led to believe; the unusual risks associated with CAA certification; the performance of the plane, including payload-range characteristics that were adequate but considerably less than either of them had understood; and the estimated operating costs and revenue-generating potential compared to the latest Constellation. I also reviewed Convair's estimates of engineering and production time; the time that would be required to produce a prototype and place the plane in production, which was substantially more than either of them was aware of; and rough estimates of the enormous amount of capital that would be required to manufacture six planes. I stated that in my judgment, production of a large number of transports would be required to make business sense. I concluded by mentioning that Boeing believed it could produce its first jet transport several months before Convair Fort Worth could produce the commercial YB-60.

I paused, expecting to be challenged or at least questioned as to my overall conclusion. After I clarified details for a few minutes, an extended pause followed, during which neither Floyd or Howard spoke. Then Floyd turned to Howard and said, "Howard, from what Bob says, this might not be a very good idea." After an equally long pause, Hughes looked soberly at Floyd and responded, "Yes, Floyd, I think you're right. It might not be very productive to pursue this any further."

That is how the matter was left—exactly the correct conclusion as far as I was concerned. The meeting broke up after a brief tour of the ranch and conversation on small matters. On the way back to Burbank and Hollywood, where I was staying, Howard and I had a pleasant conversation about aviation affairs and some ideas he had about the movie business. I thought the YB-60 matter had worked out well, and I made not the slightest effort to again raise this subject.

Except for my personal time, TWA had no direct involvement in the YB-60 affair other than the preparation at my request of a report by Russ Rourke and Marcy Fannon comparing the performance of theoretical four-, six-, and eight-engine jet transports with one, two, and three inoperative engines to better establish related airline operational requirements for "future planning" purposes. I was glad Howard had not requested full-scale TWA specification development activities and that only a few people knew of my investigation.

Howard's interest in the YB-60 transport program almost had to be a charade because the outcome was so obvious from the start. He may have wanted to support Odlum's drive to sell B-60's for some sort of gain or trading purpose, or perhaps he did not want to abruptly say no to the man with whom he had consummated numbers of major deals and with whom he might have many more. Whatever the fact of the matter really was, I felt I had done Odlum, Hughes, and certainly TWA a great favor by calling a spade a spade.

Project Mexico City

By the early 1950s, large jet engines had been designed that appeared to overcome most of the power plant deficiencies that had deterred the development of U.S. jet transports. P & W had the two-spool, wasp-waisted J-57's in early production and J-75's in early development, and Rolls-Royce had the bypass Conway in the works. However, all production was committed for military programs, with little indication of imminent release for commercial use.

My strong personal preference remained for jet rather than turboprop transports because of the greater speed, relative simplicity, and lack of vibration of this type plane, and my confidence that fuel efficiency would be improved. Howard was more amenable to turboprops than I, but he had agreed that the goal of deploying one rather than two basic fleets to serve TWA's domestic and international routes was desirable to provide attractive through-plane schedules and attain good operational efficiency. This called for the development of turbine transports capable of providing reliable year-round nonstop transatlantic operations.

Boeing and Douglas had kept me fully advised concerning the 367-80 prototype and DC-8 programs. Both manufacturers were convinced that the P & W J-57's (later designated JT-3's), which they proposed to use when cleared by the military, would provide over-ocean range. They seemed content with the idea that the jets would frequently require landing for fuel in Gander, Newfoundland, or Shannon, Ireland, which the majority of piston aircraft had been doing for years. My current negotiations with Lockheed over the Constellation 1049E were intended to produce true nonstop transatlantic planes. I was convinced that nonstop piston services would become commonplace, as in fact they soon were. Because the time lost for refueling jets en route would seriously undercut the flight time saved by the jets compared to the anticipated long-range pistons, I believed nonstop capability of the jets to be essential.

Detailed analysis by my staff confirmed that transatlantic nonstop services could not be achieved with acceptable schedule reliability with any of the proposed four-engine J-57-powered airplanes. Higher thrust engines were required. (Shortly after the Boeing and Douglas jets were introduced in 1958 and 1959, respectively, P & W developed a bypass version of the J-57, which produced adequate thrust; however, while bypass thermodynamic cycles were well understood in 1953, design conversion was yet to come.)

The more powerful P & W J-75's (later, designated the "JT-4's") were also being developed for military projects but were not yet in production. The J-75's gave promise of enabling nonstop transatlantic operations, but only after operational experience had been accumulated. Because they were not slated for early production, it seemed that the proving period would require considerable time. P & W representatives judged that J-75's could not reasonably be offered for civil transport applications until several years after the J-57's, if at all. If this point of view were taken at face value, it appeared that early transatlantic nonstop jet services could only be realized by six-engine, J-57-powered; or four-engine, turboprop transports, which though slower burned less fuel. I thought the mechanical complexity, 100-mph nominal speed disadvantage and greater vibration of the turboprops would quite obviously make them less attractive than jets, and the use of six rather than four jet engines was questionable. I also believed that the discouraging comments of P & W's representatives were in part the result of their natural reluctance to push a new engine when the older one was doing so well and might conceivably be satisfactory. Once the need for more powerful engines was generally recognized, I was sure that P & W would not allow the market to go begging.

In mid-1954, Project Mexico City appeared to offer an alternative solution to the range problem. AVRO Canada's Jim Floyd suggested the development of transport versions of A. V. Roe's (the parent company) Vulcan delta-wing jet bomber. He wrote a confidential follow-up letter, October 27, to summarize pertinent discussions between Hughes and Crawford Gordon and present two design concepts: the Atlantic I for coast to coast, and the Atlantic II for transatlantic services.

The Atlantic I was essentially a new design except for use of the Vulcan outer wing and some landing gear and control system components. The proposed wing was 22 feet greater in span than the Vulcan, and had a new wide-span center section. The fuselage was elongated and increased in diameter to accommodate 120 passengers. The Atlantic II was smaller overall, configured to accommodate only 100 passengers. Both models were to be powered by four Rolls-Royce Conway engines buried in the wing roots and were expected to cruise at high subsonic speeds.

Both concepts were intriguing, but they contained some preliminary design proposals I thought unsuited for airline operations: thrust augmentation for takeoff by rockets or engine afterburners, two 16-foot-diameter parachutes for slowing the plane after landing, engines buried in the structure, and delta wings. I thought airport noise ruled out rockets and afterburning; drag parachutes appeared to be an abomination for airline use; buried engines raised serious questions of fire and maintenance accessibility; and precious little operational experience had been accumulated with delta wings compared to decades of tough pioneering with conventional aircraft, during which bitter experience generated many improvements. The fact that it was necessary to propose such unorthodox features to achieve acceptable performance demonstrated the marginal nature of jet transport design in 1954.

During early 1955, after I discussed my concerns, Jim proposed a new six-engine conventional design that eliminated most of my objections and which appeared to have excellent international range capability. I discussed it with Howard. He took immediate interest, insisted on absolute secrecy, and tabbed the project "Mexico City."

Jim claimed the plane, equipped with a distinctive, double-deck fuselage, would routinely be able to fly 138 passengers against winter head winds from Rome to New York at high subsonic speeds—a demanding design objective indeed for mid-1955, when the Boeing and Douglas jets could not be shown to fly nonstop New York-London with good schedule reliability. The AVRO was to be powered by six P & W J-75 engines, the most powerful in the offing. Single-deck and mid-wing variations were also proposed.

To save development time and cost, Hughes suggested that consideration be given to the use of Boeing B-52 wings, engine nacelles (eight J-57 engines), and empennages with fuselages to be designed by AVRO. Floyd examined this idea. The resulting preliminary design incorporated a conventional tricycle-type landing gear rather than the B-52 bicycle type, four double nacelles slung below the wing as in the B-52, and long, torpedo-shaped external auxiliary fuel tanks extending ahead of and behind the wing between the inboard nacelles and the fuselage. While use of the B-52 components would have saved time and money, conversion engineering would still have been formidable. Except for the care and feeding of eight rather than six engines, the design looked fairly attractive.

I was not at all surprised when William M. Allen, Boeing's chief executive officer, indicated he had no interest whatsoever in undertaking special arrangements with the Air Force for permission to use the B-52 components or in helping AVRO become a competitor in the large transport market, particularly because PAA, AAL, and other airlines had already expressed serious interest in Boeing 707's. (PAA and AAL ordered 707's a little later, during October and November 1955, respectively.) Allen closed the subject by flatly refusing to seriously entertain Howard's joint venture suggestion, which did not enhance Howard's feeling toward Boeing.

Mexico City, however, was not terminated. Jim Floyd continued to offer long-range jet proposals in profusion. He forwarded technical data from time to time, which was discussed by phone or during personal meetings, some involving Hughes. We had considered no less than 14 different designs—Schemes A through N—by April 1956. All were intended to leapfrog the Douglas and Boeing jets by providing substantially greater payload-range capability: not only a desirable operational feature for TWA, but also an important sales consideration for AVRO because initial production would lag appreciably behind the other manufacturers.

In the spring of 1956, two or three months after Toolco's initial jet orders were placed, Jim Floyd, several AVRO executives, and I met with Howard at the Beverly Hills Hotel to review the latest AVRO design. While walking to the car after the meeting, one of the executives told me that AVRO had placed that morning with Hughes Aircraft a major order for advanced armament fire-control systems for its fighter program. That very evening Howard called me at the Bel Air Hotel and asked that I drop the Mexico City project. He said, "Bob, don't do it precipitously. Don't you see? Let it die over a period of months."

Was the AVRO affair only a charade to land a lucrative contract for Hughes Aircraft? It might have been, but I believe there was much more to it than that. After the Boeing JT-4-powered long-range jets were offered during the fall of 1955, and Howard finally faced up to the fact that they would be good planes, available much sooner than the AVROs, he may have decided against the AVRO program but elected not to make this known until after the fire-control contract matter had been settled, lest he upset the negotiation and dissuade AVRO from committing. The enormity of the financial undertaking that would have been involved by ordering both Boeings and AVROs also may have been a deterrent, although this consideration did not stop him from subsequently making further major fleet buy commitments. His initial interest in the AVRO transports was probably sincere, at least to the extent of exploring a potential opportunity;

266

had delivery timing been favorable, he might have elected that course. I never doubted that Jim Floyd and his team could have produced excellent jet transports well tailored to satisfy TWA's operational requirements, notwithstanding the shadow of possible government interference cast by Minister C. D. Howe's untoward actions in the Jetliner affair. The design of AVRO's Jetliner was superb, and given the freedom to perform, comparable results seemed likely.

During 1958–59, Jim Floyd proposed several supersonic transports for TWA's transatlantic operations—as far as I know, the first supersonic proposal by a responsible, major manufacturer. The first was designed to operate at 900-mph supersonic speeds; the final one was an attractive, extremely sleek, 1,200-mph jet with a double-ogee wing plan-form. It would have been years ahead of anything else. Nevertheless, by late 1959, Howard's jet programs were in such an acute state of disarray that serious procurement consideration was utterly inappropriate—indeed, impossible.

The inviting AVRO designs, like so many early attempts that produced paper rather than real airplanes, played a significant role in advancing the art of jet transport design. Such efforts highlighted the need for research and development programs targeted toward solving important operational needs, for example, more efficient, higher-thrust engines; more effective flap systems for swept-back wings to reduce takeoff and landing distances; reverse thrust for landing safety; the development of external noise attenuation devices; and improved interior sound proofing. I, with some other airline representatives, helped define research programs through membership on NACA advisory committees, as well as through negotiations and by taking advantage of every opportunity to press for constructive action by the manufacturers.

Notes

1. The manufacture of transports by Hughes was prohibited by the Federal Aviation Act and the CAB orders permitting his original acquisition of interest in TWA. Implausible as it may seem, Howard's plan was to somehow obtain immunity from the CAB to manufacture aircraft for TWA and, after manufacture was well under way, obtain expanded authority to sell planes to other airlines.
2. Jim has chronicled A. V. Roe Canada's turbulent history, including the successes, tribulations, and disappointments encountered in the Jetliner development program, in *The AVRO Canada C102 Jetliner* (Boston Mills Press, 1986). I commend this book to those who wish to know more about this technically

advanced company, which produced superb, world-beating civil and military aircraft, but which nonetheless was destined for dissolution. One can only wonder what success the pioneering Jetliner project might have enjoyed if AVRO had been permitted to develop and market the planes in a timely manner, as it wanted. While a great disappointment for Jim Floyd and his associates, the Jetliner demonstrated close at home the great promise of jet transportation and thus helped pave the way for the spectacular jet age.

17.

The Vickers Viscount Diversion— 1951–1957

Our efforts to develop or acquire turbine-powered aircraft for TWA were not limited to the jets. Among the turboprops Hughes and I considered was the Vickers Viscount. Our interest in the Viscount increased considerably after I shared with Howard the enthusiasm of my first Viscount ride—my first in any turbine aircraft—taken over southern England and the Channel as a guest of George Edwards during September 1951 while attending the Third Anglo-American Technical Conference, held in Brighton, England. I reported that the contrast between the Viscount and the pistons was striking, that the high-altitude, over-weather ride passengers would enjoy in relaxed comfort was such that in my opinion they would never fly in pistons if turbines were standing by. Howard reacted by requesting that I closely follow pertinent developments and keep him fully advised.

The Viscount was the world's first four-engine turboprop-powered transport. It was a medium-range, 32-passenger (later increased to 47 passengers by a seven-foot increase in fuselage length), low-wing plane powered by four Rolls-Royce Dart engines. It was developed by Edwards working in collaboration with BEA.

Our first serious Viscount negotiation occurred the following spring. After an exhaustive appraisal of the offerings and TWA's ability to deploy the aircraft, I agonizingly recommended against procurement at that time despite my strong preference for turbines. Howard reluctantly agreed. My primary reasons were: (1) TWA's engineering, operational, and corporate plates were full. TWA was digesting the purchase of 52 twin-engine Martins, 25 749A Constellations, and 10 long-body 1049's. (2) The United States had not promulgated certification rules for turbine-powered transports, which I thought would thwart certification reciprocity between the United States and England and likely prevent on-time aircraft delivery. (3) I did not like single-spar wings and tail surfaces. With all the structural eggs in one basket, undetected minor flaws or cracks could all too easily lead to catastrophic failures, a consideration exacerbated by lack of industry experience with the airplane. (Subsequent Viscount history showed this concern to be unjustified. However, the British government set a relatively low flight-hour limit, which could be exceeded only if the spars were replaced at great expense.) (4) The purchase of airplanes offshore raised questions concerning Vickers's lack of demonstrated in-service support capability in the United States.

Years passed before the right time arrived. The second negotiation started during early 1956 at Howard's instigation after Viscounts had demonstrated great popularity in Europe and North America. Capital Air Lines had recently increased its order from 60 to 75 ships, an enormous order for that period, and was expanding Viscount services as rapidly as Vickers could deliver the planes. Viscounts were also making their mark at TCA and would be successful at other U.S. airlines.

Christopher Clarkson, Vickers's U.S. representative, had sent an avalanche of information on real and study models, which were analyzed in depth. My reports, which Howard routinely received, again aroused his interest and led to extended discussions with Clarkson and Edwards concerning price, delivery, and other pertinent matters.

At that time Howard was belatedly engaged in active discussions with Boeing and was on the verge of committing for the purchase of long-haul jets—a circumstance I did not want interrupted lest he turn away. Ordering jets for TWA was seriously overdue and much more important than Viscounts. I presented every other logical reason I could think of to persuade Howard to defer Viscount negotiations. He agreed, but requested that I maintain active dialogue with Vickers toward maintaining as long as possible the stipulated purchase price and favorable delivery positions. After Vickers agreed several times to postpone firm commitment dates, Clarkson finally made it eminently clear on September 26, 1956, that the delivery positions could no longer be held and that if Howard wanted the planes, the contract would have to be signed immediately.

Howard usually did not react well to pressure tactics, but he accepted my recommendation that the acquisition of Viscounts continue to be deferred because delivery of them would be too nearly coincident with anticipated initial TWA jet operations. Also, the jets would likely displace piston aircraft, moving them from long- to medium-haul services well suited for the Viscount, thus relieving need for the immediate purchase of Viscounts.

I advised Clarkson of Howard's decision. We lost the delivery positions, and I heaved a sigh of relief, hoping Howard would permit me to concentrate on problems associated with the jets he had belatedly ordered the preceding March. He did not.

Howard's Plan

Only a few months later, shortly before Carter Burgess became president, Howard resumed negotiations with Sir George Edwards, now Vickers's managing director (he had recently been raised to knighthood because of outstanding contributions to British aviation). However, as had not been the case in our earlier work with Vickers, Howard directed that no one was to get even a hint of this activity except those who were directly and unavoidably involved, whom he identified.

Howard had long wanted to manufacture transports for TWA and saw the Viscount as a great opportunity. He asked me to consider how to best achieve earliest possible production at competitive costs.

Obviously, manufacturing Viscounts required appropriate contractual arrangements with Vickers, production tooling and facilities (Howard ruled out doing this work in California), and a production organization and manpower. Howard envisioned starting a new factory from scratch with a core of management personnel and production engineers from the Hughes Aircraft Division of Toolco.

After mulling Howard's question over several weeks, I recommended that the airplanes be built backwards. I explained to him that to minimize risk and produce airplanes at the earliest possible date, the first step should be to assemble major components imported from England, such as fuse-

271

lages, wings, tail surfaces, and landing gear, thus avoiding investing initially in related tooling and manpower required for detailed parts and subassembly manufacturing. I suggested that rights to ultimately manufacture all components be obtained from Vickers at the outset so that the manufacturing of any components that future circumstances might justify could be undertaken with minimal negotiations. I pointed out that this approach would require initially less factory space and a smaller work force—factors that should permit delivery of finished aircraft and the attaining of competitive proficiency much sooner than if a complete facility were established from scratch.

"In other words," I said, "instead of starting with small parts, start with major assemblies and work in reverse order. Build the small components and assemblies only if and when volume justifies. However, the practicality of this approach does depend on Vickers's production capability, willingness to provide the assemblies, and pricing policies." Howard thought this approach made sense and requested that I discuss production aspects with Sir George on a super-secret basis as soon as he "laid the groundwork."

Within a few weeks Howard called and requested me to discuss cost and production aspects with Edwards. This involved making numbers of transatlantic telephone calls from home. I could not charge the calls to TWA without risking breaches in security or at least the raising of eyebrows. The fact was that with five children and a wife to support, I simply could not afford the $50 to $80 calls and should never have been placed in the position of having to do so. So, after my personal budget had been badly bent by numbers of calls, I discussed remuneration with Howard. He said he would make suitable arrangements and asked me to make a call to Sir George on his behalf.

Howard called back in a few days and asked if I had made the call. I said, "Sorry, Howard, I didn't know how to charge it." Bill Gay called me about 10 minutes later. He arranged for payment of past calls and set up a procedure for charging such expenses to his office.

This incident opened the door with Howard for long overdue (as far as I was concerned) discussions concerning pay for special services rendered. The result was that I was placed on the payroll of the Hughes Tool Company with the full consent of TWA's Board of Directors. This was supposed to be a lifetime arrangement, but it lasted only until Howard lost control of TWA.

Carter Burgess

Controversy soon arose concerning Vickers's ability to produce the volume of major assemblies required for early stateside production, associated purchase prices, and the early availability of a small fleet of British-made Viscounts for introductory TWA operations to bridge the lag in manufacturing planes in the States. Our secret negotiations continued well into Carter Burgess's short regime as president.

I felt Carter should be apprised of our Viscount negotiations as a matter of courtesy and mentioned this to Howard as I had done before. Howard's response was the same: I should maintain secrecy. He would advise Carter when the time was "right."

One of the first things Carter undertook was a sweeping fleet planning project called "Super Overlord." In deference to the new president (I did not know what Howard might have requested from or discussed with him), I made available all pertinent information I could without breaching Howard's secrecy directives. Under the Super Overlord label, evaluations were undertaken by his New York staff of the possible acquisition of 22 Viscounts, 20 Bristol Britannia intercontinental-range turboprops, 3 additional 1649A's, and the lease of a small fleet of 1049H Constellations. Of those possibilities, Carter concluded that TWA should procure 20 Britannias for coast-to-coast and international services.

I disagreed because delivery of the Britannias would have been nearly contemporary with the clearly superior jets Howard had ordered through Toolco, although in partial defense of Carter's position, TWA had no legal rights to Toolco's jets. Viscounts were not chosen for procurement because Vic Leslie's department showed the operating costs to be exorbitant. This was exactly contrary to my projections and industry experience.

I discovered that Leslie's people had assumed that 22 Viscounts would be deployed throughout TWA's domestic system. The multiplicity of stations and flight segments to be served under this plan ensured high costs and disastrous financial results. My studies had assumed, with the concurrence of TWA's Traffic Department, that Viscount services would be concentrated east of Kansas City on a limited number of carefully selected segments. I discussed this with Leslie and Burgess, who requested a new Finance Department study. I was not anxious to obtain Viscounts—just the opposite—but I did not want Carter's position based on unsound premises. The new study showed the Viscounts to be profitable.

Chris Clarkson surprised me by phone on May 10, 1957, by offering for early delivery at a price of £400,000 per airplane the last 15 Viscounts Capital had on order, explaining that Capital was strapped for funds and would be unable to accept delivery. He wanted to know if Howard wanted the planes.

I immediately briefed Bill Gay by phone and asked him to ask Howard to call me. Howard called right back. Then Howard called Sir George Edwards, expressed interest, and agreed to try to make a firm decision by the following Wednesday. He did not. Much later he called back and asked me to brief Burgess, Leslie, and Oz Cocke on the Clarkson offer, emphasizing that I was not to mention any part of our negotiations concerning his interest in manufacturing Viscounts.

An intense flurry of activities immediately followed. TWA's senior management undertook new studies. Specification and contract negotiations were expedited. Carter sent Leslie and Harry West to London to discuss sticky contractual aspects with Vickers's representatives. I sent a technical team headed by W. H. ("Bud") Spannuth, who had joined my department as a structures and systems expert, to review maintenance and operational aspects of Capital's and TCA's Viscount operations. And, on Howard's request, I contacted Gordon McGregor, TCA's president, to see if he could make a Viscount available to Hughes for 48 hours for flight tests. McGregor regretted he could not do so because of an advertised increase in TCA flight schedules. However, he did offer to make a Viscount available to Howard for four hours and insisted that this be done fully at TCA's expense. However, Howard's busy schedule did not permit acceptance.

Then Vickers made a Viscount available. When it arrived at La Guardia Airport, Howard had it placed under armed guard, even though he had no right whatsoever to do so. No one was allowed to approach it, even to remove food from the galley. Howard provided the crew, who remained on standby status, with top accommodations at a New York hotel at his expense. Despite Vickers's pleadings and protestations, the plane remained under guard for months, presumably waiting for Howard to fly it. He never did.

While the Viscount was resting at La Guardia, Howard asked whether I thought we should continue to develop or drop the Viscount deal. The planes were in production, and Sir George desperately needed a commitment—even a verbal one—to justify continuing with the program.

I said that before responding to his question I would prefer to talk with Carter. I did not feel entirely comfortable about expressing TWA's views because of the recent change in TWA's senior management. He said, "Absolutely, by all means. Do so, and let me know as soon as possible."

Carter called a New York management meeting the same day I discussed this issue with him. George Spater confirmed the conclusions of the meeting by letter of June 7, 1957:

In view of the proposal to limit the operation of the Viscount to a restricted number of points [cities] east of Kansas City, it was agreed that the indirect costs assignable to the airplane would not reasonably be expected to exceed 92% of direct cost, exclusive of passenger service and depreciation. On this assumption, the Finance Department has conservatively estimated a break even load factor of 66.4%. Depreciation was based on seven year life with 15% residual. A passenger yield of 5.8 cents [per passenger mile] was used, based on domestic average for 1956, although a yield of at least 6 cents can be expected in the area in which the Viscount is to be operated.

Based on these figures and the belief that the drawing power of the airplane will attract traffic to the rest of TWA's fleet, the purchase of 22 Viscounts [Carter's number—Howard's deal was for 15] is recommended.

The Spater letter carried the "concur" signatures of Oz Cocke, senior vice president of sales; and John H. Clemson, vice president of passenger service.

Carter confirmed by telephone that the letter represented his position and that I should so advise Mr. Hughes. I called Howard and relayed Carter's position, reminding him of the tremendous TWA task ahead to prepare for and integrate the jets, which would be doubly difficult while acquiring Viscounts if, indeed, the Toolco jets were to go to TWA.

Based on his understanding that TWA wanted the planes, Howard called Sir George and personally committed to procure the 15 Viscounts, leaving open final resolution of the specifications and a number of contract details. Sir George accepted Howard's word as his bond and authorized the continuing construction of the planes.

Manufacturing Facilities

The 15 Viscounts fit Howard's plan. They were available for early delivery and would bridge the period required for tooling and initial stateside production.

275

TWA's principal maintenance and overhaul facility, at Fairfax Airport (KCK), Kansas City, Kansas, was scheduled to move during late 1957 to larger, custom-designed facilities at the new Kansas City Mid Continent International Airport (MCI), located north of town. The large, double-span KCK complex had been constructed by North American for predelivery modifications of B-25 bombers and was well suited for the manufacture of Viscounts.

I discussed the forthcoming availability of the KCK facility with Howard. When I mentioned that TWA planned to cancel the lease, he said, "Make absolutely certain that it remains available. Get a handle on it. Bob, don't lose it under any circumstances. Work it out and let me know."

My private letter of June 4, 1957, to Carter Burgess stated:

For reasons that can be best explained in person when I see you next, Mr. Hughes has requested that I arrange for retention of the complete KCK overhaul facility until a controlling decision can be made. I anticipate that the final decision will be made later this year, perhaps during the next three months.

The KCK facility is the only suitable facility for the intended purpose in the Kansas City area. . . . A summary of the lease terms is attached for your information.

The letter also explained that Ray Dunn needed the facility until November 15 and that Hughes's decision might be made before then, suggesting a method for handling the budgets in event he did not. It also attached a letter for Carter's signature to George H. Clay, vice president of administrative services. Carter wrote to Clay the next day as follows:

"This is to request that you not finalize arrangements for subletting or otherwise disposing of any or all of the KCK facility without first clearing such action with either Bob Rummel or myself."

"Vacation" in Estes Park

At the most critical time of my negotiation with Vickers, when final resolution of numbers of items required clearance with Hughes, he suddenly left the country without comment. To make an awkward situation worse, no one knew where he was or when he would return. As a stopgap measure, I urged Vickers to complete and submit for review a new draft of the airplane procurement specifications as a desirable prerequisite for finalizing open matters. Derek Lambert, Vickers's sales engineer, agreed, indicating several weeks would be required.

I had promised Bobby, my eight-year-old son, for an entire year to take him camping. After Howard could not be reached for nearly two weeks, we tossed camping gear in the Chevrolet convertible and set out for Colorado for a week's vacation: a rare and long-sought event. After a really great trip, we camped at the head of Eleven Mile Canyon near the base of the dam. It was a perfect setting, deep in a lush canyon near a cascading whitewater stream. After a day and a half there, I decided we needed a bath and checked into a motel near Florissant with the idea of returning to the campsite the next day.

I called home from the motel to see if all was well. Margie said Howard had been trying to reach me by phone ever since the day I left town. He was upset because neither she nor my secretary, Jacqueline Canada, could tell him where I was. Margie was certain Howard believed I was trying to avoid him. Within minutes, I called Bill Gay at Howard's Romaine Street headquarters and explained why I had been out of touch and how I could be reached.

About an hour later, Howard called from Nassau, the Bahamas: "Bob, where in hell have you been? I've been trying for days to reach you and all I've gotten is double-talk. Edwards is putting the heat on to execute the Viscount deal, and here I am in the Bahamas with lousy communications and can't reach you. Where in Christ's name are you?"

I told him, with a reminder that ever since he had left Hollywood the deal had been on dead center waiting further word from him and that neither I nor anyone else had been able to reach him.

"Yes," he said, "but how in hell can I give you the word if I can't get you?" Then in a hurt voice, "Bob, I just *assumed* that since I'm in the Bahamas pretty much out of touch that you would automatically pick up on the deal and follow through. I just *assumed* that *naturally* you would do this and bring this thing to a conclusion."

How could he possibly make such an assumption? We had not finally agreed on purchase price, payments, and several critically important items concerning Howard's prospective production of Viscounts. What if I had assumed full authority, pressed negotiations to what I considered to be an acceptable conclusion, only to find that Howard disagreed? Besides, with

Howard out of touch, how could I know he might not be negotiating directly with Sir George? A fine situation if I had proceeded, only to find Howard doing the same thing but singing a different tune!

I responded, "Howard, that is exactly what I would never do" and explained my position. "I certainly would have been glad to proceed if I had had a clear understanding of terms and conditions acceptable to you and that I had authority to bring things to a conclusion." This seemed to go down okay.

After a pause, Howard continued, "Sir George has pressing reasons to bring this deal to an early conclusion. Maybe we can make some hay on that. He has a team ready to come over—Derek Lambert and Bert Dymet— and we just have to get on with it. We can't afford to lose a single day."

I glanced at Bobby. "Okay, Howard. It will be a keen disappointment for my son, but I'll pack up and return to Kansas City in the morning."

"Oh, hell!" Howard exclaimed. "Bob, you can't do that! That will take too long. Find a suitable place where you are and get Harry West and any one else you need from Kansas City. The Vickers people will be there in the morning."

In the morning? How in hell could they be here in the morning? Howard had not even known where I was until an hour ago. Weybridge, the site of the Vickers plant in England, was at least a day and a half away. It would be at least two days, probably more. But I did not think it was a good time to argue.

For another hour, Howard discussed negotiating objectives and strategy and the importance of maintaining absolute secrecy re his plan to manufacture Viscounts. He said that Bert Dymet, Vickers's manufacturing and cost expert, was coming over to discuss privately the open manufacturing issues. Our conversation was cut short by heavy static. All telephone conversations to the Bahamas were via radio. Depending on the weather, they were often impossible.

I requested the Romaine Street office to make suitable hotel accommodations and requested Harry West, Norm Parmet, and Bud Spannuth to come out with the necessary documentation. Arrangements were made at the old Stanley Hotel, a resort in Estes Park near Rocky Mountain National Park. The usual Hughes security precautions prevailed. Bobby and I occupied a corner suite in a bungalow several hundred feet from the main building. Unoccupied suites were rented on both sides so telephone conversations could not be overheard. The Vickers and TWA groups were in the main building in widely separated areas. Additionally, special security personnel were arranged to protect the confidentiality of our activities, even though the fact of our negotiations for the 15 planes had been widely known within TWA and industry circles ever since Clarkson had advised that Capital could not accept delivery of the planes.

Howard called within 10 minutes of my arrival at the Stanley. The call lasted for hours until static killed all hope of continuing. This went on for the next two days—the TWA and Vickers groups had not yet arrived— during which Bobby and I were virtual prisoners in the suite. I felt sorry and guilty about Bobby's confinement. I called Margie and asked her to send one or two of his older sisters to show him the area. She said she would.

Heavy static ruled out phone conversations with Howard around noon the next day. Bobby and I took advantage of this lull and escaped for the first time. We went horseback riding on a wonderful mountain trail. On returning nearly three hours later, I was surprised to find Margie and the four girls parked by our rooms in our Ford station wagon. When she found that the girls would have to transfer between airlines, she had decided to drive. Margie was tired from the all-night drive and visibly annoyed. Hotel personnel had followed Howard's security directives to the letter and re- fused to let her in our suite despite unquestioned identification. They had waited for two hours and had not eaten. I suggested that because the two adjoining suits were going to waste they stay for the duration. They did and had a wonderful time. I spent nearly all of my time on the phone with Howard or in meetings with Vickers and TWA people.

Derek Lambert's specification revision project was interrupted by the trip, so he arrived with only partially updated paper, costing us time. Dymet had stacks of cost and production data. It became obvious during private meetings with him that much more time would be required to achieve detailed agreements concerning stateside Viscount production. Howard, recognizing the impracticality of holding up production, agreed reluctantly that the 15-plane deal would have to be executed first.

When tempers began to unravel, I suggested the men take time to go horseback riding on the pristine mountain trails. Our British friends did not tell me they had never ridden horses.

Bert Dymet was a large, big-boned man. He tried to mount on the right side with his left foot in the stirrup and realized too late he would face backwards. With Bert's great weight well off center, the poor horse could

279

do nothing but try to trot sideways. With the horse swinging toward him, Bert was afraid to get down. He very nearly rolled the horse but managed, amidst our laughter, to scramble off just in time. After mounting correctly, Bert did very well.

Derek mounted and lagged behind the rest of us. In fact, he never really started down the trail. When I saw his horse turn slowly toward the stables, I loped back to learn if he had changed his mind. I heard him growl, "Get going, you blasted, bloody blighter! Move, you ornery bastard! Damn you, beast, move!"

I interrupted with, "Have a problem, Derek?"

"Oh, no," he said, "Heavens no, but I just remembered that Sir George planned to call, so I think I better go back." He dismounted and led his horse to the stables.

Our adventures on horseback cleared the air and permitted us to complete the Estes Park work fairly rapidly.

The Refusal

The contract papers were ready for execution shortly after the Estes Park meetings except for a misunderstanding between Howard and Sir George on the purchase price. Efforts to resolve the matter dragged on until early November, when Sir George brought matters to a head. He called me and said Vickers had extended itself beyond reasonable measure to cooperate with Howard and simply had to have a duly executed contract and overdue progress payments. He said Howard should make an offer—any offer— and he would consider it. Because the papers were otherwise ready for execution, any Hughes offer made at that juncture, if accepted, would have closed the deal. I had kept Carter Burgess, Vic Leslie, and others at New York headquarters advised. They understood that the purchase of the 15 Capital Viscounts, which TWA had approved earlier, was about to be closed.

While Howard was mulling over his offer, Vic Leslie phoned with a blockbuster surprise. He said that Carter had reevaluated the project and decided he did not want and would not accept the Viscounts. Vic explained why and made it emphatically clear that this position was in accord with senior management's views and would not change.

I immediately placed an urgent call to Howard. On hearing the news, he said, "What? You mean to tell me that TWA is turning its back on the Viscount deal? Holy Christ! Bob, are you serious?"

"Yes, Howard, I'm serious. It's a hell of a note. I'm just as surprised as you are. I called the very minute Leslie hung up."

"What did he say?" Howard demanded. I explained that Leslie, TWA's senior vice president of finance, had come up with a brand-new financial forecast showing a financial downturn, which Carter deemed ruled out the Viscounts.

"That's too damn bad," said Howard. "TWA has made its bed and is going to have to lie in it. My reputation in Europe is worth a damn sight more than the price of 15 planes, I'll tell you that! TWA will just have to take the planes."

After a pause, I said, "Howard, I don't think TWA will, unless you force the issue. Carter called a special meeting—I'm not sure who all was there—and came to a corporate position. Leslie called right afterwards saying TWA would not accept the planes and that I had absolutely no authority to conclude a deal for TWA. No, Howard, I don't think TWA will change. After our months and months of effort, which I'm sure they understood, it certainly is a hell of a note."

"Jesus, yes! You know, after TWA said it wanted the planes, I committed verbally to Sir George for all 15, and I'm not going back on my word."

This unpropitious confrontation between Carter and Howard seemed to me in retrospect to represent just one more nail Carter drove into his presidential coffin. He had made the right decision at the wrong time.

Carter remained adamant, and Howard did not force TWA to accept the planes. Nor did he buy them, but, good to his word, he did arrange for their disposal in ways that would not diminish Vickers's total sales volume.

I was surprised when Howard accepted Carter's refusal to buy the Viscounts. Noah Dietrich's firing (see Chapter 19), the fact that no discernible effort had been made to finance the huge jet transport orders recently placed by Toolco, and the softening of the travel market may have accounted for Howard's submission.

Howard personally assured Sir George that he would see that every one of the 15 planes was disposed of to Sir George's complete satisfaction. Assisted by a number of key employees and business associates, including Leonard Schwartz, he worked in close collaboration with Sir George to

281

that end. Progress was slow, a circumstance that only seemed to reinforce Howard's determination.

About one year later, after all the planes had been placed, Howard called me at home with a single message. He said with some pride, ''I just talked to Sir George Edwards. He said I have discharged every obligation and he's completely happy with the outcome of our Viscount deal. Bob, I know you were concerned, and I just wanted you to know.''

I deeply appreciated Howard's call and thanked him for his thoughtfulness. Many years later, while I was visiting Sir George in his suite at the Gotham Hotel in New York, he told me how much he appreciated Howard's role in disposing of the 15 Viscounts. He commented, ''He is truly a good friend and a great gentleman.''

Of course, Howard's plan to manufacture Viscounts did not work out. When this became apparent, I released the KCK overhaul base to George Clay for disposal.

18.
The Convair Digression

Having concluded at the end of 1952 that British turbine designs should be passed over in favor of prospective U.S. aircraft, it became immediately incumbent on us to try to determine the manufacturer or manufacturers most likely to produce those better planes and to work with them in developing the best possible planes for TWA's use. Busy as we were with Constellation and other piston-aircraft problems, I eagerly found time for this.

I have already described the abortive YB-60 investigation with Convair and the far more serious consideration given the AVRO Jetliner and subsequent AVRO proposals. Indeed, Project Mexico City was actively discussed through 1955 and not dropped until 1956. The major programs, however, seemed certain to be at Boeing and Douglas. In 1953 another would-be player entered the arena, shrouded in a secrecy extreme even for Hughes.

The Romaine Street boys left word during early July with Ralph Ellinger at his Lockheed office that Howard wanted me to meet him at the Beverly Hills Hotel. I excused myself from one of my fairly frequent Lockheed 1049E meetings and drove to the hotel in one of Howard's Chevrolets.

One of Howard's Mormons met me at the door and directed me to the grand ballroom. It was completely empty except for one small table in the center of the dance floor and four nearby chairs. A few minutes later, Howard entered with Jack Zevely, Convair's vice president of sales; and Ralph Bayless, chief engineer. Howard had posted guards outside every door to the ballroom. No one was allowed to enter, and all discussion, which lasted about two hours, was at the table so as not to be overheard. After preliminaries, Ralph unrolled drawings, showing a slick, 68-passenger, highly swept-wing jet transport. I thought the plane looked great and probably showed my enthusiasm.

Examination of the preliminary data indicated that the proposed jet lacked range and might be too small for our purpose. This led to technical discussions the next several days at the Beverly Hills Hotel, during which Zevely and Bayless were requested not to leave for any purpose. Because I was staying at the Hollywood Roosevelt I had permission to leave, but only to sleep.

Jack and Ralph had been hoping for the meeting with Hughes for several weeks. When Howard finally called the meeting, he gave hardly any notice. As a consequence, Ralph rushed to Beverly Hills from San Diego without taking time to collect personal essentials. Just after arrival, before hurrying to the meeting, he asked one of the boys to buy him a white shirt and some other things at "any convenient" Beverly Hills store. Ralph of course expected to reimburse the boy, but when the merchandise was delivered, the boy refused to accept payment. Howard had instructed his Mormon team that Ralph and Jack were to be accorded every courtesy, and their every need or whim was to be accommodated (within the confines of the hotel) at his expense. When Ralph insisted that he pay—it was against his grain to accept any form of charity, no matter how well intended—and was again refused, he asked, "If I can't pay you, how and who should I pay?" The boy, confronted with the dilemma of how to abide by Howard's directive and still keep Ralph happy, instantly saw Ralph's question as a solution. He exclaimed, "That's it! How and who? I'll have to let you know." Ralph never heard.

During ensuing private discussions, Howard asked me to center my investigative efforts at Convair but to maintain familiarity with the Boeing, Douglas, and any other similar jet or turboprop transport development projects. Howard insisted that only an absolute minimum number of my

284

staff be involved and that secrecy surround all work with Convair. This project was ultimately called "Southern Comfort."

During the next year, a host of airplane designs were developed with Convair and evaluated, including four-engine and six-engine jets, four-engine turboprops, and hybrid configurations. Various jet and turboprop power plants were considered, including P & W J-57 and J-75 and Wright Aeronautical J-67 jets; the ill-fated P & W T-34 turboprop; and the Wright T-47 and T-49 and Bristol Proteus turboprops. Single-deck and double-deck fuselages, wings with different sweep angles, and other design variables were evaluated to find the best design formula.

It was through such exchanges, reinforced by appreciable interim engineering efforts, that acceptable design proposals were finally produced. Howard discussed the relative performance and competitive aspects of the various designs but did not involve himself in the evolutionary design process per se, relying on Convair and me for this.

Technical discussions and design review meetings were held in numerous cities, including Beverly Hills, Culver City, Kansas City, Las Vegas, San Diego, Santa Monica, and Washington. These exercises were extremely interesting for me and commanded the attention of Hughes, who found time to attend numbers of the conferences. Each meeting that Hughes attended was cloaked in the same kind of protective secrecy that accompanied the initiating Beverly Hills Hotel meeting. One meeting called by Hughes was held in the Santa Monica beach house of Marion Davies, movie star and William Randolph Hearst's long-time girlfriend, which Howard borrowed for the purpose. The large, attractive beach house had a gabled roof and was situated on a smallish lot between the Pacific Coast Highway and the ocean on the north side of town. The house was unoccupied at the time: furniture in the spacious rooms was covered with drop cloths except in one room filled with wicker furniture, which had been hurriedly prepared for the meeting by one of Howard's Mormons.

One of the more interesting design studies was reviewed during October 1953 in the third-floor library of my Kansas City residence. I played hooky from TWA by feigning illness to maintain secrecy. Only Al Reidler (Convair's performance expert) and I were present. The primary concept we examined was the use of a common airframe but with different types engines for domestic and international operations. The domestic model was to be propelled by six P & W J-57 jet engines, and the international model by four P & W T-34, Wright T-47, or Wright T-49 turboprops to achieve the desired New York-Paris range. For comparison, a hybrid arrangement with four turboprops mounted in wing leading-edge nacelles along with two jets mounted in outboard underslung nacelles was also considered. While these designs were not fully suitable, the idea of propelling a single airframe with two types of engines was examined repeatedly during the next year and became an inherent part of the project.

Ralph Bayless was hesitant to endorse the feasibility of turboprops for commercial use because of probable excessive propeller noise (the blade tips would exceed the speed of sound) and marginal propeller efficiency at high altitudes. In addition to sharing his concern over noise, I did not like the complexity of contra-rotating propellers and questioned whether sufficient empirical data existed to reliably predict the efficiency and vibration characteristics of propellers located ahead of highly swept wings.

The most inviting solution for the development of international nonstop aircraft remained the installation of four large jet engines, but suitable engines were not available. P & W JT-4's appeared to be the most promising but remained unavailable; the Wright J-67 jet lacked strong military support; the Rolls-Royce ducted-fan Conway was only in the early stage of development; and the P & W J-57's developed insufficient thrust. Indeed, ever since my first direct encounter with jet design, when I responded to Jack Frye's early 1945 request by laying out a transcontinental mail plane, the lack of suitable jet engines with acceptably low fuel consumption and sufficient operational experience to assure reasonable operational reliability had been the principal technical obstacles to jet transport development.

I never knew Howard to take a drink of liquor, but once he seemed to come close. During one of the private Las Vegas project review meetings, he decided to take a night off and asked if I would like to see a few shows. While passing through the hotel bar on the way to the Chevrolet, we were invited to join the swimmer and movie star Johnny Weissmuller and two starlets, who were in a nearby booth. Howard did it again. He introduced me as "Bob Rummel, *the* airplane designer."

Howard ordered a crème de menthe frappe. The young bartender brought Howard a glass of crème de menthe filled with ice cubes. Howard looked at it, sloshed it a while, and motioned to the bartender. When he came over, Howard said quietly, "Jesus, I didn't want icebergs. Can't you break this up?"

We heard hammering, after which the bartender returned with a frappe filled with broken ice cubes about half the original size and handed it to Howard. Howard looked at it a moment, handed it back, and said, "For Christ's sake! Don't you know what a frappe is? Bring me one with chipped ice."

The bartender returned once more—by now we had been in the booth about 20 minutes—this time with a proper frappe. Howard held it a while, asked me the time, said we had to leave, and excused us from Weissmuller and friends without ever having taken as much as a sip of the crème de menthe.

The evening was unusual but enjoyable. We saw parts of four shows, had several pleasant chats, and not once discussed business. All the shows were seen from standing in the shadows just inside the entrance doors. Howard elected not to be seated, probably so as to avoid public attention. However, the entire evening cost him absolutely nothing, including a late meal provided gratis by the hotel.

Our exploratory investigations at Convair extended through 1954 and 1955, right through the traumas we experienced with the Lockheed 1449-1649A's. When Howard was out of touch, I continued the dialogue and associated engineering efforts with the usual able input from my staff. Ralph Bayless and his capable design team continued their helpful exploratory efforts throughout this extended exercise.

Boeing

Ever since Boeing announced the development of the 367-80 prototype jet transport on August 30, 1952, various Boeing officials had tried to establish liaison with Hughes and periodically kept Ralph Damon and me informed concerning Boeing's plans to offer and produce jets for the airlines. I welcomed Boeing's sales initiatives, the associated technical information flow, and the opportunity these activities afforded to discuss the 707 and related airline requirements. Whenever occasion permitted, I brought Howard up to date.

Ken Gordon of Boeing called me on October 27, 1954, and advised that Boeing was having serious contractual discussions with PAA and an unnamed airline. Ken said Boeing expected to have contractual specifications completed by November 15 and to shortly work out option arrangements guaranteeing relative delivery positions between airlines. However, he did not expect Boeing to be able to make firm commercial delivery commitments until January. Such commitments would be contingent on obtaining clearance from the Air Force to manufacture commercial transports using facilities common to its KC-135 tanker-transport program. The KC-135, the military version of the 367-80, had been ordered to limited production during July.

Ken volunteered that Howard had contacted Wellwood Beall, Boeing's executive vice president, several weeks earlier, but since then Howard had not returned Wellwood's calls. Ken said Boeing was anxious to work with us and suggested early specification conferences. Before closing, he invited TWA's senior management to visit Seattle and inspect the 367-80 prototype. I was told later that Howard had expressed interest to Wellwood in procuring the first 50 Boeing jets, and Wellwood refused, explaining that such exclusivity was self defeating and contrary to Boeing policy because excluded airlines would likely turn to other manufacturers. If this account is true—it would have been typical of Howard to make such a request—Howard probably never forgot.

Bill Allen, Boeing's intrepid, far-seeing president, wrote to Ralph Damon on November 19. He advised that the 707 delivery schedule for any customer would be based on the order in which commitments were made and would take into account the quantity purchased by each. He also invited TWA to undertake specification and contract negotiations. Allen sent a copy to Hughes and identical letters to other major American airlines as well as some of the larger foreign airlines. Shortly thereafter, PAA, AAL, and UAL commenced negotiations in response to the invitation.

I advised Howard of this development and recommended that exploratory negotiations be undertaken with Boeing without delay and that investigative work at Convair be continued. I said that in this way we could develop a good negotiating position at Boeing while maintaining a strong position with Convair so the best plane could be selected for TWA after Convair had completed the design investigation, which appeared to be imminent. I reminded him that Convair was still working with paper, while Boeing was flying a prototype and was ready to deal.

"I know of no technical reason why Boeing can't develop a stretched JT-4-powered model for international operations," I said. "Let's bet on both horses until we know for sure which will be the winner." Howard said the time "wasn't right" to deal with Boeing, that he would "handle that," and that I should continue to work with Convair "to design the best damned airplane for TWA that can be designed."

During December Boeing mounted what appeared to be an all-out campaign to get Howard and TWA to participate in its 707 program. Wellwood sent Howard a wire directed to his personal attention on December 23 reconfirming Boeing's readiness to undertake procurement negotiations and soliciting Howard's interest and participation. On December 27, Bill Allen wrote a letter to Ralph Damon repeating essentially what was in Beall's wire to Hughes, but adding details concerning Boeing's proposed option terms. Notwithstanding, Hughes, possibly enamored by the Convair project, still did not authorize negotiations with Boeing.

Ralph Damon, like me, recognized the inherent competitive superiority of the prospective U.S. jets and was eager for TWA to be the first or among the first to operate them. He knew in general terms of my activities at Convair, and, also like me, wanted to keep our options open. However, as far as I knew, he had not pressed Hughes for clearance to work with Boeing. So, on January 12, 1955, I wrote a letter to John Collings and sent a copy to Ralph Damon to encourage them to somehow influence Howard to permit negotiations. If they made the effort, it was not effective.

I may have tried too hard. During early 1955, in spite of my protestations, Howard expressly ordered me not to contact or negotiate with either Douglas or Boeing.

Project Southern Comfort

My work with Convair continued. During February 1955, Ralph Bayless and his Convair associates produced the N-2 series of proposed transport designs. They appeared to satisfy our requirements. By this time the commercial availability of P & W JT-3's was certain, and in my opinion, shared by Bayless, that of JT-4's was probable.

TWA could not afford to wait for the later availability of engines with truly adequate thrust such as the JT-4 because competing airlines were certain to deploy Boeing and Douglas jets powered by JT-3 engines significantly before the higher-powered jets could become available. Thus, as a practical matter of market preservation, it had become clear that TWA would require both types of aircraft, hopefully, however, using essentially common airframes and systems.

Bayless presented domestic and international versions of the N-2's with essentially common airframes. The domestic N-2's, with space for 101 five-abreast luxury seats or 123 six-abreast coach seats, were to be powered by four P & W JT-3's. The international model was to be configured identically except for a longer fuselage capable of accommodating up to 147 coach passengers, the installation of four JT-4's in lieu of JT-3's, and higher operating weights. The N-2 design schemes reflected our joint efforts to develop advanced planes with unsurpassed competitive attributes. For example: (1) The wing sweep was greater than in the Boeing or Douglas jet transport designs for low drag at higher cruising speeds. (2) The diameter of the fuselage, tailored to comfortably accommodate six-abreast coach seating, was greater than then offered by Boeing or Douglas. (3) True transatlantic nonstop range capability was shown to be feasible with the JT-4 version, whereas the Boeing and Douglas jets lacked this capability. (4) The great commonality between the domestic and international versions offered the potential for realizing significant production and operating cost savings.

Attesting to the soundness of the N-2 plan, during the fall of 1955 both Douglas and Boeing offered JT-4-powered transports for international operations in response to airline pressure generated primarily by PAA (Hughes's orders that I not work with Douglas and Boeing had remained in effect). The width of the fuselages was also increased, matching that of the Convair N-2.

Howard adopted the long-range game plan of obtaining early delivery of a fleet of JT-3-powered Convairs for domestic and limited international use, followed as soon as possible by acquisition of a fleet of the JT-4-powered model for international and through-plane West Coast-Europe services. He of course understood that stops would be required on many of the JT-3-powered flights when deployed in over-ocean operations. Howard tabbed this plan "Southern Comfort." Convair called the airplane the Model 18. During early March 1955, Howard requested me to expedite the preparation of a contract and specifications for procurement of a fleet of domestic Convair Model 18 jets.

Ralph Damon and I were convinced the jets would pull passengers on board the way flowers attract bees, and after the jets were sold out, TWA would have an opportunity to book passengers on the pistons. Thus, it was considered extremely important for TWA's jets to be deployed at the earliest possible date. Without at least maintaining a pari passu delivery relationship with prime competitors, the airline's market share would all too easily deteriorate. With earlier deliveries, it could increase.

Convair planned to achieve initial CAA certification by March 1958 and final certification by the end of July, when 16 planes were to be ready for delivery.[1] Had this happened, TWA would probably have been the first airline to operate United States-built jets because revenue operations could have begun during the third quarter, whereas PAA in fact commenced service with Boeing 707's on October 26, 1958. Convair's design and production schedules, however, were extremely demanding, left little time for contingencies, and required the earliest possible implementation if they were to succeed. In hindsight, such early deliveries were probably never in the cards.

Boeing had continued to contact me regularly and tentatively discuss 707 delivery positions, which were somewhat earlier than Convair was willing to offer for the CV-18. However, because Boeing had not yet obtained the necessary permission from the Air Force to manufacture commercial transports, its delivery estimates remained speculative.

The availability of Douglas DC-8 jet transports was even more speculative because the Douglas decision to formally offer DC-8's had not been made. I had no doubt that Douglas would enter the jet transport race and that William A. ("Pat") Patterson, UAL's chief executive, would be the first customer, or among the first, as had been his long-standing habit. The probability of TWA's obtaining early deliveries from Douglas seemed remote in any event, and nonexistent unless Howard changed his prohibition against working with it.

My judgment of the comparative early availability of jet transports produced by the three manufacturers was that Douglas probably would not be competitive; Convair could easily suffer acute production indigestion or constipation; and Boeing, if it could obtain timely manufacturing permission from the Air Force, could achieve early, probably the earliest commercial production. After all, Boeing had enormous experience manufacturing large swept-wing jets, had flown the prototype 367-80, and was in early production on the KC-135 jet tanker. It had learned the score the hard way. However, I had no specific reason to doubt Convair's ability to do what it represented.

The deal Convair offered was for Howard to purchase the first 30 CV-18's at a base price of $4,750,000 each. Convair's willingness to sell the first 30 planes to one customer was astonishing, notwithstanding Hughes's inflexible demands. The other manufacturers refused to close out early delivery positions for any one customer lest this discourage sales to prospective customers.

291

Hughes had agreed that Convair would need to concentrate first on detailing the J-57-powered model to meet the stringent proposed delivery schedule, but appropriately, he wanted this done to minimize development time for the heavier, stretched-fuselage, J-75-powered model, which was to follow. Howard intended to place a follow-on order for the long-range J-75-powered model as soon as circumstances permitted, even if this required renegotiation and reconfiguring some of the J-57-powered planes. Had this happened, Howard's intended CV-18 monopoly conceivably might have extended through as many as 50 planes, possibly more, assuming he had the financial wherewithal to follow through on such an enormous undertaking.

Shortly after Howard had requested me to expedite the Southern Comfort negotiations, Bill Gay called. He said that Howard thought I would probably be spending a great deal of time in the San Diego area, and to help maintain secrecy, he requested that I use a pseudonym, all business activities be conducted at some location other than the Convair plant, and any personnel involved on account of Hughes's interests be required to maintain anonymity while in the San Diego area.

Bill suggested that I use the name "Howard Lundeen." I did not like the idea of using a pseudonym and checked the legal implications with Harry West before agreeing. Because I did not have a better name in mind, I accepted Bill's suggestion. I did not know then that the real Howard Lundeen was one of Howard's Mormons. When I found out later on, I called Lundeen, explained the situation, and retroactively obtained his permission.

Howard also suggested through Bill that I might want to bring my family to San Diego for the duration, and if so, to please charge the expenses to Toolco—this would be considered an entirely legitimate expense. I did not like being alone, which happened all too often during my tenure with Hughes and TWA, and I knew Margie and the children would enjoy spending more time in San Diego, so I asked, "Does Howard know that I have five children?" Bill responded, "No problem, Bob, no problem. By all means bring them out, if you wish." I asked Bill to thank Howard for me and did so directly at the first opportunity. My family joined me in San Diego during the summer vacation.

I checked in at the La Jollian Motel, La Jolla, as Howard Lundeen on Saturday, March 19, 1955, for CV-18 contract and specification negotiations. I called Jack Zevely to arrange for meetings that evening or the following day to plan the work agenda. Jack could not get his people together until Monday but invited me to join him at dinner with Bob Loomis Sunday evening. Ralph Bayless called a few minutes later to make arrangements for the Monday meeting, which we agreed would be held at the La Jollian to maintain secrecy.

Howard called Saturday evening to discuss the Convair offer and our negotiating objectives, and again to urge expeditious action. He called again early Monday evening and inquired why Harry West was not with me. I explained that Harry was required to attend a CAB accident hearing in Albuquerque, and he would be in La Jolla as soon as possible, certainly within a few days. Howard discussed for over an hour whether the hearing could be postponed and whether someone could substitute for Harry. He insisted that I discuss this with John Collings, who of course agreed that this was out of the question. Howard called again on Tuesday, asked about Harry, and once more urged expeditious development of the specifications and contract.

During the Saturday evening telephone discussion, I had proposed to Howard that a brief, objective type specification, rather than a detailed one, be written along with a short-form letter contract to tie down deliveries, base price, payment schedule, aircraft certification, and other minimum essentials, but which deliberately left details open for resolution during the final contract negotiations. I pointed out that if Convair agreed to comply with the design principles and objectives I wanted, good negotiating leverage would exist for favorable resolution of design details in accordance with TWA's requirements during the preliminary design phase, when such decisions would be timely. He enthusiastically endorsed this approach, which would allow more time to develop contract terms to our liking.

At the Monday meeting, Convair agreed with this approach, noting this would dovetail nicely with the need to obtain general project approval from the General Dynamics Board of Directors (Convair was a division of General Dynamics). The next weeks were spent developing papers accordingly.

On March 29, 1955, the General Dynamics board appointed the Special Project Committee to develop a recommendation for Executive Committee action. The committee's report, dated May 23 and supplemented June 2, 1955, recommended that Convair be authorized to proceed with the Model 18. The committee noted in its report that "the Douglas Aircraft Company, Inc. would, it was believed, change from its present plans for a turboprop for American Airlines to a turbojet"; that "Boeing was not believed to be a serious factor in view of the Air Force's insistence that it take no more work''; that ''Lockheed might or might not be a factor''; and that ''based on the sale of only 30 aircraft, the resultant loss would be $27,000,000.'' On June 7, 1955, the Executive Committee gave the necessary approval, authorizing management to negotiate and enter into a contract for the manufacture and sale of Model 18 aircraft. Contract negotiations and preliminary design activities continued on an expedited basis.

The Convair principals involved at this stage were Gen. Joseph T. McNarney, president; J. V. (''Jack'') Naish, executive vice president; Jack Zevely; Ralph Bayless; and Bernie Simons, CV-18 project engineer. Harry West and I handled detail negotiations for Howard; however, Howard was also directly involved with Convair, mostly by telephone with McNarney, Naish, or Zevely. Howard's nearly daily telephone conversations with me provided essential coordination for our respective activities.

After working out of the La Jollian for about a month, Ralph Bayless suggested that it would be extremely helpful if my headquarters could move closer to the Convair plant to save his staff transit time between San Diego and La Jolla. I agreed to check into it. A vacant apartment in a small, one-story building, conveniently located on Kettner Boulevard just across the tracks from Convair's ''blockhouse'' headquarters building, appeared to be adequate, but barely so. It consisted of two rooms, a small kitchen, and a bath. One of the rooms, extending from front to rear, was an ideal size for a conference room.

When I discussed relocation with Hughes, he agreed but insisted that the conference room be made soundproof, even though the adjoining apartment was packed solid with used furniture and did not appear to have been visited for years. The landlord agreed to the construction of an additional wall without an increase in rent provided I (Lundeen) paid for the installation and its removal on vacating the premises. Convair, per industry custom, provided the furniture, file cabinets, and office equipment.

When the Kettner Boulevard office was activated and I was about to move from the La Jollian to the Town & Country Motel in Mission Valley, Bill Gay suggested I change my pseudonym from Howard Lundeen to Jack Clark lest my identity as Lundeen had become suspect. I agreed, but somewhat against my better judgment. My fear was that I might encounter a mix of people, some who knew me as Howard Lundeen and some who knew me as Jack Clark. This proved to be unavoidable one night during an intermission at the Old Globe Shakespeare Theater in Balboa Park. I felt awkward introducing Margie only as "my wife," but because I managed to keep fairly lively conversation going concerning the play, the embarrassment of having two names did not arise.

I found use of pseudonyms to be difficult. Little things bothered. For example, if someone from across the way called, "Hi, Bob!" I'd try to remember not to respond unless I recognized that the person calling knew my true name. Or, perhaps most difficult, when addressed as "Howard," and later "Jack," I had to remember to answer in a relaxed, easy manner.

On evenings after dinner at the Town & Country I sometimes took time to play shuffleboard with Bobby. One evening I sensed that I was being watched and turned to see two men dressed in business suits staring at me from the shadows. When I looked again, they approached, and one asked if my name was Jack Clark. I responded with a smile and said, "That's what I'm called." They were plainclothes police officers who wanted to know why I was at the Town & Country, what my business in San Diego was, my home address, who my associates were, and, really, about almost everything I could not answer without breaking my security commitment to Howard. They were polite but obviously unhappy with my unresponsive answers. Nonetheless, they left quietly without having learned much.

The next day, Margie called me at the Kettner office and said two men had moved numbers of "black boxes" into the adjoining suite, but only one of the men had left. She thought it was unusual and I should know. Like her, I assumed they had installed listening devices. I explained the situation to Bill Gay and called Jack Naish. I asked Naish to call the San Diego police chief and ask him to call his dogs off, and for Naish to guarantee that "Jack Clark" was clean, but to do so without breaching security. Naish handled it. That afternoon Margie saw the black boxes being removed from the motel.

I had become suspect because the motel rosters in the San Diego area were regularly examined by the police, who were perpetually on the look-out for underworld characters, con artists, and the like. At that time I had about 15 associates at the hotel, all registered under the name Jack Clark. I had asked them to sign "Jack Clark" to the motel, restaurant, and incidental expense checks to avoid bookkeeping confusion that might have arisen from the use of 15 pseudonyms. When the police saw so many Jack Clarks, they understandably became curious.

The Town & Country was developed and operated by a fine old gentleman named Brown. We became friends, and he graciously asked me and Margie to accept the honor of becoming the king and queen of the Pacifico del Rio Fiesta. We were flabbergasted. Under ordinary circumstances we would have accepted without hesitation, but because there was certain to be considerable publicity associated with the affair, we declined. We could not bear the thought of having false names ascribed publicly, and our presence as king and queen would undoubtedly have spilled Howard's security beans.

Howard's CV-18 venture, however, was not a well-kept secret. Boeing and Douglas knew something was going on and could no doubt tell what from the way TWA personnel reacted to their overtures. Indeed, I discovered later that they were aware of many of the CV-18 design details. In the end, the security breach did not harm the CV-18 project because Convair decided not to go ahead. On July 28, the Executive Committee formally resolved that it was "inadvisable to proceed with any further sales efforts." Two primary reasons were given: conflicting military production requirements and excessive competition. This was the second time Convair pulled the rug out from under us, the first being Cohu's Super 240 withdrawal.

This decision no doubt reflected several events that had recently occurred: Lockheed had announced the sale of turboprop Electras to AAL on June 8, 1955, making clear that Douglas was out of that race; Douglas announced the DC-8 go-ahead on June 9; and the Air Force approved Boeing to manufacture commercial jets along with KC-135's on July 13, which signaled the 707 program go-ahead. Thus, it was clear that Convair would be confronted with two major jet transport competitors—a sobering development, but one that I thought should have been anticipated.

For some reason I could never fathom, some of General Dynamics' senior executives had hung on to the unrealistic notion that Douglas would offer long-range turboprops rather than jets even long after the jet-powered DC-8 was generally known to be in preliminary design. I knew Donald Douglas, Sr., and could not imagine his agreeing to forego the civil transport market, in which he had long been firmly entrenched, or undertaking the development of anything other than the most competitive vehicle, which clearly had to be jet rather than turboprop powered.

I was also surprised by the persistence of view expressed to me by several Convair executives that the Air Force would not allow Boeing to enter the civil jet transport market. I knew Bill Allen was determined to do so and believed it was only a matter of time until formulae for the equitable allocation of costs between Boeing's military and commercial programs would be agreed upon, permitting the Air Force to release Boeing to manufacture commercial jets and KC-135's in the same facilities.

In retrospect, General Dynamics-Convair's final decision was probably in the best interest of their shareholders because the market most likely could not have supported three types of U.S. jets designed to fulfill essentially the same missions—in my opinion, a circumstance that should have been foreseen all along.

Lost Opportunity

After the CV-18 program aborted, I hoped sufficient time remained, albeit marginal, to obtain good Boeing 707 delivery positions. I urged Howard, as I had done before, to immediately authorize negotiations. He did not. He considered just about every potential alternative except Douglas DC-8's.

At that time, Douglas seemed no more interested in dealing with Howard than Howard was in dealing with Douglas. Douglas had even stopped sending DC-8 technical data to TWA before the CV-18 program aborted, as if they had given up on selling Howard, or possibly in the belief that Howard and I were somehow trying to copy the DC-8. The fact of the matter was that I had no interest whatsoever in urging Convair to duplicate a design that calculations showed could not do the required job. (Later on, after Douglas produced the international JT-4-powered model, the DC-8's performed very creditably in overseas services.)

During the next six weeks, Convair engineering inexplicably came forward with new preliminary designs, which I presumed represented a last-ditch effort to maintain our interest and generate a basis for seeking the approval of the General Dynamics board for a new program. Three-view drawings of Convair Models 19 and 20, in multiple variations, appeared in quick succession. All were large, six-engine JT-4- (J-75) powered designs intended to surpass the payload range and speed capability of the Boeing and Douglas jets then in the offering. "Long-tube" and "double-deck" versions with various length fuselages, some with low wings and some with mid wings, were presented for consideration. The maximum takeoff weight considered was 370,000 pounds, compared to 260,000 pounds for the CV-18.

It was at this time that my old friend Benny Howard visited me at my Kettner Boulevard office to promote the development of a sweet-looking, extremely clean, four-engine jet transport design he had recently developed. Unfortunately the engines were buried in the aft section of the fuselage in such a manner that catastrophic failure of any engine, such as a burst turbine wheel, could cause failure of other engines and the empennage, possibly including the flight control system. For this reason, I declined. Other than that, the design looked great.

As an engineer, I found these exercises intriguing (I had drawn similar designs a few months earlier as part of Hughes's ongoing AVRO Mexico City project). However, because such aircraft quite obviously could not be made available until at least one year after the 707's, I tried again to direct Howard's interest toward Boeing. Again, my effort did not succeed, or at least I could discern no perceptible progress. Instead, he thrashed about in all directions, demanding investigation of everything except the single obvious choice.

During a "visit" to my family in Kansas City, Howard called over the weekend and requested immediate handling of an "urgent" matter. He wanted me to explore the practicality of acquiring a fleet of Mark IV de Havilland Comets for use throughout TWA's system until the six-engine Convair or AVRO jets could be made available, after which they would be confined to domestic routes. Howard considered early deliveries of 15 Mark IV's to be "absolutely essential." He wanted me to meet in secret with F. H. M. ("Frank") Lloyd of de Havilland to discuss the situation and obtain the best possible delivery positions for 15 Mark IV Comets.

I knew Frank quite well from previous occasions when we had considered acquiring Comet fleets. Howard emphasized that I was to talk to absolutely no one else and that I was to contact him at once. He reiterated several times that the meeting was to be "absolutely secret" and directed me not to give my name, affiliation, or any other information to telephone operators, hotel clerks, or anyone I might encounter that might "tip our hand." He even said, "Bob, don't give the operator the number you're calling from, and don't let anyone in the de Havilland organization or anyone else other than Lloyd know that you are calling." I said I would try, but privately, I questioned if it would be possible to contact Lloyd following Howard's restrictive directions, which I considered excessive to the point of absurdity.

I did not know where Lloyd was. All I knew was that he was on an around-the-world Comet demonstration flight, and he was probably somewhere in Canada. I assumed he would demonstrate the plane to the central

Canadian government and TCA officials first, so I decided to start trailing him in eastern Canada.

My first call was to the residence of a Canadian official I had not met. Luck was with me. A child answered the phone. He confirmed that Lloyd was in town and had been at his house earlier. He gave me the name of Lloyd's hotel where he said Frank was attending a dinner meeting. I called Lloyd's hotel. Lloyd, who had momentarily returned to his room to pick up some papers, answered. He was as surprised to hear from me as I was to have reached him so easily without having breached Howard's security instructions.

Frank was delighted with the renewed interest and agreed to meet me in Chicago the next evening. Bill Gay's office arranged for a lavish suite at the Blackstone Hotel. I do not know how Bill arranged it, but I used a code word to register and sign checks and was not required to use or sign my name at all. On leaving I found that payment of the bills had been prearranged. I asked Frank not to register or check with hotel personnel but to come directly to my suite, which he did.

We had a late dinner in the suite, reviewed the current Mark IV situation, discussed de Havilland's ability to comply with Howard's delivery requirements demand, and per instructions placed a call to Howard around midnight to review Lloyd's position. Howard called back within minutes. We talked about an hour and a half, after which he talked to Frank another hour, and then to me for another 30 minutes. Lloyd offered the 15 Comets for delivery in 1958 at $3 million each, subject to clearance from the British Air Ministry, which he, on Howard's request, agreed to obtain. By the time our investigation had been brought to maturity, Howard had finally agreed to buy Boeings, and the Comet project was dropped.

Howard also suddenly renewed interest in acquiring a fleet of long-range Bristol Britannia turboprops. He asked me to obtain up-to-date information on available delivery positions, performance, and the purchase prices to be paid by other airlines. The latter request was unreasonable and, as Howard well knew, would be nearly impossible to fulfill because aircraft procurement contracts almost always prohibited any participant from divulging such information without the formal consent of the others. Notwithstanding, I was able through personal contracts to obtain some useful data. He also said we should consider whether a small fleet of around 15 planes would give TWA a worthwhile competitive edge.

After talking it over a bit, I suggested that in any event such a fleet be limited to no more than 5 planes. That way, TWA could offer minimal high-speed New York-Los Angeles and New York-San Francisco nonstop services and obtain turbine experience at minimal investment and expense. Most importantly, I suggested that the purchase or lease of only a small fleet of Britannias would conserve funds and permit the allocation of primary resources to the acquisition of jets, which would be faster and more competitive than the Britannias and likely be available within one year after such planes were acquired. I also questioned whether we could rely on Bristol delivery estimates because production had been running late, emphasizing that all indications were that our competition would not purchase Britannias, but go straight to jets.

This was one of the most frustrating and hectic periods of my long association with Hughes. His refusal to deal with Boeing was especially galling because TWA's arch competitors, PAA and AAL, were actively negotiating specifications and contracts at that time, as were other airlines. The AVRO Mexico City project also continued throughout this period. Indeed, it continued for several months after Howard finally agreed to purchase Boeings.

Ralph Damon was also frustrated. It was painful for him to observe competing airlines getting a head start. His report to TWA's Board of Directors during its December 1955 meeting reflected his concern and, among other things, forecast that in 1959–60 "every airplane TWA now owns or has on order or option will be either totally obsolete or heavily outclassed."

Nothing came of any of Howard's equipment divagations. Unfortunately, the precious time lost in the CV-18 exercise and in exploring acquisition of six-engine Convairs, de Havilland Comets, Bristol Britannias, and the AVRO jets could not be made up.

Note

1. The responsibilities of the CAA were subsequently transferred to the FAA when President Dwight D. Eisenhower signed the Federal Aviation Act of 1958 into law on August 23, 1958.

19.

A Jet
Program—
But Whose?

Back to Boeing

During the fall of 1955, most major airlines except TWA, which could not move without Howard, placed large orders for jet transports. During that eventful fall, Boeing and Douglas announced the development of JT-4-powered international transports to complement the JT-3-powered versions, which were then termed "domestic" planes. Our calculations confirmed that both of the proposed JT-4-powered models would be capable of performing satisfactory transatlantic services, virtually the same as the passé JT-4-powered CV-18.

PAA placed two huge jet transport orders on October 13, 1955: 20 JT-3-powered Boeing 707's and 25 Douglas DC-8's. On December 19, shortly after Boeing announced the availability of its long-range JT-4-powered model, PAA modified its Boeing order by reducing the number of transcontinental range 707's on order from 20 to 10, with an option to cancel the last 4. At the same time, PAA ordered 12 long-range 300-series 707's. UAL ordered 30 DC-8's on October 25, and AAL ordered 30 707's

on November 9. By December 9, 1955, airlines had placed firm orders for
a total of 186 jet aircraft, including 95 Douglas and 59 Boeing jets:

Airline	Manufacturer and Type	Quantity
PAA	Boeing 707	20
PAA	Douglas DC-8	25
UAL	Douglas DC-8	30
National	Douglas DC-8	6
EAL	Douglas DC-8	26
BOAC	de Havilland Comet IV	20
AAL	Boeing 707	30
Braniff	Boeing 707	5
Air France	Sud Aviation Caravelle	12
KLM	Douglas DC-8	8
Continental	Boeing 707	4

Confronted with these developments, Hughes finally authorized negotiations with Boeing in late December 1955 for the acquisition of a "stopgap" fleet of 8 domestic 707's. I was happy Howard had turned toward
Boeing but shocked and disappointed when I discovered that he intended
to purchase such a limited quantity of domestic planes and none of the
international model.

Ralph Shepard Damon

TWA's problems compounded when it lost one of its truly great presidents
on January 4, 1956, when Ralph Damon died. Some months earlier, Ralph
had gone on a severe diet and lost a great deal of weight, which unquestionably undermined his resistance. Shortly before year's end, on a raw,
blustery, black night, he became bone chilled while dedicating a new
lighted TWA billboard from the roof of the old Astor Hotel at Times
Square, New York. He died only a few days later from pulmonary complications. His death was a terrible shock. I knew of his illness, but like
most, had no idea of its seriousness.

Ralph was always completely straightforward and entirely open to suggestions and new ideas. He was easy to work with and most understanding
of my association with Hughes. Ralph and Howard worked well together,
but Ralph did not hesitate to disagree when he thought he was right. He

took a personal interest in employees, was extremely well liked throughout the ranks, and knew an astounding number of people by their first name.

Ralph Damon's competent leadership had been good for TWA. During his tenure the company had expanded operations and moved away from incipient bankruptcy. Constellation Models 749A, 1049, 1049G, and 1649A were all evolved and ordered, along with the Martin 202A's and 404's. Mixed-class and luxurious "Ambassador" services were introduced, setting industry trends. His accomplishments were many. Ralph's early passing was a tragedy for family, friends, and TWA.

The Orders

In the final days of Damon's life, Hughes's belated authorization triggered an intense negotiation in Seattle between Harry West and me for Howard; and Wellwood Beall and J. B. ("Bruce") Connelly, director of contract administration, for Boeing. It culminated in a letter agreement for the 8 planes and executed January 6, 1956, only two days after Damon died, by F. W. Ayers for Toolco, and Bruce Connelly for Boeing. The detail contract and specifications, not "completed or perfected" at that time, were left open to agreement by February 15 or an agreed extended date.

Howard reconsidered his stopgap position and during the first week of January agreed to negotiate for a sizable fleet of international Boeings. On the same day the letter agreement for the 8 planes was executed, Boeing tendered an offer to sell between 22 and 30 international 707's at a base price of $5,150,000 each, subject to cost escalation and adjustment for changes in the detailed specification, which remained to be negotiated. Now it appeared that if Howard followed through, although TWA would have a late start, it might be able to compete on its international routes quite well, and a limited number of the large planes could be assigned to operate through plane West Coast-Europe services via New York.

By the time Howard had authorized negotiations, the majority of Boeing's early production had been contractually committed to PAA and AAL, Braniff and Continental having agreed to later delivery positions. Boeing offered Howard some of the early delivery positions it had reserved to attract new customers. However, PAA and AAL had already obtained the earliest delivery positions, which, of course, was exactly what the Boeing delivery allocation system was designed to do: reward early customers with the best available positions while retaining some ability to attract additional business.

Howard claimed preemptive understandings on delivery positions, which Boeing refused to acknowledge. This immediately led to intense arguments that continued well after contract execution, indeed, almost until the aircraft were delivered in 1959. I found myself negotiating repeatedly with Bill Allen on delivery matters, including Howard's reported understandings with Bill, which Bill emphatically denied. It was sometimes a delicate, even embarrassing, situation. Harry West; Ray Cook, who had become more active in aircraft contractual matters; and later on, Leonard Schwartz, who had joined Hughes after the Lockheed 1049H, participated in the continuing wrangle.

Bill Allen, like the vast majority of aviation executives I had worked with, was a candid, forthright, and knowledgeable executive. Bill was highly respected throughout the industry. He was always pleasant and positive—the kind of straightforward person I enjoyed working with. He had demonstrated more than once his unique ability to rely on the informed judgment of his extremely competent engineering staff while making major investment decisions, which shaped the course of Boeing and to a major extent that of aviation. His decision to develop the 707 prototype, Model 368-80, was such a case. The principal Boeing executives involved in our 707 negotiations in addition to Allen were Wellwood Beall, executive vice president; Bruce Connelly; George R. Sandborn, sales; Ed Wells, now vice president of engineering; Maynard L. Pennell, chief project engineer; R. L. ("Dick") Rouzie, project engineer; and Jack Steiner, preliminary design.

The Boeing management had been extremely stable through the years, which I viewed as a positive, attractive attribute. The persistence of knowledge of service problems was especially noteworthy. For example, I encountered engineering executives who recalled in accurate detail problems encountered with TWA's Boeing 307 Stratoliners (the fleet was delivered to TWA during 1940) and who had never lost sight of the advisability of avoiding such problems.

Typically, Howard wanted the Boeing negotiations conducted in secret, and they were, at least in the beginning. When the detail specification development period was reached, secrecy became impossible because of the need for my staff, assisted by other TWA technical experts, to participate in concert with representatives from other airlines in detail design standardization activities, which I had pressed Boeing to sponsor. Even so, secrecy was maintained in key contractual matters.

Because AAL and PAA specification negotiations had preceded ours, Boeing's standard specification was essentially what AAL had negotiated, revised somewhat to accommodate PAA's unique requirements. TWA also had unique requirements: flight deck instrumentation and instrument arrangements, air-conditioning system design and performance, the design of certain key aspects of the hydraulic and electrical systems, selection of accessories standard to TWA, autopilot selection, and others. Had Hughes been an earlier customer, Boeing could have complied with many more TWA requirements than was feasible under the circumstances. The specification standardization conferences were effective in many areas, and, while complete standardization was not expected or achieved, they were helpful to all concerned because of the savings ultimately realized through these efforts. Because TWA was able to convince other airlines to adopt some of its unique requirements, Boeing was able to comply with more of our specification objectives than had the conferences not been held.

The definitive contract for the 8 domestic Model 707-131 Boeings was executed on March 2, 1956, by Ayers for Toolco and Connelly for Boeing. Eight domestic Boeings, while better than none, were not sufficient to preserve TWA's markets against the forthcoming onslaught by AAL and UAL. Armed with marketing data, I pressed Hughes to increase the order in his own best interests and urged that Raymond Holliday and Ray Cook do the same if they had the chance. Howard responded but took painfully long. He increased the order in three stages to 15 ships, the last amendment being executed January 10, 1957. Each stage involved extensive efforts to obtain earlier airplane delivery positions, which to a modest extent were successful.

A contract for the purchase of 18 international Model 707-331 Boeings was executed March 19, 1956, by C. H. Price for Toolco and Connelly for Boeing. Thus, on January 10, 1957, when the 15th domestic 707 was ordered, Toolco had on order a total of 33 Boeing jets. I felt that having that many jets on order was something of a personal victory. However, because the 33 Boeings would be flown in competition with that portion of AAL's, PAA's, and UAL's combined fleet of 105 jets, which those airlines would elect to operate in competition with TWA, as well as against competing Lockheed turboprops and jets flown on TWA routes by other airlines, TWA's competitive outlook was sobering, indeed. TWA's principal competitors would clearly have greater latitude in deploying their jet fleets to a strategic advantage than would TWA because of the sheer number of jets available to them. Worse was to come.

A few days after the January 10 contract had been executed, Howard called with a clear, crisp message: *"TWA has no rights whatsoever to the Toolco jets."* After repeating and emphasizing this, he asked that I so advise TWA management. Then he requested that I handle the technical and business aspects of the two Toolco contracts on his behalf as I was doing for Toolco's Lockheed 1649A program. I agreed, hoping some of the authorization problems recently encountered in the 1649A program would not arise. The question of TWA's rights to the jets was troubling, but it seemed inconceivable that the company would not receive the planes.

Howard's Renewed Plans to Manufacture Jets

Howard surprised me when he called within days of closing the initial Boeing contracts and asked that I confer with George Spater, Ray Cook, and Rae Hopper, who was in charge of the Hughes Aircraft Division of Toolco, about obtaining permission from the CAB for Hughes to manufacture jet aircraft for TWA. He indicated, "If we are successful, we should be able to expand the authority later to include other airlines after TWA's requirements are met, so while this aspect should not be mentioned at this time, ask Spater and Cook to consider this when drafting papers so nothing will be done to preclude this possibility."

Howard had in mind manufacturing larger, longer-range jets than had been offered by Boeing and Douglas, similar in concept to the six-engine AVROs and Convair Models 19 and 20, which we had considered earlier. He intended the 18 international Boeings just ordered to tide TWA over until the more advanced planes could be produced. He saw this as an opportunity to establish himself in the large transport market, leapfrogging Boeing and Douglas, who were committed to manufacture 707's and DC-8's for years, and he envisioned TWA's obtaining the same kind of competitive advantage originally foreseen for the initial Constellation program.

I was astonished. Howard was proposing an enormous undertaking that would require years to implement and hundreds of millions of dollars to be invested before any return could be expected. The fact that he could seriously entertain such a huge project after just having ordered 27 Boeings suggested to me that he must have nearly unlimited resources available, which of course was reassuring. I wondered if his interest in manufacturing had anything to do with his delay in buying Boeings.

I met with Spater and Cook in New York to discuss Howard's request. It would be necessary to modify the CAB order of October 17, 1944, which approved control of TWA by Toolco, so the terms of that order would not restrict the right of TWA to purchase jet aircraft from Hughes. The draft Toolco motion that ensued, dated April 20, 1956, which Howard subsequently approved and had submitted to the CAB with hardly any change, limited the number of jets for TWA to 25:

Thorough studies have been made by TWA of the characteristics of all jet aircraft available in this country and abroad. None of these aircraft have the range desirable for all-year around operations across the Atlantic so as to permit non-stop operations under the extreme conditions frequently encountered . . . . During the past few years important new developments have occurred affecting jet aircraft which make it possible to design aircraft at this time that are superior in performance, safety, and economy to the commercial aircraft now being constructed. . . . Hughes Tool Company . . . has advised TWA that the aircraft would be constructed by the aircraft division of the Hughes Tool Company in a new factory to be located in accordance with the recently announced policy of the Air Force to insure the widest possible dispersal of aircraft production facilities.

The motion also indicated that TWA had been advised by Toolco that the jets would be constructed "on terms at least as favorable in every respect as those that can be secured from any manufacturer" and concluded with the request that the 1944 CAB order be amended "so, that the terms of such order will not restrict the right of TWA to acquire from Hughes Tool Company the aircraft . . . and . . . further relief as appropriate." It was filed with the CAB on May 10. Howard called the plan "Greenland" and authorized preliminary studies of possible land acquisition in Florida for the proposed factory.

The CAB responded by issuing on June 8, 1956, an "Order Instituting Investigation." Then, on July 10, John J. Stowell, bureau counsel, issued a "Statement of Issues and Request for Evidence" seeking detailed information on every conceivable aspect of the proposed relationship with TWA and the characteristics of the new plane, which at this point had not been designed.

Howard asked me to develop specifications "which would satisfy the CAB but permit wide latitude in the design of the plane." "Don't you see?" he said. "We can't be tied to specific dimensions, passenger capacity, detailed performance, purchase price and the like at this stage. Bob, confer with Cook and Hopper and see if you can develop suitable responses." I agreed it was much too soon to be specific but expressed doubt that anyone could draft general language that would satisfy the specific questions asked by bureau counsel. We tried, but none of us knew how.

It was the CAB's intention to hold a public hearing on the issues following receipt and review of the requested information. It requested through bureau counsel that "Toolco supply Mr. Howard Hughes as a witness" at such time as the hearing might be held. Howard elected neither to serve as a witness nor even to respond by submitting the requested information. Toolco's filing became dormant and was finally abandoned, but not until 1958. Howard's long-standing desire to produce transport aircraft again came to naught.

Dramatic Engine Purchases

During early 1956, before Toolco's Boeing orders had been placed, P & W offered by wire to sell JT-3 and JT-4 jet engines to the airlines. P & W stated the purchase price would be increased by 5 percent on a specified date, but if engines were ordered before that date, the current price would apply and only a 5-percent down payment would be required. It looked like a no-lose situation for any buyer-furnished or spare engines that might be required.

I knew how many jets TWA needed but did not know when, how many, or what kind of airplanes Howard would finally agree to order. I thought that if a few too many engines were ordered, Howard could likely dispose of any surplus because of the price increase and the obvious budding demand; and that he should "roll dice" and authorize the purchase of a reasonable quantity of spares. This seemed safe enough on firm belief that acquisition of jets for TWA was unavoidable and that they would likely be powered with P & W engines.

I explained this situation to Howard at the Beverly Hills Hotel and recommended that 60 engines be purchased for spares. He immediately authorized the purchase of not 60, but 210 engines—30 JT-3's and 180

JT-4's—for the earliest possible delivery! The order was placed through Toolco during February 1956, after I had conferred with Raymond Holliday and Ray Cook.

T. E. ("Tillie") Tillinghast, P & W's sales manager (no relation to Charles C. Tillinghast, Jr., who became president of TWA in 1961), opposed accepting Hughes's immense order because he feared that Howard might sell the engines or broker the early delivery positions in competition with P & W, as Howard had done when he purchased an excess quantity of engines from Tillie for TWA's Martin 404 program. When P & W hesitated to accept Toolco's order, Howard reacted overnight by ordering an additional 90 JT-4's and forwarding the down payment for all 300 engines. Surprisingly, P & W accepted the orders.

Arguments immediately arose concerning engine delivery dates. I did my best to obtain the earliest possible dates per Howard's request and did quite well, but Howard claimed to have prior understandings, which P & W did not acknowledge, so I was in the middle of a sticky affair that dragged on for months.

Ordering 300 engines that had no clear, assigned purpose was astonishing—bordering on the unbelievable. At a time when a 20-plane order was considered huge, 300 engines were sufficient to equip 60 four-engine transports and provide 60 spares. I assumed that Howard either had in mind providing engines and spares for AVROs, Boeings, or possibly for Hughes-produced jets; or that he indeed intended to tie up the market. Later, after Howard encountered cash-flow problems, a large quantity of Toolco's surplus engines were painstakingly sold with P & W's cooperation.

Noah Dietrich's Firing

It was about this time that Noah Dietrich and one of Howard's Houston lawyers raised questions concerning Howard's sanity. They were concerned with the enormity of his commitments, the fact that he continued to negotiate for still more airplanes, and that no effort whatever was being made to make suitable financing arrangements. They considered his actions irresponsible with respect to the engines. However, I feel sure that Howard had plans never disclosed to turn this near corner on jet engines to his advantage.

During late 1956, while I was at the Hollywood Roosevelt Hotel, Nadine Henley, Howard's private secretary, called with the request that I meet with Noah Dietrich to "discuss Howard's jet programs." I had assumed that Howard had told Noah all he thought Noah needed to know and felt awkward about the proposed meeting because Howard had not personally requested it. When I inquired, Nadine assured me that Howard wanted me to meet with Noah and tell him everything I could that he wanted to know. I agreed.

Noah began the meeting by discussing the scope of Howard's jet program. It quickly became apparent that he was either misinformed or was feigning ignorance for some reason. This surprised me. The facts were widely known within Toolco: The Toolco board had already authorized execution of the airplane and engine procurement contracts, albeit in a somewhat mechanical manner. I had provided Raymond Holliday and Chuck Price, secretary, Toolco, with cash-flow and other program implementation information.

I briefly reviewed the financial scope, the contract delivery dates, broad cash-flow requirements, and the current status of the programs. Additionally, I answered all of Noah's questions that I could, but in a categorical rather than an expansive manner. The meeting was pleasant, but Noah was visibly shocked on hearing of the enormous financial obligation Howard had taken on. It was inconceivable to me that Howard had not kept his chief financial officer fully informed or that he might not have consulted with him before making such major financial commitments and proposing still others, such as Project Greenland.

I should have learned by then not to be surprised by anything that occurred in the Hughes's empire. Even so, I could not have been more surprised when Howard telephoned me at our Mission Hills home on March 11, 1957, with one clear, crisp message: "Bob, Noah Dietrich is out. I want you to call Raymond Holliday, Chuck Price [C. H. Price, secretary, Toolco], and Harry West and tell them of this. Make it clear that it is my request that none of you are to have any more business relations whatsoever with Dietrich that involve my interests. Also, make it clear they are not to say anything about this to anyone until tomorrow, since Noah doesn't know about it yet."

I was shocked because of lack of prior warning, Dietrich's good standing in the financial community, and his long association with Howard. Noah had been Howard's kingpin, who for many years handled Howard's complex fiscal affairs and the financing of major programs. It struck me as an extremely poor time to fire Noah because financing had not been arranged for the Boeing and Convair jet fleets Toolco had belatedly ordered the preceding year.

When Noah went to his office at 7000 Romaine Street the next morning, he found a padlock on the door and brand new locks on all of the other offices. The padlock was the first notice Noah had that he was out.

Noah tells a different story. He claims he suddenly resigned after being refused a capital gains position he had been seeking "for 15 years." On hearing Noah resign over the telephone, Howard said, "Jesus, Noah, you can't mean that. Noah, I can't exist without you."[1]

This is one of a number of things in Noah's book that do not agree with my personal recollections and research. It is true, of course, that Howard's activities almost always involved complex interrelated moves, sometimes taken over extended periods. When recalled years later events might have easily become confused and twisted into a somewhat different scenario. Noah's overall thesis that he was calling the shots, however, whether or not true in other areas, is to my knowledge incorrect in connection with aircraft purchased for TWA. In that field, Howard Hughes might have taken advice, but the decisions were his alone.

The Convair 880

During the third week of March 1956, only a brief period after Howard ordered the 18 international Boeing jets, Howard advised that during recent Las Vegas meetings, Jack Zevely and Ralph Bayless of Convair had proposed a new, smaller jet for domestic use. Howard requested that I examine the proposed Convair design at the earliest opportunity and advise him concerning the potential benefits that TWA could realize from operating such a fleet.

Howard explained that Convair claimed the new model, called the Model 22 Skylark, would be a down-sized, 80-passenger Model 18, designed to efficiently serve medium-range route segments and be capable of nonstop coast-to-coast operations. The nonstop transcontinental capability was extremely attractive because Howard had ordered only nine domestic Boeing 707's at that time, which would be a woefully shy fleet during the inevitable assault by competitive jets. It is noteworthy that at that time, Convair claimed the Skylark could routinely carry in scheduled service 80 passengers and cargo 2,940 nautical miles, which indeed would be sufficient

311

range for transcontinental nonstop service. Even so, my immediate reaction was that Skylarks, if procured, should not be a substitute for acquiring more Boeings but should supplement that fleet.

I commented to Howard that if operational factors including economics were favorable, such planes would unquestionably attract more passengers than would the competing turboprop Lockheed Electras recently ordered by AAL and EAL because of the higher speed and almost complete lack of vibration that could be expected in the jets. Also, the smaller size of the Convairs compared to the Boeings might permit increased flight frequencies in coast-to-coast services by flying during off-peak hours when the Boeings might prove to be too large for a number of years for economical operations. I reminded him that the Electra could not fly coast to coast nonstop and said that procurement of a fleet of the new Convairs was worth serious consideration.

Howard knew I was scheduled to work with Boeing in Seattle on interairline standardization matters. Nevertheless, he asked that I contact Zevely "right away" to arrange for briefings. He said:

I want as good an analysis as you can work out within the next few days since I need to have some answer within a week or so that I can discuss with Collings. . . . Give me the best analysis you can. I don't want this to interfere in any way with your work on the specifications for the 320 [international Boeing]; therefore I made sure Convair's people will be happy to spend as much of this week as you like either in Los Angeles, Seattle, or Kansas City. . . . Convair is waiting to send people tomorrow because I promised General McNarney [Convair's president] an answer right away.

This was one of the fairly frequent periods when TWA had no president. However, John Collings had been named chief executive officer shortly after Ralph Damon's death. Howard had in mind executing a letter of intent to purchase a fleet of Convairs if analysis showed this to be advisable and wanted Collings's pro forma concurrence before confirming his interest to General McNarney.

The initial Skylark briefing was held in Kansas City because the Seattle standardization meetings had been postponed one week. This was followed by Seattle meetings with Convair at the Ben Franklin Hotel during late afternoon and evening sessions every day for a week following the Boeing standardization meetings. Howard had personally arranged for packages of

312

Convair data to be flown to me in Seattle to expedite the study, but the Convair group did not need prodding. Additional Skylark conferences were also held in Washington, D.C., and Los Angeles to examine the merits of the proposed design. The net result of our evaluation was that Howard confirmed to General McNarney serious interest in exploring procurement possibilities.

Almost immediately, intense competitive negotiations erupted between Boeing, Convair, and Lockheed. Lockheed sought to sell Howard turboprop-powered Electras, as it had been doing ever since the AAL order had been announced in 1955, and Boeing vigorously renewed efforts to sell additional domestic 707s.

Howard requested that I accord the highest priority to developing a detailed comparative analysis of fleet operations with Skylark, Electra, and Boeing fleets, again, without interfering with my work "in any way" on the specifications for the 320. This was, of course, impossible, and I am sure Howard knew it.

Bob Gross fired Lockheed's opening negotiating gun in its renewed sales campaign by sending a confirming letter to Hughes, April 3, which read in part:

Following my conversation with you last night, I am sending you herewith four pieces of paper which I think are quite significant in the analysis of the Electra versus the so-called small jet application problem. . . . We have tried in our analyses to lean over backwards to give the Convair and the little Boeing every break; in fact we think we have been somewhat unfair to the Electra. But even so, it indicated that no jet airplane will do everything and that the Electra has a very significant place in TWA's system. . . . I only hope you will allow us to sit down with you personally and point out many aspects of the whole problem that cannot be covered in four brief pieces of paper.

Gross assigned his lead salesman, Kirk Yost, to follow through with TWA. Kirk did his best to work directly with Howard, as did some of the top Boeing and Convair representatives, but unlike Leonard Schwartz, Kirk kept me fully advised, and to my best knowledge he attempted no negotiating end runs.

My staff and I had followed the Electra program from its inception and analyzed potential fleet applications on TWA's domestic system. This work was updated and put in perspective with the other contending fleets.

313

The Electras appeared to be promising airplanes, but I remained convinced that jets could give TWA a strong competitive advantage. I hoped Howard agreed, but I could not be certain.

I had no doubt whatsoever that Lockheed Electras would attract passengers from competing piston flights and that AAL's and EAL's combined fleet of 45 Electras would seriously erode TWA's market if an adequate fleet of offsetting medium-range jets could not be procured. Of course, acquisition of a fleet of Electras for TWA would tend to equalize the competitive equation, but it would not generate the advantage I sought for TWA.

In addition to acquiring a fleet of medium-range jets, I considered the purchase of additional domestic Boeing 707's to be extremely important for TWA because of the large orders for transcontinental jets placed by TWA's primary competition, AAL and UAL. Toolco had ordered 9, whereas AAL and UAL had each ordered 30, with the declared intention of using most of them on their principal domestic routes. TWA could relieve the anticipated severe competitive pressure somewhat by using some of its 18 international 707's in through-plane West Coast to Europe services, but its ability to do so would be limited because the majority of TWA's 18 international 707's would be required to compete in Atlantic services with PAA's jets and those of other international flag carriers. PAA alone had 47 jets on order, many of which would unquestionably be deployed in Atlantic services in competition with TWA.

The domestic Boeing 707's seemed well sized for coast-to-coast and other domestic long-range markets. However, because projections prepared by TWA's traffic department indicated that the 707's would be too large for many of TWA's domestic medium-range markets, even if two piston flights were combined into one jet flight, I undertook with Howard's concurrence to convince Boeing to develop a smaller version of the 707.

The development of a small Boeing seemed inviting because of the likelihood that important standardization advantages could accrue from operating an all-Boeing fleet: common flight decks and flight crew training, which would save considerable expense; commonality of spare parts and accessories, with attendant provisioning savings; common maintenance tooling and practices.

The principal Boeing technical negotiators were my old friend Ed Wells, along with Maynard Pennell and Dick Rouzie. Ed explained that while Boeing had been quietly considering a smaller version of the 707, he was

314

reluctant to undertake another major airplane development project at that time because Boeing's commercial plate was quite full. Nonetheless, because the advent of the Convair Skylark had introduced a new competitive factor, Ed agreed to study the problem to see what could be done without impairing existing programs.

The Boeing men presented within weeks a preliminary design proposal that was severely constrained by Boeing's need to use 707 tooling and components to the maximum feasible extent and the necessity for avoiding extensive new design effort because of engineering manpower limitations. The small Boeing was an almost identical, slightly foreshortened, lightweight version of the standard domestic 707. It was not very attractive compared to what could have been designed had the development constraints not existed. The predicted operating costs were nearly equal to costs expected to be generated by the standard 707. However, because the proposed plane would have had fewer passenger seats, the estimated operating costs were unacceptably high.

Boeing knew perfectly well how to propose a more efficient small jet, but not without downsizing the wing and making other changes, which would have added considerable development expense and usurped manpower from committed programs. With continuing negotiations, Boeing improved its small jet offering, but not enough. However, Boeing persisted with efforts to develop a smaller version of the 707, designating it the "Model 720." During late 1957, over a year after Howard agreed to purchase Convairs, it sold small fleets of 720's to UAL and AAL. Subsequently, six were ordered by Northwest.

Howard continued to insist on the highest order of secrecy concerning our negotiations, despite the fact that little secrecy existed. All three manufacturers produced detailed comparative studies of the four contending planes. Consequently, many people were knowledgeable concerning the Skylark, and leaks occurred. Even so, Howard required the use of pseudonyms in the San Diego area until shortly before contract execution.

The basic strategy for dealing with Convair was set during a telephone conversation between Hughes and me that occurred when I was in Palo Alto attending a NACA Operating Problems Committee meeting. Harry West had sent to me in Seattle copies of a short form contract prepared by Convair, which Howard had asked him to review and discuss with me. I did not like its tone or substance, and asked Harry to meet me at the Palo Alto hotel for discussion.

To my surprise, when I objected to the terms, Harry led me to believe that Howard had already indicated by phone that he considered the terms acceptable. After discussing the reasons for my views with Harry, I placed a call to Hughes, an act that Harry did not fully appreciate, possibly for fear that my call might agitate Howard or contradict viewpoints Harry may have already expressed.

Howard returned my call within a few minutes, as if he might have been expecting to hear from me. I explained that the Convair paper as written would give Convair the right to charge extra for any and all items, possibly hundreds of them—even changes in language—which arguably should be included in the detailed specification at no extra cost as a pro forma matter or as a result of mutual determination of the design details that should be adopted as part of the standard design configuration. I did not suggest that Convair would in fact take undue advantage of this language, which according to Harry, Convair representatives had indicated was inviolate; I just wanted to close the door of opportunity to exorbitant price increases and set the stage for negotiating on a more equitable basis. I also indicated that I did not like the certification language and the requirement that the customer pay for the full costs of compliance with any changes in CAA regulations promulgated after contract signing.

All this got Howard's attention. I recommended the same approach that I had suggested earlier for the Model 18 negotiation, which had worked well, that is, to write a brief rather than detailed specification, setting forth design and performance objectives, and a letter contract that tied down only minimum essentials such as base price, airplane delivery schedule, payment schedule, and mission guarantee, but which deliberately left open details for future resolution for inclusion in a long-form contract and specification to follow.

With respect to the cost of design changes, I proposed that agreement be held in abeyance until just before execution of the long-form contract. I suggested that would be the most opportune time to negotiate, our negotiating position would be the strongest, and "package" prices could be discussed meaningfully. However, I concluded, "The practicality of this overall approach is dependent on changing the proposed short-form contract as I suggest."

Howard agreed with this strategy and asked Harry and me to proceed accordingly. Convair agreed in principle with the objective language approach, but the compromise language finally made part of the short-form contract was not nearly as objective as I had wanted.

Convair required a minimum of 40 Skylarks to be ordered because anything less represented an unacceptable risk for incurring excessive program losses. In response to Howard's request, I had recommended that 30 be purchased for TWA, based on an exhaustive route analysis that attempted to take into account TWA's future competitive situation and which reflected the opinions of TWA's Traffic Department, my staff, and me.

When the preliminary detail specification discussions were well under way, Delta agreed to order 10 Skylarks on Hughes's acquiescence. The short-form contracts were executed June 7, 1956. An unusual aspect of the Toolco 30-plane contract was that an airplane delivery schedule for 40 planes was included, along with the proviso: "Prior to execution of the definitive purchase agreement . . . , Buyer shall designate the aircraft by manufacturing number to be delivered to Buyer with due regard to delivery positions desired by Delta Air Lines as an initial purchaser of Model 22 aircraft with Buyer." The final contract required Delta to agree to Toolco's designation of Delta's 10 delivery positions.

J. F. ("Nick") Nycum, Delta's Manager Flight Equipment Development, handled specification negotiations and served as the technical liaison agent for Delta. Every effort was made through joint meetings between TWA and Delta representatives to achieve complete standardization, except for passenger accommodations. The degree of standardization achieved through these efforts was exceptional, stood to expedite construction, and reduced the cost for design changes common to the two airlines.

Convair had selected General Electric's CJ-805 jet engines to power the Skylarks. The CJ-805 was new, a commercial derivative of GE's J-79 engine, which had performed quite well in military service but had never been exposed to the intensity of operations common to commercial transports. I was apprehensive, perhaps experience-shy because of the unsatisfactory Lockheed 1449A turboprop engine situation, and I had never considered it good policy to purchase new airplanes powered by new engines. It was risky enough to buy new planes with proven power plants. However, because all available jet engines were new to commercial aviation, little choice existed. The contending engine, which I understood Convair had ruled out during formative Las Vegas discussions with Hughes, was P & W's brand new bypass JT-8 engine. It was heavier but developed greater thrust and would have made a good engine for a somewhat upgraded Skylark. P & W representatives made repeated efforts to interest Howard and me in requiring Convair to install JT-8 engines. Because it would have required basic design changes and delayed airplane delivery beyond the peak-traffic summer period of 1960, which was our delivery target, we rejected this idea.

GE was extremely anxious to enter the commercial engine field. Jack S. Parker, then head of GE's Aircraft Gas Turbine Division and later of the president's office, saw the development of the CJ-805 as a means to accomplish this goal. Neil Burgess, GE's manager of engine products, had been assigned the task of selling the CJ-805 to the airframe manufacturers and had convinced Ralph Bayless and his associates that the CJ-805 was the right engine for the Skylark.

I wanted direct assurance concerning GE's intention to support the engine by expediting any revision engineering that service experience might prove to be necessary, ensuring the adequate availability of spare parts, and establishing acceptable warranted maintenance expense ceilings and parts pricing policies. I spent two days with Jack Parker and his associates in Cincinnati to discuss points of concern and to become more familiar with background military operations with the parent engine. Jack was most cooperative and convincing concerning GE's long-term intention regarding the commercial engine business. To help prove the point, he offered to reduce the price of any spare CJ-805's purchased by Hughes or TWA by $25,000 per engine. Later, 58 spare engines were ordered at a savings of $1,450,000.

The GE engines proved to be troublesome and expensive to operate. It was even necessary to operate at reduced thrust for extended periods because of stubborn hot-section problems. Confronted daily with pressure to maintain flight schedules, TWA's maintenance and provisioning people complained and grumbled incessantly about GE's product-support performance, including cost-recovery aspects. They produced charts and data that convinced me that GE had failed miserably to live up to both the spirit and letter of its obligations.

After this had gone on long enough to establish the facts, I requested a detailed accounting of related technical and cost factors with the intention of personally pounding the table and exacting financial retribution from Jack Parker and his associates. The TWA report required nearly one year to complete and was presented to me somewhat sheepishly. Contrary to the rampant TWA criticism that existed almost from the first, the report indicated that GE had met its after-delivery obligations in a satisfactory manner, including cost-recovery aspects. I heard little carping after that.

TWA's and Delta's poor experience with CJ-805's generally undermined GE's position and tended to discourage additional engine sales. The fact that GE had met its support obligations overcame much of this and helped pave the way for it to become one of the world's major suppliers of commercial aircraft turbines. Reminiscing in the late 1980s, Jack Parker said, ''The CJ-805 had too many operational problems, but the fact that we bent over backwards to support the using airlines established our reputation and opened the commercial transport world to GE.''

Not long before execution of the detailed contract, Convair dropped the name ''Skylark'' and gave the aircraft a new designation: Model 880. For reasons that were never made clear to me, the 880 project, including Howard's and Delta's intentions, was announced considerably before the definitive contract was executed by either airline. This seemed to be especially undesirable because it tended to weaken our negotiating position by leading Convair to believe an affirmative buy decision was a foregone conclusion.

Howard insisted that the announcement emphasize that the planes would look like ''shimmering gold'' and be called ''Golden Arrows.'' This caught the imagination of the press, which I suppose was part of his intention. Howard had not bothered to discuss with me the ''shimmering gold'' aspect, which was not part of the specifications, and which I knew to be impractical. The Convair sales group was enthusiastic, but Bayless and his engineers saw this as I did. At the first opportunity, I explained to Howard that the exterior surfaces of the 880 would consist of several different aluminum alloys, and even the best-controlled anodized gold finishes would be of somewhat different hue for each alloy. Color bleeding could be anticipated; the aluminum rivets would appear as aluminum, not gold, because the flush-headed rivets would be automatically machine polished after being driven. Thus, I said, ''The planes would appear something like a stitched crazy quilt, despite everyone's best efforts.''

Howard thought Convair could work this out. ''This is too good a sales gimmick not to move forward,'' he said, and told me to ''see that this is done.'' I reviewed this matter with Ralph Bayless and Aluminum Company of America representatives, who reconfirmed what I had told Howard.

319

About that same time, Bob Six, president of Continental Air Lines (CAL), called and objected to the reference to "shimmering gold" and "Golden Arrow" in the Convair press releases, saying that any such references in future advertising would be completely unacceptable because of the "gold" service theme CAL had been using for some time. However, Bob's comments did not seem to phase Howard in the least.

I suggested to Ralph Bayless that the impasse might be solved if Convair would agree to a "best-efforts" side letter of agreement to the contract, but cautioned that if Convair did, a further serious effort to comply would of course be required. He agreed. I discussed this approach with Howard, explaining that Convair still did not know how to produce acceptably uniform shimmering gold, but that it would formally agree to use its best efforts to produce the desired result. I warned him that I doubted that Convair would succeed. Howard reluctantly agreed to this approach. Convair's further efforts only confirmed previous findings, and the shimmering gold idea was eventually dropped.

The definitive contract between Toolco and Convair for the purchase of 30 Convair 880's shows it was executed on September 10, 1956, by Raymond Holliday for Toolco and Jack Naish for Convair, but the deal was not in fact concluded at that time. Convair had forwarded to Toolco at Houston by letter of September 8 for execution two copies of the definitive contract, which had been signed by Naish and postdated on September 10, 1956. This was done in anticipation that Howard would immediately authorize contract execution. Instead, he and I continued to negotiate because open items remained.

Three days later, September 13, Howard telephoned and discussed at great length unresolved pricing issues concerning the cost of design changes and the restoration of the original airplane delivery dates, in lieu of the two-month slippage Convair had claimed was unavoidable. He requested that I provide him with "a current statement of [TWA] management's position on the advisability of proceeding with the Golden Arrow program."

The same day, after calling John Collings to relay Howard's request for "management's position," I called Jack Zevely to discuss the cost of design changes and the other open items I had just reviewed with Howard. As anticipated, TWA and Delta had requested a large number of design changes during detail specification negotiations. In accordance with the stratagem agreed to with Howard during June before the preliminary agreement was negotiated, neither I nor any of my associates had agreed that any of Convair's prices for design changes were reasonable or acceptable. We simply deferred all discussions on costs until all of the information had been made available for all of the changes. Convair Engineering did not like this, but they were cooperative.

I reminded Zevely of this during the call, adding that I had been reviewing the whole price situation fast and furiously in relation to what the airplane might be expected to do for TWA. The lengthy item-by-item discussion with Jack that followed and meetings held during the next week or so resulted in Convair's agreement to reduce the price of changes for Howard's 30-plane fleet by approximately the price of one airplane. The strategy worked. Howard seemed pleased but expressed little appreciation for my efforts.

In response to my having relayed Howard's request to John Collings, John called a meeting the following morning attended by Busch; Cocke; Henry D. Fellows, schedule planning; Clyde S. Fullerton, general sales manager; Rourke; Weller; and me to develop TWA's final position concerning the purchase of the 30 880's. John reconfirmed the results of the meeting early Friday evening after checking the recommended position with absent TWA officers.

I recorded TWA's position, which agreed with my personal recommendations, in my letter of September 17 to John, which stated in part:

1. Not interested at $4,000,000. per airplane.

2. Thinks it is the best airplane for TWA if purchased in the realm of $3,100,000.

3. Thinks market is limited, but on information that PAA may buy 30, thinks Convair may sell 150 ships and, therefore, recommend going forward with the deal provided the contract is changed to exclude the principle of "fundamentally dissimilar" and substitute the principle of "outgrowth of design. . . ." [Convair had agreed to rebate a portion of the purchase price of each of the 30 planes because of TWA's contributions to the design of the 880's, the amount being dependent on the number of aircraft sold in addition to the first 40, but they had refused to define derivative aircraft models to be included in the count, as I wanted. The sale of a total of 150 planes would have reduced the unit price to approximately $3,150,000.]

4. If the contract is not so changed, recommend not purchasing these aircraft. [This item was included at my request to provide Howard and me with a stronger negotiating position.]

TWA also recommended seeking further monetary protection against changes in CAA regulations but concluded that Howard should not consider this a go-no-go issue. My letter also recorded that I had reminded Hughes, "There could be no positive assurance that PAA would buy 30 Golden Arrows."

I reported TWA's position to Howard on the evening of September 14, shortly after John's call. He accepted this as TWA management's concurrence that he procure the 30-plane fleet for TWA's use.

Howard also discussed important open issues with me during the same call. He asked me to call Jack Zevely and tell him I was calling "as an authorized representative of the Hughes Tool Company," and I was calling for Howard inasmuch as Howard had been unable to reach him by phone. Howard asked me to emphatically demand of Convair that the original airplane delivery schedule be reinstated and to tell Jack that he would personally settle the question of allocation of the 10 Delta delivery positions with C. E. Woolman, the president of Delta. Howard "regretted that Convair got into the Delta act" and repeated that he would handle this and that I should so advise Zevely. He concluded, "Tell Zevely that if he could agree with our points, I will immediately authorize signing the papers in Houston."

Howard never functioned on the Delta delivery allocation matter. Later, after manufacture of the planes in compliance with Delta's special requirements had been unconscionably delayed by his procrastination, Convair proposed to fairly allocate essentially every fourth delivery position to Delta. Toolco tacitly acquiesced, but Howard never formally agreed.

I followed through during a lengthy telephone discussion with Jack Zevely the following morning, September 15, after Howard's Romaine Street Mormons had located him. Jack agreed to comply with most of our positions, discuss the remaining issues with General McNarney and Jack Naish, and let me know the result.

After agreement had been achieved on the controversial items, Toolco wrote a letter to Convair on September 20 and sent a confirming telegram the same day to the effect that it had executed the contract for the purchase of 30 880's with the proviso that telegrams of understandings dated September 17, 19, and 20 had been deemed to have been included as part of the contract. The agreements were conditioned on execution of a contract for the purchase by Delta of 10 of the 40 880's covered by the Convair-Toolco agreement of June 7. On September 21, 1956, Convair confirmed by telegram to Toolco that the Delta contract had been executed.

A few days later, Howard called with the now familiar message, "TWA has no rights whatsoever . . . ." He asked me to represent Toolco as its special representative during the 880 contract implementation period, with authority to act in all matters except for changes in aircraft mission and delivery dates. As before, he set no personal financial limits of authority but said that progress payments and other financial obligations would be handled by Houston. Later, I formally set financial limits for myself, which made my signature in the name of Toolco worth about $19 million.

When Howard increased his order for domestic Boeing jets to 15 during January 1957, a total of 63 jets were on order by Toolco, presumably for TWA's use. I was certain this fleet would satisfy TWA's needs during the initial jet age but that TWA would likely need additional jets within two, possibly three years.

Because all 63 planes were to be manufactured in accordance with TWA specifications, because Howard had chosen at long last to purchase fleet quantities that corresponded to TWA's recommendations, and because all of Toolco's contracts permitted it to assign the jets to TWA without the manufacturer's consent, TWA's management, including me, believed that TWA should plan on receiving all 63. Now, the job ahead was to help ensure that the jets measured up to specifications and for TWA to prepare to make efficient use of the 63-plane fleet. Or so we thought.

Note

1. Noah Dietrich and Bob Thomas, *Howard: The Amazing Mr. Hughes* (Greenwich, Connecticut: Fawcett Publications, 1972), p. 294.

20.

Jet Program Implementation

Howard's order for 30 Convair 880's was greeted with enthusiasm and relief at TWA. Now, instead of standing on the sidelines while our competitors equipped, it appeared that TWA would be fully competitive. The news that TWA "had no rights" had not spread. Morale picked up, more smiles were seen, and brighter days seemed assured.

One of my first jobs was to man our construction surveillance offices at Boeing and Convair. It had been TWA's practice since the DC-1 development program to establish "plant representative" offices at airframe manufacturers during production to ensure compliance with the procurement specifications and provide liaison between the home office and the manufacturer. In addition to the representative, small staffs of carefully selected inspectors were provided to better ensure compliance and help keep the shop personnel aware of customer requirements. Such inspectors usually became TWA lead inspectors or training instructors after aircraft delivery. The plant representative offices had more than proved their worth through the years.

Ralph Ellinger, who had a wealth of engineering knowledge and valuable operating experience, was easily the number one candidate to head our factory offices. However, because Ralph was thoroughly established as TWA's plant representative at Lockheed, where he was sorely needed because of 1649A problems, I placed him in a policy-overview relationship with our representatives at Boeing and Convair to better enable TWA to benefit from his knowledge. Ralph contributed significantly to our jet programs, just as he had done on every TWA aircraft since the DC-1, until his untimely passing on September 11, 1960.

One of the potential candidates for the plant representative position in Seattle was Edwin Zak, who was in charge of maintenance for TWA's entire International Division. Ed had joined TWA in 1942, served as an instructor at TWA's Eagles Nest wartime flying school near Albuquerque, and worked in various management positions for Ray Dunn and then Jim Davis, who had preceded him as head of international maintenance. Ed's background seemed to ideally suit him for the plant representative job. While I was on a quick trip to Europe for conferences with de Havilland and Sud Aviation, I met Ed in Paris to learn if he might be interested. His wife, Juanita, joined us for dinner in a small, intimate restaurant near the Champs Elysees. It was a fine evening, but nothing definite developed.

After returning to Kansas City, I contacted W. L. ("Larry") Trimble, who was in charge of TWA's International Division, and requested that Zak come in for an interview if he were interested. Zak had the impression that an interview would be a waste of his and my time because he had not had a great deal of formal engineering education. Larry said, "Ed, I don't know about that, but why don't you do it? It's a free ride to the States, and you could stop in Chicago and see your parents."

Ed said later that he did not expect to get the job and figured he was just "going along for a free ride." When he expressed the same reservations to me that he had to Trimble, I said, "Hell, Ed, Boeing is full of engineers. What we need is a manager with a practical background: someone who can spot potential problems before they develop and knows what to do to avoid them." Ed accepted the job. He discovered later that being involved in a Hughes project was not exactly a small corner of paradise.

Ralph Ellinger called me about the same time and indicated that John Guy might be interested in leaving his Oregon ranch and returning to TWA. I had met John shortly after I joined TWA, worked with him, knew of his contributions, and was altogether confident he would do an outstanding job as Zak's assistant and our chief inspector at Boeing. After several telephone calls, John agreed to accept the Seattle position. With John and Ed on board I knew the Seattle office was in competent, experienced hands. In 1964, when Ed accepted the plant representative job at Douglas, I placed John in charge at Boeing.

Somewhat later, a search was undertaken to locate someone with the proper qualifications to handle the plant representative job at Convair. The result was the appointment of J. William Bew to this position during June 1957. Neither Bew, nor I, nor anyone else then had the slightest inkling of the debacle that would befall Convair's 880 program.

I explained to the three men that they and those working for them would represent the Hughes Tool Company through me as its special representative; the planes were on order by Toolco, not TWA; their salaries would be paid by TWA; and company seniority and other personnel matters would be unaffected by this circumstance.

Seating Plans

I was absolutely certain that the superb passenger comfort attributes of the jets—I had recently flown from Chicago to Seattle in Boeing's 367-80 prototype—ensured the enthusiastic acceptance of jet transportation by the flying public, and that the public preference for jet transportation would overwhelm the piston fleets and render them prematurely obsolescent at great loss, just as Ralph Damon had predicted.

To postpone this eventuality and the need for expanding the jet fleets, and because it would have been patently impractical and ineffective for TWA to act alone, I proposed that TWA take the lead in establishing a unified industry program as follows: (1) Place a moderate surcharge on jet passenger fares. (2) Offer five-abreast, all-first-class seating on the Boeings and four-abreast, all-first-class seating on the Convair 880's (the Convair fuselage was not wide enough to accommodate five-abreast seats), rather than mixed-class interiors. (3) Offer all-skycoach piston flights on schedules paralleling the prime jet flights, but without a fare surcharge. (4) Later, after the life of the pistons had been extended by these means and marketing conditions so required, provide mixed-class service on the jets, retaining the jet surcharge as long as possible.

I wrote letters proposing this approach to Oz Cocke and Vic Leslie, and discussed this subject with them and others in senior management. My plan did not elicit enthusiastic support.

327

The most important deterrent was that discussions with other airlines could not take place without first obtaining permission from the CAB because of the antitrust laws. Because I saw important advantages to TWA if CAB permission could be obtained and the airlines convinced of the soundness of my plan, I urged that the effort be made. However, TWA did not take action at that time on belief that it was untimely to do so, and on the supposition that the effort would not be likely to succeed.

Then I suggested that TWA file with the CAB for the fare surcharge and proceed with the five-abreast, all-first-class Boeing interiors, and the CAB filing be made well in advance of the anticipated service dates so the filing could be withdrawn and replacement seats ordered if other airlines did not join. TWA's Finance and Traffic departments approved the five-abreast plan for the domestic Boeings, and I arranged for the design of the Toolco planes to proceed accordingly in confidence that the CAB fare filing would be handled at the opportune time.

Later on, after five-abreast, first-class seats had been ordered for TWA's domestic Boeings, C. R. Smith and Pat Patterson announced, respectively, that AAL and UAL would provide four-abreast, first-class and six-abreast coach seating compartments on its jets. This killed my plan. Almost overnight, at considerable effort, our five-abreast seats became four abreast by the removal of seat cushions and backs and the insertion of a table between seats on the left, three-abreast side; and the construction of six-abreast coach seats was expedited. TWA's domestic Boeings were initially delivered with first-class and coach compartments so configured. Later, more spacious four-abreast, first-class seats were installed with a central aisle.

With this turn of events, the course of the industry was set. The pistons would compete head-on with the jets, which I claimed would unquestionably cause premature economic obsolescence of the pistons, and generally cause the airlines to accelerate the procurement of jet fleets. I knew that if history proved me to be correct, which it did, the price to be paid by the industry would be extremely high from rushing unnecessarily rapidly into the jet age. On the other hand, the public would have a wider choice of jet flights and services available sooner than if my plan had been followed.

The existence of the Convair 880 program may have contributed to Smith's and Patterson's decision to offer four-abreast, first-class services because the Convairs were deliberately designed to have the advantage of four-abreast, first-class seats, compared to five abreast in the Boeings. I had hoped the revenue advantage of five-abreast seats in the Boeings would prevail, but for whatever reason, Smith and Patterson decided otherwise.

The CAB came forward before U.S. jet services were inaugurated with permission for the industry to levy a jet surcharge for a defined period.

Carter Burgess's Participation

One of the first things I did after Burgess was elected president of TWA on January 23, 1957, was apprise him of Toolco's orders for the Boeing and Convair jets, including Howard's admonition that "TWA has no rights whatsoever" to the transports. On March 5, I sent Carter a confidential letter listing Toolco's anticipated jet delivery dates by airplane type and month of delivery to aid in the planning of future TWA jet operations. It was prepared on the assumption that TWA would receive all 63 of the Toolco jets, and necessarily contained the following qualifications:

1. There is no assurance that TWA will receive any or all of the jets currently on order by the Hughes Tool Company.
2. Boeing is currently scheduling production three months in advance of the dates shown.
3. Final determination of delivery sequence of Delta's ten Convairs out of the first forty to be manufactured has not been made.

Clearly not a satisfactory planning premise for TWA, this was the best I could produce that accorded with Howard's directives. I hoped that Howard would soon offer TWA a contractual arrangement validating that TWA would receive the jets, and thereby permit TWA to prepare for their use in a timely and efficient manner, including making the necessary associated financial commitments. However, I could offer Carter no encouragement along this line.

TWA's not having jets directly on order wore heavily on Burgess, who was painfully aware of minority stockholders' interests and the fact that TWA's future competitive position appeared to be entirely a matter of decision by Hughes rather than TWA's management. Carter appreciated the vital need for TWA to have fully competitive fleets for the long-term survival of the corporation and became deeply concerned over the lack of resolution of the jet availability issue.

329

Carter called me in mid-1957 and requested that I contact Boeing to see if it would be willing to sell TWA fleets of Boeing jets equal in number to those Toolco had on order. I tried to discourage this approach because I thought it would be received extremely poorly by Howard, and I was confident that Howard would ultimately release the Toolco jets to TWA. Nevertheless, Carter insisted that I take this up with Boeing.

I discussed Carter's request with Bruce Connelly by telephone. After thinking it over a few minutes, Bruce responded, "Bob, there isn't any way Boeing can agree to sell jets to TWA without first receiving Howard's permission and without knowing of the disposition of the jets Howard already has on order." He explained his position, which I thought was reasonable, after which I passed the word on to Carter. As far as I ever knew, that ended Carter's inquiry into TWA direct-purchase possibilities.

Carter's concern was understandable. It was important for TWA to prepare to deploy the jets if indeed it were to receive them. This would involve expending millions of dollars. I wanted TWA to move forward with implementation planning and make the necessary financial commitments in a timely manner; but I did not know how it could do so without Howard's agreement to assign the jet contracts to TWA or to bear the associated TWA costs if he did not make the jets available. This knotty problem was not completely solved until well after TWA introduced jet services.

Carter had taken a keen interest in the passenger accommodations planned for TWA's Convair 880's. He, a fairly large group of senior executives, selected members of my staff, and I flew to San Diego in the fall of 1957 to examine, critique, and hopefully approve Convair's full-scale passenger interior mock-up. Convair had worked closely with TWA during the development phase and complied nicely with our requirements, including a red, white, and blue color scheme selected by Carter. Having checked out the mock-up and display material the day before, I was expected to take the lead with Carter during the conference.

It was to be a big day. Convair had prepared an elaborate conference room adjacent to the mock-up filled with diagrams, fabric samples, carpet-swatch boards, photographs, and artist's renderings of the interior. Convair's top brass and technical experts were to be on hand to meet Carter and present briefings. I arrived about a half hour early and was greeted by a Convair guard at the outside gate with an "urgent" message to call Bill Gay.

I called Bill from a nearby booth. Bill said that Howard was "extremely anxious'' to talk to me and that the matter was ''exceptionally urgent.'' I explained that I was obligated to introduce Carter and would call Howard ''in about an hour.'' Bill said Howard was standing by for my call, which I should make at once; I should do nothing to alter the mock-up review meeting plans; Howard did not want me to call from any telephone on Convair property, including public telephone booths; and Howard wanted me to return immediately to the Town & Country Motel, where I was staying, to receive his call. When I attempted to argue with Bill, he said, ''No, Bob, this is urgent and important. You must immediately return to the T & C. Howard will call you when you arrive. Don't even wait to explain this to Convair. I'll take care of that.''

I reluctantly returned to the Town & Country, but before doing so I asked Russ Rourke to explain to Carter and the Convair people that I would be a bit late, and I would return as soon as possible.

The phone was ringing when I arrived at the motel. It was Howard. He began by asking what Carter was doing in San Diego. Then he wanted to know who else from TWA and Convair would attend the conference. I explained and indicated the need for me to attend the conference and introduce Carter. Howard said, ''Fine, Bob, fine. Just as soon as we are through talking.''

Howard talked about airplane design, performance, safety, and recent airline accidents, but said nothing about active current projects, including the mock-up conference. I saw nothing urgent about any aspect of the call. Except for one 10-minute relief break, the call lasted until 7:15 in the evening, 30 minutes after Carter had left San Diego for New York. I was exhausted from not having eaten anything since breakfast, 10 hours of the kind of intense concentration that usually accompanied technical conversations with Howard, and probably as a reaction to being disappointed with myself for having responded to Howard's ''urgent'' call instead of attending the mock-up conference.

Howard's call did not make much sense to me. He obviously did not want me at Convair that day, possibly to cause Carter embarrassment, but I do not think my absence could have had that effect. And it certainly was not necessary to show who was the big boss. Later, when I explained the reason for my absence, Carter did not appear to be aggravated, and I thought he had dismissed the incident as an example of Hughes's sometimes oddball antics. Not long afterwards, however, he resigned from TWA.

Jet Integration Planning

It was clear that every sector of TWA would ultimately be affected by its transition from piston to jet operations: airport terminals, fuel farms, ground support equipment, reservation systems, flight operations, maintenance facilities and practices, flight training, airport runways, aircraft gates, and all the rest. Making ready to deploy the jets meant the virtual creation of a new airline. It was also obvious that millions of dollars would be required to properly prepare the airline, and sound planning and efficient implementation activities would be required to minimize investments and help ensure efficient operations.

TWA's initial jet integration planning effort, which began shortly after the Toolco jets were ordered, was centered in the Flight Operations Department. Plans being made with respect to flight operations appeared to be satisfactory, but the planning either lacked authority or was not using it to firmly establish company-wide premises, goals, and schedules. Many of the plans the department had developed lacked acceptance and support by senior management. I wrote a letter to Carter Burgess on December 24, 1957, pointing out the need for establishing a top-level "jet planning" function to assure the development of coordinated programs acceptable to senior management and compatible with the function Toolco's jets were intended to fulfill.

I do not know if Carter ever read the letter before he left office on December 31. A management committee was established after Carter's departure consisting of Warren Lee Pierson, chairman; Oz Cocke; and Vic Leslie. Around mid-January, Pierson, who had read my letter to Burgess, called and asked me to take over TWA's jet planning function. I agreed to propose a new planning organization for his acceptance and suggested that a top-level management meeting be held at New York headquarters in two weeks to review and approve the organization plan, adding, "If my proposal is agreeable with all concerned, I will be glad to serve as chairman of the jet planning function." Warren agreed to call such a meeting and to have all officers and key flight operations personnel present.

Two concepts were the cornerstones of the organizational plan I advanced: Jet planning must function within the existing TWA organization; and those responsible for implementing the programs must participate in the development of the premises and plans, agree that the mutually developed objectives are reasonably attainable, and approve the plans prior to submitting the plans to the president for acceptance. Once presidential approval was obtained, the plans were to become corporate objectives. The practice of directly involving those ultimately responsible for program implementation in the planning process and requiring their concurrence that the plans were practical and achievable (if not, they would be revised accordingly) worked very well indeed for TWA's jet planning program. Industry and government alike would be far better off if this practice were generally followed.

I proposed the establishment of a Jet Planning Staff consisting of the two senior vice presidents, six vice presidents, the corporate secretary, the director of personnel, and me as chairman. Its primary function was to approve plans and premises for submission to the president and make certain that jet integration plans were implemented on schedule. I also proposed the establishment of a Jet Working Group consisting of designated action representatives of every major department. The group's charge was to formulate significant action recommendations for submission to the jet planning chairman and jet staff for approval, take cognizance of the detailed planning activities of their departments, and keep the jet planning chairman currently advised of overall departmental planning and implementation activities.

During the New York meeting, I suggested that Russ Rourke serve as deputy jet planning chairman and Marcy Fannon as coordinator to maintain detailed surveillance over the program and record its status. The primary function of this three-man jet planning management team was to ensure that realistic interdepartmental project completion schedules were established, all essential work was covered, associated costs were minimal, troublesome areas were flagged out and corrected, and funding and consolidated cash-flow forecasts were provided to the senior vice president of finance and the president. Pierson and those present approved the proposed jet planning organization and personnel, as proposed.

Only three control documents were used by the Jet Planning Staff throughout the planning and implementation exercise. One contained the plans and premises: Each page set forth a premise or plan that had been agreed to by all affected departments, such as aircraft delivery dates, start of service dates, stations to be served, assignment of aircraft by division, and the like. A second document listed and summarized the status of each project—there were hundreds of them—and showed if they were on schedule. The third report contained capital and cash flow requirements, and showed current financial commitments. Each was kept continuously up to date.

The financial commitment status reports were especially helpful because they were always appreciably more up to date than reports prepared by the Finance Department. The weeks normally required for routine paper flow were circumvented by knowing of the detail commitments when they were made. Additionally, special status reports were issued by my office from time to time when occasion required. The most frequent cause for such reports was to emphasize the critical need to receive supplemental commitment authority for implementation of the approved projects.

In order to cope, Vic Leslie established two nonduplicative capital budgets, one for regular corporate affairs, and one for the jet implementation program. Funding the jet implementation program was extremely troublesome because of the inability of TWA's board to authorize funds—it would not have done so anyway without Howard's approval—because TWA had no bona fide rights to the jets.

At this point my plate was overflowing. In addition to regular departmental duties, managing the Toolco jet programs, and handling special assignments from Howard, I had a new major corporate obligation: jet planning. Seventy-hour work weeks were the norm, and 80-hour weeks were not exceptional. I had little time for the family, which was not fair to them, and which bothered me deeply. Today, when I hear people complaining about the stress of 40-hour-per-week jobs, I have difficulty understanding what their problems are.

During the year that followed execution of the 880 contract, Howard was largely out of touch, sometimes for a month or more at a time. He was out of the country much of that period and would occasionally call, but he was extremely difficult to reach. Lack of commitment authority from Toolco for TWA (or anyone else) to purchase BFE and spare parts for the Boeing program became hypercritical, just as it had for the 1649A Constellations. These types of expenditures were considered an inherent part any of aircraft procurement program and were normally authorized by the board on program approval.

When I was unable to reach Howard, I tried to persuade Raymond Cook, Raymond Holliday, and Chuck Price of Toolco to arrange for the necessary commitment authority. I argued that spare parts and BFE would be required if the jets were to be operated by TWA or any other airline, and in any event, the purchase of this equipment was necessary to protect Howard's investment in the jets and ensure profitable use. After all, transports without spares could not be legally or effectively deployed. The Toolco officers and counsel were sympathetic, but their hands were also tied.

Earlier, Jim Shaunty; H. I. ("Red") Reynard, director of provisioning; and I, without Toolco authority, had persuaded numbers of the vendors to manufacture equipment for Toolco without receiving purchase orders because the aircraft were being manufactured and certain to be deployed by some airline, the equipment would be needed, and little or no financial risk would be incurred. Boeing's policy was to manufacture spare airframe components concurrently with the aircraft, so while the lack of timely orders was annoying, Boeing continued to manufacture an appropriate quantity of spare parts for the Toolco planes without having received purchase orders. However, the time came when the vendors and Boeing ran completely out of patience.

At that time, Ray Cook at long last reached Howard and persuaded him to authorize TWA to order to Toolco's account a limited quantity of airplane spare parts and BFE for the Boeings, and GE CJ-805 spare engines for the Convair program through me as its "Special Agent"—the same solution that had been reached earlier for the 1649A's. However, much greater authority was needed to fully prepare the airline. To obtain the customary airline discounts not available to nonairline customers, the TWA purchase orders contained the following stipulation: "The parts ordered are intended solely for the use of Trans World Airlines in its scheduled airlines operation and . . . Trans World is acting here as the agent for Hughes Tool Company, solely for the purpose of financing this purchase order for TWA's use." The inclusion of this language was contrary to Hughes's "no rights" admonition and caused a flap between Toolco and TWA lawyers after most of the orders had been placed, notwithstanding that use of this language had been cleared verbally with Houston at the outset.

Ray Cook believed that it was appropriate for Toolco to provide funds for the purchase of items that could be sold with the jets such as BFE and spares; however, he did not consider it appropriate for Toolco to provide funds for items that were an inherent part of and unique to TWA's operations, such as facilities, ground equipment, personnel training, and the like. This position, which was adopted by Howard, was not unreasonable, but as a result, implementation of many aspects of TWA's unique jet integration plans remained on dead center because of the inability of the TWA board to provide funding.

335

After repeated efforts, I was finally able to discuss the acute nature of this bottleneck with Hughes by phone from the old TWA terminal at Los Angeles on March 17, 1958. I apprised him of TWA's jet planning activity, pointing out that it embraced all phases of TWA's operations: facilities, tooling, airport construction, personnel training, and so on. I emphasized that lack of commitment authority had created crises on virtually all fronts, and it was necessary for TWA to proceed expeditiously to permit the efficient and timely initial use of the jets, if indeed TWA were to receive them. I also said I would appreciate an opportunity to meet with him personally at an early date to review TWA's plans and obtain his concurrence or alternate recommendations or directives so the program could move forward.

Howard was most cordial and gave me the impression that he had been quite oblivious to the arresting influence his "no rights" position had had, notwithstanding prior discussions on funding. He said he had neither the inclination nor the time to judge the suitability of TWA's jet planning, and if I was satisfied with the plans, TWA was free to proceed, provided two directives were strictly adhered to. These were: (1) Whenever and wherever possible, rent or lease on a reasonable basis facilities and equipment of all kinds. Invest the minimum cash. Use outside money. Conserve our financial resources. Do not buy unless no other way can be worked out. (2) Be economical. If we can get along without equipment or facilities, do not commit. Arrange for no more than is necessary.

Then, as an example, I raised the question of the Chicago hangar construction project, which had been on hold for months. He said that if I were personally satisfied with the specific hangar plan, and if his two directives were met, TWA could proceed.

I viewed this conversation as assurance of his intention that TWA would receive the jets—nothing else made any sense—and a clear declaration of authority for TWA to proceed with our jet implementation program provided I was satisfied with the plans and Howard's two directives were adhered to. I advised Warren Pierson, Ray Cook, and TWA's senior officers of my conversation with Howard and his directives by letter of March 19. My letter was well received, but to my disappointment, TWA's outside lawyers did not consider Howard's verbal directive to me to be sufficient justification for the board to grant the necessary commitment authority while TWA still had no legal rights to the jets.

Great ingenuity was required to move forward under these circumstances. For example, the fuel suppliers were persuaded to invest in new tank farms—jet fuel could not be mixed with gasoline—and then recoup the investment over an extended period, thus eliminating the need for TWA cash, and the construction of facilities was promoted to the maximum extent using outside money on a lease-back basis. Most vendors and parties with whom we dealt were remarkably cooperative. Even so, progress with the implementation program was slow and tedious.

Charles Sparks Thomas

Howard's search for a new TWA president ended July 2, 1958, with the election of Charles Sparks Thomas, most recently Eisenhower's secretary of the navy. Thomas had no airline experience and knew little about the business. However, he brought a fresh outlook and a wealth of administrative ability, a welcome change from six months of the sometimes bickering leadership by committee since Carter Burgess's departure.

Thomas had saved Foreman and Clark, a West Coast chain of men's clothiers, from bankruptcy during the 1930s. Foreman and Clark stores were generally located on second floors. Its radio and newspaper advertising theme was, "Climb a flight of stairs to the low rent district, buy a suit and get an extra pair of pants free." It was depression time. Business flourished, and Charlie became known as "Two-Pants Charlie." While there, Thomas earned a reputation as an outstanding executive.

Bob Gross had been impressed with Thomas's demonstrated success as an organizer and administrator. He thought Charlie could do a fine job for TWA and called Howard's attention to his impending availability during the closing period of Thomas's tenure as secretary of the navy. Howard, who had met Thomas earlier and been favorably impressed, contacted him, but found he had little interest in running an airline. Howard was convinced Thomas was the right man for the job and persisted over several months until he finally accepted the presidency.

Howard called me on Saturday, July 5, with the same message he gave after Carter Burgess became president: "Bob, you and I will continue to handle aircraft selection and procurement matters just as we have been doing, and Thomas will run the rest of the airline." I did not see how Thomas could willingly accept being president of only part of the airline, any more than Burgess had, but I had to assume that he had agreed to this limitation when accepting the position.

337

I wrote Thomas on July 16 to acquaint him with the Toolco jet procurement program. The letter explained my position with Toolco and stated:

In all instances, the Hughes Tool Company has agreed to reimburse TWA its costs for administration and handling [of the contracts and other authorized expenditures] in the event the jet aircraft now on order are not tendered to and accepted by TWA. In the past I have arranged for monetary authorities to be extended by Toolco to TWA to the extent needed for [BFE and spare parts for] the Boeing program, and am currently attempting to make funds available for Convair spares and BFE.

The Toolco has not made funds available for ground support equipment, construction, training, or any category other than the three mentioned above, because it believes capital items other than these should more appropriately be handled by TWA. In this respect it is *imperative* if we are to operate jets on time and efficiently that funds be provided to permit committing those jet items that have been approved by the Jet Staff and the Capital Appropriations Committee.

Tables showing Toolco's jet program investments and my personal limits of authority were attached. TWA's jet implementation expenditures forecast at that time totaled $28.5 million.

Thomas called me on July 31 and requested that jet implementation expenditures be reduced by $9 million, saying that $28.5 million was "out of the ballpark." Complying with this request appeared to be an impossible task because the initial "asking" figures had already been cut in half through jet planning activities.

Week-long meetings with all using TWA functions were held at the Jack Frye Training Center in Kansas City in an effort to comply with the Thomas request. The participants were disappointed with this turn of events, but they bent over backwards to cooperate. Every project was examined. Wherever possible, new solutions were devised, short cuts developed, and expenditures deferred. As an example of deferred projects, the group elected to forego the purchase of cargo containers for the carriage of luggage and cargo and modify existing boarding stairs rather than procure new covered, powered units. Such deferments reduced immediate commitment levels and thereby helped permit the program to move forward. We recognized, and I warned Thomas, that over the long term, the deferments would increase costs. The result of this exercise was a reduction in the forecast of $15.5 million. We had bettered the Thomas request by $6.5 million, which was very well received, indeed!

Charlie Thomas was quick to undertake a sweeping review of TWA's organization. He obtained studied opinions and suggestions from TWA's top echelon and separately sought independent ideas from second-echelon representatives in every department. Additionally, outside consultants were hired to assist. This all took considerable time. The result was a major organizational change, in which I was elected corporate vice president of planning and research on April 27, 1959.

My portfolio was expanded to include long-range corporate planning, and I was expected to move to New York. I welcomed the promotion but was a bit queasy about the move for two reasons. First, I questioned the advisability of uprooting the family. Second, I did not know if this would be agreeable with Howard. When I could not reach him after a number of calls, I asked Bill Gay if Howard knew of the promotion and the upcoming move to New York. Bill assured me that he did, Howard was all for it, and I should go ahead with the move.

The family question was more difficult because of our school-age children. I finally decided that my choice came down to whether I should stay with Hughes and TWA or seek other employment in the Kansas City area. Earlier, I had concluded it would be a mistake to turn down the promotion and remain with the company. I found no acceptable job alternatives, so, with Margie's concurrence, we moved to Weston, Connecticut, during August 1959, and I became a commuter.

About a month after the move, Howard called. His first words were, "Bob, what in hell are you doing in New York?" I explained that I had been assured by Bill Gay that he (Hughes) knew about and approved the move. He was displeased. Then he asked me exactly what my new job was, whether my added responsibilities would interfere with handling his flight equipment programs, and the effect of this change on my Kansas City staff. I assured him that my obligations to him had not been disturbed, I was expected to discharge my responsibilities to him, and because I was now in charge of long-range corporate planning, I could likely be of even greater service. This seemed to placate him.

Howard and Boeing

The arguments between Hughes and Bill Allen over jet delivery positions became intense during the first half of 1958. Howard continued to contend that Allen had offered him an equal position with AAL and agreed to

339

deliver the Toolco jets much closer to the time Boeing planned to deliver PAA's. Boeing continued to claim it was required to deliver 6 planes to AAL 60 days in advance of the delivering of jets to any other U.S. customer and to maintain the 60-day advantage throughout the AAL delivery period. It also said its contract with PAA required it to deliver 6 jets 60 days before it delivered jets to any other commercial customer. Hughes and Boeing were far apart, and Ray Cook, Harry West, and I were in the middle.

At this time Boeing was fabricating the first 6 707's for PAA and the next 10 for AAL. Toolco's first delivery was to be the 18th plane, the 17th being the prototype for the international J-75-powered version. However, manufacturing sequence and the sequence of airplane delivery were two different matters.

During December 1957, Hughes had asked me to call Bill Allen and discuss the relative delivery position question in his behalf. A quotation attributed to C. R. Smith had appeared in the *Aviation Daily* indicating that AAL would start jet service in January instead of March 1959. If true, this would give AAL an even greater lead over TWA than anticipated.

My conversation with Bill went like this: "Bill, Howard asked me to call in his behalf on a matter he considers to be extremely important: the relative delivery positions of AAL and TWA, especially with regard to start of jet service dates. The *Daily* indicated recently that AAL could start jet service during January 1959, which would be months before TWA. If true, Howard says that isn't right or proper, because he had been led to believe his deal with Boeing was on the basis that TWA would be able to start service the same day as AAL."

Bill responded, "Well! I don't know where he got that."

"That's what he says, Bill."

"I sure as hell never told him that! That isn't correct, and I can't believe Howard thinks it is."

"Well, I'm sure he wouldn't say it if he didn't think it's correct."

Bill then reviewed briefly the earlier Toolco negotiation and totally closed the door on opening delivery position discussions by saying, "There is no use to our spending a lot of time discussing this situation because this has been long since fixed and it has been long since understood, and as far as Howard is concerned—you can take my word for this—considering the time he came into the program, he got excellent deliveries."

I concluded with, "Well, Bill, I think you should understand that

Hughes feels very strongly about this. He's positive about it, and he wants you to understand that he feels this is most important as far as our future business is concerned."

On March 29, 1958, Hughes left unusually lengthy instructions at his Romaine Street operations headquarters with orders that they be read to me twice, and that if I had any questions, they be read to me a third time. When Howard's instructions were transmitted through Romaine Street, which seldom occurred except to arrange for phone calls, they were usually short and crisp. In this case, they were long and involved, and they changed as he dictated. The typed copy of Howard's words, which I requested after the second reading, required three closely typed pages.

"Be very careful not to say anything to anyone," the message began. It continued, "We [Toolco] are going to write a letter to Boeing charging all manner of collusion, misrepresentation, etc." He discussed at great length the need for me and my associates to avoid any discussion with Boeing that might undermine his position on jet delivery positions, warned that he might want my testimony, and asked that all TWA telephone calls to Boeing cease at once. He then asked that I confer with Cook and West to develop instructions to Ed Zak for handling routine, ongoing technical affairs with Boeing such as those involving design changes, transmittal of contract change orders, and the like, and requested that all discussions with Boeing by anyone in TWA be in person in Seattle or Kansas City.

He became more restrictive as he continued. He asked for a "complete blackout and cessation of any correspondence, telegrams, telephone calls, etc." and concluded, "The only thing left to discuss with Cook and West are memos and Change Orders, but because I don't like memos, the only thing left is Change Orders."

It was obvious that strict implementation of Howard's instructions would cause an almost complete curtailment of technical liaison with Boeing. This might defeat Howard's delivery position initiative because lack of cooperation on TWA's part in pending technical matters could interfere with construction of the planes and be construed as an excuse for delay in airplane delivery. His directive was also most untimely with respect to obtaining the desired design improvements then under investigation.

After discussions with Cook and West the same afternoon, I tried to phone Howard to convince him to ease his restrictions. The pressure tactic was more apt to be successful if TWA conducted technical liaison with Boeing in a routine manner and avoided creating technical bottlenecks.

However, I could not reach him despite repeated tries through Romaine Street and Nadine Henley's office, so I had no choice as Toolco's special representative but to implement his instructions.

The next day, Sunday, I tried all day to reach Ed Zak to request him to be in my office Monday morning so I could personally review and discuss Howard's distasteful instructions. I did not reach him until evening because he and his family had taken a long-overdue, all-day tour of Whidbey Island and points north of Seattle. Even so, he arrived in my office early Monday morning. Ed's reaction was even more negative than mine.

That same day Toolco sent a letter to Boeing, directed to the attention of Bill Allen. It concluded, "Unless immediately rectified, Boeing's threatened discrimination in deliveries and its breaches of basic obligations will expose Hughes and TWA to ruinous losses. Responsibility for these losses must be borne by Boeing. . . . Despite the seriousness of these developments and the urgency of solution, Hughes is willing to discuss them. . . . Pending a satisfactory explanation and revision of these matters, the progress payments are being withheld." The withheld progress payment funds totaled nearly $5.9 million.

Bill Allen responded with an equally strong letter, which concluded, "The failure of the Hughes Tool Company to make payment . . . constitutes a material breach of each contract [for domestic and international jets] and subjects the Hughes Tool Company to responsibility for any and all damages incurred by Boeing as a result thereof."

Ed Zak was a conscientious person. He did his best to faithfully implement Howard's March 29 instructions, knowing full well such actions could damage the program and certainly cause him a great deal of extra work. After nearly a month had passed, I asked Ed to write me a no-holds-barred letter describing how Howard's directive had handicapped his work and the impact this could have on Toolco's Boeing program. This was a calculated move: Enough time had gone by to establish the fact of the matter, so I would not be simply expressing an opposing opinion to Howard. Ed wrote the letter and attached a long list of specifics.

This time, I was able to reach Howard. When I started to explain the situation and pointed out that his instructions were largely self defeating, he said, "Why didn't someone tell me?"

"Jesus, Howard," I answered, "I tried to. I tried to call you twice the same day the instructions were read to me. Then I tried through Ray Cook and Nadine. Then through Bill Gay. Nothing worked. You didn't return any of the calls.''

Howard said, "Bob, I know that at times I'm hard to get. I've been so goddamn busy lately with so damn many balls in the air, I've barely had time to breathe. But, damn it, Bob, in a case like this with so much at stake at Boeing—"

I interrupted with, "What more could I have done, Howard?"

Howard paused for what seemed like a long time, cleared his throat, and admitted, "Well, Bob, I guess not much at that." Then I explained the situation in detail. By the time our conversation ended, Howard had agreed that TWA's technical liaison with Boeing could be resumed on a normal basis. Ed Zak was delighted to be able to hand to Boeing over three dozen TWA letters and technical position papers, which had been withheld, and to be in the position of renewing normal working relationships.

Boeing made a few concessions during the next few months, including verbal assurances that AAL would never receive at the end of any month more than a five-plane advantage, but noted that if TWA got the breaks during flight test acceptance operations, the five might be reduced to four or possibly two during the monthly periods. (Aircraft were accepted only after flight tests established functional compliance with the specifications; frequently, malfunctions would cause delay in delivery). However, if AAL got the breaks, the five could become eight. Boeing also agreed to make the prototype 367-80 available for TWA flight training. This would have the beneficial effect of reducing the interval between initial airplane deliveries and TWA's start of service date.

Although such concessions cooled somewhat the contractual firestorm that had been building, delivery arguments continued. However, parity with AAL and a reduction in PAA's lead were never achieved.

Ed Zak confirmed that Boeing had continued its manufacturing operations exactly as scheduled without regard to the Hughes-imposed technical blackout, Toolco's withholding of funds, or the extended arguments with Allen. Zak recalled during my 1984 interview:

Boeing's management team just would not quit. Its system was a blessing, but it was also a curse. It had difficulty implementing customer changes in reasonable time and at reasonable costs. On the other hand, Boeing's ability to produce planes on schedule was absolutely phenomenal.

Boeing's management was always well informed. If a customer wrote a letter on a technical matter, within two days everyone—sales, engineering, contracts, and production personnel—knew about it. Boeing made 18 copies of everything and distributed them to all who could possibly be concerned with the subject matter. If a manager found he had no legitimate interest, he wasn't obligated to file it and chucked it into the wastebasket. If it had to do with his own affairs or those of his customer, he would take note and handle it accordingly. The system worked. The Boeing team just wouldn't quit.

Bill Allen sent the prototype 367-80 to Los Angeles for Howard to inspect and flight demonstration during the late fall of 1958. Brien Wygle, a fine Boeing pilot, was in command, with Harley Beard serving as copilot. Hughes took the controls on the first flight out of Los Angeles International Airport with Wygle as copilot and Beard as flight engineer. Howard had had very little jet experience. The 367-80, like most jets, was difficult to slow down during descent. During the final approach, Howard exceeded the structural speed limit for the landing flaps, and one eight-foot section broke off. While difficult to fly, the plane landed without further damage.

The flap section, however, impacted near the airport fence on a car owned by an FAA inspector. When the plane taxied in, the FAA was on hand. Howard was extremely sensitive concerning his reputation as an aviator. Immediately after the plane stopped, when the attention of the FAA men was centered on the damaged area, Lee Flanigan, a TWA pilot and a friend of Hughes, whisked Howard off in a waiting car before he was spotted by the FAA.

The flap incident made great fodder for the press. It was known that Howard had been on the plane, but he had not been seen, and confirmation that he had been flying when the incident occurred was lacking because everyone knowledgeable kept quiet. The fact that the plane was the experimental forerunner of the widely publicized 707 program only added fuel for the press.

Robert J. Murphy, a leading Boeing executive, had been having fairly frequent phone conversations with Howard for some time prior to the incident and helped shield his image in the aftermath. The FAA conducted an official investigation, during which it was unable to establish that Hughes had the controls when the flap broke. At the conclusion of the investigation, Ed Zak received a phone call from Bill Gay, who requested Ed to purchase, gift wrap, and deliver to Bob Murphy a case of his favorite liquor: Chivas Regal.

Not a single case of Chivas Regal was to be had in any of the Seattle-area stores. Ed enlisted the aid of Boeing's customer relations representative, Bill Huston, who checked with the restaurants Boeing patronized, including the Canlis Restaurant, to round up a case. Nothing was available. Bill then recalled that Bob Murphy also liked Remy Martin cognac. After clearing this change with Romaine Street (he had learned that specific instructions from the Hughes organization were to be followed exactly), Ed bought a case of Remy Martin and had Boeing's driver deliver it one evening when Bob was home in time for him to have a good after-dinner cognac. Nothing was said, but Bob knew what it was for.

Disaster

During early 1959, Leonard Schwartz and Raymond Cook asked that I meet them at the Waldorf. They dropped a bombshell. Schwartz said he had talked to Howard, and they thought Toolco had too many jets on order for TWA. He had discussed this subject with Charlie Thomas, and steps would most likely be taken to reduce the size of the international Boeing and 880 fleets to something "more compatible with TWA's needs."

I was convinced that all of the jets ordered by Toolco were needed for TWA and strenuously objected to the idea of reducing the size of the fleets. I might have been more amenable had he said that financial resource limitations made fleet reduction necessary, but he did not.

Leonard continued by advising that TWA might receive only about 10 of the 18 international Boeings and possibly only 20 of the 30 880's Toolco had on order. He thought I should be cognizant of this because of my TWA jet planning activities and added that the matter would likely be resolved soon. He intimated that Charlie Thomas was in accord with this cutback, and he believed that all airlines had committed to buy too many jets.

I was appalled. I tried to convince Leonard and Ray that such a move would be a serious error that would handicap TWA competitively for years. They seemed somewhat sympathetic but did not agree to try to alter what I believed to be direct instructions from Hughes, possibly supported by Thomas.

I discussed this with Charlie Thomas, who had the peculiar notion that reducing the size of the anticipated TWA fleets while its principal competitors maintained their equipment status quo would not be harmful competitively. I could not have disagreed more. Charlie also mentioned the

345

economic downturn, which I considered to be transient—certainly of shorter duration than the lead-time required to purchase replacement aircraft—and indicated that if TWA cut back now, better jets could likely be procured later. Better jets could indeed likely be available later, but, I argued, would TWA be able to afford them if it did not maintain a strong interim competitive position?

Several years after Thomas had left the company, he said he never fought with Hughes over fleet size. After all, he indicated, the planes and the airline were Howard's, and if he wanted to slow down delivery it was okay. I did not see it that way. As a corporate officer, I felt an obligation to try to build a strong airline, believing this to be in everyone's best long-term interests, including Howard's.

I did my best during the next month or so to persuade Thomas, Schwartz, Cook, and Holliday to join me in persuading Hughes not to cut the size of the fleets. I did not succeed, and Hughes, who was having trouble making the Boeing and Convair progress payments, made it very clear that he did not need any suggestions from me concerning this matter.

When Hughes decided to permit TWA to receive only 20 880's, Cook and Holliday suggested I plan on an allocation of Toolco's 30 aircraft on a proportional basis—that is, Toolco and TWA would receive 1 plane each initially, after which TWA would receive 2, and Toolco would receive 1. They thought that chronological order should continue until all 30 were delivered. However, as will be explained later, deliveries did not follow this order, and Howard had not approved the suggested allocation, nor did he ever devise one of his own.

Juan Trippe and Raymond Holliday executed an agreement on June 25, 1959, assigning 6 of Toolco's 18 international Boeings to PAA, subject to acceptance of the arrangement by Boeing, which quickly agreed. Hughes had agreed to transfer planes I was convinced TWA needed to compete with its prime overseas competitor: a double-barreled shot bound to hit TWA hard in the future. TWA would lose 6 planes and PAA would gain 6: an adverse swing of 12 planes. Holliday indicated later that Trippe was astounded that TWA would agree to release the planes.

These changes required a complete reworking of TWA's jet implementation plans on an expedited basis, on the assumption, still, that the remaining planes would be delivered on time. But which Convairs? Hughes had not designated which 10 880's would be retained by Toolco. I provided the best delivery estimates I could, which nevertheless proved to be incorrect because of subsequent delays in the Convair program caused largely by Howard's impeding actions. My Jet Planning Staff and Group tackled the job and developed new detailed plans in remarkably short order.

Difficulties at Boeing

Hughes held tight reins on the delivery of the jets. It had been a regular practice to obtain authorization from the TWA board for my plant representatives to formally accept aircraft deliveries on completion of satisfactory acceptance flight tests and on signal that final payments were ready for transfer. In this case, Howard telegraphically granted power of attorney to Zak through Toolco, one Boeing at a time, and then only when Howard considered it to be appropriate. He no doubt considered this degree of control necessary because of difficulty in mustering the necessary funds. Later, Howard asked me to negotiate interim storage arrangements on Boeing property for two 707's when lack of Toolco funds prevented acceptance and delivery. Boeing charged Howard $55,500, at $1,100 per plane-day of storage.

Shortly before the flight test phase, Hughes insisted that no one be allowed on the Toolco Boeings except the absolute minimum number of Boeing employees required to accomplish essential work and those known to be closely associated with Hughes. Many Boeing people were involved. I advised Ed, who enlisted the assistance of Boeing to help police the planes on a 24-hour basis. I was at Boeing a few weeks later. When I started to climb the ladder to inspect the plane, one of the foremen yelled, "Hey, Bub, who in hell do you think you are getting on that plane?" I whirled around to respond, but before I could speak, Zak explained.

Howard also required Ed to report to Romaine Street operations before each test flight on how long the flight would take, who would be on board, and specifically what was to be checked. Additionally, Ed was to collect all raw data and penciled notations taken on each flight and transmit this information to Romaine Street immediately after the plane landed, which of course was out of the question because the flights were Boeing flights and Boeing needed the data for reduction purposes. Many of Howard's detailed requests to Zak were unreasonable, remained effective throughout the delivery period, distracted Zak and the men from the main work at hand, and caused a great deal of unproductive effort. Later, after Hughes

347

lost control of TWA, Zak said, "Working at Boeing without Hughes is like heaven."

He had this to say in the late 1980s, however, about the integrity of both Boeing and Hughes:

As far as Boeing was concerned, I always felt that I was dealing with responsible people whom I could trust. I don't know of any case that anybody in any
position of consequence ever tried to lie to me. I'm sure there were times when
they didn't tell me the whole story, but I don't know of a single Boeing untruth.
Also, I don't know of a single case of Hughes telling Boeing a falsehood. There
may have been times when Boeing may have deluded themselves on some
points, but I doubt if Hughes ever actually lied. With Hughes, it wasn't prudent
to assume anything.

It proved to be extremely difficult for Boeing to make the first Toolco
707 ready for delivery. Repeated flight tests and some time-consuming
modifications were required before proper system functioning was demonstrated. I was in Seattle and was obliged to make reports every few hours
to Howard, sometimes through Romaine Street. Howard did not interfere
with making the plane ready except for the distraction of the reporting
exercise. He seemed just as anxious as Charlie Thomas and I for the plane
to be delivered so TWA jet services could be operated on the publicized
date.

The start of service contingency time was all but used up by the time the
plane was ready. The plane had remained Toolco's, but last-minute arrangements had been made to lease it to TWA on a day-to-day basis,
arrangements that applied to all subsequent domestic and the first four
international 707's. After delivery, I flew in this first 707 with TWA
Captain Gail Storck to San Francisco, where I turned it over to Flight
Operations for FAA route proving flights. The inaugural flight occurred on
schedule, March 20, 1959, with only minutes to spare.

That single plane flew daily round trips between San Francisco and New
York, and it performed flawlessly. It was operated a phenomenal 21 days
without a single flight delay. And it operated with full passenger loads plus
oversales passengers, who occupied the lounge seats. This incredible operating record is a tribute to effective jet planning and the fine TWA
operations team that made it work.

21.

Howard's
Defeat

The Convair 880 manufacturing program proved to be a nightmare. Hughes's disruptive actions included the forced removal and roping-off of planes by armed Hughes guards without the consent of Convair; the bailment of incomplete planes to Toolco, which otherwise would have been the first to be delivered; the curtailment of aircraft flight tests; and the outright refusal to accept delivery. Howard's maneuvers resulted in unconscionable aircraft manufacturing and delivery delays, with devastating impacts on Convair and TWA that nearly drove both corporations into bankruptcy.

Howard's primary motivation for this unexpected and pernicious behavior stemmed from failure to finance Toolco's jet programs and the consequent inability to pay for the 880's. Several financing plans had been developed by TWA and Toolco representatives working in coordination with eligible institutions, but none had met with his approval. With Toolco strapped for funds—it had taken every ounce of ingenuity to arrange for Toolco to pay for the Boeing fleet while refusing to allow TWA to engage in the conventional financing, which would have been possible if he had dropped the "no rights" position—Howard bought time to obtain financing to his liking by delaying the Convair program.

Howard's attitude as I observed it changed during this period of acute financial frustration, a period that must have been personally vexing and stressful, perhaps especially so because of the contrast of this circumstance to his nearly continuous run of previous industrial successes. He remained friendly but was sometimes cryptic. Sometimes he spoke rapidly, as if he were excited, and he was considerably less prone to discuss technical matters and seek advice than had been typical of our relationship from the outset.

During this disappointing period all of Howard's contacts with me were by phone rather than in person. His calls became less frequent, and instructions were more often passed through Romaine Street rather than in person. This made objecting to demands I considered to be imprudent difficult or impossible. Several times, somewhat against my better judgment, I enlisted the aid of Ray Cook and Raymond Holliday to convince Howard to alter his position, usually without success. They were having similar difficulties.

I was not personally involved in efforts to resolve Howard's financing problem, and at first I was unaware of how close Toolco had moved to severe financial embarrassment. Howard no doubt was acutely aware of this, although his actions did not seem to reflect much concern, possibly because he still had enormous resources. Unfortunately, liquidity was lacking because a large part of his empire, tied up in the Hughes Medical Institute and real estate investments, was not available for jet acquisition purposes. He was also completely unwilling to enter into any arrangement that might jeopardize his absolute ownership of Toolco. Thus, Toolco, an immensely wealthy company, found itself without the cash to meet pressing current needs.

The Convair-Hughes-Lockheed Financing Attempt

TWA's bottom-line prospects had brightened considerably during 1959 because of the great popularity of the leased Boeing jets, the outstanding corporate efficiency that had been gained through jet planning, and the management leadership of Charlie Thomas. After losing $5.7 million during the preceding three years, by the end of 1959 TWA had earned a profit of $9.4 million. It was the second best year TWA had ever enjoyed. Lease payments on the jets, however, were booked by TWA and Toolco but not paid, pending permanent financing, so Toolco's cash-flow problems were not helped.

TWA's strong showing did strengthen Howard's position with the financial institutions, but he rejected their advice to engage in conventional financing, which involved transferring ownership of the jets to TWA. During the later part of 1959, Howard turned to Convair and Lockheed for aid through use of their credit instead of his. He dangled in front of the manufacturers enticing prospects for receiving large Toolco orders for Convair 990's and Lockheed Electras, if agreeable financing, adequate to dispose of his current problems and accommodate the added fleets, could be arranged.

The 990's were GE aft-fan-powered, heavy, long-range, follow-on versions of the 880, then under development for AAL. Convair agreed to hold open for Hughes 36 990 delivery positions, with the first Toolco deliveries to occur during the second half of 1961. Howard simultaneously expressed serious interest at Lockheed for the procurement of as many as 40 turboprop Electras.

Neither manufacturer was financially healthy, and both jumped at the apparent opportunity to receive major new plane orders. Convair was hurting because of the high cost of its commercial jet development programs, and Lockheed had only recently suffered the consequences of disastrous Electra airline accidents, which required it to modify at great expense the wing structure of delivered and production Electras. Working in concert with Hughes, both manufacturers undertook to arrange satisfactory financing to solve Hughes's problem. By so doing, they hoped to make significant corporate gains.

The jointly developed Hughes-Convair-Lockheed financing proposals that resulted might have succeeded, but the involved Lockheed and Convair bankers did not believe that the three sick "partners" could make each other well. After trying for several months, Howard abandoned this approach during early 1960. The negotiation with Convair for 990's, however, kept Convair quiet for many months about Hughes's deliberate efforts to delay its 880 production.

Production Debacle

Bill Bew had confirmed in mid-1959 that the Convair 880 production line was essentially on schedule—that is, all 40 planes, including the 10 for

Delta, which were interspersed with the 30 for Toolco, were on schedule so far. Deliveries were expected to commence in the fall of 1959 and end in September 1960, as stipulated in the contract. However, Bill cautioned that the cushion-time Convair had reserved for those development modifications, which were an inherent part of any new airplane development program, had been all but used up.

On July 30 Bill phoned me in New York to advise that a group of inspectors employed by Toolco had arrived at the Convair factory to observe the progress being made on various 880's. Neither of us had been forewarned. Bill had a competent staff of TWA inspectors on station. He wanted to know why the Toolco inspectors were there and how their presence would affect his duties and obligations, if at all. I asked him to proceed as usual and to let me know what developed.

During this period approximately 15 880's were in various stages of assembly in the San Diego plant. The first three, scheduled for airworthiness and FAA certification tests, were to be delivered to Toolco after certification and the installation of TWA interiors. The fourth 880 was to be the first delivered to Delta. The next five Toolco planes were scheduled to be delivered from November 1959 through February 1960. The second Delta 880 was scheduled to be delivered to Delta during January. The overall deliveries so scheduled were in accordance with contractual understandings. However, while the allocation between Toolco and Delta had been proposed by Convair and agreed to by Delta, this aspect had never been acceded to by Toolco.

Bew advised on August 6, 1959, that the Toolco inspectors began to take particular interest in the two aircraft scheduled for delivery November and December, which were to be the first aircraft delivered to Toolco. Two months later, the Toolco inspectors, with no warning whatsoever, placed the first such airplane under armed guard at the Convair factory.

Hughes called me on October 10, the month before the first 880 was scheduled to be delivered to Toolco. Without discussion, he ordered that I instruct my "chief inspector" not to commit Toolco to the acceptance of any of the contract airplanes that had any appreciable defects. I assured Howard it was our policy and practice not to accept "appreciable defects" and to require that such discrepancies be corrected. He said he understood that and explained that his concern was that Convair's correction of such squawks might infer acceptance. I pointed out that the contract required Toolco to accept aircraft only after demonstration flight tests showed them to be functionally acceptable and Toolco's "technical approval" had been indicated by endorsement on the packing sheets. After those events occurred, Toolco would, indeed, be obligated to accept the aircraft.

Notwithstanding, Howard asked that I confer with Harry West "to make certain that nothing any inspector might say or sign, or by omission of saying or signing, might be construed as acceptance of any airplane." I discussed this with Harry, who thought we should continue our regular practices. I then advised Bew to be mindful of Howard's concerns when discharging his duties.

Bill Gay called Bew the next day to relay modified instructions. Gay said that Howard had directed that he, Bew, should never indicate final acceptance of any aircraft without prior direct clearance from Hughes. Howard had elected to play it super safe.

Bill Bew called during early December 1959 and advised that Toolco guards had taken control of the two 880's scheduled for delivery in December and January. He said these planes, along with the 880 scheduled for November delivery, had been roped off, and no one was allowed to board. Consequently, the TWA inspectors could not complete necessary inspections, and Convair personnel could not complete outstanding work. These were the first three planes expected to be tendered to Toolco for delivery. Convair had installed a prototype crew seat for customer demonstration and acceptance purposes in the December aircraft just before it was roped off. Neither TWA nor Convair was allowed to remove the seat so it could be placed in another 880 for the same purpose, despite repeated pleadings. This stalled seat production until after the vendor reluctantly produced and demonstrated another prototype.

During January 1960, the month under terms of contract in which Toolco should have received its third 880, and Delta in fact received its first, Hughes directed Convair to advise Bew of all contemplated demonstration 880 flights so Bew could keep him currently informed and requested Bew "to tighten up control" of flight test aircraft. When representatives of AAL and Braniff requested a ride in an early Toolco 880, they were refused by Hughes. Then, on February 22, Bew was instructed to place an agent at each 880 that might be flown to prevent demonstration of such aircraft to would-be purchasers. The assigned TWA personnel made a sustained effort during March and thereafter to prevent demonstration flights because none had been cleared with Hughes. Howard may have been concerned with the remote possibility that Convair might receive an offer for some of the Toolco planes and thereby force his hand. Obviously, however, this and similar Hughes actions severely handicapped Convair's marketing efforts for added planes, in spite of the fact that additional sales would have resulted in reducing the price of Toolco's planes.

On February 8, I wrote to Charlie Thomas and pointed out the urgent need for TWA's jet planning function to undertake "full scale review" of our jet implementation plans. The key questions requiring resolution were, "How many 880's, and when?" I added that when I had been on the West Coast the preceding week, I had found no positive confirmation that TWA would or would not receive 880's from Toolco. I recommended to Charlie that to enable the review, I be given a directive concerning how many 880's TWA should plan on receiving and whether the company should plan on continuous delivery sequence; a "pari-passu" (equally proportional) relationship between Toolco and TWA, which Cook and Holliday had recommended; or some other delivery order. This recommendation was not entirely unreasonable because I had not been able to obtain a declaration of intent from Howard or any of the Toolco people saying which 880's would be made available to TWA, and because I knew Thomas to be involved in financing discussions, which necessarily had to address the delivery question.

In my capacity as special representative for Toolco and vice president of planning and research for TWA, I should have had a solid delivery position for Charlie. However, Howard would not commit, probably because an agreeable financing plan had not been consummated, and he simply did not have the answer. I had hoped that Charlie would somehow be able to resolve the issue with Howard, but he could not.

Convair had scheduled flight tests so as to receive FAA certification of the 880 several months in advance of the contract-required date of May 1, 1960. (The Toolco 880's scheduled for delivery prior to FAA certification were to be "NP"—provisionally certified—aircraft for pilot training and other preparatory operations.) I suggested to Thomas that TWA plan on certification by May 15 because I considered this more realistic. To Convair's credit, however, it satisfied a major contractual commitment by obtaining certification on May 1.

Shortly after my letter of February 8 to Thomas, in response to a Hughes directive, Raymond Holliday caused the three Toolco 880's that had been roped-off and were nearest completion and delivery to be placed under bailment to Toolco, thus removing them from Convair's control. Howard's

354

ostensible excuse was that he wanted to personally test fly the planes, but he never did. Later, a fourth 880 scheduled for delivery during early February was also placed under bailment. All four planes were towed away from the Convair plant but remained immobile at Lindbergh Field.

Hughes requested Bew and his staff during February to refrain from participating in any discussions with Convair or any one else with regard to delivery schedules. By this time Hughes had assumed direct control of all Toolco's early deliveries, and he had the planes under armed guard.

The four bailed aircraft were exposed to the salt-laden, highly corrosive seaside atmosphere. Bew noticed that action had not been taken to preserve the engines and urged that this be done. Notwithstanding the obvious need, Toolco guards would not allow Convair, GE, or TWA personnel to approach the planes to protect the engines. Corrosion did occur, causing added expense later on.

The impact of all this on Convair was devastating. Shop personnel were repeatedly reassigned jobs, with little hope of attaining proficiency in any one job. As a result, Convair's overall production learning curve was abysmal, and operating costs were inordinately high. Production, which could not keep up with Hughes's surprises, was in chaos. Perhaps worst of all, no one knew what to expect next or when Hughes would release his grip and permit Convair to resume orderly production.

About this time, Thomas asked me to go to San Diego and personally talk to Convair, inspect the 880 production line, and provide him with a personal estimate of when Toolco's aircraft could be delivered. When I indicated that I was up to date—my presence at Convair would not resolve the question because the matter was in Howard's court—he said he understood but insisted nonetheless that I make the trip.

I flew to Los Angeles and drove to La Jolla, where I had reserved a room in a brand-new motel by the Cove. When I arrived, an urgent call from Bill Gay awaited me. Bill said Howard did not want me to go to Convair or talk to any Convair employee until after I had talked to Howard. He requested me to stand by for Howard's call, which he expected to make soon. I received similar messages every day for a solid week. I reported this unpalatable development to Thomas and asked what he thought I should do. He said to follow Howard's instructions and do the best that I could.

After another week, Howard called. I explained my purpose and gave several other good reasons why my visit to Convair would be timely. Howard said it would be fine for me to visit Convair, but he would appreciate it if I would "postpone my visit for a while," explaining that nothing was to be gained at that time, and he did not want to risk stirring up Convair. He said he would let me know when a visit would be timely. He was sure Charlie would understand and told me to return to New York or wherever business required. My trip was completely a dry run, and I am not sure Howard's position was received entirely graciously by Charlie Thomas.

During March 1960, five more Toolco 880's were pulled out of production and stored on the Convair flight line. One of the 880's that had been bailed earlier to Toolco was supposed to be returned to Convair for FAA airworthiness certification tests in March, but it was not returned until September 13. The other three bailed aircraft were not returned until October 21.

In an effort to establish more realistic Convair production targets, Amendment No. 4 to the purchase agreement was executed March 2 by Holliday and Naish. It contained a new airplane delivery schedule, which provided that 4 880's would be delivered to Toolco during May, 4 in June, 5 each in July and August, 4 in September, 5 in October, and 3 in November. This would have provided an updated schedule for TWA's planning purposes, but Hughes would not identify the 10 planes Toolco planned to retain out of the 30 on order. Even so, this amendment seemed to permit the development of more realistic jet implementation plans. I did not know then that further delivery delays would render this time-consuming exercise meaningless.

During early April, Charlie Thomas, who had supported the cutback to 20 880's, asked if I thought TWA could effectively deploy 25 880's. After reviewing TWA's jet implementation preparedness activities and conferring with our marketing and schedule planning people, I advised Thomas by letter of April 6 that TWA could effectively deploy the first 25 planes listed in Amendment No. 4. (I of course had no doubt that 30 could be used and were needed.) This was then reflected in a financing plan under development for the acquisition of 52 rather than 45 jets for TWA. Later, this plan aborted.

Later on, Thomas again asked me to investigate the advisability of increasing the 880 fleet, this time by adding 4 planes, making up a 24-plane Convair fleet. In response, I indicated by letter that 4 additional 880's would generate an additional operating profit of $2.6 million in 1961 and recommended that they be procured. Again, nothing happened.

I was encouraged by Charlie's willingness to consider increases in the size of the 880 fleet and attributed this to the remarkable success TWA's jets had enjoyed with the flying public. Passengers who had a choice between flying by pistons and by jets had overwhelmingly chosen to travel by jets even though they paid a fare surcharge for the jets. It quickly had become obvious, just as I had predicted, that the pistons could not compete and were being driven out of the market when sufficient jets had been introduced to handle the passenger demand. Charlie had come to recognize the inadequacy of TWA's jet fleet to compete with the much larger fleets of its principal competitors.

For TWA to make efficient use of the 880's expected to be delivered per Amendment No. 4, it was necessary to undertake flight training without delay. However, Howard was not ready to make an 880 available. His acquiescence was only obtained by TWA's agreeing to pay for a training 880 with its own funds although no financing was in place. It was delivered May 18, 1960.

Capt. Gordon Granger flew the 880 training plane nonstop from San Diego to Kansas City on its delivery flight. Immediately after landing, Granger stormed into Russ Rourke's office with disconcerting news. Granger claimed that the 880 had consumed from 7 to 15 percent more fuel than the Convair performance manual indicated it should.

Convair reacted to Granger's claim with disbelief. It had run comprehensive fuel consumption tests during the flight test program, was sure of its "facts," and had based its flight manuals on the "validated" results. Table pounding immediately occurred. Convair agreed to recheck its accumulated test data, including calibration of the test equipment. On recheck, it was discovered that the fuel mass-flow meters on the test airplane had been calibrated on the wrong frequency, which recorded lower than actual fuel flows, and the volumetric flow meters installed for check tests were in error by about the same amount. Thus, the test results, which were in substantial agreement with predictions, had been erroneously verified. Additional Convair flight tests provided correct definitive data and confirmed Granger's claim.

This disappointing shortfall was just enough to make it wholly impractical to plan on operating 880's in coast-to-coast nonstop services, which calculations had already shown to be marginal. And payload capabilities on the longer flights and those from runways that limited the maximum operating weight of the planes would be adversely affected, as would the cost of fuel on all 880 flights. However, it appeared that the TWA operating plan for initial 880 services could still be effectively flown.

Shortly after delivery of the training plane, a letter agreement dated May 9, 1960, was signed between Toolco and TWA providing for the assignment of 19 880's to TWA. (Convair's agreement to the assignment was not technically required because the September 10, 1956, purchase agreement permitted Toolco to assign 880's to TWA without Convair's consent.) It appeared that a major breakthrough was about to happen and TWA would soon receive its Convair fleet. However, despite execution of the letter agreement by Raymond Holliday and Gordon L. Gilmore, TWA's vice president of public relations, Convair refused to honor the assignment without confirmation from Hughes—which was not forthcoming. Consequently, the assignment agreement never became effective, and Howard continued to exercise personal control over the remaining 29 880's still on order.

The Delta 880 Accident

During this period Convair delivered to Delta substantially on schedule its first three 880's. Delta commenced scheduled services on May 15, 1960, on its nonstop New York to Atlanta, Houston, and New Orleans segments. Only a few days later, on May 23, Delta suffered a tragic 880 training accident at Atlanta, killing the crew of four. According to the official CAB summary description of the accident, "Immediately after liftoff the aircraft assumed an extremely nose high attitude and banked steeply to the left. It then rolled to a vertical right bank, the nose fell through, and the aircraft struck the ground."

The Delta accident was immediate cause for great concern, lest its origin be some hazardous design deficiency. After clearing the matter with Delta, I sent Norm Parmet to Atlanta to learn all he could and assist Delta in the investigation. He remained in Atlanta several weeks and kept me advised, but pending the result of minute, detailed examination of the wreckage by teams of experts, which would require months, the cause could not be established.

Howard was deeply concerned about the accident—we all were—a fact that I thought might contribute to his reluctance to move forward with the Convair program. But as I was to appreciate more fully later, Howard's dominant restraining factor was lack of funds, not the accident. However, I believe his concern over the safety of the design to have been sincere.

Delta had been experiencing considerable difficulty with the 880 hydraulic system, which immediately became suspect. TWA had also encountered hydraulic problems while flying at Convair and requested Convair considerably before the accident to qualify and install higher-pressure pumps—the same type that had been performing satisfactorily on the Boeings—and to make some plumbing changes to improve system reliability. The principal hydraulic problems encountered were slow flap retraction and incapacitating plumbing failures. Immediately after the Delta accident, TWA set out to undertake hydraulic and control system flight tests in its training 880 to determine if any unknown control system shortcomings existed.

Hughes called me on June 5, during a St. Louis layover. I was on my way to attend a one-day meeting at Lockheed, to be followed by meetings with Convair concerning the accident. I also planned to take the occasion to make a further attempt to inspect and personally evaluate Convair's chaotic production situation. Howard said that he did not want any "explanation, study, or investigation of the [Delta] accident on our ship." He then directed that a TWA man be on every 880 flight conducted on planes destined for Toolco, regardless of whether they were Convair or TWA flights, to make sure that his directive was followed.

Howard's directive was exactly what I did not want to hear. After he closed the door on further discussion, I passed his instructions about having a TWA observer on all flights on to Bew and Rourke. I was not given to breaching Howard's instructions, but in this case, in good conscience as an airline operator, I did nothing to interfere with tests on TWA's training 880. Later on, I reviewed the test results with Howard and explained why I had permitted the carefully planned tests. I thought he might react angrily, but he did not. Apparently his strong interest in safety overcame his previous objections.

The CAB aircraft accident report, adopted January 12, 1962, 19 months after the accident, contains the following:

Examination of the wreckage did not reveal evidence of structural failure prior to impact. In addition, no malfunction or failure in the control surfaces, control cables, or systems was found which could have caused or contributed to the unusual flight attitudes described by witnesses.

The Board determines the probable cause of this accident to be the stalling of the aircraft, for reasons undetermined, at an altitude too low to effect recovery.

Even though the CAB ultimately found that the design of the plane was not at fault, Convair, under extreme pressure from TWA and Delta, had replaced the hydraulic pumps at no cost to its customers and made other needed hydraulic system improvements.

When I arrived on schedule at the airport Hyatt House in Los Angeles the evening of June 5, a message from Bill Gay was waiting for me. Bill requested that I remain at the hotel, where Russ Rourke was to meet me, until Howard called later that evening. Howard did not call until the next afternoon. Leaving no room for discussion, he gave a brief order: No flight tests of any kind were to be made on any of Toolco's 880's by either Convair or TWA. He added that he would call me back as soon as possible to discuss the Delta accident. I reluctantly passed the word along to Bew. Within a few days, Convair flew airplane No. 20 to Edwards Air Force Base at Mojave for tests. On its return, Howard saw that it was promptly stored.

Howard's Romaine Street Mormons reminded me at least twice every day for the next week of Howard's request to stand by, which had been expanded to include Rourke. Nonetheless, we moved to the Hollywood Roosevelt, much more convenient for attending the Lockheed meeting, which I had postponed rather than breach Howard's standby instructions. When I insisted through the Mormons, Howard approved the Lockheed meeting provided I was not out of touch more than 20 minutes at a time!

On Friday, June 10, Howard left the following message: "Tell Bob that if he has finished at Lockheed, I don't want him to go to San Diego until Monday morning. I have spoken to the people at Convair and made arrangements for Monday morning . . . to negotiate with Convair concerning a number of matters . . . . This evening I will [call] without fail." He did not call until late the following evening around 11:00 P.M. Before calling, Howard left precise directions. I was to be alone in the hotel room, with Rourke standing by in an adjacent room in case consultation became advisable.

Howard and I talked for several hours, but not about the Convair production situation. The entire conversation related to the Delta accident. The accident investigation teams had made available to Parmet a considerable amount of information, even though the investigation was continuing. I had passed to the Romaine Street office items of significance for transmittal to Howard, which he wanted to discuss. For example, based on the postmortem examination, suggestions had been made that the pilot might have suffered a heart attack immediately before the accident. Howard had discussed with a group of prominent doctors such aspects as whether the pilot would pull the wheel toward him in a severe attack or whether he would release the wheel and grab his chest. He arranged for Rourke and me to meet with the doctors, but after I reminded him that neither of us had any medical training whatsoever, and we were in no position to judge the validity of such considerations, important as they might be, the meeting was canceled. Although no evidence to confirm it was ever developed, the heart attack theory continued to be accepted by a number of those concerned with the accident.

Virtually all aspects of the Delta accident were discussed that evening, with special regard to how the accident might affect the design. We were interested in the direct cause, whatever that might prove to be, and also in any lessons being learned from the investigation. The teams of experts that investigate the majority of airline accidents usually uncover design deficiencies or suspect areas that should be corrected in operating aircraft, but which have nothing to do with the accidents. Howard concluded our conversation by saying he would appreciate it if Rourke and I could stand by until he had completed ''ground work'' for our trip to Convair.

While Rourke and I were on ice in Hollywood, I requested Ed Zak to visit Convair to appraise the delivery situation. Ed's report did not flatter Convair. When he asked the person responsible for production what kind of production status reports he received, Ed was handed a three-inch-thick stack of computer sheets and told that everything was in the sheets, which were produced every day. Ed said to me, ''You couldn't even look through them in a day. I don't know how in hell anybody could tell what was going on. What I was looking for was a simple piece of paper like Boeing issues daily. You know, Bob, everything shown pictorially on one piece of paper: where the airplanes are and when they will deliver.''

My experience that fall was similar. Convair had hired a production man who had had years of experience at General Motors. After meeting him, I was ushered into a windowless war room with a large conference table in the center. Every wall was filled with beautifully prepared colored bar charts and graphs showing the exact status of construction in every shop and hangar, and on the flight line. It was an extremely impressive display.

The only problem was, as Bew quickly pointed out, that the charts bore little resemblance to the facts. In fairness to Convair, I do not believe any production control system could have kept up with Howard's unpredictable maneuvers.

Rourke and I stood by in Hollywood until June 24, when Rourke was released to return home. What a waste! We did what work we could, but being forced to stand by with the concurrence of TWA's president at such a critical time could not have been more disappointing or frustrating. Soon after Rourke left, Howard asked me to go to Convair to ''attend negotiating sessions.'' When I arrived in San Diego, he called and said he still had preparatory work to do with Naish. He requested for me to please remain in the area, but not to meet or talk with any Convair people.

Now, the general status of active Toolco 880's was that three had flown, one was in Field Operations, and two had been moved out of the hangar for system checks. During July, work on all of the active Toolco aircraft slowed down. Convair began taking weekends off, and delivery prospects faded even farther into the future. At about the same time, Hughes visited Convair and personally flew two of the Toolco 880's. He then directed that no acceptance flights be flown except as he directed, and only when he was present.

Thomas's Resignation

Charlie Thomas resigned as president on July 28, 1960. This bombshell was extremely poorly received by the financing institutions, and morale at Convair and TWA hit rock bottom. ''Thomas is out,'' Howard advised by phone. He released me to return to New York that same evening without my having been permitted to set foot on Convair property.

Review of the Romaine Street call sheets for William A. Forrester, Jr., of Merrill, Lynch, Pierce, Fenner, & Smith (Merrill Lynch) show that Hughes had this to say about Thomas several months after Charlie resigned:

Charlie Thomas negotiated and developed the financing plan with Dillon Read without my authority or any encouragement from me. He forced it down my throat. Then, at a Board meeting he created a coalition of my directors and turned them against me and faced me with a mass resignation of all but one of the TWA directors. I have never liked this plan; I have never been in favor of

362

this plan; I have fought it from the very beginning and I am still fighting it. I assure you that if it is employed, it will be over my dead body.

If you would like to come up with any suggestions of an alternate plan or any way whatsoever by which I can avoid being forced into the Dillon Read program, I would be most grateful. It is very flattering of you to say that you don't think I have ever been forced to do anything and maybe there was a time when this might have been a fairly accurate statement, but I assure you it is not true today and has not been true concerning the Dillon Read program from its inception. I have fought it hammer and tong from the very first day I ever heard of it.

Thus, Thomas, working no doubt in good faith and trying to solve TWA's life-or-death problems, had breached one of Howard's sacred precepts. Like negotiating for the procurement of aircraft, negotiating financing arrangements required his personal authorization and approval.

Financing Dilemma

The Dillon Read plan was intended to raise $290 million for TWA. One hundred million was to come from insurance companies, $90 million from a group of banks, and $100 million from Toolco, which would take TWA subordinated debentures in return for the money it had already invested in the jets. The bank and insurance company participation was later scaled down when the proposed fleet was reduced from 52 to 45 jets. On the insistence of the financing institutions, who had grown tired of Howard's financial machinations, restrictive covenants and limitations on Hughes's prerogatives, which proved to be completely unacceptable to him, were added during the evolutionary development of the plan. The proposed restrictive covenants included the placing of Hughes's TWA stock in a voting trust in event TWA defaulted on its debt or if any changes in TWA's management occurred that the lending institutions considered to be adverse, provided they were not corrected within 90 days. Such covenants were an anathema to Howard and ran totally against his grain. When the TWA board threatened to resign, Howard actually signed a formal approval prepared by Equitable Life Assurance Society leading all to believe he had generally accepted the Dillon Read plan. Later, he made it exceedingly clear that he had not.

During that fall, in response to a Hughes request, the Irving Trust Company developed an alternate financing plan that would have involved a group of banks and eliminated the Metropolitan Life Insurance Company. Howard wanted Metropolitan out because of its earlier insistence on the voting trust, which he wanted the bank plan to eliminate or at least soften. In addition to bank participation, General Dynamics Corporation was to provide substantial funds in return for which Hughes would order additional 880's and 990's for TWA. Hughes approved this plan, but it failed to clear a principal General Dynamics creditor, the Prudential Insurance Company of America, presumably because of its concern over the heavy losses being incurred by General Dynamics' Convair division. The bank plan was abandoned for this reason, but Hughes tried to resurrect it later by offering to assume through new borrowings an amount equal to the General Dynamics planned participation. Irving and the banks doubted that Hughes could raise the required funds and rejected his offer during early October, an act that permanently disposed of the plan.

During the period that followed Thomas's resignation, Convair tendered six Toolco 880's for acceptance flights. Hughes continued to refuse to allow such flights because if the aircraft were found to be acceptable, Toolco would have been obligated under the contract to accept and pay for them. All six aircraft were placed in storage. Convair tendered two more 880's during September and October. They were also placed in storage when Hughes refused to authorize acceptance flights. Four other 880's were pulled off the production line during October. Many of the planes were preserved with yellow-green acrylic paint. The San Diego factory lots were a disheartening forest of irregularly parked 880's in various stages of completion. At that point, Convair ceased work on all Toolco aircraft and began a substantial layoff of personnel.

I have never understood why Convair's executives permitted Howard to encroach, even though they were sympathetic to his desperate financial situation, and notwithstanding that he held out the carrot of a sizable 990 order. In my opinion, this never could have happened at Boeing. I believe Bill Allen never would have permitted disruptive intrusions, and certainly not outside guards and roped-off airplanes. In the interest of minimizing costs, Convair should have completed the planes on schedule and then parked them until payment could be made, just as Boeing did. Instead, Convair bent repeatedly to Howard's will, a little at a time, until Howard gained complete control.

Howard's performance at Convair was driven by lack of available credit, his habitual, stubborn unwillingness to give up even one jot of control or to share the fruits of any of his business enterprises, and his persistent treatment of TWA as a wholly owned subsidiary rather that as a privately held corporation. Factors of this nature and his apparent disdain for the financing institutions angered the financial magnates, who finally rebelled and dictated the circumscribing terms contained in the Dillon Read plan.

Howard's overall strategy also reflected pragmatic business considerations. His plan to retain ownership of the jets and to lease them to TWA on a long-term basis would have permitted Toolco to deduct the depreciation of the jets from pretax earnings, thus dramatically reducing the amount of Toolco's taxable income. Thus, Toolco would have paid relatively little corporate income tax. Additionally, the leases would have permitted Toolco to invest its profits in the jets and treat the income from the leases as capital gains while avoiding all risks of the penalty rates of the excess profits tax. And, while TWA could not depreciate the jets, the cost of the Toolco leases could be charged by it as a business expense.

Throughout this period Convair succeeded in delivering aircraft to Delta in substantial accord with its contractual obligations. Had Convair met its delivery obligations to Toolco as originally agreed upon, all 30 would have been delivered by the end of September 1960. As matters stood, only one 880, which TWA had purchased with its own funds for crew training, had been delivered to TWA. And no one knew when Howard would authorize delivery of the remaining 19 planes.

TWA needed the 880's. The Boeing jets continued to perform exceptionally well, attract full payloads, and generate record revenues. In my view, the ability of the jets to attract business had been demonstrated, TWA's need to receive the 63-plane rather than the 47-plane fleet was evident (Howard had allowed 12 international Boeings to go to TWA in lieu of the planned 10), and Howard's disruptive incursions at Convair seemed completely inappropriate. I continued throughout this period to take every opportunity to cite TWA's need to receive more jets faster to Ray Cook, Raymond Holliday, and, when feasible, to Howard. This probably did not endear me to Howard, but I do not remember any harsh words between us, perhaps because he knew I was right.

During September, Howard asked by phone if I would like to work for him full-time rather than continue to divide my time between TWA and his interests. I did not expect this. After we discussed what he had in mind, which was somewhat vague, I thanked him and said I thought I would prefer to continue with TWA, but I would think it over. This position no doubt at least partially reflected my frustration over the Convair situation.

Hughes's financial predicament worsened during October. Years before, Toolco had borrowed $14 million from Irving for purposes related to Hughes's acquisition of RKO. This loan was due for repayment at month's end, and certain other Toolco loans were already overdue. This provided Irving with a heavy club: If these loans were not repaid on schedule, Irving could force Toolco into receivership and force the sale of its assets to the extent necessary for repayment. Such a seizure would devastate Howard's remaining prospects for saving his empire and almost certainly cost Hughes his Toolco money fountain. With a bankruptcy trustee and court taking over, he would probably have been forced to testify publicly under oath about financial matters. As far as Howard was concerned, this had to be avoided at all costs.

The financiers decided that Hughes's procrastination had gone on long enough and the only acceptable way for him to avoid financial ruin for TWA was to implement the Dillon Read plan. They lowered the boom on Hughes by threatening to confiscate Toolco's and TWA's bank balances and declaring Toolco in default on delinquent loans. With this turn of events, Howard agreed, but he wanted the right to pay off the loans at any time without penalty. All of the prospective loan participants agreed except Metropolitan, which insisted that the lenders were entitled to the full 6½-percent return on the 10-year loan regardless of whether or not it was paid off early. This was unacceptable to Hughes and arrested early implementation of the Dillon Read plan.

During late October, Col. Henry Crown, who had merged his Materials Services Corporation (construction services) into General Dynamics, came forward with a plan to help Hughes and General Dynamics. He offered to arrange a bank loan of $150 million and purchase a large block of TWA stock. A supplemental $150 million was to be raised through the sale of TWA debentures to the public. In return, Hughes was expected to purchase Convair transports for TWA for an indefinite period. Howard welcomed this as a way to avoid the voting trust and retain control of TWA. Unfortunately for the Crown plan, the selected securities agent, Merrill Lynch, was doubtful of the success of the sale of the proposed TWA debentures because of the generally depressed value of airline securities and refused to guarantee the results of the sale. Confronted with this, Hughes reluctantly dropped the Crown plan, but not forever.

Shortly before the Crown deal was developed, Raymond Cook, for Toolco, and Dudley Diggs, for Convair, prepared Amendment No. 6 to the Toolco-Convair 880 purchase agreement to reflect agreements achieved between Hughes and Naish. The amendment, executed September 10, reduced the number of 880's Toolco had on order from 30 to 24. The other 6 880's were simultaneously leased by Convair to Northeast Airlines (NEA). This killed any remaining hopes I harbored that somehow, if adequate financing could be arranged, Hughes would change his mind and permit TWA to receive all 30 Toolco 880's.

Toolco also placed an order at that time with Convair for the purchase of 6 Convair 990s to be manufactured in compliance with AAL specifications. Earlier, during the spring of 1960, Raymond Holliday with the concurrence of Charlie Thomas had requested me to prepare a "feasibility study" to show the effect of TWA operations of a fleet of Convair 990's. The study showed such an operation to be profitable; but, as I pointed out to Raymond at that time, it did not project or compare the results of operations with a counterpart supplemental fleet of Boeings, which might show to be more profitable than the Convairs.

During that summer, Raymond Cook, who was in close touch with Hughes, asked me to undertake 990 specification negotiations at Convair to determine what changes to the basic AAL specifications would be required for TWA standardization purposes in event Howard ordered 990's for TWA's use. In response, I sent a small task group to San Diego.

Within the week after the group arrived at Convair, Howard called me in New York and asked that our 990 specification activities cease. He explained that this activity had put him "in a terrible crack with Convair" because it enabled Convair to put pressure on him—Bob Loomis, who was now president of Convair's San Diego division, had objected to detailed specification review activities without an expression of further interest from Hughes. Howard requested that I pull out the men one at a time so it would not be obvious to Convair that negotiations had been called off.

A few days after the November 990 Toolco order had been placed, Howard called me and unequivocally directed that neither I, nor Bew and his San Diego staff, nor anyone else in TWA was to have anything to do with the Toolco 990's. I pointed out to Howard that if the 990's were destined for TWA, it would be advisable to renew the standardization specification negotiations at Convair. He said the planes would be manufactured in strict compliance with the AAL specifications and that TWA was not to become involved in any way. At the same time, Bill Bew received instructions through Romaine Street that he was "not to inspect, discuss, or even recognize the fact that 990's were on the production line."

Similar instructions were received with regard to the Convair Model 22M, called the 880M, aircraft then in limited production; however, none had been ordered by Toolco. The 880M's were heavyweight versions of the 880 equipped with wing leading-edge flaps to improve takeoff characteristics. TWA, joined by Delta, had tried for over a year during the early period of construction of the 880's to convince Convair to install leading-edge flaps as standard equipment. Convair was finally persuaded fairly late in the program to do so, but at a cost to Toolco of $1.65 million—nearly $2 million less than the initial Convair asking price—for the 30-plane Toolco fleet. Even so, this amount exceeded the personal limits of authority for individual changes that I had set for myself at the beginning of the program. It was a worthwhile change, especially advisable because of changes in FAA operating requirements promulgated after the planes were ordered. I urged Howard to authorize this expenditure, but he refused because of the cost.

Other adverse impacts on TWA's fleets because of Howard's financial foot-dragging were less visible. For example, not long after production was well under way on the domestic 707's, Boeing offered an advanced B version powered by the recently developed, bypass-type, forward-fan versions of P & W's JT-3 engines. Boeing also offered kits for the retrofit of such installations in delivered nonfan planes, or alternately, to accomplish the retrofit at the Boeing factory. Later, Boeing also offered the fan engine as standard on new production international 707's in lieu of P & W JT-4's.

The principal advantages of the 707B's were increased speed, reduced takeoff distances, lower fuel consumption with significant increases in payload-range capability, and lower airport noise. Our studies showed that conversion to the B model would pay for itself in five years through a combination of avoiding revenue loss to TWA's competition, increased fleet utilization because of faster speeds, and increased revenue from the ability to carry greater payloads on many long-range flights. The cost, including estimated lost revenue from the time out of service required for this highly desirable modification, was $33.8 million for TWA's 15 domestic Boeings.

AAL had taken the lead in this program with Boeing and P & W, but Boeing undertook nearly simultaneous negotiations with TWA. By this time, AAL had ordered 50 Boeing transports, primarily for U.S. domestic operations. Boeing agreed to install the advanced engines in 25 AAL jets, upgrade the next 10, which were nearing completion at the factory, and modify the remaining 15 before delivery by installing the fan engine and making other related changes. Later on, AAL standardized power plants by installing fan engines in the 10 nearly completed planes as well.

At that time, AAL also had 25 Convair 990's on order; and UAL had 68 four-engine jets on hand or on order and 20 Caravelles on order, and was negotiating with Boeing for a fleet of 40 727's—a total combined fleet of 203 jets that would be flown by TWA's principal domestic rivals in services largely competitive with TWA. In sharp contrast, TWA had only 15 domestic and just a few international Boeings available for domestic services, with unknown prospects for obtaining 20 Convairs.

Because a bad competitive situation would become worse if TWA did not modify its 15 Boeings, I recommended that it do so, but that priority be given to obtaining the Convair fleet. Spending $33.8 million for the modification program without having first solved the acute financial crisis Howard found himself in was totally out of the question, no matter how desirable the engine change was. Anyway, it was more important to obtain additional jets than to modify the existing fleet, so the engine conversion project was held in abeyance. Later on, when TWA's financial health had improved sufficiently to warrant renewed serious consideration of the installation of the fan engines, the cost had risen so sharply that the program could not be justified.

When Howard was trying to work out an acceptable financing arrangement, Jack Naish had sent numbers of demand letters to Toolco, which pointed out:

The General Dynamics Corporation has been under heavy and continuing financial burdens by reason of the failure of the Hughes Tool Company to take delivery of completed Model ''880'' aircraft; [and] by reason of its failure to pay the balances due thereon, including both the remainder of the purchase price and the charges and costs incurred by General Dynamics Corporation as

a result of failure to take delivery. . . . Accordingly, I must and do herewith . . . make formal demand that these failures of performance by the
Hughes Tool Company be remedied.

Convair knew Toolco could not respond affirmatively and was making a
record that might be needed to reinforce its future legal position. Contrary
to the implications in Naish's demand letters, the Toolco 880's were not
entirely ready for acceptance. The updating of aircraft systems, completion
of equipment and interior installations, and customer acceptance flight tests
were required.

I had been led repeatedly to believe that Howard's financing problem
might be close to solution. I wanted a clear understanding with Convair on
TWA's current minimum acceptable 880 configuration requirements to
enable factory preparatory work at the earliest feasible date and minimize
further delays in delivery. Because Howard no longer had objections, I met
with Bob Loomis to review the production status of the planes. I encouraged Bob to do all the necessary planning and prepare to update and
complete the aircraft at the earliest practicable date.

Loomis and his Convair associates wanted desperately to resume production, make deliveries, and receive payment, but quite understandably
they were unwilling to resume full-scale operations without proof that
Howard or TWA could and would pay for the planes. Nonetheless, as the
end of 1960 approached, Convair, encouraged by the apparent progress
being made in financing the 880's, did undertake a moderate level of
factory work to prepare the most nearly complete aircraft for delivery.
Because of continuing liaison with Loomis, Convair was well apprised of
TWA's current requirements, and I was well acquainted with Convair's
delivery capabilities.

Hughes's Final Days at TWA

Howard's wily maneuvering, extended procrastination, and denial of jets
for TWA took a heavy emotional toll. TWA's management became ex-
cruciatingly frustrated and extremely tense during Howard's final days at
TWA. So did the financiers involved in TWA's and Toolco's affairs. Each
day the crises seemed to worsen, as Hughes frequently refused to accept
phone calls or otherwise respond to deadlines.

TWA and Toolco had come precariously close to insolvency because of

Howard's delay in concluding a financing program; the fact that he had stretched his immediately accessible resources to the limit to pay for the Boeings, which Toolco was leasing to TWA on a day-to-day basis (all 15 domestic and 4 of the 12 international); and because of other Toolco debts. Unfortunately, Howard's considerable remaining resources simply were not available to help.

Shortly after the Crown plan failed, concerned CAB investigators reported to the board that TWA's financial affairs had reached a critical stage. One of the investigators advised Hughes through Raymond Cook that if TWA's financing program were not soon finalized, the CAB would consider it in the public interest to hold a hearing to determine if Hughes should be permitted to retain control of TWA. A public CAB hearing would likely require months for completion and the issuance of findings and would destroy what little opportunity remained for Hughes to come to terms with the financing problem. Also, unquestionably, such a hearing could cost Howard his control of the airline, if not by CAB edict, then by the forced establishment of a voting trust, and it might result in bankruptcy.

Howard, now under extreme pressure from all sides, responded by asking if the Dillon Read plan could be reinstated. He was advised on the concurrence of the participants that it could, but the terms would be tougher: This time, the voting trust would be required to be implemented as a prerequisite to advancing funds. Also, a deadline to end all deadlines for execution of all aspects of the plan was set for year's end. After that, if the Dillon Read plan were not implemented, insolvency would be unavoidable. Appearing to accept this dictum, Howard ordered his lawyers to work with the Dillon Read lawyers to expedite preparation of the necessary papers, thereby permitting timely execution of this complicated multiparty deal.

During a special meeting of the TWA board held December 2 to review the progress being made by the lawyers, Raymond Cook announced that his firm no longer represented Hughes. This unexpected development was a good-sized bombshell, fired by Hughes at an extremely crucial time. Raymond said that Gregson Bautzer, a prominent Hollywood lawyer who for years had handled Hughes's personal legal problems and been involved in developing the Crown plan, was his replacement. I was shocked when I heard of this development. The TWA board and the financing institutions were nonplussed.

Bautzer arrived in New York in a few days. Instead of vigorously pursuing the Dillon Read plan, he set out to revive the aborted Crown deal, no doubt on instructions from Hughes, who had not given up on finding some way to avoid the voting trust. The CAB heard of this development and volunteered that any financing plan through which an airframe manufacturer gained an interest in an airline would be unacceptable. Because this is precisely what would have happened had the Crown plan been implemented, Bautzer then concentrated on finalization of the Dillon Read plan.

Howard's cliff-hanging tactics continued, however, through December. At times he could not be reached for days at a time for clearance of critical details. Most of the informed people I talked to had expected him to authorize execution of the Dillon Read plan rather than accept bankruptcy, but his prolonged evasive antics raised doubts about his true intentions. It was announced shortly before the scheduled closing that Greg Bautzer had entered a Wilmington, Delaware, hospital and would be unavailable to give his legal opinion at the closing.

On Friday, December 30, the last working day of the month, at 7:25 P.M., after the FAA had made special arrangements to keep its Oklahoma City office open until 7:30 P.M., Raymond Holliday executed the last of the Dillon Read papers in New York. The lenders, on the advice of their counsel, waived the Toolco legal opinion, so Bautzer's absence, whatever the reason for it, did not prevent the closing. Within minutes, the Oklahoma City FAA had been advised to register the titles on all TWA aircraft in the names of the lenders. The Dillon Read plan had been adopted and was in full operation. Howard had lost control of the airline.

Howard had appointed Raymond Holliday to serve as his trustee on the three-man voting trust. The financing institutions appointed to serve as their representatives Ernest R. Breech, the former chairman of the Ford Motor Company, who had been long importantly associated with aviation affairs, including TWA's predecessor companies; and Irving S. Olds, the former chairman of the U.S. Steel Corporation, who was associated with the New York firm of White and Case. Their duties commenced with Holliday's execution of the last official document. The CAB, which had given prior approval to the concept, volunteered that the trustees would not be restricted in their power to approve further financing for TWA or in their ability to manage the assets.

The majority of TWA executives, including me, remained in the office that evening until the closing had been confirmed. I had mixed, conflicting feelings. I was deeply distressed that Howard had lost control of the airline and greatly relieved over the prospect that once again TWA could start moving. I had no idea what the future might hold for me and wondered if my close association with Hughes would irreversibly tarnish me with TWA's new board and the new president, whoever that might turn out to be.

The impact of what had happened hit me more forcibly the next day. As the day passed, I became almost numb from the realization that Howard was really out, even though I had known full well that it was exceedingly unlikely, despite his great ingenuity, that he could pull any last-minute remedial rabbits out of this particular hat. I tried to assimilate what had happened and began to worry about how my family might be ultimately affected. I knew loss of control must have hurt Howard deeply, and I felt sympathetic. He had never been a quitter, and I suspected that he would make every effort to regain control at the earliest possible opportunity. But I really had no idea what to expect. Altogether, it was a black, terrible day.

That evening was New Year's Eve. Margie and I had been invited to a neighborhood party in the woods of Weston, Connecticut. It was to be a lavish affair that we both had looked forward to. The last thing I felt like doing that evening was attending a party, but because I did not want to disappoint Margie, I decided to forget TWA and celebrate the new year. But I could not get Hughes out of my mind. The result was that for me, the party turned out to be absolutely the worst I had ever attended, and I was certainly the most unresponsive guest. I noticed that everyone else seemed to have a fabulous time. In truth, it was a great party, but I just could not appreciate it.

My attitude toward Howard had begun to change with the sale of the Toolco Boeings to PAA and his denial to TWA of the 10 Convair 880's that he had purchased initially for TWA's use. Despite my long-term admiration for Howard, I became increasingly disenchanted by these developments, the Convair production fiasco, and the escalating negative impact of Howard's calculated stratagems on TWA. Through the years we had had differences of opinion in fleet-selection matters, but I dismissed such instances as honest differences in judgment until Howard's airplane withholding and disposal actions convinced me his decisions had been governed by empire considerations rather than what was best for TWA.

My loss of esteem for Howard slowly increased, but at no time did I feel angry, although I intensely disliked his cavalier subversion of TWA. I felt sorry for him and would have had considerably more compassion except that numbers of TWA and Toolco executives who were well versed in financial matters—I had no significant independent expertise in this area—assured me that Howard could have quite easily financed Toolco's jet programs had he done so much earlier, when it was timely.

It was a wrenching experience. Emotionally, I did not want Howard to lose control. Intellectually, I knew TWA would be better off being its own master.

22.

Twenty-Seven Years in Court

I suspected that my close association with Hughes and Toolco would raise questions concerning my loyalty to TWA, so I resigned from Toolco effective January 1, 1961, to at least allay suspicions concerning any conflict of interest. Even so, I knew that if management gave me the chance, only my future conduct would finally put such concerns to rest. Hughes's loss of control of TWA left an immediate wake of apprehension, confusion, disappointments, and high expectations. Hughes did not accept graciously the fact that he had been forced to place his TWA stock in the voting trust. Toolco's TWA directors were directed not to attend TWA board meetings, thus preventing quorums and thwarting reconstitution of the board so that the trustees were deprived of the anticipated immediate control of the airline. Hughes ordered additional Convair 990's stated to be for TWA's use without consulting TWA. He tried to force TWA to buy the 990's and a fleet of Lockheed Electras. He tried to disrupt TWA's fleet procurement programs even after the new Boeings had been ordered. Soon TWA sued Hughes, Toolco, and Raymond Holliday.

After a good financial showing in 1959, due substantially to effective jet

375

planning and the excellent productivity of the initial Boeing fleet, jet-starved TWA suffered a decline in profits in 1960 to just under $6.5 million. The 1960 slide in profits continued throughout the year, exacerbated by not receiving either the six international Boeing jets or any of the Convair 880's except the single training plane, which had been delivered in May 1960. A general depression had overtaken the U.S. airline industry, which did not help. TWA's jet fleets had produced profits, but barely enough to overcome the losses generated by TWA's piston flights. The truly alarming fact was that, unlike its competition, TWA had no additional jets on order.

During early 1961, TWA's business trends remained negative, with alarming losses a daily occurrence. And as if that were not enough, TWA flight engineers went on strike during February, making a bad financial situation much worse. This was not a welcome or reassuring backdrop for the trustees in their task of recruiting new directors, but a circumstance that the Hughes interests no doubt welcomed because the increasing losses being incurred as the year advanced reinforced their strong endeavors to regain control. By the end of 1961, TWA would incur a whopping net loss of $38.7 million.

A New Equipment Program

I thought it entirely clear that TWA's principal problem was insufficient jets to command a profitable share of the market and permit the timely retirement of the comparatively inefficient pistons. My best hopes for the widespread enthusiastic acceptance of the jets and my worst fears that the pistons could not compete successfully against them were being realized every day. I resolved to be prepared to present the new president, whoever he might turn out to be, with a comprehensive fleet procurement plan designed to restore TWA's competitive position and reverse its bleak profit outlook.

Consequently, I undertook on my own initiative during early January of 1961 to develop such a plan for submission to the new president at the earliest feasible date. My market and technical planning staffs, under Henry Fellows and Russ Rourke, respectively, and I were the principal participants. I simultaneously undertook direct negotiations with Boeing and Convair to secure the most favorable delivery positions and contract terms if the plan should be implemented.

376

The Executive Committee, established when Charlie Thomas resigned, continued to function until March 1, 1961, when the interim Management Committee, consisting of W. L. Pierson, Vic Leslie, and Oz Cocke, was established to serve until the election of a new president. I advised them of the development of the new equipment plan, probable capital requirements, and key decision dates, and told them that once the plan was ready, I would press hard for approval of the fleet procurement recommendations it contained.

The plan, entitled "TWA Fleet Requirements, 1961–1970," was issued March 1, 1961. It reflected a thoroughgoing team effort and contained historical and projected marketing data, key aircraft operational characteristics and delivery information, an analysis of past and future TWA competitive situations, and recommendations concerning TWA fleet composition. All eligible types of Boeing, Convair, and Sud Aviation transports were considered. I had ruled Douglas out of contention for reasons of standardization and lack of early availability.

Quite deliberately the report did not expressly recommend selection of specific types of aircraft; rather, it recommended procurement of fleets by category because I did not wish to prejudice negotiations still under way with the manufacturers. This approach provided no basis for Howard to attempt to interfere with our negotiations because as far as the report was concerned, manufacturers had not been selected. Specific recommendations, including selection of the manufacturer and particular airplane models, were contained in a concurrent, tightly guarded summary document.

The fleet requirement report recommended procurement of 6 international long-range turbo-fan transports and 20 domestic long-range turbo-fan transports for deployment beginning in 1962. I also recommended that TWA plan on procuring specific quantities of additional turbo-fans for use beginning in 1963 and beyond, and that before the end of 1961, TWA procure approximately 20 Boeing 727's or Sud Aviation Caravelles to satisfy TWA's shorter-haul requirements. It was an appropriate but ambitious proposal.

During the last working day of Howard's control of TWA, December 30, 1960, Toolco had assigned to TWA rights to 19 of the 23 880's it still had on order. This effectively broke the Convair logjam. Convair had followed the late-1960 Toolco financing developments closely. As year's end approached, it had reassigned factory manpower to expedite completion of Toolco's undelivered 880's. Bew was able to accept TWA's second

880 on January 1, 1961 (the first had been accepted during the preceding May for training purposes), which Capt. Gordon Granger flew to Kansas City the same day. Bew accepted a total of 6 880's during January, 5 more by April, and the 20th on October 13. TWA's 880 fleet had been delayed 198 airplane-months, or an average delay of 9.9 months per airplane, whereas Delta's fleet had been delayed only 14 airplane-months, or a total of 1.4 months per airplane. It is reasonable to believe that except for Hughes, TWA's 880's would have been delivered with no more average delay than Delta experienced. TWA began scheduled 880 services on January 12, 1961; we had planned to begin in May 1960, as Delta did. A critical high-traffic season had passed us by.

Almost at once TWA operated with near-capacity payloads on its 880's, which proved capable of drawing passengers from competing turboprop flights. With the start of 880 services, TWA was poised to accomplish a reversal in its downward trend, but it was obvious that appreciable time would be required to stem and make up the losses, regain market share, and return TWA to profitability. Receipt of the 880's also permitted solid planning concerning the retirement of TWA's economically obsolescent piston aircraft. The Lockheed 1649A Jetstreams, which Howard had insisted on buying over my objections, were among the heaviest losers and the first to be listed for disposal.

Operation with the 880's went smoothly except for the engines, which proved troublesome. After the engine maintenance problems had been brought up to barely acceptable standards, we found that the design changes we had incorporated altered the combustion process just enough to produce highly visible smoke trails during takeoff and climb operations. This offended airport communities and caused political problems, and it was one of the reasons for the early retirement of TWA's 880's in 1973.

The durability and fatigue-resistance characteristics of the 880 airframes, however, were perhaps the best in the business. Convair had found through special tests conducted at my urging that heavier than normal fuselage skin combined with the right degree of soundproofing material produced optimum internal noise attenuation compared to the usual design practice of basing skin thickness on structural considerations alone. This new concept—combined with heat-bonded wing components, which were also attached by normally spaced rivets—was largely responsible for the superb structure.

While the first group of TWA's 880's was being delivered and the fleet

378

requirement plan was under development, Ernie Breech and Irving Olds, the trustees appointed by the financial institutions, were having their problems. Howard's orders to the Toolco-appointed TWA board members not to attend TWA board meetings until the annual meeting, scheduled for April, prevented a quorum of the board and made it impossible for the majority trustees to reconstitute the board during regular board meetings and take over active control of the corporation. After the February 23 board meeting was aborted for this reason, Breech and Olds had had enough. They called a special stockholders meeting for February 28, at which time new board members were elected.

It was an illustrious board indeed. Included were George R. Brown, executive vice president at Brown & Root; Charles S. Hobbs, president of Hale Brothers Stores; Clifford F. Hood, former president of U.S. Steel; Barry T. Leithead, president of Cluett, Peabody & Company; Houston M. McBain, former chairman of Marshall Field & Company; and others. The new board was a powerhouse of experience and seasoned judgment that would do well for TWA.

During the first meeting of the reconstituted board, Tom Slack, who for years had worked closely with Hughes and had served as a TWA board member since 1950, stated that TWA should employ independent counsel to look into the liability of everyone who had been involved in permitting TWA to muddle into such a chaotic condition. In response, Breech, over the strong objections of Raymond Holliday, who had remained a board member, appointed a committee of three directors to recommend within 60 days a law firm to investigate.

A new president was urgently needed. On the suggestion of Francis Reed, a prominent New York lawyer serving as counsel for the trustees, Breech contacted Charles C. Tillinghast, Jr., vice president for international operations for the Bendix Corporation. Tillinghast, a successful lawyer and corporate executive, was happy at Bendix but disliked being away from home almost continuously because of international business obligations. Breech decided Tillinghast was the right man for the job and invited him to attend the March TWA board meeting, where he was greeted warmly and encouraged to accept the job. He did so during the meeting, effective April 17, 1961, following the annual stockholders meeting.

At the same meeting, the board selected the New York law firm of Cahill, Gordon, Reindel & Ohl to determine if any cause for legal action on behalf of TWA existed. A team of lawyers from that firm under the direction of John Sonnett, a former assistant attorney general in charge, successively, of the Claims Division and the Antitrust Division of the Justice Department, quickly began to investigate Hughes's activities during the period of his control of TWA. I became one of the centers of attention because of my direct involvement in fleet procurement matters and my long association with Hughes.

Within days of his election I phoned Tillinghast at Bendix for an appointment to review my March fleet plan and point out that decisive action would be required shortly after he became president because of Boeing's lead-time production requirements if the most favorable airplane delivery positions were to be obtained. He agreed to meet me the next day. He was most cordial and listened intently while I summarily described TWA's equipment situation, the derivation of the plan, the cash requirements, and the recommendations. I explained that all eligible transports had been considered in detail and that I had concluded that the best course for TWA would be to procure 6 international fan-powered Boeings and 20 fan-powered domestic versions. I was encouraged that he did not appear to be shaken by the enormous sums involved, even including the additional 20 727's or Caravelles scheduled for procurement later that year. After a discussion that lasted about two hours, I departed after leaving a copy of the report and my definitive recommendations.

To my absolute delight, on April 30, only days after Charlie Tillinghast took office, the board on his recommendation approved the purchase of 5 international and 18 domestic type Boeing fan-jets. Additionally, the board authorized the short-term lease that I had negotiated for 4 Boeing 720B's. Boeing had manufactured these aircraft for NWA, which was unable to take delivery, and they could be made quickly available for interim TWA use. Suitable contracts were executed the same day, subject to TWA's concluding financing arrangements, which occurred on schedule on May 31. Now, TWA would have an excellent chance over the years immediately ahead to reverse its deteriorating competitive position.

TWA's use of the NWA 720B's was especially valuable. In addition to permitting early supplemental services, the FAA-authorized time between overhauls (TBOs) for TWA's own fan engines was governed by the date of receipt of the leased aircraft. The FAA established TBOs separately for each operating airline, the permissible hours between engine overhauls depending on a number of factors, including extent of prior usage by the particular airline. Thus, a greater number of hours between overhauls for

TWA's entire 23-plane fan fleet was permitted because of the earlier introduction of the leased aircraft into TWA's system. Additionally, experience gained by TWA personnel with the 720B's permitted more efficient initial use of TWA's own 23 fan-jets than otherwise would have been the case.

The announcement that TWA had purchased the fans was greeted with unbounded enthusiasm throughout TWA's ranks. Employees were encouraged not only by the size of TWA's Boeing order, but also by the rapidity with which it had been executed after Tillinghast became president. Morale visibly improved, job interest increased, and brighter days ahead seemed assured.

Howard, however, was chagrined over TWA's order. On February 22, 1961, he had ordered 7 additional 990's, making a total of 13, which he stated were intended for TWA's use, although he had them built to another airline's specification, and no TWA personnel were permitted to take any part in supervision of production. Moreover, he continued to entertain the idea that TWA should acquire a sizable fleet of Lockheed Electras. He claimed that the trustees should have sought his recommendation before approving the Boeing deal. He was acting as if he had never surrendered control by putting his stock in a voting trust.

It was obvious that Howard's burning ambition was to end the voting trust and regain actual control of TWA at the earliest possible moment, even if this required paying a heavy penalty for early debt retirement. As part of the Dillon Read plan closing, TWA had paid Toolco $157.5 million, which corresponded to the amount Toolco had invested in the jet aircraft and support equipment to which TWA took title. Of this, $100 million was in the form of a 6½-percent interim note and the rest was in cash. Toolco's unpaid obligations for the 19 Convair 880's were assumed by TWA. Howard's financial health had improved considerably. The threat that he might regain control appeared real, possibly imminent.

Howard's interest in having TWA acquire 990's and Electras reflected his desire to reassert his dominance over TWA's equipment planning and pass off on TWA his financial obligations for the 990's (and the few 880's that he had held back for his own purposes), and his concern over the negative impact that conditions and covenants contained in TWA's financing arrangements for the new Boeings might have on his ability to regain control. The $147 million loan needed to acquire the new Boeings—an additional $40.5 million was to come from TWA cash—was to be made by the same financial institutions that had forced Hughes to give up control of TWA. Because the $147 million would become immediately payable if Hughes paid off the $165-million Dillon Read plan loan (plus a 22-percent penalty for early repayment), Hughes would be confronted with the need to raise the enormous sum of $348 million to regain control if the Boeing order remained in effect. On the other hand, if TWA canceled the Boeing order and purchased Convairs and Electras through Toolco, and if Convair and Lockheed would assist in making financing arrangements independent of the Dillon Read plan participants, the two financing arrangements would be uncoupled, and Howard might be able to regain control of TWA much earlier.

Howard mounted a major campaign headed by Chester Davis, an attorney who had recently been retained by Hughes and was then a senior partner in the trial department of the New York firm of Simpson, Thacher & Bartlett. Davis's charge was to persuade TWA to substitute additional Convairs and Lockheed Electras for the recently ordered Boeings. A continuing flurry of telegrams (including telegrams to Boeing and letters to the Securities and Exchange Commission asserting that TWA had no legal right to place the orders), phone calls, and meetings resulted. Davis advised one of the involved New York financiers that Hughes had every intention of doing everything he could to "bust up the Boeing deal."

During late May 1961, days before the financing for the Boeing deal was to be closed, Charlie Tillinghast received additional delivery information about Convair 990's and asked me if, in light of that data, it was still my opinion that TWA should adhere to our decision to procure the Boeings. After studying the new data, I responded by letter of May 25, as follows:

It remains my opinion that for a variety of reasons the best interests of TWA would be served by adhering to our original decision to purchase Boeing 707-131's rather than Convair 990's.

The attached forecast cost and revenue summary, based on the very latest information available including the delivery information referred to in your letter, supports this view.

Further, it is important to note that Boeing's historical delivery performance fully supports the idea of firm TWA planning and implementation activities whereas Convair's 880 delivery performance and its current 990 situation [Convair had recently encountered serious 990 performance deficiencies] strongly suggests that this would not be the case if 990's were to be acquired.

On Chester Davis's insistence, a conference to consider "vital new technical information" was held in TWA's board room, Friday, June 2, just two days *after* financing arrangements for the new Boeing fleet had been closed. It was attended by Tillinghast; a few other TWA executives, including me; and Chester Davis and several Toolco representatives.

I formalized my appraisal of the "vital new information" by letter of June 8 to Tillinghast, with copies to the other senior officers. The letter, followed by seven pages of explanation addressing Chester's major points, stated:

My understanding of the purpose of the conference was to obtain certain vital new technical information from the Hughes Tool Company which could possibly bear upon TWA's decision to purchase Boeing flight equipment. Much of the conference seemed vague as to technical particularity and much of it had nothing to do with the technical or engineering aspects. . . . My general comments are:

1. The information that was presented was not new . . . and in almost all particularity had been given prior consideration by TWA.
2. The presentation was a "lawyer's" presentation rather than that of a technical expert. Much of the information presented was vague and general in character and none of it was backed up with documentation, studies, or other technical data or reports.
3. Nothing was presented which could be reasonably viewed as providing a basis for changing the over-all appraisal of Boeing vs. Convair equipment for TWA's intended use of the aircraft.

The letter concluded with, "All in all, our earlier recommendation stands."

My appraisal of the contending aircraft had been based on thoroughgoing evaluations of the technical and business aspects with regard to what would be best for TWA. It had nothing to do with financing considerations or how TWA's Boeing order might bear on Howard's ability to regain control of TWA. I thought such considerations were the clear prerogative of the president and TWA's new board of directors. My job was to recommend the best fleets for TWA's long-term use. I was of course well aware that bucking Howard's equipment plan as I had done would likely cost me my job if he should regain control. Even so, I thought that what I honestly considered to be best for TWA had to take precedence over

383

personal considerations, and I had proceeded accordingly. Despite what appeared to me to be endless arguments between opposing lawyers and unrelenting attacks engineered by Howard and Chester Davis, TWA stayed with its decision to acquire the Boeings.

Subsequent events confirmed that acquisition of 990's would have been a serious mistake for TWA. Among other problems, the cruising speed of the aircraft was found to be seriously deficient—over 20 knots slower than promised. Convair hired Art Raymond, who had recently retired from Douglas, to explore what redevelopment, if any, would permit attaining the original performance objectives. The combined efforts of Raymond and Convair only partially restored the performance, and AAL retired its 990 fleet years early in favor of more efficient aircraft.

TWA's Federal Suit

John Sonnett's investigation of whether TWA had a basis for legal action culminated in his recommendation that a suit be filed in the federal court against Hughes, Toolco, and Raymond Holliday. On June 30, 1961, with board authorization, concurred in by Tillinghast, Sonnett filed a suit charging antitrust violations at the Federal Courthouse in lower Manhattan. The papers were sealed (made unavailable to the public) until July 11, and later until August 1, to permit settlement negotiations without incurring publicity if Hughes should be so disposed. Along with the antitrust complaint, Sonnett filed a petition requesting a court order for Hughes to appear as the first witness.

By this time, Hughes had virtually withdrawn from the world except for phone lines, TV monitors, and written messages. He still ran his empire, but behind closed doors and opaque windows. Hughes did not enjoy good health, possibly as a result of early airplane accidents and his atrocious eating and irregular sleeping habits. Now, he was surrounded by only a few trusted Mormons, who served as secretaries and took care of his personal needs. Hughes, the white knight who in the shining armor of righteous indignation had so fearlessly charged and successfully fought the "evil" Washington empire of Senators Brewster and Ferguson in 1947 and thereby once again become an acclaimed public hero, no longer seemed capable of facing the public at large or prosecutors in particular. His withdrawal was tragic and, I thought, incomprehensible. One of the richest men in the world had deliberately committed himself as a prisoner in circumscribed, extremely limited jails of his own making. Sonnett's petition for Howard to appear as a witness struck raw nerves.

The complaint in the case charged that Hughes had controlled and manipulated TWA and its affairs for his own benefit in violation of the antitrust laws. Specifically, the complaint alleged that Hughes had prevented TWA from ordering jet aircraft and making independent financing arrangements and that he had required TWA to purchase its jet fleets from Toolco, preventing TWA from dealing with alternative sources or obtaining necessary related financing, instead retaining the TWA market for himself.

When the seal was broken, the suit commanded intense interest throughout America and in many foreign countries. The idea that a corporation would sue its 78-percent owner under the antitrust laws for monopolizing and running his own company's purchasing and financing arrangements was unique and startling. The legal basis for the suit was bewildering to me because I knew that Howard's lawyers had sought and obtained the approval of the CAB for all financial transactions that had occurred through the years between Toolco and TWA and that the CAB had confirmed and reaffirmed Howard's right to control the corporation. The CAB, a quasi-judicial body, had been empowered by Congress to grant antitrust immunity, the extent of which was now being challenged by John Sonnett's suit. TWA's damages as initially claimed were $35 million, which if awarded would be trebled under antitrust law to $105 million. Sonnett later increased the claim by $10 million.

Serious settlement discussions were undertaken while TWA's suit was still under seal, possibly because of Howard's fear that he might be ordered by the court to appear as a witness. During this period Howard made repeated efforts through Chester Davis and Greg Bautzer to persuade TWA to cancel the Boeing orders and purchase 990's and Electras through Toolco. Some of the settlement efforts appeared promising, but the parties could not come into final agreement for various reasons, including the flight equipment matter.

Howard's Strategy

Howard's subsequent strategy to regain control of TWA through a series of maneuvers before the CAB in Washington nearly succeeded. Almost accidentally he had come to own an interest in NEA when he merged RKO

Studios into Floyd Odlum's Atlas Corporation during the mid-1950s. As part of the merger deal, Hughes received 11 percent of the Atlas stock. Because Atlas owned 55 percent of NEA, Hughes would have been a factor in the control of NEA had it not been for a CAB order requiring him to place his Atlas stock in a voting trust to comply with the statute prohibiting any one person from controlling more than one airline without CAB approval.

Capitalizing on this situation, Hughes devised a scheme to regain control through a flank attack. The plan was to find ways to control NEA; pay off the Dillon Read plan loan and dissolve the voting trust, thus reacquiring control of the TWA board and management; merge NEA and TWA; and find a cosmetic way to settle the TWA suit once he was in control of both prosecution and defense.

NEA, a regional New England airline that had obtained temporary routes to Florida in 1955, was operating pistons against National's and EAL's turboprops on the Florida routes, with disastrous financial results. The six Toolco 880's Hughes had permitted Convair to lease to NEA in 1960 (instead of making them available to TWA) gave promise of helping, but the full financial benefit to be realized from implementation of jet services required more time than was available. NEA was operating on the ragged edge of bankruptcy.

The CAB wanted to avoid the embarrassment of any U.S. airline's being forced into bankruptcy because, after all, it was the federally designated guardian of the health of the industry. Hughes recognized this and that his hand in dealing with the CAB would be strengthened if NEA remained weak. He seized upon this circumstance to regain the good graces of the CAB by seeking permission to advance funds to NEA. The CAB, attentive and cooperative, probably did not realize that Howard intended to advance only those minimal funds required to keep NEA alive until his objectives at TWA were attained. Howard even succeeded in avoiding a personal appearance and a full evidential hearing before the CAB, which, in its anxiety to find some way to rescue NEA, settled for a one-day hearing in which the history of Hughes's relationship with TWA was ignored as irrelevant.

On December 4, 1961, Hughes obtained permission from the CAB to provide NEA with emergency funds to permit continuing operations. The CAB withheld approval for Hughes to exercise control over NEA, but its permission was tantamount to the same thing. It was clear that it would be politically untenable for the CAB to withhold such approval at a future time after his financial backing alone had made it possible to continue operations of NEA's New England routes. Thus, within one year after Hughes lost control of TWA, he had through adroit maneuvering gained working control of another airline. All that remained before acquiring legal control was to obtain the official blessing of the CAB when the time was right. The first step of Howard's grand strategy to regain control of TWA was close to realization.

Hughes advanced just enough money from time to time to keep NEA alive. By gambling around $20 million on NEA, he hoped to win control of an airline worth 10 times that amount.

The Search

From the first, John Sonnett had argued over the objections of Chester Davis that the court should require Hughes to appear as the first deposition witness in TWA's case. Because Hughes could be served as a defendant in the case only in the New York federal district in which the suit had been filed, a subpoena was obtained from the federal court of the Southern District of California for Howard to appear as a witness.

Sonnett had the authority, but where was the man? The elusive Hughes had no intention whatsoever of accepting service and remained unavailable. His faithful Mormons knew the drill and blocked every move to find and approach him.

Sonnett placed an associate, Fred Furth, later a successful San Francisco lawyer, in charge of the search, assisted by an ex-FBI agent, Albert E. Leckey, who hired other detectives to help track Howard down. Their search was centered in the Los Angeles, San Diego, and Las Vegas areas. They searched everywhere that even the flimsiest of leads took them. Hughes's homes in Bel Air and Rancho Santa Fe, the Beverly Hills Hotel, and his 7000 Romaine Street operations headquarters were focal points. Personal service was necessary, and, this being a civil case, the detectives had no right to enter on Hughes's (or anyone else's) private property without permission. They found driveways leading to Hughes's homes chained off. The Mormon guards were perpetually watchful, and they seemed to appear everywhere Sonnett's detectives attempted to search.

The fact that Howard was avoiding the subpoena came to the attention of the press, which at times carried daily accounts of the intrigue of the

attempts to locate him. Well-meaning citizens offered numerous suggestions and leads, which complicated and extended the search and proved to
be fruitless. The subpoena was never served. Later, however, after considerable legal jockeying by Sonnett, the pressure on Hughes came to be
such that, to have the search called off, Chester Davis sought and obtained
permission from the New York federal court to accept service of the
subpoena on Hughes's behalf.

Toolco's "Countersuit"

Chester Davis filed what were called "counterclaims" in the Federal District Court in lower Manhattan on February 13, 1962. To nearly everyone's
surprise, Toolco did not sue TWA, except nominally. Instead, the thrust of
its counterclaims was that both Toolco and TWA had been damaged by the
financial institutions that had made or arranged for the $165-million loan
and required Howard to place his TWA stock in the voting trust. The real
defendants named in the counterclaims were Equitable, Metropolitan, Irving Trust, Dillon Read, and those key individuals who had opposed Hughes
in his battle to maintain control of TWA: James F. Oates, president of
Equitable; Harry C. Hagerty, vice chairman of Metropolitan; Ben-Fleming
Sessel, senior vice president of Irving Trust; Ernie Breech; and Charlie
Tillinghast.

The counterclaims alleged that the four institutions had illegally deprived Toolco of control of TWA and that they had engaged in self dealing
to extend the voting trust beyond the initial 10-year period. They also
alleged that Metropolitan and Equitable through their extensive involvement in airline financing were engaged in a phase of aeronautics and that
in forcing Hughes to accept the voting trust by withholding financing they
had gained control of TWA without the approval that the CAB required of
anyone so engaged. Additionally, the counterclaims charged that the financial institutions violated the antitrust laws by conspiring to restrain
interstate commerce through forcing Toolco to borrow from themselves,
rather than from the market at large.

The counterclaims alleged that TWA had been damaged in excess of $45
million, $10 million more than the TWA suit had claimed. It in effect said,
"Yes, TWA was damaged, but Toolco didn't do it. It was all the fault of
the financing institutions." Because the antitrust laws were alleged to have
been violated, Davis claimed treble damages: $135 million for TWA and

$308 million for Toolco, a total of $443 million. (Later, Sonnett accepted Davis's figures on TWA damages and increased the claims in TWA's suit from $35 million to $45 million.)

Chester Davis was generally credited for devising the exceedingly clever and ingenious counterclaims. This may have been the fact of the matter, but I would be surprised if the guiding hand of Hughes were not also involved. First, TWA might be ahead by $30 million if it could find ways to dump its own suit and jump on the Davis bandwagon. Second, if Hughes won, dissolution of the voting trust and his resumption of control of TWA were certain. If this happened, ways could certainly be found to settle the TWA suit.

TWA's Second Suit

A few weeks later, on April 18, 1962, Sonnett filed a second suit on behalf of TWA against Howard and Toolco in a Delaware state court. The underlying facts on which the claims were based were essentially the same as in the federal case, but the legal theories underlying the charges were different: mismanagement and breach of fiduciary responsibility. The claimed damages totaled $35 million. Because no antitrust violation was charged, any awarded amount would not be trebled.

The second suit was filed in the Court of Chancery, Wilmington, Delaware, because Toolco was a Delaware corporation and Delaware law then permitted the stock in any Delaware corporation owned by a defendant in a civil suit to be sequestered. Once a sequestration order is entered, if the defendant does not appear and defend, the court may sell the stock to the extent necessary to pay any judgment. Thus, jurisdiction over an absent defendant such as Hughes would be acquired to the extent of his stock interest in a Delaware corporation, without any personal service whatever.

Sonnett obtained a sequestration order against Hughes when he filed the Delaware suit. All of Hughes's Toolco stock was seized and placed under the control of Jacob Kreshtool, a Wilmington lawyer who was appointed to act as sequestrator. This was a sharp blow to Howard. Toolco was Howard's perpetual money fountain and the anchor for many investments, and it was now subject to confiscation to the extent required to pay the damages if Howard failed to appear as a witness. The cornerstone of his empire was under attack, but the battle was just getting under way.

The Northeast Judgment

CAB public hearings in the NEA control case were held April 2, 1962, in Washington. By then Toolco had bought out Atlas's controlling position and arranged for a $1-million revolving credit, barely enough to keep NEA alive. Toolco's primary opponents were National and EAL, but five other airlines either opposed or raised challenging questions concerning Hughes's control. TWA chose to take no part because it was unwilling to have the critical issues in its dispute with Hughes dealt with in any other place than the courts in which they were being vigorously litigated. Nonetheless, the CAB staff raised questions as to whether the history of Hughes's actions while in control of TWA should disqualify him from control of NEA.

Despite Toolco's having withheld evidence requested by the CAB, including tax records, CAB Examiner Merritt G. Ruhlen announced his decision on April 20. It could hardly have been more favorable to Hughes. Ruhlen found that ''the record will not support a finding that Toolco engaged in improper or unlawful activities in regard to TWA or Northeast,'' and the charge that Hughes had managed TWA's aircraft procurement programs to his own benefit was without merit. Ignoring the fact that TWA was not a party to the proceeding before him and had presented no evidence, the examiner's opinion hit hard at several major tenets of the two TWA lawsuits.

Alan Boyd, chairman of the CAB, announced the decision of the full board on June 19. The CAB approved Toolco's control of NEA, just as recommended by Ruhlen. Because there were no other known parties willing to aid NEA and NEA's survival was in the public interest, said Boyd, approval was appropriate.

Thus, the first step of Hughes's strategic plan had been fulfilled. It was a major victory for Hughes. Howard, who only a short time before had been severely criticized by the CAB for his involvement in TWA affairs, was in good graces once more. The second step, payment of the outstanding loan arranged by Dillon Read, proved to be more difficult.

Merger Attempts

Part of my long-range planning obligation at TWA was to study airline merger possibilities. During the final months of Charlie Thomas's tenure as president, he asked me to evaluate a proposal to merge NEA and TWA, which had been recently instigated by Hughes and offered by NEA. Hughes had agreed to loan Floyd Odlum $9.5 million for NEA on condition that NEA seek to merge with TWA. I placed Henry Fellows in charge of the study.

The study concluded that NEA's East Coast-Florida routes would be a valuable addition to TWA's system not only because of the profit potential offered by the routes themselves, but also because the north-south routes would correct part of the seasonal imbalance of TWA's predominately east-west routes. The Florida business peaked during the winter months, when east-west travel was slack. On the other hand, the study showed NEA's New England routes to be an economic disaster area. Because we knew of no acceptable way to merge with half of an airline or cast off the New England routes after a merger had been effected (it was most unlikely that the politically sensitive CAB would approve dropping the losing routes), the report recommended against the merger. However, Thomas left before this issue came to a head. The matter was put on hold during the chaotic period following his departure.

Shortly after Tillinghast became president, tough economic times forced the airline industry to give serious consideration to mergers. Due substantially to the prevailing poor business conditions, the majority of airlines were experiencing minimal profits or heavy losses. It appeared that mergers might provide an avenue to better times and quite possibly in TWA's case a way to ensure the survival of the corporation, which had continued to suffer excessive losses.

Tillinghast requested a full-scale study of all reasonable merger possibilities. He believed that TWA might be given only one chance by the CAB to merge and wanted the best opportunity for TWA—that is, if any merger appeared feasible under all the constraining circumstances that confronted the corporation. Hughes was almost certain to oppose a TWA merger with any airline but NEA because it would dilute his stock interest and substantially impair his ability to ever again direct the affairs of the corporation. We considered single partners and combinations of airlines. Our studies narrowed the field to EAL, PAA, NWA, and a combination of Western, Continental, and TWA. All such studies were reviewed during the bimonthly meetings of the Management Policy Committee, which consisted of the corporate officers.

The earlier NEA study was updated as part of this exercise. Except for

391

the Florida routes, this study held little interest for TWA notwithstanding Hughes's known interest in having a TWA-NEA merger consummated. When Tillinghast advised NEA during August 1961 that Atlas and NEA had been named co-conspirators in a lawsuit against Hughes, negotiations chilled and were soon abandoned.

During late 1961, Breech and Tillinghast undertook exploratory merger discussions with Captain Rickenbacker and Malcolm MacIntyre, chairman and president, respectively, of EAL; and separately with Juan Trippe, chairman of PAA. Later on, Tillinghast discussed similar possibilities with Donald W. Nyrop, president of NWA; and Ted Baker, president of National. At Tillinghast's request, Oz Cocke met with Bob Six, chairman of Continental; and Terrell C. Drinkwater, president of Western, to determine what interest they might have in undertaking three-party merger discussions. The two most promising possibilities were EAL, which offered excellent synergistic opportunities, including significant leveling of the seasonal business swings historically experienced by both airlines; and PAA, which had never given up on obtaining a "chosen instrument" position in the Atlantic and access to U.S. domestic routes. By then, because of heavy continuing loses, many TWA executives believed that consummating a merger was the only way for TWA to survive.

As far as TWA was concerned, discussions with EAL, which preceded talks with PAA, were serious. When discussions were quite advanced, Tillinghast noticed that MacIntyre was less than enthusiastic and appeared to be holding back. The fact of the matter was that EAL was simultaneously negotiating a merger with AAL. On January 18, 1962, the two airlines announced their intention to seek the approval of their shareholders to merge and filed a joint application to the CAB on January 23, thus killing all hopes for a TWA-EAL deal. During April 1963, the CAB rejected the AAL-EAL application.

TWA's merger discussions with PAA were another matter. Tillinghast and Trippe personally negotiated the framework, and Thomas F. Huntington, TWA's vice president of organization and procedures, carried out detailed negotiations on Tillinghast's behalf.

Trippe devised a clever plan designed to keep Hughes from gaining control of the merged airline. He proposed that PAA become a holding company whose principal asset would be the majority of shares in the new PAA-TWA airline. The airline would be a separate company. Those holding PAA stock would only receive stock in the holding company, and none in the airline. Hughes and TWA minority stockholders would only receive shares in the airline, and none in the holding company. Trippe would become chief executive officer in both the holding company and the airline and would always be able to outvote Hughes through his control of the holding company. The PAA-TWA merger might have succeeded except that by the time the lengthy negotiations were nearing completion, TWA experienced an upturn in business, which made the marriage seem less compelling.

These merger discussions, which were hardly secret, only provided Hughes with further incentive to win back control of TWA at the earliest possible date, certainly before any merger could be implemented that would restrict his ability to control the airline.

Legal Imbroglio

With two major lawsuits and the CAB proceedings simultaneously confronting the lawyers for the multiple parties involved, matters quickly became exceedingly complex and intertwined. For example, during pre-trial depositions I was confronted by as many as eight opposing lawyers who sat at the table with the special master, who presided over the depositions, along with four or five friendly lawyers. It was an interesting experience, but it was most certainly not fun to be grilled for seemingly endless weeks by batteries of some of the best lawyers in the business.

When I first learned that I would be a witness, I resolved to comprehensively review the period of Hughes's control from the time I joined TWA. I thought the greatest disservice I could do either side of the controversy was to withhold information or be less than candid. This required exhaustive review of all that had transpired involving Hughes and me and necessitated extensive research. Much of my personal effort occurred during late evening hours to minimize interference with my regular TWA duties. I quickly discovered that one's recollections of events may seem clear, but they sometimes become clouded or enigmatically distorted with passing time. Keeping straight the exact sequence of specific incidents that occurred years before during my simultaneous handling of multiple projects for Howard was especially challenging.

I learned quite early during the deposition period to confine my responses to categorical answers. Completeness was in the hands of the lawyers. Quite often I was abruptly cut off when I approached the crux of the matter under interrogation, probably because the opposing lawyers did not want to risk hearing answers that might prejudice their position. At other times, the lawyers asked incredibly expansive questions such as, "Mr. Rummel, please take your time and tell us all you know about the purchase of TWA's Martin fleets." Answers to such memory-jogging questions were voluminous and time consuming. Hughes's lawyers frequently challenged my accuracy, sometimes by sly inferential returns to controversial subject areas covered weeks or years before. Repetitive review of the facts proved necessary throughout my continuing but intermittent participation as a witness over the years, until the trial of the second case was finally concluded in 1985.

The deposition proceedings were conducted with considerably less formality than is customary during courtroom trials. The early discovery sessions were conducted by the lawyers; the later sessions were presided over by a court-appointed special master, James Lee Rankin, who had been solicitor general of the United States during the last three years of the Eisenhower administration. The interrogations usually occurred in some conveniently located conference room. The witness was sworn in, and a court reporter was always present, as were the sizable groups of lawyers from all sides.

In theory, the purpose of discovery was to acquaint the lawyers representing the defendants with the facts on which the allegations were based and the lawyers representing the plaintiffs with pertinent insights concerning the defendants' defense. The lawyers representing the financial institutions had their own, separate axes to grind.

The defendants had the first turn. Tillinghast, the first witness, was sworn in January 5, 1962. His deposition, continuous except for interspersed court proceedings, spanned almost seven months, to July 30. During this time he managed the nearly impossible task of ably serving as TWA's chief executive while being compelled to suffer long days away from the office under interrogation. It was a hard time for Tillinghast and TWA. Instead of being able to take the time he wanted to address the corporation's critical economic problems and become better acquainted with his new charge, he sat across the table from Chester Davis. He was running the corporation during early mornings, evenings, weekends, and recesses.

I do not remember Tillinghast's ever saying so, but I am quite sure he found the performance of Chester Davis to be just as annoying as I did.

394

Davis, who was undoubtedly a highly accomplished lawyer, had a brusque, caustic, vexatious manner, which proved to be perpetually irritating and disagreeable. I thought many of the gratuitous comments and innuendoes he uttered while attempting to slant the record were unconscionable and unfair. But as a witness, I was not allowed to comment. Davis seemed to do everything possible to prolong the depositions and thereby buy time to help implement Hughes's grand game plan. By the time Tillinghast was excused, an astonishing 6,000 pages of testimony had been recorded. I fared somewhat better—mine came to only 2,000 pages—but my explication had barely begun.

The Supreme Court handed down an opinion on January 14, 1963, in an entirely separate case (*PAA* v. *United States*) dealing with the division of authority between the CAB and the courts in matters involving conflicts between the principles of the antitrust laws and the Federal Aviation Act. The decision strongly favored the position Hughes was taking. The Court ruled that the CAB's regulatory powers took precedence over the federal antitrust laws in certain instances and that the courts could act in such cases only after the CAB had ruled. Even though the ruling was not all inclusive, it struck hard at Sonnett's position that the federal courts had jurisdiction over the antitrust matters his suit addressed. This circumstance appeared to be a major setback for Sonnett. Davis lost no time in preparing arguments to have Sonnett's case thrown out of the courts.

Davis moved swiftly because pressures were building. On January 9, 1963, Judge Charles Metzner, who presided over the antitrust case, had entered an order that the deposition of Hughes would "go forward" on Monday, February 11, 1963, and that this date would "be adhered to in the absence of extraordinary circumstances." After further motions seeking to avoid or delay the Hughes deposition, including a fruitless attempt to get the Court of Appeals to intervene, on Friday, February 1, 1963, Davis filed a motion to dismiss based on Toolco's CAB defense arguments, supported by a 27-page printed brief.

At 11:00 A.M. the next day, John Sonnett filed an 81-page printed answering brief for TWA. Sonnett was making good on his oft-stated intent to "keep their feet to the fire" and had a team of lawyers working for months drafting the answering papers to the motion that was sure to be filed. Chester Davis telephoned Sonnett in outrage, complaining that Hughes was accusing him of letting Sonnett place a spy in Davis's office.

Because all the papers were before him, Judge Metzner scheduled arguments on the motion for February 6. The argument was short—both sides had said what they could in the briefs. When it was over, Judge Metzner announced he would deny the motion in an opinion to be filed shortly. He also ruled he would not delay Hughes's deposition for an interlocutory appeal. But the long-awaited deposition would never take place.

On February 8, the Friday before Hughes was to begin testifying on Monday, Chester Davis once more went before Judge Metzner and announced that Toolco had made a "business decision" not to produce Hughes for his deposition. After questioning Davis closely as to his authority to take this step, Judge Metzner ruled that the Hughes deposition would not go forward but that TWA could move for a judgment by default.

These events made it clear that Howard was no longer the enthusiastic, innovative, and aggressive entrepreneur that I had worked with during the 1940s and early 1950s. At that time, I think Howard would never have gotten himself into the type of financial mess he found himself in later, but if he somehow had, he would have leaped at the chance to meet Sonnett head-on. That had been his nature as I observed it.

Judge Metzner handed down his written opinion on May 3, 1963, entering a default judgment against Toolco. He decided that Toolco's refusal to produce Howard after it had assured the court that it would was "deliberate and willful." The allegations in TWA's suit had been legally admitted, and Toolco was liable for commensurate restitution to TWA. However, in the same opinion Judge Metzner granted Toolco's motion to seek an interlocutory appeal.

The U.S. Court of Appeals agreed to hear the interlocutory appeal, but then it dealt Howard a further sharp blow on June 2, 1964, when it affirmed Judge Metzner and ruled that the CAB's 1944 and 1950 rulings concerning Toolco's control of TWA did not immunize Hughes from the effect of the antitrust laws—that the federal courts, not the CAB, had primary jurisdiction in dealing with the antitrust charges contained in the TWA complaint.

The Court of Appeals went even further. It seemed clear that the federal judges did not like the cavalier manner in which Davis and his client had handled the federal court proceedings, almost as if the court's judgments were to be taken lightly or ignored. This attitude perhaps did not affect the legal rulings per se, but when choices existed, it may have caused the judges to levy more severe penalties against Hughes than otherwise might have been the case. The Court of Appeals concluded, "The District Court was not obligated to employ sanctions less severe than the dismissal of the counterclaims with prejudice.'' The term *with prejudice* means that decisions are final and can never be reopened. Davis made an immediate motion for a rehearing but was turned down. Thus, Toolco's $443 million counterclaims were irrevocably dismissed by the Court of Appeals. It was a bad day for Howard Hughes.

But matters suddenly took a different turn. Barely a month later, on July 10, 1964, in seeming defiance of the Court of Appeals, the CAB issued Order E-21507, which granted Hughes's motion to resume active control of TWA by paying off the financial institutions and dissolving the voting trust as soon as the CAB approved any plan he might submit which divesting Toolco of the power to simultaneously control both TWA and NEA. Because no merger had occurred between NEA and TWA, Howard would have to divest himself of control of NEA to regain control of TWA. It appeared that Hughes's strategy to regain control of TWA and dissolve the voting trust was very close to succeeding.

Sonnett petitioned the Court of Appeals to review the July 10 CAB decision. It did so and handed down a decision on December 7, 1964, ordering the CAB to suspend Order E-21507 until after a full evidential hearing had been held. Such a hearing was certain to require Hughes's personal appearance, and because he had only recently defaulted on allegations that had the potential of costing $135 million, it seemed unlikely he would agree to appear before the CAB. Yet this appeared to be his best chance of quickly regaining control of TWA and beating the trustees and financing institutions.

That was not the end of the appeals process, however. Chester Davis, aided by Abe Fortas, a prominent Washington attorney who was appointed to the U.S. Supreme Court the following year, petitioned the Supreme Court to review the decisions of the district and appellate courts in the antitrust case. On November 16, 1964, the Supreme Court agreed to review both the default judgment and dismissal of the countersuit.

The Supreme Court hearing was held on March 3, 1965, before Chief Justice Earl Warren and the eight associate justices. Sonnett and Davis were allotted only one hour each to argue their exceedingly complex cases, and Sonnett's time had to be split with the financial institutions. A tall order, indeed. Sonnett devoted almost all his time arguing that the Supreme Court should not have agreed to hear the matter at all because at this stage nothing was involved but the disciplinary powers of the district court over the defendants and witnesses disobeying discovery orders; the innumerable other arguments were left to the briefs. His performance was reported as absolutely superb.

Five days later, the Supreme Court issued a terse, single-sentence opinion stating that its earlier decision to review the cases had been "improvidently granted." In other words, the Court had changed its mind and decided not to review the prior rulings of the district and appellate courts. This was devastating news for Hughes. To complete matters, on October 11, 1965, the Supreme Court refused to hear Davis's appeal from the decision of the Court of Appeals that the CAB could not grant Toolco and Hughes permission to reacquire control of TWA without a full evidentiary hearing.

Now, all that seemed to remain was for the New York court to conduct a hearing to determine the extent of damages. Preparations for the hearing were undertaken shortly after the Supreme Court opinion had been rendered. It became my job to project the TWA jet fleet that would have existed had Hughes not controlled TWA, so that the results of operating such a fleet could be projected and compared with what in fact happened.

In reconstructing the fleet on paper, I assumed that TWA would have ordered the same number of jets that in fact had been ordered by Toolco, but that TWA would have ordered them at least as early as TWA's competitors, just as I had repeatedly recommended to Hughes; and that TWA would have received all 63 jets instead of 47. Actual airplane delivery dates were used for the Boeings, and I assumed that Convair would have delivered all 30 880's with no more average delivery delay than Delta had experienced.

It was necessary to reallocate Boeing's early delivery positions between AAL, PAA, and TWA on the assumption that all three airlines would have placed their initial jet orders simultaneously, or nearly so. I did this based on Boeing's sales and delivery allocation policies, with which I was closely familiar because of my participation in extended negotiations concerning delivery positions with Bill Allen, Bruce Connelly, and other Boeing executives. To be doubly certain that I had projected what Boeing would have done under the assumed circumstances, I arranged for a Seattle meeting attended by Bruce Connelly; Ed Wells; Harold F. Olsen, Boeing's outside counsel; Corydon Dunham, then an associate of John Sonnett and later general counsel of the National Broadcasting Company, and me. Because Bruce was still recovering from an illness, we met at his home. I reviewed my understanding of Boeing's policies; discussed various ramifications, including the need under my assumptions for Boeing to have initially certified its jets for use by three rather than two airlines; and reviewed the process I had used in developing my projections. The Boeing representatives agreed that my understandings were correct and that my projections were reasonable. Later, Bruce Connelly said the same thing under oath.

My projections showed a much more competitive TWA than had historically existed. Sonnett hired consultants to compute the financial results of operating the projected fleets, which, when compared to TWA's actual results, provided the basis for a large part of TWA's damage claims.

The damage hearing commenced on May 2, 1966, and continued for nearly two years. A new special master, Herbert Brownell, former attorney general of the United States, replaced Lee Rankin, who had resigned to accept an appointment as corporation counsel for New York City. Chester Davis employed new counsel to represent the defendants, the well-known New York law firm, Donovan, Leisure, Newton & Irvine.

I was TWA's chief witness. I did not want it that way; there simply was not anyone else who was sufficiently knowledgeable. After all, I had worked closely with Hughes for 18 years, been privy to his participation in all of TWA's aircraft procurement programs, and was familiar with all the negotiations. Indeed, I had conducted many of them on his behalf. I was again subjected to months of interrogations.

TWA's fortunes had turned around from the fearful days of 1961–62. The fan-powered Boeings had been delivered, six additional Convair 880's had been purchased from Convair after they had been repossessed from NEA, and the Convair "house" 880 had been purchased and standardized in TWA's shops. (I had also successfully negotiated with Raymond Cook for the purchase of the remaining four Toolco 880's, only to have Howard angrily declare to Raymond—Howard and I had no direct contacts after he lost control—that under no circumstances would he agree to the sale of the aircraft to TWA.) The added lift combined with the renewed enthusiasm apparent in TWA's management under Tillinghast's leadership was working wonders. TWA's net profit had climbed from $19.8 million in 1963 to $37 million in 1964 and $50.1 million in 1965. From a low of $7.50 per share in 1962, TWA's stock rose to a high of $62 in 1965.

On April 8, 1966, Toolco surprised almost everyone by announcing its intention to sell all its TWA shares. The TWA stock had closed the preceding day at 80⅜. On May 3, the day after the damage hearing started, Toolco sold 6,584,937 shares at $86 per share, with net proceeds of $545,814,771—an enormous gain for Howard's years with TWA. Shortly thereafter, TWA's stock peaked at just over $100. Many thought Hughes should have offered to sell his stock as a giant chip to bargain for settlement of the TWA suit. He had specifically ordered, however, that this not be done, perhaps realizing that any settlement discussions would take considerable time, during which the price of the stock might fall, as it in fact did during the following months. Howard's timing was excellent.

Howard was out of TWA, but the damage hearing and legal maneuvering continued for the next two years. After exhaustively studying the conflicting information presented during the damage hearing, Special Master Brownell awarded TWA trebled damages of $137,611,435.95 on September 21, 1968. Somewhat over one year later, Judge Metzner confirmed Brownell's award. Still later, on April 14, 1970, Judge Metzner awarded TWA costs plus an attorney's fee, increasing the total to $145,448,141.07. The wheels of justice had turned slowly, but they had turned well.

John Sonnett, who had won all of the important legal battles while Davis had won some skirmishes, died suddenly of brain cancer in 1969, before Judge Metzner's decisions came down, and the direction of TWA's case passed to his chief of staff for the case, Dudley B. Tenney, an accomplished lawyer in his own right, who had handled the main part of the damage hearings.

TWA appealed Judge Metzner's decision along with Toolco. TWA wanted an even larger award and a higher interest rate, whereas Toolco wanted Judge Metzner's ruling reversed. The appeal was argued by Tenney before the Court of Appeals on May 7, 1971. The three appellate court judges unanimously affirmed the award and increased the interest rate from 6 percent to 7.5 percent as requested (interest would now accumulate at about $30,000 per day). It was a tremendous victory for Sonnett, Tenney, and TWA.

Tenney had hoped the case would end with the Court of Appeals decision, but nevertheless he was prepared to see it through the court of last resort: the Supreme Court of the United States. As all expected, Chester Davis petitioned the Court for a writ of certiorari. During late February 1972, the Court announced it would hear Toolco's appeal and TWA's cross-appeal during its coming October term.

Davis elected to recruit yet another new legal team to handle the case before the Supreme Court, although he remained chief counsel for Toolco. He hired two prominent Washington law firms to assist and selected a highly respected and well-recognized lawyer to make Toolco's argument to the Supreme Court—Charles Alan Wright, a law professor at the University of Texas who had specialized in federal procedure in civil cases. Dudley Tenney represented TWA and hired famed Yale professor J. William Moore, Wright's former teacher, as an advisor. Exhaustive briefs were prepared by both sides, followed by a series of reply and rebuttal briefs and memoranda.

By this time the judgment with interest amounted to over $165 million, larger by far than any previous judgment in American legal history. It was with a mix of optimism and concern that TWA awaited the final outcome. Sonnett and Tenney had won decisive victories at every level, and surely, the Supreme Court would not overrule such a long string of consistent court decisions, particularly after it had decided they were not worth ruling on in 1965—or at least so we thought. After all, the litigation had proceeded for over six years in the lower courts on the assumption that the Supreme Court's 1965 decision had settled the question of whether the CAB orders had conferred on Toolco and Hughes immunity from antitrust claims. On the other hand, at least four justices had voted to grant certiorari.

Tenney and Wright squared off before the Supreme Court on October 10. The justices were extremely attentive during Wright's presentation, which preceded Tenney's, but constantly interrupted Tenney during his presentation, as if they were arguing with him. Unexpectedly, their interest was concentrated on proceedings before their 1965 refusal to review rather than on the matters which had been the subject of the intervening six years of arduous litigation. Tenney was not given much of a chance in the 30 minutes allotted to him to make his case. He left the court room with a sense of indignation and foreboding.

On January 10, 1973, the Supreme Court handed down a devastating opinion: Hughes had not violated the antitrust laws because his acts at TWA had been immunized by the CAB approvals. Thus, after only a few hours before the Court, Hughes was off the hook as far as the federal case was concerned, and TWA's $145-million award (plus interest) had been thrown out. We had known this was a possibility, but the Court's opinion was shattering and a lasting disappointment, especially considering that Sonnett and Tenney had won every legal battle for the preceding 11 years,

401

including three unanimous decisions by the appellate courts. That the chief justice, joined by Justice Harry A. Blackmum, wrote a vigorous dissent, indignantly refuting the arguments of the majority, was no help. The majority decision of course stood.

Tenney considered the Court's adverse opinion a personal defeat. What would have been the largest damage award in history had suddenly vanished. His disappointment was as hard felt as the loss of the case was within TWA. Those millions would have healed many problems. Tenney considered resigning from the case and mentioned this to Raymond R. Fletcher, TWA's inside general counsel, just before the next TWA board meeting, which was held in Jamaica (TWA owned Hilton International Hotels at the time and was opening a new hotel), where Tenney was scheduled to explain the results of the case to the board. Fletcher dissuaded him. It is a good thing he did, considering Tenney's subsequent success in the Delaware case.

Losing the case was bad enough, but matters were in fact worse than that for TWA. A heartbreaking fight occurred over Toolco's rights to collect its "costs" from TWA—a term that does not legally include such major costs as attorney's fees, travel, experts, and the like, but which does cover certain specific printing and other costs, including most importantly the cost of an appeal bond. The clerk of the Court allowed Toolco costs of $1,853,453.15. Tenney appealed this to Judge Metzner, who disallowed $683,805.40 of audit expenses that the defendants had incurred to get permission to avoid a standard appeal bond, substituting other guarantees.

Davis promptly appealed Judge Metzner's ruling, and on March 7, 1975, the appellate court reinstated costs totaling $1,867,827.60. Tenney unsuccessfully applied for a rehearing and petitioned for certiorari, denial of which in 1976 brought the federal case to a final conclusion. By this time the judgment on costs amounted to over $2 million, which TWA was obliged to pay.

The Delaware Case

It was not until late 1975 that Dudley Tenney knew TWA would be allowed to proceed in Delaware. The first problem that confronted him in the Delaware case was to dispose of the threat that the rule of res judicata would apply, that is, that the Supreme Court's 1973 decision would be held to have disposed of TWA's Delaware case as well because essentially the same facts provided the foundation for both cases. Had this happened, the Delaware case would have become history, with no hope of revival. The threat was real because the U.S. Supreme Court decision was certainly final, although it made no reference to the Delaware case.

When the Supreme Court decision had come down in early 1973, one tough question was how to handle its impact on the Delaware case. Should Tenney ask the Supreme Court to phrase its mandate to expressly be without prejudice to TWA's rights in the state courts, or should he just let the usual bare-bones mandate come forth, in the hope subsequent proceedings would hold that the decision had no effect on the Delaware case? Once asked, if the Supreme Court gave the wrong answer, the battle would be forever lost. If it gave the right answer, Tenney could proceed as he wanted. With adroit maneuvering, however, possibly he could do that anyway—and the Supreme Court at the moment seemed less than sympathetic to TWA's problem, to say the least.

Tenney decided not to risk petitioning the Supreme Court but to apply to Judge Metzner instead for entry of a final judgment, which would state that dismissal of TWA's antitrust case was without prejudice to its Delaware case. Tenney argued that the Supreme Court's decision should not be construed as having dismissed the Delaware case grounded in charges that Hughes had breached his fiduciary responsibilities to TWA. This position was of course hotly contested by the Hughes forces.

Judge Metzner wrote an opinion stating that dismissal of TWA's federal case as ordered by the Supreme Court did not necessarily bar TWA's prosecution of its nonfederal claims, but he was reluctant to tamper with the Supreme Court's final mandate. Accordingly, his judgment of dismissal was devoid of any express permission to go ahead with the Delaware case. On the other hand, his words gave strong support to Tenney's position that there should be no automatic bar. The res judicata issue remained in contention until 1975, when the Delaware Supreme Court put it to rest. Chester Davis again sought intervention by the United States Supreme Court, but certiorari was denied. The Delaware courts also held that the CAB's approvals of Hughes's control of TWA by no means immunized him from liability for violating his fiduciary obligations under state law to TWA and its minority stockholders.

The Delaware case could at last go ahead. While it was based on essentially the same facts as the federal case, the charges were different: Hughes and Toolco had breached their fiduciary responsibility to TWA and its minority stockholders by preventing TWA from purchasing an adequate number of jet aircraft on its own account on a timely basis and by self-dealing in exercising their dominance and control over the affairs of TWA. Self-dealing by a controlling person is not in itself a wrong, but it is a wrong when unfair advantage is taken, and the burden of proof of complete fairness rests with the controlling person. Specifically, Tenney claimed the defendants had interfered with TWA's management; prevented TWA from purchasing an adequate number of aircraft for its own account; delayed placing the jet aircraft orders; dominated and controlled TWA's financing; prevented TWA from obtaining adequate financing; and harassed and delayed the Convair program and prevented delivery of the planes. He contended that these harmful acts, largely motivated by Hughes's and Toolco's tax considerations, had involved self-dealing in the defendants' own interests and at TWA's expense.

Because the TWA factual allegations had been legally admitted during the federal case by the defendants because of Hughes's failure to appear as a witness, Tenney's strategy was to narrowly limit the Delaware case proceedings to the same facts and essentially the same claimed damages, anticipating that these facts would either be admitted again or proved from defendants' own files and records. Once the Delaware Supreme Court had acted and the U.S. Supreme Court had denied certiorari, Tenney moved in the trial court to commence discovery—starting with Hughes's deposition. The Hughes forces responded by filing amended answers, admitting "the well pleaded allegations of the complaint except as to damage," and then filed a motion seeking summary judgment on the ground that the facts TWA had alleged did not add up to a violation of Delaware law.

Tenney's response was a cross-motion for partial summary judgment on liability in favor of TWA. After extended briefing and argument, Delaware Chancellor William Marvel entered an order on June 6, 1977, which found the defendants liable to TWA for breaches of their fiduciary responsibility as charged in TWA's complaint, except for the charges based on the sale of 6 Boeings to PAA and the retention of 10 out of the original 30 Convairs (including the 6 leased to NEA). He also specified that these exceptions did not relieve Hughes of responsibility for not permitting TWA to acquire an adequate fleet of jet aircraft on its own account. Chancellor Marvel directed the defendants to account for the resulting damages.

While the cross-motions were pending before the Delaware court, Howard Hughes died on April 5, 1976. Howard, who from all reports had suffered fragile health and led a self-inflicted miserable life during his final years, was returning or had just returned to Texas—I am not sure exactly when he passed away—by chartered plane to die in the United States. The press reports of his wasted and unkempt appearance were hardly believable. Poor Howard! He could have contributed so much during his later years. His was a sad, totally inappropriate ending. I chose to remember only the vibrant, aggressive aviator and industrialist that I had known years before.

Chester Davis had little to do with the Delaware case after the 1973 U.S. Supreme Court decision, although he continued for several years as chief counsel for Toolco. His partner, Max Cox, handled the case until late 1977, when Davis was dismissed by William R. Lummis, who was named administrator for Howard's estate. Lummis was a relative of Hughes, and a former partner in the same Houston law firm that Raymond Cook had worked for. Cook, who had been Howard's lawyer in so many matters and for so many years, had recently died in an automobile accident. Toolco's oil drill business had been sold to the public under the name of the Hughes Tool Company. Raymond Holliday became chief executive officer, and the remaining Toolco enterprises were renamed the Summa Corporation. At that point, the defendants were changed to Summa and William R. Lummis.

In June 1978, two years after Hughes's death, the defendants applied for permission from the court to amend their answers yet again to withdraw the admissions they had made, claiming that Hughes had not been competent when their answers were filed in late 1975 and that he had not authorized the filing. At the same time, newspaper articles based on what must have been planted "sources" mysteriously appeared in the local press suggesting that Hughes indeed had become incompetent. (I was assured by Nadine Henley, Howard's long-time private secretary, over dinner years after Hughes's death that she had been in contact with him on business matters until shortly before he passed away and that he had been alert and lucid in all such instances.) Chancellor Marvel was not convinced and turned down the application.

A number of law firms became involved in the case on behalf of Summa before and after the departure of Chester Davis. Andrew B. Kirkpatrick of Morris, Nichols, Arsht & Tunnel of Wilmington, Delaware, handled most of the proceedings in which I was personally involved.

After Marvel's 1977 Delaware Supreme Court rulings, Tenney moved to go immediately to trial without further discovery. Chancellor Marvel gave Summa permission to undertake discovery proceedings even though his 1977 ruling appeared to have established the basic facts concerning the harm done to TWA by the defendants and the extent of their legal liability. This led to five more years of slow action—sometimes only one deposition was taken by the defendants in a six-month period. Defendants obtained court permission to take further depositions provided repetitive questions were not asked of Edward L. Wemple, an expert consultant in airline revenues and operating costs matters, and me. However, I cannot think of a single question asked during the deposition that I had not already answered at least once under oath!

During this period, Tenney, who had been intimately familiar with every aspect of the case from the first, undertook a searching review to see if any opportunity had been overlooked or if somehow the case strategy could be improved. He decided to supplement the damage claim papers based on the 63-plane fleet by adding a fallback position based on a 52-plane fleet. Tenney had noticed that the Dillon Read financing plan advanced in March 1960 gave TWA an option to finance a 52-plane fleet (15 domestic Boeings, 25 Convairs, and 12 international Boeings) in lieu of the 45-plane fleet, provided TWA made that election by April 11. Howard had approved this plan in writing shortly after the entire TWA board except Raymond Holliday threatened to resign. The 52-plane fleet was never implemented because Howard permitted the option to lapse, but the financing papers established without question that this fleet could have been successfully financed.

During September 1983, Tenney submitted a memorandum to the Court of Chancery requesting that a trial for the determination of damages finally be scheduled. Chancellor Marvel had retired by then, and the trial did not get underway until the spring of 1985. Vice Chancellor Joseph T. Walsh presided.

I was again TWA's principal witness and was rated by the court as an expert witness (that is, one entitled to express professional opinions) as well as a fact witness. The trial was held in Wilmington and lasted six weeks. On May 15, 1986, Justice Walsh (in the interim he had been appointed to the Delaware Supreme Court) handed down a decision awarding TWA damages based on the 52-plane fleet rather than the 63-plane fleet, which he concluded TWA might not have been able to finance.

Tenney's strategy paid off. The defendants were required to pay TWA about $17 million plus prejudgment interest.

The rate of interest immediately became a hot issue. The defendants insisted that the legal rate of 6 percent be applied and that no interest should be charged for the period the Delaware case had been held in abeyance while the federal case was in process. TWA contended that a higher rate, reflecting TWA's actual borrowing costs, should be applied from January 1, 1960, on. Justice Walsh ruled on January 21, 1987, that an interest rate of 7.32 percent would be applied and that the term would run from January 1, 1960. Interest thus computed raised the award to $48,346,600.

The defendants appealed to the Delaware Supreme Court. Dudley Tenney had retired after the liability phase of the case was completed in trial court but agreed to serve as a consultant to Bill Hegarty and Marshall Cox, two accomplished Cahill lawyers. Hegarty, who was now in charge, had only become involved in the case in the last few years, but Cox (no relation to Max Cox, Davis's partner) had been directly and importantly involved in the two cases from day one. In due course, the court affirmed Justice Walsh's opinion in every respect. As expected, the defendants petitioned the U.S. Supreme Court for a writ of certiorari, and that petition was denied on October 3, 1988. TWA had already been paid in full by Summa after both the Delaware Supreme Court and then Justice Brennan refused to stay execution on TWA's judgment. Thus, TWA's suits against Hughes were finally brought to a close.

From the time the federal case was filed in 1961 to the close of the Delaware case, the litigation had been before the U.S. Supreme Court no less than six times, the U.S. Court of Appeals five times, and the Delaware Supreme Court three times. The total elapsed time for the two cases was an astonishing 27 years.

23.

Reflections

I look back on my long association with Howard Hughes with a sense of personal pride for having effectively participated with him in the evolutionary development of air transportation. His interest in aviation was genuine, and posterity will surely consider his contributions noteworthy. It was a great privilege to have worked with him during his prime. I owe Howard a debt of gratitude that can never be repaid for having permitted me to work with the greatest leaders in aviation's development.

I also look back with a tinge of personal disappointment for not having been able to influence Howard more effectively in TWA aircraft procurement matters, but I doubt that any rationale or argument would have caused him to change direction. His insatiable drive was to expand his empire no matter what the costs to its components, and his consuming interest in minimizing taxes and maximizing the overall results was too strong. His frequent avoidance of recommended courses of action and the pursuit, instead, of patently unproductive or mistimed ventures proved as I had anticipated to be extremely costly for TWA. TWA was a great airline, but it could have been much greater. It also could have been much worse off except for actions I undertook from time to time on my own initiative that minimized the damage caused by Howard's equipment procrastinations and divagations. TWA remained one of America's leading airlines until the 1980s, when it dropped out of the top group.

As for Howard's later life, one can only wonder what circumstance or possible psychopathy could have fostered such extreme reclusion and physical debasement. I did not once see or converse with him after he lost control of TWA, but consistent descriptive information leaves little doubt about his chosen mode of living. Despite his billions, one must feel compassion because of his miserable final years and what must have surely been lack of human warmth and friendship.

The stable management that TWA enjoyed in my last years was a refreshing experience indeed after the frequent changes of presidents and extended periods of management by committee during the Hughes regime. Best of all, I had only one boss. I stayed with TWA until early 1978, when Margie and I moved to Arizona, and I established and operated a successful aviation consulting business until I decided to give precedence to writing this book.

While at TWA, I continued to handle aircraft development and procurement matters along with other corporate duties and enjoyed participating in the Douglas DC-9, the Boeing 727 and 747, and the Lockheed L-1011 development programs. My advisory work at NASA continued, along with serving on other government and industry groups. Numbers of honors unexpectedly came my way as the years passed. Those which I am most proud of are my election to the National Academy of Engineering in 1973 and receipt of the Distinguished Public Service Medal from NASA in 1979. It also was my privilege and honor to have been appointed a commissioner by President Ronald Reagan to serve on the Presidential Commission on the Space Shuttle Challenger Accident.

As for Margie, her love, the wonderful family life she provided, and her acceptance without complaint of the unusual burdens my chosen work imposed all gave me strength and reinforced my determination to persevere. With humility and boundless gratitude to God that she is still by my side, I dedicate this book to her.

In the future, I look forward with the same enthusiasm and excitement that for me has always enveloped cutting-edge discovery and invention. The continuously expanding technological horizons remain just as bright and alluring as ever.

410

Bibliography

Angeluccia, Enzo, ed. *World Encyclopedia of Civil Aircraft*. New York: Crown Publishers, 1982.

Barton, Charles. *Howard Hughes and His Flying Boat*. Fallbrook, California: Aero Publishers, 1982.

Betts, Ed. "Fifty Years Ago." *TWA Skyliner* 39 (8): 1, 2, 4 (April 19, 1976).

Boyne, Walter J. *The Smithsonian Book of Flight*. Washington, D.C.: Smithsonian Books; New York: Orion Books, 1987.

Carey, Edwin F., Jr. *These We Honor*. International Aerospace Hall of Fame, 1984.

Davies, R. E. *Airlines of the United States Since 1914*. Washington, D.C.: Smithsonian Institution Press, 1972.

Day of Trial and Triumph. Burbank, California: Lockheed Aircraft, 1969.

"A Deadline for Howard Hughes?" *Fortune* 60 (1): 112ff. (July 1959).

Dietrich, Noah, and Bob Thomas. *Howard: The Amazing Mr. Hughes*. Greenwich, Connecticut: Fawcett Publications, 1972.

Flight Plan for Tomorrow: The Douglas Story. A Condensed History. Santa Monica, California: Douglas Aircraft, 1962.

Floyd, Jim. *The AVRO Canada C102 Jetliner*. Erin, Ontario: Boston Mills Press, 1986.

Hickerson, J. Mel. *Ernie Breech*. Des Moines, Iowa: Meredith Press, 1968.

Ingells, Douglas J. *L-1011 Tri Star and the Lockheed Story*. Fallbrook, California: Aero Publishers, 1973.

Jet Aviation: Threshold of a New Era. Waşhington, D.C.: National Air and Space Museum, Smithsonian Institution, 1981.

Johnson, Clarence L. "Kelly," with Maggie Smith. *Kelly: More Than My Share of It All*. Washington, D.C.: Smithsonian Institution Press, 1985.

Killon, Gary L. *The Convair Twins, 240 to 640*. London: MacDonald and James, 1979.

Mansfield, Harold. *Billion Dollar Battle*. New York: Van Rees, 1965.

Marson, Peter J. *The Lockheed Constellation Series*. Tonbridge, England: Air-Britain (Historians), 1982.

Masefield, Peter G. *Aviation and the Environment of the 1970's*. Society of Automotive Engineers, Littlewood Memorial Lecture, November 18, 1971. New York: David McKay, 1972.

Maynard, Crosby. *Fifty Years of Service to the Community, the Nation and the World*. St. Louis: McDonnell Douglas, 1970.

Murphy, Charles J. V., and T. A. Wise. "The Problem of Howard Hughes." *Fortune* 59 (1): 79ff. (January 1959).

Newhouse, John. *The Sporty Game*. New York: Alfred A. Knopf, 1982.

"Pan American Orders Fleet of 26 Giant DC-7 Douglas Clippers at Cost of $40,000,000." News release, Douglas Aircraft, October 24, 1944.

Pedigree of Champions—Boeing Since 1916. Seattle: Boeing, 1977.

Scott, J. D. *Vickers: A History*. London: Weidenfeld and Nicolson, 1962.

Scotti, Rose, comp. "Milestones." *TWA Skyliner* 39 (8): 3–5 (April 19, 1976).

Serling, Robert. *Howard Hughes' Airline: An Informal History of TWA*. New York: St. Martins/Marek, 1983.

Shrader, Welman A. *Fifty Years of Flight: A Chronicle of the Aviation Industry in America, 1903–1953*. Cleveland: Eaton Manufacturing, 1953.

Solberg, Carl. *Conquest of the Skies: A History of Commercial Aviation in America*. Boston and Toronto: Little Brown, 1979.

Taylor, J. H., and David Mondey. *Milestones of Flight*. London: Jane's Publishing, 1983.

412

Tinnin, David B. *Just About Everybody vs. Howard Hughes.* New York: Doubleday, 1973.

"Trans World Airlines, Inc., Further Control by Hughes Tool Company: Decided October 6, 1950." Docket No. 2796 (E-4701), *Civil Aeronautics Board Reports* 12 (12): 200, 223.

Williams, Nicholas M. "Globemaster: The Douglas C-74." *AAHS Journal* 25 (2): 82–106 (Summer 1980).

Williams, R. E. "Yesteryear: The Douglas C-124 Globemaster II." *Douglas Service,* September/October 1981, pp. 32–39.

Wise, T. A. "The Bankers and the Spook." *Fortune* 63 (3): 142ff. (March 1961).

Index

421

429